Practical Industrial Data Communic

Best Practice Techniques

Other titles in the series

Practical Cleanrooms: Technologies and Facilities (David Conway)

Practical Data Acquisition for Instrumentation and Control Systems (John Park, Steve Mackay)

Practical Data Communications for Instrumentation and Control (John Park, Steve Mackay, Edwin Wright)

Practical Digital Signal Processing for Engineers and Technicians (Edmund Lai)

Practical Electrical Network Automation and Communication Systems (Cobus Strauss)

Practical Embedded Controllers (John Park)

Practical Fiber Optics (David Bailey, Edwin Wright)

Practical Industrial Data Networks: Design, Installation and Troubleshooting (Steve Mackay, Edwin Wright, John Park, Deon Reynders)

Practical Industrial Safety, Risk Assessment and Shutdown Systems for Instrumentation and Control (Dave Macdonald)

Practical Modern SCADA Protocols: DNP3, 60870.5 and Related Systems (Gordon Clarke, Deon Reynders)

Practical Radio Engineering and Telemetry for Industry (David Bailey)

Practical SCADA for Industry (David Bailey, Edwin Wright)

Practical TCP/IP and Ethernet Networking (Deon Reynders, Edwin Wright)

Practical Variable Speed Drives and Power Electronics (Malcolm Barnes)

Practical Centrifugal Pumps (Paresh Girdhar and Octo Moniz)

Practical Electrical Equipment and Installations in Hazardous Areas (Geoffrey Bottrill and G. Vijayaraghavan)

Practical E-Manufacturing and Supply Chain Management (Gerhard Greef and Ranjan Ghoshal)

Practical Grounding, Bonding, Shielding and Surge Protection (G. Vijayaraghavan, Mark Brown and Malcolm Barnes)

Practical Hazops, Trips and Alarms (David Macdonald)

Practical Machinery Safety (David Macdonald)

Practical Machinery Vibration Analysis and Predictive Maintenance (Cornelius Scheffer and Paresh Girdhar)

Practical Power Distribution for Industry (Jan de Kock and Cobus Strauss)

Practical Process Control for Engineers and Technicians (Wolfgang Altmann)

Practical Power Systems Protection (Les Hewitson, Mark Brown and Ben. Ramesh)

Practical Telecommunications and Wireless Communications (Edwin Wright and Deon Reynders)

Practical Troubleshooting of Electrical Equipment and Control Circuits (Mark Brown, Jawahar Rawtani and Dinesh Patil)

Practical Hydraulics (Ravi Doddannavar, Andries Barnard)

Practical Batch Process Management (Mike Barker, Jawahar Rawtani)

Practical Industrial Data Communications

Best Practice Techniques

Deon Reynders Pr.Eng, BSc (ElecEng) (Hons), MBA,
Senior Staff Engineer, IDC Technologies, Perth, Australia

Steve Mackay FIE (Aust), CPEng, BSc (ElecEng), BSc (Hons), MBA,
Gov.Cert.Comp., Technical Director – IDC Technologies

Edwin Wright MIPENZ, BSc (Hons), BSc (ElecEng),
Senior Staff Engineer for IDC Technologies, Perth, Australia

Series editor: Steve Mackay FIE (Aust), CPEng, BSc (ElecEng), BSc (Hons), MBA,
Gov.Cert.Comp., Technical Director – IDC Technologies

ELSEVIER

AMSTERDAM • BOSTON • HEIDELBERG • LONDON
NEW YORK • OXFORD • PARIS • SAN DIEGO
SAN FRANCISCO • SINGAPORE • SYDNEY • TOKYO

Newnes is an imprint of Elsevier

Newnes

Newnes
An imprint of Elsevier
Linacre House, Jordan Hill, Oxford OX2 8DP
30 Corporate Drive, Burlington, MA 01803

First published 2005

British Library Cataloguing in Publication Data
Reynders, D.
  Practical industrial data communications : best practice
  techniques. – (Practical professional)
  1.
  2. Computer network resources
  3. I. Title II. Mackay, S. III. Wright, E.
  4. 621.3'981

Library of Congress Cataloguing in Publication Data
A catalogue record for this book is available from the Library of Congress

ISBN   0 7506 6395 2

For information on all Newnes Publications
visit our website at www.newnespress.com

www.integra-india.com
Transferred to Digital Printing 2009

Contents

Preface

The objective of this book is to outline the best practice in designing, installing, commissioning and troubleshooting industrial data communications systems. In any given plant, factory or installation there are a myriad of different industrial communications standards used and the key to successful implementation is the degree to which the entire system integrates and works together. With so many different standards on the market today, the debate is not about what is the best – be it Foundation Fieldbus, Profibus, Devicenet or Industrial Ethernet – but rather about selecting the most appropriate technologies and standards for a given application and then ensuring that best practice is followed in designing, installing and commissioning the data communications links to ensure they run fault-free.

The industrial data communications systems in your plant underpin your entire operation. It is critical that you apply best practice in designing, installing and fixing any problems that may occur. This book distills all the tips and tricks learnt with the benefit of many years of experience and gives the best proven practices to follow.

The main steps in using today's communications technologies involve selecting the correct technology and standards for your plant based on your requirements; doing the design of the overall system; installing the cabling and then commissioning the system. Fiber Optic cabling is generally accepted as the best approach for physical communications but there are obviously areas where you will be forced to use copper wiring and, indeed, wireless communications. This book outlines the critical rules followed in installing the data communications physical transport media and then ensuring that the installation will be trouble-free for years to come.

The important point to make is that with today's wide range of protocols available, you only need to know how to select, install and maintain them in the most cost-effective manner for your plant or factory – knowledge of the minute details of the protocols is not necessary.

This book will be useful to anyone working with or required to follow best practice in the installation of industrial data communications systems ranging from RS-232 to Fieldbus and Ethernet systems, including:

- Instrumentation and Control Engineers/Technicians
- Process Control Engineers
- Network Planners
- Electrical Engineers
- Test Engineers
- System Integrators
- Designers
- Electronic Technicians
- Consulting Engineers
- Design Engineers
- Plant Managers
- Systems Engineers
- Shift Electricians

We would hope you would gain the following knowledge from reading this book:

- Best practice in industrial data communications design, installation and commissioning
- Practical hands-on experience in jointing, splicing and testing of copper and fiber based cabling
- How to design and install your own fully operational industrial data communications systems
- How to integrate different industrial communications protocols and standards into a complete working system

You should have a modicum of electrical knowledge and some exposure to industrial automation systems to derive maximum benefit from this book.

1

General topics

1.1 Overview

This book can be divided into several distinct sections.

1.1.1 Introduction

This introductory chapter deals with general topics such as the OSI model, systems engineering concepts, physical (layer 1) connections, protocols, and noise and ingress protection.

1.1.2 Media

Chapters 2 and 3 deal with media – specifically conductive media viz. copper (coax, UTP, STP) and fiber.

1.1.3 Physical layer standards

Chapters 4–6 (inclusive) cover RS-232, RS-485, and 4–20 mA.

Note: Throughout this book, we will refer to RS-232, RS-422, and RS-485. One is often criticized for using these terms of reference, since in reality they are obsolete. However, if we briefly examine the history of the organization that defined these standards, it is not difficult to see why they are still in use today and will probably continue as such.

The Electronics Industry Association (EIA) of America defined the common serial interface RS-232. 'RS' stands for 'recommended standard', and the number (suffix-232) refers to the interface specification of the physical device. The EIA has since established many standards and amassed a library of white papers on various implementations of them. So to keep track of them all, it made sense to change the prefix to EIA. (It is interesting to note that most of the white papers are NOT free.)

The Telecommunications Industry Association (TIA) was formed in 1988, by merging the telecommunications arm of the EIA and the United States Telecommunications Suppliers Association. The prefix changed again to EIA/TIA-232 (along with all the other serial implementations, of course). So now we have TIA-232, TIA-485, etc.

It should also be noted that the TIA is a member of the Electronics Industries Alliance (EIA). This alliance is made up of several trade organizations (including the CEA, ECA, GEIA . . .) that represent the interests of manufacturers of electronics-related products.

Now when someone refers to 'EIA', they are talking about the Alliance, not the Association!

If we still use the terms RS-232, RS-422, etc., then they are just as equally obsolete as the 'RS' equivalents. However, when they are referred to as TIA standards some people might give you a quizzical look and ask you to explain yourself . . . So to cut a long story short, one says 'RS-xxx' – and the penny drops. 'RS' has become more or less a *de facto* approach, as a search on the Internet will testify.

Copies of the relevant standards are available from Global Engineering documents, the official suppliers of EIA documents. A brief perusal of their website (http://global.ihs.com) will reveal the name changes over time, since names were not changed retroactively. The latest '232' revision refers to TIA-232, but earlier revisions and other related documents still refer to TIA/EIA-232, EIA-232, and RS-232.

1.1.4   Industrial protocols

Chapters 7–10 (inclusive) deal with a few well-known industrial protocols such as TCP/IP, Modbus, DNP3, and IEC 60870.

1.1.5   Industrial networks

Chapters 11–18 (inclusive) deal with some popular industrial networks (both old and new) such as Industrial Ethernet, AS-i, DeviceNet, Profibus, Foundation Fieldbus, Modbus Plus, Data Highway Plus, and HART. Although the topic of troubleshooting only follows towards the end of the workshop, each chapter has been divided into an A and a B section, where the A section deals with the operation of the system and B deals with troubleshooting the same system. This has been done for ease of reference.

1.1.6   Other technologies

Chapter 19 deals with several wireless technologies, including VSAT, IEEE 802.11, and wireless point-to-point.

1.1.7   Selection methodology

Chapter 20 covers the appropriate steps to be taken in choosing the components for an industrial data communications system.

1.1.8   Installation, commissioning, troubleshooting

Chapter 21 covers recommended practice in installing, commissioning, and trouble-shooting industrial data communications systems.

1.2   OSI reference model

Faced with the proliferation of closed network systems, the *International Organization for Standardization* (ISO) defined a 'Reference Model for Communication between Open Systems' in 1978. This has become known as the Open Systems Interconnection Reference model or simply as the OSI model (ISO7498). The OSI model is essentially a data communications management structure, which breaks data communications down into a manageable hierarchy of seven layers.

Each layer has a defined purpose and interfaces with the layers above and below it. By laying down standards for each layer, some flexibility is allowed so that the system designers can develop protocols for each layer independent of each other. By conforming to the OSI standards, a system is able to communicate with any other compliant system, anywhere in the world.

At the outset, it should be realized that the OSI reference model is not a protocol or set of rules for how a protocol should be written, but rather an overall framework in which to define protocols. The OSI model framework specifically and clearly defines the functions or services that have to be provided at each of the seven layers (or levels).

Since there must be at least two sites to communicate, each layer also appears to converse with its peer layer at the other end of the communication channel in a virtual ('logical') communication. These concepts of isolation of the process of each layer, together with standardized interfaces and peer-to-peer virtual communication, are fundamental to the concepts developed in a layered model such as the OSI model. The OSI layering concept is shown in Figure 1.1.

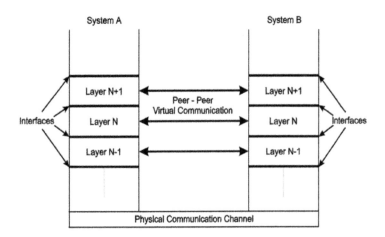

Figure 1.1
OSI layering concept

The actual functions within each layer are provided by entities that are abstract devices, such as programs, functions, or protocols that implement the services for a particular layer on a single machine. A layer may have more than one entity – for example a protocol entity and a management entity. Entities in adjacent layers interact through the common upper and lower boundaries by passing physical information through *service access points* (SAPs). A SAP could be compared to a predefined 'post-box' where one layer would collect data from the previous layer. The relationship between layers, entities, functions, and SAPs are shown in Figure 1.2.

In the OSI model, the entity in the next higher layer is referred to as the $N + 1$ entity and the entity in the next lower layer as $N – 1$. The services available to the higher layers are the result of the services provided by all the lower layers.

The functions and capabilities expected at each layer are specified in the model. However, the model does not prescribe how this functionality should be implemented. The focus in the model is on the 'interconnection' and on the information that can be passed over this connection. The OSI model does not concern itself with the internal operations of the systems involved.

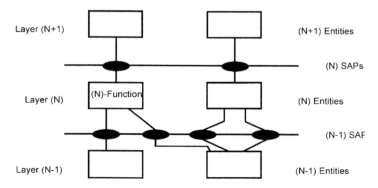

Figure 1.2
Relationship between layers, entities, functions, and SAPs

When the OSI model was being developed, a number of principles were used to determine exactly how many layers this communication model should encompass. These principles are:

- A layer should be created where a different level of abstraction is required.
- Each layer should perform a well-defined function.
- The function of each layer should be chosen with thought given to defining internationally standardized protocols.
- The layer boundaries should be chosen to minimize the information flow across the boundaries.
- The number of layers should be large enough that distinct functions need not be thrown together in the same layer out of necessity and small enough that the architecture does not become unwieldy.

The use of these principles led to seven layers being defined, each of which has been given a name in accordance with its process purpose. Figure 1.3 shows the seven layers of the OSI model.

Application
Presentation
Session
Transport
Network
Data Link
Physical

Figure 1.3
The OSI reference model

At the transmitter, the user invokes the system by passing data and control information (physically) to the highest layer of the protocol stack. The system then passes the data physically down through the seven layers, adding headers (and possibly trailers), and invoking functions in accordance with the rules of the protocol. At each level, this combined data and header 'packet' is termed as protocol data unit or PDU. At the receiving site, the opposite occurs with the headers being stripped from the data as it is passed up through the layers. These header and control messages invoke services and a peer-to-peer logical interaction of entities across the sites.

At this stage, it should be quite clear that there is *no* connection or direct communication between the peer layers of the network. Rather, all communication is across the physical layer, or the lowest layer of the stack. Communication is down through the protocol stack on the transmitting stack and up through the stack on the receiving stack. Figure 1.4 shows the full architecture of the OSI model, whilst Figure 1.5 shows the effects of the addition of headers (protocol control information) to the respective PDUs at each layer. The net effect of this extra information is to reduce the overall bandwidth of the communications channel, since some of the available bandwidth is used to pass control information.

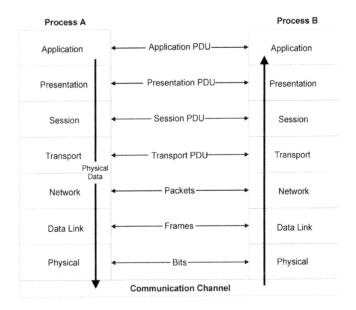

Figure 1.4
Full architecture of OSI model

1.2.1 OSI layer services

Briefly, the services provided at each layer of the stack are:

- *Application (layer 7)*: The provision of network services to the user's application programs (clients, servers, etc.). Note: the user's actual application programs do *not* reside here.
- *Presentation (layer 6)*: Maps the data representations into an external data format that will enable correct interpretation of the information on receipt. The mapping can also possibly include encryption and/or compression of data.
- *Session (layer 5)*: Control of the communications between the users. This includes the grouping together of messages and the coordination of data transfer between grouped layers. It also affects checkpoints for (transparent) recovery of aborted sessions.

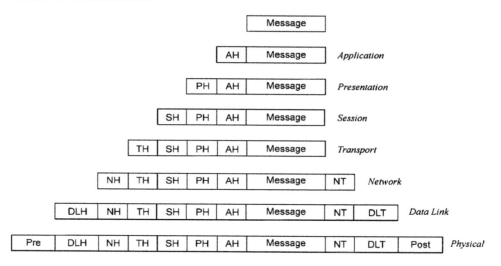

Figure 1.5
OSI message passing

- *Transport (layer 4)*:   The management of the communications between the two end systems.
- *Network (layer 3)*:   Responsible for the control of the communications network. Functions include routing of data, network addressing, fragmentation of large packets, congestion, and flow control.
- *Data link (layer 2)*:   Responsible for sending a frame of data from one system to another. Attempts to ensure that errors in the received bit stream are not passed up into the rest of the protocol stack. Error correction and detection techniques are used here.
- *Physical (layer 1)*:   Defines the electrical and mechanical connections at the physical level or the communication channel itself. Functional responsibilities include modulation, multiplexing, and signal generation. Note that the physical layer defines, but does *not* include the medium. This is located below the physical layer and is sometimes referred to as layer 0.

A more specific discussion of each layer is now presented.

Application layer

The application layer is the topmost layer in the OSI model. This layer is responsible for giving applications access to the network. Examples of application layer tasks include file transfer, electronic mail services, and network management. Application layer services are more varied than the services in lower layers, because the entire range of application and task possibilities is available here. To accomplish its tasks, the application layer passes program requests and data to the presentation layer, which is responsible for encoding the application layer's data in the appropriate form.

Presentation layer

The presentation layer is responsible for presenting information in a manner suitable for the applications or users dealing with the information. Functions, such as data conversion from EBCDIC to ASCII (or vice versa), use of special graphics or character sets, data compression or expansion, and data encryption or decryption are carried out at this layer. The presentation layer provides services for the application layer above it and uses the session layer below it. In practice, the presentation layer rarely appears in pure form and is the least well-defined of the OSI layers. Application or session layer programs will often encompass some or all of the presentation layer functions.

Session layer

The session layer is responsible for synchronizing and sequencing the dialogue and packets in a network connection. This layer is also responsible for making sure that the connection is maintained until the transmission is complete and ensuring that appropriate security measures are taken during a 'session' (i.e. a connection). The session layer is used by the presentation layer above it, and uses the transport layer below it.

Transport layer

In the OSI model, the transport layer is responsible for providing data transfer at an agreed upon level of quality, such as at specified transmission speeds and error rates. To ensure delivery, outgoing packets are assigned numbers in sequence. The numbers are included in the packets that are transmitted by lower layers. The transport layer at the receiving end checks the packet numbers to make sure all have been delivered and to put the packet contents into the proper sequence for the recipient. The transport layer provides services for the session layer above it and uses the network layer below it to find a route between source and destination. In many ways, the transport layer is crucial because it sits between the upper layers (which are strongly application dependent) and the lower ones (which are network based).

The layers below the transport layer are collectively known as the subnet layers. Depending on how well (or not) they perform their function, the transport layer has to interfere less (or more) in order to maintain a reliable connection.

Network layer

The network layer is the third lowest layer or the uppermost subnet layer. It is responsible for the following tasks:

- Determining addresses or translating from hardware to network addresses. These addresses may be on a local network or they may refer to networks located elsewhere on an internetwork. One of the functions of the network layer is, in fact, to provide capabilities needed to communicate on an internetwork.
- Finding a route between a source and a destination node or between two intermediate devices.
- Establishing and maintaining a logical connection between these two nodes and to establish either a connectionless or a connection-oriented communication. The data is processed and transmitted using the data-link layer below the network layer. Responsibility for guaranteeing proper delivery of the packets lies with the transport layer, which uses network layer services.
- Fragmentation of large packets of data into frames which are small enough to be transmitted by the underlying data-link layer. The corresponding network layer at the receiving node undertakes re-assembly of the packet.

Data-link layer

The data-link layer is responsible for creating, transmitting, and receiving data packets. It provides services for the various protocols at the network layer, and uses the physical layer to transmit or receive material. The data-link layer creates packets appropriate for the network architecture being used. Requests and data from the network layer are part of the data in these packets (or frames, as they are often called at this layer). These packets are passed down to the physical layer and from there the data is transmitted to the physical layer on the destination machine. Network architectures (such as Ethernet, ARCnet, token ring, and FDDI) encompass the data-link and physical layers, which is why these architectures support services at the data-link level. These architectures also represent the most common protocols used at the data-link level.

The IEEE 802.x networking working groups have refined the data-link layer into two sub-layers: the logical link control (LLC) sub-layer at the top and the media access control (MAC) sub-layer at the bottom. The LLC sub-layer must provide an interface for the network layer protocols and control the logical communication with its peer at the receiving side. The MAC sub-layer must provide access to a particular physical encoding and transport scheme.

Physical layer

The physical layer is the lowest layer in the OSI reference model. This layer gets data packets from the data-link layer above it and converts the contents of these packets into a series of electrical signals that represent 0 and 1 values in a digital transmission. These signals are sent across a transmission medium to the physical layer at the receiving end. At the destination, the physical layer converts the electrical signals into a series of bit values. These values are grouped into packets and passed up to the data-link layer.

The mechanical and electrical properties of the transmission medium are defined at this level. These include the following:

- The type of cable and connectors used. A cable may be coaxial, twisted pair, or fiber optic. The types of connectors depend on the type of cable.
- The pin assignments for the cable and connectors. Pin assignments depend on the type of cable and also on the network architecture being used.
- The format for the electrical signals. The encoding scheme used to signal 0 and 1 values in a digital transmission or particular values in an analog transmission depends on the network architecture being used. Most networks use digital signaling and some form of Manchester encoding for the signal.

1.3   Systems engineering approach

1.3.1   System specifications

Systems engineering, especially in a military context, is a fully fledged subject and proper treatment thereof will warrant a two-day workshop on its own. However, the basic principles of systems engineering can be applied very advantageously throughout the life cycle of any project, and hence, we will briefly look at the concepts. The project, in the context of this workshop, would involve the planning, installation, commissioning, and ongoing maintenance of some sort of industrial data communications system.

The question is: what is a system, where does it start and where does it end? The answer is a bit ambiguous – it depends where the designer draws the boundaries. For example, the engine of a motor vehicle, excluding gearbox, radiator, battery, and engine mounts, but including fuel injection system, could be seen as a system in its own right. On the other hand, the car in its entirety could be seen as a system, and the engine, one of its sub-systems. Other sub-systems could include the gearbox, drive train, electrical system, etc. In similar fashion, a SCADA system integrator could view the entire product as the 'system' with, for example, the RTUs as sub-systems, whereas for a hardware developer the RTU could be viewed as a 'system' in its own right.

The point of departure should be the physical, mechanical, and electrical environment in which the system operates. For a car engine, this could include the dimensions of the engine compartment, minimum and maximum ambient temperatures, and levels of humidity. An engine operating in Alaska in mid-winter faces different problems than its counterpart operating in Saudi Arabia.

In similar fashion, an RTU developer or someone contemplating an RTU installation should consider:

- Minimum and maximum temperatures
- Vibration
- Humidity
- Mounting constraints
- IP rating requirements
- Power supply requirements (voltage levels, tolerances, current consumption, power backup and redundancy, etc.).

These should all be included in the specifications. Let us return to the engine. There are five attributes necessary to fully describe it, but we will initially look at the first three attributes namely inputs, outputs, and functions.

Inputs

What goes 'into' the system? Inputs would include fuel from the fuel pump, air input from the air filter, cold water input from the radiator, and electrical power from the battery. For each input, the mechanical, electrical, and other details, as required, must be stated. For example, for the electrical inputs of the engine, the mechanical details of the +12 V and ground terminals must be given as well as the voltage and current limits.

For an RTU the inputs could include:

- Digital inputs (e.g. contact closures)
- Analog inputs (e.g. 4–20 mA)
- Communication input (RS-232)
- Power (e.g. 12 V DC at 100 mA).

Specifications should include all relevant electrical and mechanical considerations including connector types, pin allocations, minimum and maximum currents, minimum and maximum voltage levels, maximum operating speeds, and any transient protection.

Stated in general, in the mathematical equation $y = f(x)$, where x would be the input.

Outputs

What comes 'out of' the system? Engine outputs would include torque output to the gearbox, hot water to the radiator, and exhaust gases to the exhaust system. For each output, the exact detail (including flange dimensions, bolt sizes, etc.) has to be stated. The reason for this is simple. Each output of the engine has to mate exactly with the corresponding input of the associated auxiliary sub-system. Unless the two mating entities are absolutely complementary, dimensionally and otherwise, there will be a problem.

For an RTU the outputs could include:

- Relay outputs
- Open collector transistor outputs.

Specifications should include maximum voltages and currents as well as maximum operating speeds, relay contact lifetime, and transient protection.

Stated in general, in the mathematical equation $y = f(x)$, y (the output) occurs as a result of x, the input.

Functions

What does the system (viewed as a 'black box') do? The functions are built into the system black box. They convert the input(s) to the output(s) according to some built-in transfer function(s). The system can be seen as having a singular function with several sub-functions, or as simply having several separate functions. The overall function of the engine would be to convert fuel plus air into energy. Its main sub-function would be to convert the fuel plus air into torque to drive the car, another sub-function could be to provide electrical energy to the battery. In the mathematical equation above, this refers to the $f(\ )$ part, in other words it takes 'x' and does something to it in order to produce 'y'.

The three items mentioned so far describes the behavior of the system in terms of 'what' it has to do, but not 'how'. It has, in other words, not described a specific implementation, but just a functional specification. Once this has been documented, reviewed (several times!), and ratified, the solution can be designed.

The full (detailed) specification has to include the 'how'. For this, two additional descriptions are necessary. They are the structure of elements and couplings, and the state transition diagram.

Structure of elements and couplings

It is also referred to as the EC diagram. This refers to all the 'building blocks' of the system and their inter-relationship, but does not elucidate the way they operate. In a car engine, this would show the engine block, pistons, connecting rods, crankshaft, etc., and the way they are attached to each other.

For an RTU, this would include a full electronic circuit diagram as well as a component placement diagram.

1.4   State transition structure

This is also referred to as the ST diagram. This is the 'timing diagram' of the system. It explains, preferably in diagram form (e.g. flowchart), how all the building blocks interact. For the engine, it would show the combustion cycle of the engine plus the firing sequence of the spark plugs, etc.

For an RTU, this would be an explanation of the system operation by means of a flowchart. Flowcharts could be drawn for the initial setup, normal system operation (from an operator point of view) and program flow (from a software programmer's point of view), etc.

1.4.1   System life cycle

Our discussion this far has focused on the specification of the system, but not on the implementation thereof. Here is a possible approach. Each phase mentioned here should be terminated with a proper design review. The further a system implementation progresses, the more costly it becomes to rectify mistakes.

1.4.2   Conceptual phase

In this phase, the functional specification is developed. Once it has been agreed upon, one or more possible solutions can be put together and evaluated on paper.

1.4.3   Validation phase

If there are any untested assumptions in the design concept, now is the time to validate it. This could involve setting up a small pilot system or a test network, in order to confirm that the design objectives can be achieved.

1.5   Detailed design

Once the validation has been completed, it is time to do the full, detailed design of the system.

1.5.1   Implementation

This phase involves the procurement of the equipment, the installation, and subsequent commissioning of the system.

1.5.2   Maintenance/troubleshooting

Once the system is operational, these actions will be performed for the duration of its service life. At the end of its useful life, the system will be replaced, overhauled, or scrapped. In fact, often overlooked is the monetary cost of maintaining a system over its useful life, including the cost of parts, maintenance, and service infrastructure that could exceed the initial purchase cost, be a factor of five or more.

1.6   Media

For any communication to take place between two entities, there must be some form of medium between them. The OSI model does not include the actual medium (although it may specify it). The medium is sometimes referred to as 'layer 0' (being below layer 1) although, in fact, there is no such thing. In the context of data communications, we can distinguish between two basic groupings, namely conductive media and radiated media.

In the case of conductive media, there is a physical cable between the two devices. This cable could be either a copper cable or an optic-fiber cable.

In copper cable, the signal is conducted as electrical impulses. This type of cable can be in the form of:

- Coaxial cable, e.g. RG-58
- Twisted-pair cable (single or multi-pair), e.g. EIA/TIA-568 Cat 5, or
- Untwisted (parallel) cable, e.g. the flat cables for DeviceNet or AS-i.

Twisted-pair cable can be unshielded or shielded with foil, woven braid, or a combination thereof.

In the case of optic fiber, the signal is conducted as impulses of light. There are two main approaches possible with fiber-optic cables, namely:

1. Single mode (monomode) cabling and
2. Multimode cabling.

This is widely used throughout industrial communications systems because of immunity to electrical noise and optical isolation from surges and transients. As a result, fiber is tending to dominate in all new installations that require reasonable levels of traffic (Figure 1.6).

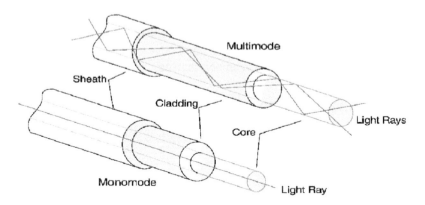

Figure 1.6
Single mode and multimode optic fibers

An alternative to conductive media is radiated media. Here, the medium is actually free space, and various techniques are used to transmit the signal. These include infrared transmission as well as VHF transmission (30–300 MHz) and UHF transmission (300 MHz–3 GHz). A very popular band is the unlicensed 2.4 GHz ISM (industrial, scientific, and medical) band as used in IEEE 802.15 Bluetooth and most wireless LANs e.g. IEEE 802.11.

In microwave transmission, a differentiation is often made in terms of terrestrial systems (i.e. transmission takes place in a predominantly horizontal plane) and satellite transmission, where transmission takes place in a predominantly vertical plane.

1.7   Physical connections

This refers to layer 1 of the OSI model and deals with the mechanism of placing an actual signal on the conductor for the purpose of transmitting 1s and 0s. Many network standards such as Ethernet and AS-i have their own unique way of doing this. Many others, such as Data Highway Plus and Profibus, use the RS-485 standard.

Here follows a brief summary of RS-485, although it is covered in detail elsewhere. RS-485 is a balanced (differential) system with up to 32 'standard' transmitters and receivers per line, speeds up to 10 Mbps and distances up to 1200 m.

The RS-485 standard is very useful for instrumentation and control systems, where several instruments or controllers may be connected together on the same multi-point network. A diagram of a typical RS-485 system is shown in Figure 1.7.

1.8   Protocols

It has been shown that there are protocols operating at layers 2–7 of the OSI model. Layer 1 is implemented by physical standards such as RS-232 and RS-485, which are mechanisms for 'putting the signal on the wire' and are therefore not protocols. Protocols are the sets of rules by which communication takes place and are implemented in software.

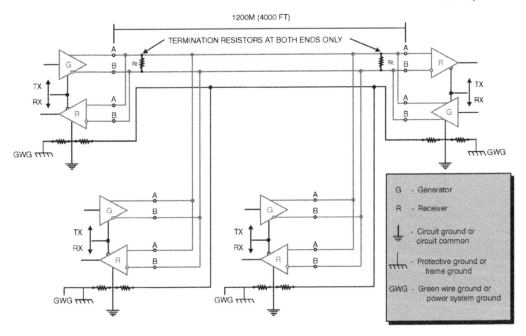

Figure 1.7
Typical two-wire multidrop network for RS-485

Protocols vary from the very simple such as ASCII-based protocols to the very sophisticated such as TCP and IP, which operate at high speeds transferring megabits of data per second. There is no right or wrong protocol, the choice depends on a particular application.

Examples of protocols include:

- *Layer 2*:　SDLC, HDLC
- *Layer 3*:　IP, IPX
- *Layer 4*:　TCP, UDP, SPX
- *Layers 5 + 6 + 7*:　CIP, HTTP, FTP, POP3, NetBIOS.

Depending on their functionality and the layer at which they operate, protocols perform one or more of the following functions:

- *Segmentation (fragmentation) and re-assembly*:　Each protocol has to deal with the limitations of the PDU (protocol data unit) or packet size associated with the protocol below it. For example, the Internet protocol (IP) (layer 3) can only handle 65 536 bytes of data, hence the transmission control protocol (TCP) (layer 4) has to segment the data received from layer 5 into pieces no bigger than that. IP (layer 3), on the other hand, has to be aware that Ethernet (layer 2) cannot accept more than 1500 bytes of data at a time and has to fragment the data accordingly. The term 'fragmentation' is normally associated with layer 3, whereas the term 'segmentation' is normally associated with layer 4. The end result of both is the same but the mechanisms differ. Obviously, the data stream fragmented by a protocol on the transmitting side has to be re-assembled by its corresponding peer on the receiving side, so each protocol involved in the process of fragmentation has to add appropriate parameters in the form of sequence numbers, offsets, and flags to facilitate this.

- *Encapsulation*:   Each protocol has to handle the information received from the layer above it 'without prejudice'; i.e. it carries/forwards it without regard for its content. For example, the information passed on to IP (layer 3) could contain a TCP header (layer 4) plus an FTP header (layers 5, 6, 7) plus data from an FTP client (e.g. Cute FTP). IP simply regards this as a package of information to be forwarded, adds its own header with the necessary control information, and passes it down to the next layer (e.g. Ethernet).

- *Connection control*:   Some layer 4 protocols such as TCP create logical connections with their peers on the other side. For example, when browsing the Internet, TCP on the client (user) side has to establish a connection with TCP on the server side before a web site can be accessed. Obviously, there are mechanisms for terminating the connection as well.

- *Ordered delivery*:   Large messages have to be cut into smaller fragments, but on a packet switching network, the different fragments can theoretically travel via different paths to their destination. This results in fragments arriving at their destination out of sequence, which creates problems in rebuilding the original message. This issue is normally addressed at layer 3 and sometimes at layer 4 (anywhere that fragmentation and segmentation takes place) and different protocols use different mechanisms, including sequence numbers and fragment offsets.

- *Flow control*:   The protocol on the receiving side must be able to liaise with its counterpart on the sending side in order not to be overrun by data. In simple protocols, this is accomplished by a lock-step mechanism (i.e. each packet sent needs to be acknowledged before the next one can be sent) or XON/XOFF mechanisms where the receiver sends an XOFF message to the sender to pause transmission, then sends an XON message to resume transmission.

  More sophisticated protocols use 'sliding windows'. Here, the sliding window is a number that represents the amount of unacknowledged data that can still be sent. The receiver does not have to acknowledge every message, but can from time to time issue blanket acknowledgments for all data received up to a point. As the sender sends data, the window shrinks and as the receiver acknowledges, the window expands accordingly. When the window becomes zero, the transmitter stops until some acknowledgment is received and the window opens up again.

- *Error control*:   The sender needs some mechanism by which it can ascertain if the data received is the same as the data sent. This is accomplished by performing some form of checksum on the data to be transmitted, including the checksum in the header or in a trailer after the data. Types of checksum include vertical and longitudinal parity, *block check count* (BCC) and *cyclic redundancy checking* (CRC).

- *Addressing*:   Protocols at various levels need to identify the physical or logical recipient on the other side. This is done by various means. Layer 4 protocols such as TCP and UDP use port numbers. Layer 3 protocols use a protocol address (such as the IP address for the Internet protocol) and layer 2 protocols use a hardware (or 'media') address such as a station number or MAC address.

- *Routing*: In an internetwork, i.e. a larger network consisting of two or more smaller networks interconnected by routers, the routers have to communicate with each other in order to know the best path to a given destination on the network. This is achieved by routing protocols (RIP, OSPF, etc.) residing on the routers.
- *Multiplexing*: Some higher-protocols such as TCP can create several 'logical' channels on one physical channel. The opposite can be done some lower-level protocols such as PPP where one logical stream of data can be sent over several physical (e.g. dial-up) connections. This mechanism is called multiplexing.

1.9 Noise

1.9.1 Sources of electrical noise

Typical sources of noise are devices that produce quick changes (or spikes) in voltage or current, such as:

- Large electrical motors being switched on
- Fluorescent lighting tubes
- Lightning strikes
- High-voltage surging due to electrical faults
- Welding equipment.

From a general point of view, there must be three contributing factors for the existence of an electrical noise problem. They are:

1. A source of electrical noise
2. A mechanism coupling the source to the affected circuit
3. A circuit conveying the sensitive communication signals.

1.9.2 Electrical coupling of noise

There are four forms of coupling of electrical noise into the sensitive data communications circuits. They are:

1. Impedance coupling (sometimes referred to as conductance coupling)
2. Electrostatic coupling
3. Magnetic or inductive coupling
4. Radio frequency radiation (a combination of electrostatic and magnetic).

Each of these noise forms will be discussed in some detail in the following sections.

1.9.3 Impedance coupling (or common impedance coupling)

For situations where two or more electrical circuits share common conductors, there can be some coupling between the different circuits with harmful effects on the connected circuits. Essentially, this means that the signal current from the one circuit proceeds back along the common conductor resulting in an error voltage along the return bus that affects all the other signals. The error voltage is due to the impedance of the return wire. This situation is shown in the Figure 1.8.

Obviously, the quickest way to reduce the effects of impedance coupling is to minimize the impedance of the return wire. The best solution is to use a separate return for each individual signal (Figure 1.9).

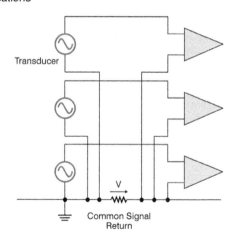

Figure 1.8
Impedance coupling

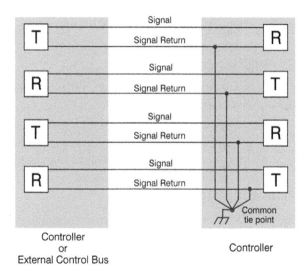

Figure 1.9
Impedance coupling eliminated with separate ground returns

1.9.4   Electrostatic or capacitive coupling

This form of coupling is proportional to the capacitance between the noise source and the signal wires. The magnitude of the interference depends on the rate of change of the noise voltage and the capacitance between the noise circuit and the signal circuit.

In Figure 1.10, the noise voltage is coupled into the communication signal wires through two capacitors, C_1 and C_2, and a noise voltage is produced across the resistance in the circuit. The size of the noise (or error) voltage in the signal wires is proportional to the:

- Inverse of the distance of noise voltage from each of the signal wires
- Length (and hence impedance) of the signal wires into which the noise is induced

- Amplitude (or strength) of the noise voltage
- Frequency of the noise voltage
- There are four methods for reducing the noise induced by electrostatic coupling. They are:

  - Shielding of the signal wires
  - Separating from the source of the noise
  - Reducing the amplitude of the noise voltage (and possibly the frequency)
  - Twisting of the signal wires.

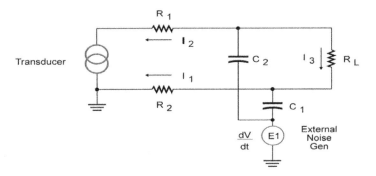

Figure 1.10
Electrostatic coupling

The problem can be addressed by installing an electrostatic shield around the signal wires. The currents generated by the noise voltages prefer to flow down the lower impedance path of the shield rather than the signal wires. If one of the signal wires and the shield are tied to the ground at one point, which ensures that the shield and the signal wires are at an identical potential, then reduced signal current flows between the signal wires and the shield (Figure 1.11).

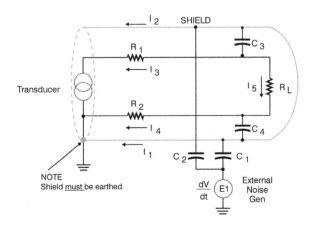

Figure 1.11
Shield to minimize electrostatic coupling

The shield must be of a low resistance material such as aluminum or copper. For a loosely braided copper shield (85% braid coverage), the screening factor is about 100 times or 20 dB. For a low resistance multi-layered screen, this screening factor can be 35 dB or 3000 times.

Twisting of the signal wires provides a slight improvement in reducing the induced noise voltage by ensuring that C_1 and C_2 are closer together in value; thus ensuring that any noise voltages induced in the signal wires tend to cancel each other out.

Provision of a shield by a cable manufacturer ensures that the capacitance between the shield and each wire is equal in value, thus eliminating any noise voltages by cancellation.

1.9.5   Magnetic or inductive coupling

This depends on the rate of change of the noise current and the mutual inductance between the noise system and the signal wires. Expressed slightly differently, the degree of noise induced by magnetic coupling will depend on the:

- Magnitude of the noise current
- Frequency of the noise current
- Area enclosed by the signal wires (through which the noise current magnetic flux cuts)
- Inverse of the distance from the disturbing noise source to the signal wires.

The effect of magnetic coupling is shown in Figure 1.12.

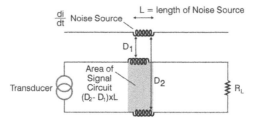

Figure 1.12
Magnetic coupling

The easiest way of reducing the noise voltage caused by magnetic coupling is to twist the signal conductors. This results in lower noise due to the smaller area for each loop. This means less magnetic flux to cut through the loop and consequently, a lower induced noise voltage. In addition, the noise voltage that is induced in each loop tends to cancel out the noise voltages from the next sequential loop. It is assumed that the noise voltage is induced in equal magnitudes in each signal wire due to the twisting of the wires giving a similar separation distance from the noise voltage (Figure 1.13).

The second approach is to use a magnetic shield around the signal wires. The magnetic flux generated from the noise currents induces small eddy currents in the magnetic shield. These eddy currents then create an opposing magnetic flux ϕ_1 to the original flux ϕ_2. This means a lesser flux ($\phi_2 - \phi_1$) reaches our circuit (Figure 1.14).

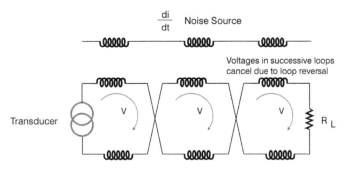

Figure 1.13
Twisting of wires to reduce magnetic coupling

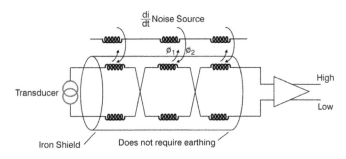

Figure 1.14
Use of magnetic shield to reduce magnetic coupling

Note: The magnetic shield does not require grounding. It works merely by being present. High-permeability steel makes best magnetic shields for special applications. However, galvanized steel conduit makes quite an effective shield.

1.9.6   Radio frequency radiation

The noise voltages induced by electrostatic and inductive coupling (discussed above) are manifestations of the near field effect, which is electromagnetic radiation close to the source of the noise. This sort of interference is often difficult to eliminate. It requires close attention to grounding of the adjacent electrical circuit, and the ground connection is only effective for circuits in close proximity to the electromagnetic radiation. The effects of electromagnetic radiation can be neglected unless the field strength exceeds 1 V/m. This can be calculated by the formula:

$$\text{Field strength} = \frac{\sqrt{2}(\text{Power})}{\text{Distance}}$$

Where
    Field strength: V/m
    Power: kilowatt
    Distance: km.

The two most commonly used mechanisms to minimize electromagnetic radiation are:

1. Proper shielding (iron)
2. Capacitors to shunt the noise voltages to ground.

Any incompletely shielded conductors will perform as a receiving aerial for the radio signal, and hence, care should be taken to ensure good shielding of any exposed wiring.

1.9.7   Shielding

It is important that electrostatic shielding is only grounded at one point. More than one ground point will cause circulating currents. The shield should be insulated to prevent inadvertent contact with multiple ground points, which could result in circulating currents. The shield should never be left floating because that would tend to allow capacitive coupling, rendering the shield useless.

Two useful techniques for isolating one circuit from the other are by the use of opto-isolation as shown in the Figure 1.15, and transformer coupling as shown in Figure 1.16.

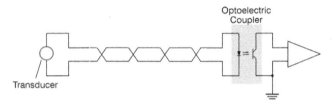

Figure 1.15
Opto-isolation of two circuits

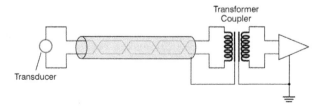

Figure 1.16
Transformer coupling

Although opto-isolation does isolate one circuit from the other, it does not prevent noise or interference being transmitted from one circuit to another.

Transformer coupling can be preferable to optical isolation when there are high-speed transients in one circuit. There is some capacitive coupling between the LED and the base of the transistor, which is in the opto-coupler, can allow these types of transients to penetrate one circuit from another. This is not the case with transformer coupling.

1.9.8   Good shielding performance ratios

The use of some form of low resistance material covering the signal conductors is considered good shielding practice for reducing electrostatic coupling. When comparing shielding with no protection, this reduction can vary from copper braid (85% coverage), which returns a noise reduction ratio of 100 : 1 to aluminum Mylar tape with drain wire, with a ratio of 6000 : 1.

Twisting the wires to reduce inductive coupling reduces the noise (in comparison to no twisting) by ratios varying from 14 : 1 (for 4 in. lay) to 141 : 1 (for 1 in. lay). In comparison, putting parallel (untwisted) wires into steel conduit only gives a noise reduction of 22 : 1.

On very sensitive circuits with high levels of magnetic and electrostatic coupling, the approach is to use coaxial cables. Double-shielded cable can give good results for very sensitive circuits.

Note: With double shielding, the outer shield could be grounded at multiple points to minimize radio frequency circulating loops. This distance should be set at intervals of less than one-eighth of the wavelength of the radio frequency noise.

1.9.9 Cable ducting or raceways

These are useful in providing a level of attenuation of electric and magnetic fields. These figures are done at 60 Hz for magnetic fields and 100 kHz for electric fields.

Typical screening factors are:

- 5 cm (2 in.) aluminum conduit with 0.154 in. thickness: magnetic fields (at 60 Hz) 1.5 : 1, electric fields (at 100 kHz) 8000 : 1
- Galvanized steel conduit 5 cm (2 in.), wall thickness 0.154 in. width: magnetic fields (at 60 Hz) 40 : 1, electric fields (at 100 kHz) 2000 : 1.

1.10 Cable spacing

In situations where there are a large number of cables varying in voltage and current levels, the IEEE 518 – 1982 standard has developed a useful set of tables indicating separation distances for various classes of cables. There are four classification levels of susceptibility for cables. Susceptibility, in this context, is understood to be an indication of how well the signal circuit can differentiate between the undesirable noise and required signal. It follows a data communication physical standard such as RS-232E that would have a high susceptibility and a 1000 V, 200 A AC cable that has a low susceptibility.

The four susceptibility levels defined by the IEEE 518 standard are briefly:

- *Level 1 (high)*: This is defined as analog signals less than 50 V and digital signals less than 15 V. This would include digital logic buses and telephone circuits. Data communication cables fall into this category.
- *Level 2 (medium)*: This category includes analog signals greater than 50 V and switching circuits.
- *Level 3 (low)*: This includes switching signals greater than 50 V and analog signals greater than 50 V. Currents less than 20 A are also included in this category.
- *Level 4 (power)*: This includes voltages in the range 0–1000 V and currents in the range 20–800 A. This applies to both AC and DC circuits.

IEEE 518 also provides for three different situations when calculating the separation distance required between the various levels of susceptibilities.

In considering the specific case where one cable is a high-susceptibility cable and the other cable has a varying susceptibility, the required separation distance would vary as follows:

- Both cables contained in a separate tray
  - Level 1 to Level 2–30 mm
  - Level 1 to Level 3–160 mm
  - Level 1 to Level 4–670 mm

- One cable contained in a tray and the other in conduit
  - Level 1 to Level 2–30 mm
  - Level 1 to Level 3–110 mm
  - Level 1 to Level 4–460 mm

- Both cables contained in separate conduit
  - Level 1 to Level 2–30 mm
  - Level 1 to Level 3–80 mm
  - Level 1 to Level 4–310 mm.

Figures are approximate as the original standard is quoted in inches. A few words need to be said about the construction of the trays and conduits. The trays are to be manufactured from metal and firmly grounded with complete continuity throughout the length of the tray. The trays should also be fully covered preventing the possibility of any area being without shielding.

1.10.1   Grounding requirements

This is a contentious issue and a detailed discussion laying out all the theory and practice is possibly the only way to minimize the areas of disagreement. The picture is further complicated by different national codes, which whilst not actively disagreeing with the basic precepts of other countries, tend to lay down different practical techniques in the implementation of a good grounding system.

A typical design should be based around three separate ground systems. They are:

1. The equipment (or instrument) ground
2. The chassis (or safety) ground
3. The earth ground.

The aims of these systems are:

- To minimize the electrical noise in the system
- To reduce the effects of fault or ground loop currents on the instrumentation system
- To minimize the hazardous voltages on equipment due to electrical faults.

Ground is defined as a common reference point for all signals in equipment situated at zero potential. Below 10 MHz, a single point grounding system is the optimum solution. Two key concepts to be considered when setting up an effective grounding system are:

1. To minimize the effects of impedance coupling between different circuits (i.e. when three different currents, for example, flow through a common impedance)
2. To ensure that ground loops are not created (for example, by mistakenly tying the screen of a cable at two points to ground).

There are three types of grounding system possible as shown in Figure 1.17. The series single point is perhaps more common; while the parallel single point is the preferred approach with a separate ground system for different groups of signals.

1.10.2   Suppression techniques

It is often appropriate to approach the problem of electrical noise proactively by limiting the noise at the source. This requires knowledge of the electrical apparatus that is causing the noise and then attempting to reduce the noise caused here. The two main approaches are shown here.

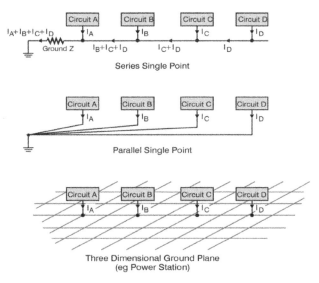

Figure 1.17
Various grounding configurations

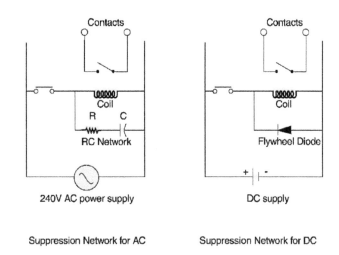

Figure 1.18
Suppression networks (snubbers)

In Figure 1.18, the inductance will generate a back emf across the contacts when the voltage source applied to it is switched off. This RC network then takes this back emf and thus reduces damage to the contacts.

The voltage can be limited by various combinations of devices, depending on whether the circuit is AC or DC.

Circuit designers should be aware that the response time of the coil could be reduced significantly. For example, the dropout time of a coil can be increased by a factor of ten. Hence, this should be approached with caution, where quick response is required from regular switched circuits (apart from the obvious negative impact on safety due to slowness of operation).

Silicon-controlled rectifiers (SCRs) and triacs generate considerable electrical noise due to the switching of large currents. A possible solution is to place a correctly sized inductor in series with the switching device.

1.10.3   Filtering

Filtering should be done as close to the source of noise as possible. Table 1.1 summarizes some typical sources of noise and possible filtering means.

Typical Sources of Noise	Filtering Remedy	Comments
AC voltage varies	Improved ferroresonant transformer	Conventional ferroresonant transformer fails
Notching of AC waveform form	Improved ferroresonant transformer	Conventional ferroresonant transformer fails
Missing half cycle in AC waveform	Improved ferroresonant transformer	Conventional ferroresonant transformer fails
Notching in DC line	Storage capacitor	For extreme cases active power line filters are required
Random excessively high-voltage spikes or transients	Non-linear filters	Also called limiters
High-frequency components	Filter capacitors across the line	Called low-pass filtering – great care should be taken with high frequency vs performance of 'capacitors' at this frequency
Ringing of filters	Use T filters	From switching transients or high level of harmonics
60 Hz or 50 Hz interference	Twin-T RC notch filter networks	Sometimes low-pass filters can be suitable
Common mode voltages	Avoid filtering (isolation transformers or common-mode filters)	Opto-isolation is preferred eliminates ground loop
Excessive noise	Auto or cross correlation techniques	Extracts the signal spectrum from the closely overlapping noise spectrum

Table 1.1
Typical noise sources and some possible means of filtering

1.11   Ingress protection

The *ingress protection* (IP) rating system is recognized in most countries and is described by several standards, including IEC 60529. It describes the degree of protection offered by an enclosure. This enclosure can be of any description, including a cable, cable assembly, connector body, the casing of a network hub, or a large cabinet used to enclose electronic equipment.

Enclosures are rated in the format 'IP xy' or 'IP xyz'.

- The first digit of the IP designation (x) describes the degree of protection against access to hazardous parts and ingress of solid objects.
- The second digit (y) designates the degree of protection against water. Refer to the appropriate sections of IEC 60529 for complete information regarding applications, features, and design tests.
- The third digit (z) describes the degree of protection against mechanical impacts and is often omitted. It does, e.g. apply to metal enclosures but not to cables or cable assemblies.

Here follows a list of meanings attributed to the digits of the IP rating.

1st	Protection Against Foreign Objects	2nd	Protection Against Moisture	3rd	Protection Against Mechanical Impacts
0	Not protected	0	Not protected	0	Not protected
1	Protected against objects greater than 50 mm diameter (e.g. hand contact)	1	Protected against dripping water (falling vertically, e.g. condensation)	1	Impact 0.225 J
2	Protected against objects greater than 12 mm (e.g. fingers)	2	Protected against dripping water when tilted 15° to either side	2	Impact 0.375 J
3	Protected against objects greater than 2.5 mm (e.g. tolls, wires)	3	Protected against rain up to 60° from vertical	3	Impact 0.60 J
4	Protected against objects greater than 1.0 mm (e.g. small tools, small wires)	4	Protected against splashing water, any direction	4	N/a
5	Dust protected – limited ingress permitted (no harmful deposits)	5	Protected against water jets (with nozzles)	5	Impact 2.00 J
6	Dust tight – totally protected against dust (no deposits at all)	6	Protected against heavy seas	6	N/a
7	N/a	7	Protection against effects of immersion	7	Impact 6.00 J
8	N/a	8	Protection against submersion	8	N/a
9	N/a	9	N/a	9	Impact 20.00 J

For example, a marking of IP 68 would indicate a dust tight (first digit = 6) piece of equipment that is protected against submersion in water (second digit = 8).

2

Copper cable

2.1 Cable characteristics

Two main types of copper cable are used in industrial communications. They are:

1. Coaxial cable, also referred to as coax
2. Twisted-pair cable, which can be shielded (STP/ScTP/FTP) or unshielded (UTP).

2.1.1 Cable structure

All copper cable types have the following components in common:

- One or more conductors to provide a medium for the signal
- Insulation of some sort around the conductors to help keep the signal in and interference out
- An outer sheath, or jacket, to encase the cable elements. The sheath keeps the cable components together, and may also help protect the cable components from water, pressure, or other types of damage.

Conductor

For copper cables, the conductor is known as the signal (carrier) wire and may consist of either solid or stranded wire. Solid wire is a single thick strand of conductive material, usually copper. A stranded wire consists of many thin strands of conductive material wound tightly together.

The signal wire is described in terms of the following:

- The type of conductive material
- Whether the wire is stranded or solid
- The carrier wire diameter, expressed directly (in inches, centimeters, or millimeters) or in terms of the wire gauge as specified in the AWG (*American wire gage*)
- The diameter of the strands, which determines some of the wire's electrical properties such as resistance and impedance. These properties, in turn, help determine the wire's performance.

Insulation

The insulating layer keeps the signal from escaping and helps to protect the signal from outside interference. The insulation is usually made of a dielectric such as polyethylene.

Some types of coaxial cable have multiple protective layers around the signal wire. The size of the insulating layer determines the spacing between the conductors in a cable and therefore its capacitance and impedance.

Cable sheath

The outer casing (sheath) of the cable provides a shell that keeps the cable elements together. The sheath differs for indoor and outdoor exposure. Outdoor cable sheaths tend to be black, with appropriate resistance to UV light, and have enhanced water resistance. Two main classes of sheath for indoor use are plenum and non-plenum.

For certain environments, local laws require plenum (a plenum is the space between a ceiling and a roof) cable. It must be used when the cable is being run 'naked' (without being put in a conduit) inside walls and above ceilings, and should probably be used whenever possible. Plenum sheaths are made of non-flammable fluoropolymers such as Teflon or Kynar. They are fire resistant and do not give off toxic fumes when burning. They are also considerably more expensive than cables with non-plenum sheaths. Plenum cable specified for networks installed in the USA should generally meet the NEC (*national electrical code*) CMP (*communications plenum cable*) or CL2P (*class 2 plenum cable*) specifications. Networks installed in other countries may have to meet equivalent safety standards, and these should be determined before installation. The cable should also be *underwriters laboratories* (UL) listed for UL-910, which subjects plenum cable to a flammability test.

Non-plenum cable uses less expensive material for the sheath, so it is consequently less expensive, but it can often be used only under restricted conditions. Non-plenum cable sheaths are made of *polyethylene* (PE) or *polyvinyl chloride* (PVC), which will burn and give off toxic fumes. PVC cable used for networks should meet the NEC CMR (*communications riser cable*) or CL2R (*class 2 riser cable*) specifications. The cable should also be UL-listed for UL-1666, which subjects riser cable to a flammability test.

2.1.2 Cable packaging

Cables can be packaged in different ways, depending on what it is being used for and where it is located.

The following types of cable packaging are available:

- *Simplex cable*: One cable within one sheath, which is the default configuration. The term is used mainly for fiber-optic cable to indicate that the sheath contains only a single fiber.
- *Duplex cable*: Two cables or fibers within a single sheath. In fiber-optic cable, this is a common arrangement. One fiber is used to transmit in each direction.
- *Multi-fiber cable*: Multiple cables or fibers within a single sheath. For fiber-optic cable, a single sheath may contain thousands of fibers. For electrical cable, the sheath will contain at the most a few dozen cables.

2.1.3 Factors affecting cable performance

Copper cables are good for signal transfer, but they are not perfect. Ideally, the signal at the end of a length of cable should be the same as at the beginning. Unfortunately, this will not be true in practice. All signals degrade when transmitted over a distance through any medium. This is because its amplitude decreases as the medium resists the flow of energy, and signals become distorted because the higher frequencies are attenuated more than the lower ones. Any transmission also consists of signal and noise components. Signal quality degrades for several reasons, including attenuation, crosstalk, and impedance mismatches.

Attenuation

Attenuation is the decrease in signal strength, measured in *decibels* (dB) per unit length. Attenuation occurs more quickly at higher frequencies and when the cable resistance is higher.

In networking environments, repeaters are responsible for regenerating a signal before passing it on. Many devices such as hubs are, in fact, repeaters without explicitly saying so. Since attenuation is sensitive to frequency, some situations require the use of equalizers.

Characteristic impedance

The impedance of a cable is defined as the resistance offered to the flow of electrical current at a particular frequency. The *characteristic impedance* is the impedance of an infinitely long cable, where the signal never reaches the end of the cable and hence cannot bounce back. The same situation is replicated when a cable is terminated. A short cable terminated in its characteristic impedance appears electrically to be infinitely long and has no signal reflected from the remote end. If one cable is connected to another of differing characteristic impedance, then there is some reflection at the junction. These reflections cause interference with the data signals and must be avoided (Figure 2.1).

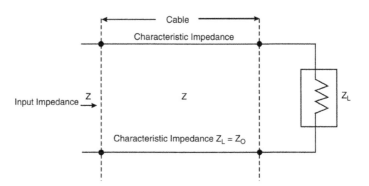

Figure 2.1
Characteristic impedance $Z_O = Z_L$

Crosstalk

Crosstalk is electrical interference in the form of signals picked up from a neighboring cable or circuits. For example, signals on different wires in a multistranded twisted-pair cable may interfere with each other.

The following forms of crosstalk measurement are important for twisted-pair cables:

- *Near-end crosstalk (NEXT)*:   NEXT measurements (in dB) indicate the degree to which unwanted signals are coupled onto adjacent wire pairs. This unwanted 'bleeding over' of a signal from one wire pair to another can disturb the desired signal. As the name implies, NEXT is measured at the 'near end' or the end closest to the transmitted signal. NEXT is a 'pair-to-pair' reading, where each wire pair is tested for crosstalk relative to another pair. NEXT increases as the frequency of transmission increases (see Figure 2.2).

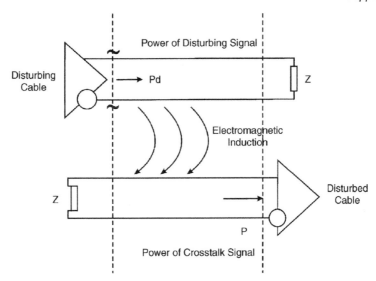

Figure 2.2
Near end crosstalk (NEXT)

- *Far-end crosstalk (FEXT)*: This is similar in nature to NEXT, but crosstalk is measured at the opposite end from the transmitted signal. FEXT tests are affected by signal attenuation to a much greater degree than NEXT, since it is measured at the far end of the cabling link where signal attenuation is greatest. Therefore, FEXT measurements are a more significant indicator of cable performance if attenuation is accounted for.
- *Equal-level far-end crosstalk (ELFEXT)*: The comparative measurement of FEXT and attenuation is called equal-level far-end crosstalk or ELFEXT. ELFEXT is the arithmetic difference between FEXT and attenuation. Characterizing ELFEXT is important for cabling links intended to support four-pair full-duplex network transmissions.
- *Attenuation-to-crosstalk ratio (ACR)*: ACR is not specifically a new test, but rather a relative comparison between NEXT and attenuation performance. Expressed in decibels (dB), the ratio is the arithmetic difference between NEXT and attenuation. ACR is significant because it is more telling of cable performance than NEXT or attenuation alone. ACR is a measure of the strength of a signal compared to the crosstalk noise.
- *Power sum NEXT*: Power sum NEXT (in dB) is calculated from the six measured pair-to-pair crosstalk results. Power sum NEXT differs from pair-to-pair NEXT by determining the crosstalk induced on a given wire pair from three disturbing pairs. This methodology is critical for supporting transmissions that utilize all four pairs in the cable such as Gigabit Ethernet (Figure 2.3).

2.2 Cable selection

Cables are used to meet all sorts of power and signaling requirements. The demands made on a cable depend on the location in which the cable is used and the function for which the cable is intended. These demands, in turn, determine the features a cable should have.

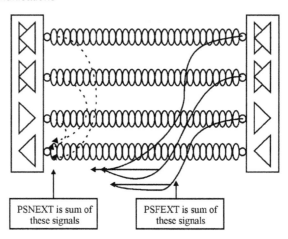

Figure 2.3
PSNEXT and PSFEXT

2.2.1   Function and location

Here are a few examples of considerations involving the cable's function and location:

- Cable designed to run over long distances, such as between floors or buildings, should be robust against environmental factors (moisture, temperature changes, etc.). This may require extra sheaths or sheaths made with a special material.

- Cable that must run around corners should bend easily, and the cable's properties and performance should not be affected by the bending. For several reasons, twisted-pair cable is probably the best cable for such a situation (assuming it makes sense within the rest of the wiring scheme). Of course, another way to get around a corner is by using a connector; however, connectors may introduce signal-loss problems.

- Cable that must run through areas in which heavy current motors are operating (or worse, being turned on and off at random intervals) must be able to withstand magnetic interference. Large currents produce strong magnetic fields, which can interfere with and disrupt nearby signals. Because it is not affected by such electrical or magnetic fluctuations, fiber-optic cable is the best choice in machinery-intensive environments.

- If you need to run many cables through a limited area, cable weight can become a factor, particularly if all that cable will be running in the ceiling above you. In general, fiber-optic and twisted-pair cables tend to be lightest.

- Cables installed in barely accessible locations must be particularly reliable. It is worth considering installing a backup cable during the initial installation. Because the installation costs in such locations are generally much more than the cable material cost, installation costs for the second cable add only marginally to the total cost.

- Cables that need to interface with other worlds (e.g. with a mainframe network or a different electrical or optical system) may need special properties or adapters. The kinds of cable required will depend on the details of the environments and the transition between them.

2.2.2 Main cable selection factors

Along with the function and location considerations, cable selection is determined by a combination of factors, including the following:

- The type of installation being planned (e.g. Ethernet or RS-485). While it is possible to use just about any type of cable in any type of network, certain cable types have been more closely associated with particular network types. In many cases, the exact type of cable is prescribed in the standard or the equipment vendor. Examples are:

  - EIA/TIA -568 Cat5 cable for 100 Mbps Ethernet
  - Belden 9841-9844 or similar for RS-485
  - Furon 1T52-8820-234 or Belden Databus 3076F for Foundation Fieldbus
  - Belden 3082A, 3083A, 3084A, and 3085A for DeviceNet.

- The amount of money available for the network. Keep in mind that cable installation can be an expensive part of the network costs.
- Whatever cabling resources are already available (and useable). There may be available wiring that could conceivably be used. It is almost certain, however, that at least some of that wire is defective or is not up to the requirements for the new application.
- Building or other safety codes and regulations.

2.3 Coaxial cables

In coaxial cable, two or more separate materials share a common central axis. Coax is used for radio frequency and data transmission. The cable is remarkably stable in terms of its electrical properties at frequencies below 4 GHz, and this makes the cable popular for cable television transmissions as well as for creating *local area networks* (LANs).

2.3.1 Coaxial cable construction

A coaxial cable consists of the following layers (moving outward from the center) as shown in Figure 2.4.

Carrier wire

A conductor wire or signal wire is in the center. This wire is usually made of copper and may be solid or stranded. There are restrictions regarding the wire composition for certain network configurations. The diameter of the signal wire is one factor in determining the attenuation of the signal over distance. The number of strands in a multistrand conductor also affects the attenuation.

Insulation

An insulation layer consists of a dielectric around the carrier wire. This dielectric is usually made of some form of polyethylene or Teflon.

Foil shield

This thin foil shield around the dielectric usually consists of aluminum bonded to both sides of a tape. Not all coaxial cables have foil shielding. Some have two foil shield layers, interspersed with copper braid shield layers.

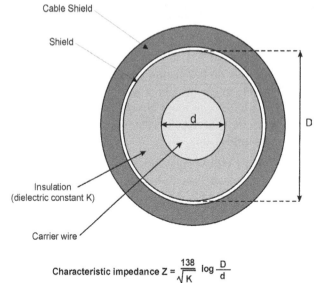

Figure 2.4
Cross section of coaxial cable

Braid shield

A braid (or mesh) conductor made of copper or aluminum that surrounds the insulation and foil shield. This conductor can serve as the ground for the carrier wire. Together with the insulation and any foil shield, the braid shield protects the carrier wire from *electromagnetic interference* (EMI) and *radio frequency interference* (RFI). The braid and foil shields provide good protection against electrostatic interference when earthed correctly, but little protection against electromagnetic interference.

Sheath

This is the outer cover that can be either plenum or non-plenum, depending on its composition. The signal and shield wires are concentric (coaxial) and hence the name.

2.3.2   Coaxial cable performance

The main features that affect the performance of coaxial cable are its composition, diameter, and impedance. The carrier wire's composition determines how good a conductor the cable will be. Cable diameter helps determine the electrical demands that can be made on the cable. In general, thick coaxial cable can support a much higher level of electrical activity than thin coaxial cable.

Impedance is a measure of opposition to the flow of alternating current. The properties of the dielectric between the carrier wire and the braid help determine the cable's characteristic impedance, which in turn imposes limits on where the cable can be used. For example, Ethernet and ARCnet architectures can both use thin coaxial cable, but they have different characteristic impedances and so Ethernet and ARCnet cables are not compatible. Most LAN cables have an RG (*recommended gage*) rating and cable with the same RG rating from different manufacturers can be safely mixed (Table 2.1).

Recommended Gage	Application	Characteristic Impedance (Ω)
RG-8	10BASE-5	50
RG-58	10BASE-2	50
RG-59	CATV	75
RG-2	ARCnet	93

Table 2.1
Common network coaxial cable impedances

In LANs, the characteristic cable impedances range from 50 Ω (RG-8/u or RG-58/u for Ethernet) to 93 Ω (RG-59/u or RG-62/u for ARCnet). The impedance of the coaxial cable is given by the formula:

$$Z = \frac{138}{\sqrt{k}} \log \frac{D}{d}$$

Where k is the dielectric constant of the insulation.

Advantages of coaxial cable

Coaxial cable has the following general advantages over other types of cable that might be used for a network. These advantages may change or disappear over time, as technology advances and products improve:

- Broadband coaxial can be used to transmit voice, data, and even video.
- The cable is relatively easy to install.
- Coaxial cable is reasonably priced compared with other cable types.

Disadvantages of coaxial cable

Coaxial cable has the following disadvantages when used for a network:

- It is easily damaged and sometimes difficult to work with, especially in the case of thick coaxial.
- Coaxial is more difficult to work with than twisted-pair cable.
- Thick coaxial cable can be expensive to install, especially if it needs to be pulled through existing cable conduits.
- Connectors can be expensive.

Coaxial cable faults

The main problems encountered with coaxial cables include the following:

- *Open- or short-circuited cables*: The cable may have an open or short circuit due to badly installed connectors or the cable may get crushed during the installation process. Check that the terminating resistors are fitted and have the correct value.
- *Characteristic impedance mismatches*: Obviously, cables must be used with the correct impedance connectors. RG-62 and RG-58 use similar BNC connectors but have different characteristic impedances (93 vs 50 Ω).

2.4   Twisted-pair cable

Twisted-pair cable is widely used, inexpensive, and easy to install. Twisted-pair cable comes in two main varieties namely shielded (STP, FTP, and ScTP) and unshielded (UTP).

It can transmit data at an acceptable rate, up to 1000 Mbps in some network architectures. The most common twisted-pair wiring is telephone cable, which is unshielded and is usually voice-grade, rather than the higher quality data-grade cable used for networks.

In a twisted-pair cable, two conductor wires are wrapped around each other. Twisted pairs are made from two identical insulated conductors, which are twisted together along their length at a specified number of twists per meter, typically forty twists per meter (twelve twists per foot). The wires are twisted to reduce the effect of electromagnetic and electrostatic induction.

For full-duplex digital systems using balanced transmission, two sets of screened twisted pairs are required in one cable; each set with individual and overall screens. A protective PVC sheath then covers the entire cable.

The capacitance of a twisted pair is fairly low (about 40 to 160 pF/m), allowing a reasonable bandwidth and an achievable slew rate. A signal is transmitted differentially between the two conductor wires. The current flows in opposite directions in each wire of the active circuit, as shown in Figure 2.5.

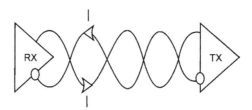

Figure 2.5
Current flow in a twisted pair

Elimination of noise

The twisting of associated pairs and method of transmission reduces the interference from the other pairs of wire throughout the cable.

The transmitted signals are in the form of changes of electrical state. An encoding process turns ones and zeroes into these signals. In a twisted-pair system, the required signal as well as its mirror image is transmitted simultaneously over the TX+ and TX– wires, respectively. Since these wires are of the same length and have the same construction, the signal travels at the same rate. Since the pairs are twisted together, any outside electrical interference will affect both wires in the same way.

The transmissions of the original signal and its mirror image reach a destination transceiver and are fed into a differential amplifier. Because the signals on the TX+ and TX– wires are of opposite polarity but of equal magnitude they add up, but any induced noise, being of the same magnitude and polarity, will cancel out (Figure 2.6).

Since the currents in the two conductors are equal and opposite, their induced magnetic fields also cancel each other. This type of cable is therefore self-shielding and is less prone to interference.

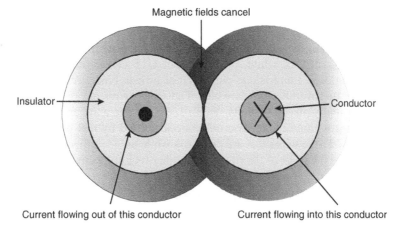

Figure 2.6
Magnetic shielding of twisted-pair cables

Twisting within a pair minimizes crosstalk between pairs. The twists also help deal with EMI and RFI as well as balancing the mutual capacitance of the cable pair. The performance of a twisted-pair cable can be influenced by changing the number of twists per meter in a wire pair.

2.4.1 Components of twisted-pair cable

A twisted-pair cable has the following components.

Conductor wires

The signal wires for this cable come in pairs that are wrapped around each other. The conductor wires are usually made of copper. They may be solid (consisting of a single wire) or stranded (consisting of many thin wires wrapped tightly together). A twisted-pair cable usually contains multiple twisted pairs; 2, 4, 6, 8, 25, 50, or 100 twisted-pair bundles are common. For network applications, two- and four-pair cables are most commonly used.

Shield

The terminology is slightly confusing as different methods are used for shielding. Some STP (*shielded twisted pair*) cables such as IBM type 1 cable have a shield in the form of a woven copper braid. In addition, each pair is individually wrapped in a foil screen. For Ethernet, screened Cat5 is normally used. Some versions of screened Cat5 have a full foil screen around all four pairs while some have individual foil screens around each pair. These are called ScTP (*screened twisted pair*) or FTP (*foil twisted pair*).

Sheath

The wire bundles are encased in a sheath made of PVC or, in plenum cables, of a fire-resistant material, such as Teflon or Kynar.

UTP cabling most commonly includes four pairs of wires enclosed in a common sheath. The typical single UTP cable is a PVC or plenum-rated plastic jacket containing four pairs of wire, and the majority of facility cabling in current and new installations is four pair cable of this type. The dedicated single connections made using four pair cable are easier to troubleshoot and replace than the alternative, bulk multipair cable such as 25-pair cable.

The jacket of each wire in a four pair cable will have an overall color: brown, blue, orange, green, or white. In a four pair UTP cable (the typical UTP used in networking installations), there is one wire each of brown, blue, green, and orange, and four wires of which the overall color is white. The white wires are distinguished from one another by periodically placed (usually within 1/2 in. of one another) rings of the other four colors.

Wires with a unique base color are identified by that base color: blue, brown, green, or orange. Those wires that are primarily white are identified as white/<color>, where <color> indicates the color of the rings of the other four colors in the white insulator.

2.4.2   EIA/TIA-568 cable categories

To distinguish between varieties of UTP, the United States Electronic Industries Association/Telecommunications Industries Association (EIA/TIA) has formulated several categories. The electrical specifications for these cables are detailed in EIA/TIA-568A, TSB-36, TSB-40, and their successor SP2840. These categories are:

Category 1 (Cat1)

Voice-grade, UTP telephone cable. This describes the cable that has been used for years in North America for telephone communications. Officially, such cable is not considered suitable for data-grade transmissions. In practice, however, it works fine over short distances and under ordinary working conditions. Be aware that other telecommunications providers have often used cable that does not even come up to this minimum standard and as such is very unacceptable for data transmission.

Category 2 (Cat2)

Voice-grade UTP, capable of supporting transmission rates of up to 4 Mbps. IBM Type 3 cable falls into this category.

Category 3 (Cat3)

Data-grade UTP used extensively for supporting data transmission rates of up to 10 Mbps. An Ethernet 10BASE-T network cabled with twisted pair requires at least this category of cable. Cat3 UTP cabling must not produce an attenuation of a 10 MHz signal greater than 98 dB/km at the control temperature of 20 °C. Typically, Cat3 cable attenuation increases 1.5% per degree Celsius.

Category 4 (Cat4)

Data-grade UTP, capable of supporting transmission rates of up to 16 Mbps. An IBM Token Ring network transmitting at 16 Mbps requires this type of cable.
Cat4 UTP cabling must not produce an attenuation of a 10 MHz signal greater than 72 dB/km at the control temperature of 20 °C.

Category 5 (Cat5)

Data-grade UTP capable of supporting transmission rates of up to 155 Mbps (but officially only up to 100 Mbps). Cat5 cable is constructed and insulated such that the maximum attenuation of a 10 MHz signal in a cable run at the control temperature of 20 °C is 65 dB/km.

TSB-67 contains specifications for the verification of installed UTP cabling links that consist of cables and connecting hardware specified in the TIA-568A standard.

Enhanced Category 5 (Cat5e)

This standard specifies transmission performance that exceeds Cat5. Cat5 supports the vast majority of existing network types such as 100BASE-T (Fast Ethernet) and ATM 155, but lacks the test parameters, are critical for support of new network technologies such as 1000BASE-T (Gigabit Ethernet). Cat5e directly supports the needs of Gigabit Ethernet. Test parameters include wire map, length, propagation delay, delay skew, attenuation, NEXT (pair-to-pair as well as Power Sum, PSELFEXT, and return loss).

Frequency range: To be measured from 1 through 100 MHz (not 100 Mbps).

Category 6 (Cat6)

Cat6 is aimed at delivering a 100 m (330 ft) channel of twisted-pair cabling providing a minimum ACR at 200 MHz that is approximately equal to the minimum ACR of a Cat5 channel at 100 MHz.

Cat6 includes all of the Cat5e parameters but extends the test frequency to 200 MHz, greatly exceeding current Cat5 requirements. (The IEEE has proposed extending the test frequency to 250 MHz to characterize links that may be marginal at 200 MHz.) It is likely that Cat6 will be the most demanding standard for four-pair UTP terminating with RJ-45 connectors. Like Cat5e, Cat6 is intended to support emerging networks such as Gigabit Ethernet. Cat6 provides a mechanism to certify to a level much greater than Cat5, providing assurance that the cabling infrastructure will support future networks that may require greater than 100 MHz bandwidth.

Test parameters include all the performance parameters that have been specified for Cat5e. Cat6 components and links are to be tested to 250 MHz even though the ACR values for the installed links are negative at 250 MHz.

Note: Several vendors are promoting 'proprietary Category 6 solutions'. These 'proprietary Category 6' cabling systems only deliver a comparable level of performance if every component of connecting hardware (socket and plug combination) is purchased from the same vendor and from the same product series.

Specially selected eight-pin modular connector jacks and plugs need to be matched because they are designed as a 'tuned pair' in order to achieve the high level of crosstalk performance for NEXT and FEXT. If the user mixes and matches connector components, the system will no longer deliver the promised 'Cat6-like' performance.

Category 7 (Cat7)

This is a *shielded twisted-pair* (STP) standard. This type of cabling may very likely only exist as the ISO Class F specification (possibly as STP-B in the USA). The cable people refer to when discussing Cat7 is constructed with individually shielded wire pairs with an overall shield around the four-shielded pairs. This cable is expensive and very difficult (i.e. expensive) to install. The cable itself provides a positive ACR value at 600 MHz but with a very weak signal (attenuation is 64 dB at 600 MHz). The installed link may be usable to 350 MHz.

Cat7 terminations will be something other than RJ-45 due to the inherent bandwidth limitations of the RJ-45 style connectors. Cat7 will not only support emerging high-speed technologies but will meet the bandwidth requirements of future networks that demand a much higher level of performance from the cabling infrastructure.

Advantages of twisted-pair cable

Twisted-pair cable has the following advantages over other types of cables for networks:

- It is easy to connect devices to twisted-pair cable.
- If an already installed cable system, such as telephone cable, has extra, unused wires, you may be able to use a pair of wires from that system – *but* see the warnings on this above.
- STP does a reasonably good job of blocking interference.
- UTP is quite inexpensive.
- UTP is very easy to install.
- UTP may already be installed (but make sure it all works properly and that it meets the performance specifications your network requires).

Disadvantages of twisted-pair cable

Twisted-pair cable has the following disadvantages:

- STP is sometimes bulky and difficult to work with.
- UTP is more susceptible to noise and interference than coaxial or fiber-optic cable.

Skin effect can increase attenuation. This occurs when transmitting data at a fast rate over twisted-pair wire. Under these conditions, the current tends to flow mostly on the outside surface of the wire. This greatly decreases the cross-section of the wire being used, and thereby increases resistance. This, in turn, increases signal attenuation.

2.4.3   Problems with unshielded twisted pairs

There are generally six types of faults with UTP cabling which will be discussed here. They are: attenuation, crossed pairs, split pairs, connector problems, termination practices, and crosstalk.

Attenuation

If the cable tester identifies a problem with attenuation, the following items should be checked:

- Excessive length of the cable (normally 100 m (330 ft) maximum between hub and node)
- Inferior quality cable (e.g. Cat3 used in place of Cat5)
- Rising temperatures (temperatures higher than 40 °C are not recommended)
- Badly installed connectors and connections.

Crossed pairs

For normal connections between a workstation and a hub, a straight-through cable is normally used. The hub port then has an X mark indicating that the connector at the hub actually performs the crossover function. In the total scheme of things, crossover is required between the network interface card and the hub (similar to a DTE connected to a DCE device where the transmitter on the one end has to be connected to a receiver at the other end).

Normally, one of the ports on the hub can be set up as a straight port or an X (crossover) port. This then allows hubs to be daisy-chained together.

Crossed-pair problems can be detected by a simple continuity check using an inexpensive cable tester or by observing the colors of the wires in the RJ-45 connectors.

Split pair problems

Physical continuity is maintained but conductors from different pairs are combined (e.g. pin-2 is twisted with pin-6 and pin-3 is twisted with pin-1). This sort of problem is unlikely to be detected with a simple continuity tester; but can be identified with low values of NEXT (22 dB or lower). The reason is that the electrical circuits in the pairs have enhanced coupling between them and do not have equal and opposite currents in each leg, resulting in greater crosstalk.

Connector problems

Ensure that the right type of connector is used. Stranded wire connectors have one blade, which pierces the strand; whilst solid wire connectors have two blades in the pin connector, which makes a firm grip on the conductor.

Termination problems

The checks that can be made here are:

- Ensure that the cable is twisted as far as possible on the connector and maintains a tight degree of twisting.
- Avoid the use of the old 66 type blocks (which have high attenuation and crosstalk).
- Ensure that voice and data cables are terminated on different punch blocks.

Crosstalk

If the cable tester indicates a high value of crosstalk check for the following items:

- Split pairs
- Use of silk line cables
- Voice and data cables mixed up
- Bad terminations.

2.5 Distribution/installation standards

There are various standards dealing with installations. These include (but are not limited to):

- ANSI/EIA/TIA-T568: Commercial Building Telecommunication Standard
- ANSI/EIA/TIA-569: Commercial Buildings, Standards for telecommunications Pathways and Spaces
- ANSI/EIA/TIA-606: Telecommunications Infrastructure Administration Standard
- ISO 11801: Generic Cabling for Customer Premises
- EIA/TIA-570: Residential and Light Commercial Telecommunications Wiring Standard
- EIA/TIA TR41.8.4 Outside Plant
- AT&T Zone Wiring Standard

- NEMA (National Electrical Manufacturers Association). Several standards, e.g. WC63.1 (Twisted-Pair, Premise Wiring Products)
- ICEA (Insulated Cable Engineers Association/Telecommunications Wire and Cable Standards/Technical Advisory Committee – (ICEA/TWCS/TAC). Several standards, e.g. S-90-661 Indoor Wiring Standard (Category Cables)
- IEEE 518: Guide for the Installation of Electrical Equipment to Minimize Electrical Noise Inputs to Controllers from External Sources.

Whereas most of these standards are of US origin, there are also specific standards originating in other countries, e.g.

- CAN/CSA-T528-93: Design Guidelines for Administration of Telecommunications Infrastructure (Canada)
- AUSTEL TS 008 and TS 009 (Australia)
- JIS X 5150 (Japan).

IEEE 518 deals with the identification of electrical noise in control circuits, the significance of electrical noise, sources of electrical noise, coupling of electrical noise, susceptibility of control circuits, electrical noise classification, electrical noise susceptibility classification, wiring type classification, shielding, filtering, buffering, noise immunity testing, installation recommendations, and wiring practices.

For situations where there are a large number of cables varying in voltage and current levels, the IEEE 518 standard provides a useful set of tables indicating separation distances for various classes of cables. There are four classification levels of susceptibility for cables. Susceptibility, in this context, is understood to be an indication of how well the signal circuit can differentiate between the undesirable noise and required signal. It follows that a data communication physical standard such as RS-232 would have a high susceptibility and a 1000 V, 200 A AC cable would have a low susceptibility.

The four susceptibility levels defined by the IEEE 518 standard are briefly:

Level 1 (high)   This is defined as analog signals less than 50 V and digital signals less than 15 V. This would include digital logic buses and telephone circuits. Data communication cables fall into this category.

Level 2 (medium)   This category includes analog signals greater than 50 V and switching circuits with voltages less than 50 V.

Level 3 (low)   This includes switching signals greater than 50 V and analog signals greater than 50 V. Currents less than 20 A are also included in this category.

Level 4 (power)   This includes voltages in the range 0–1000 V and currents in the range 20–800 A. This applies to both AC and DC circuits.

IEEE 518 also provides for three different situations when calculating the separation distance required between the various levels of susceptibilities. In considering the specific case where one cable is a high-susceptibility cable and the other cable has a varying susceptibility, the required separation distance would vary as follows:

Both cables contained in a separate tray

- Level 1 to Level 2: 30 mm
- Level 1 to Level 3: 160 mm
- Level 1 to Level 4: 670 mm.

One cable contained in a tray and the other in conduit:

- Level 1 to Level 2: 30 mm
- Level 1 to Level 3: 110 mm
- Level 1 to Level 4: 460 mm.

Both cables contained in separate conduits:

- Level 1 to Level 2: 30 mm
- Level 1 to Level 3: 80 mm
- Level 1 to Level 4: 310 mm.

Figures are approximate as the original standard is quoted in inches.

A few words need to be said about the construction of the trays and conduits. It is expected that the trays be manufactured from metal and firmly grounded with complete continuity throughout the length of the tray. The trays should also be fully covered preventing the possibility of any area being without shielding.

2.6   Connector standards

There is a wide range of connectors used by data communications equipment and to deal with all of them here would be impossible. This section will therefore discuss only a few of the more common and universally used connectors.

One of the older connectors around is the D-Subminiature connector (also called D-Submin, D-type, DB, or D connectors). They are specified for use with RS-232 and have recently also been used in Industrial Ethernet equipment, although they are not mentioned specifically in the Ethernet specification. Although they are fairly rugged, they are not dust or watertight and can only therefore only be used in IP20 environments, i.e. inside enclosures, in a plant (Figure 2.7).

Figure 2.7
DB-9 connector

Another type of connector that has become very popular due to Ethernet is the RJ-45 connector. This 8-pin plastic connector resembles a RJ-11 telephone connector; it is just a little wider. For applications in IP20 environments, requiring mounting and cabling of the equipment in a protected environment such as an enclosure, the RJ-45 has become a *de facto* standard for networking applications. New and improved connectors that fit the requirements based on the RJ-45 according to EN 60603-7 are also available. The RJ-45 is, in fact, recommended under IP20 conditions by the PNO/PTO (Profibus user organization) (Figure 2.8).

Ethernet I/O devices have become part of modern control systems. Ethernet makes it possible to use a variety of TCP/IP protocols to communicate with decentralized components virtually to sensor level. As a result, Ethernet is now installed in areas that were always the domain of traditional fieldbus systems. These areas demand IP67 class protection against dirt, dust, and fluids. This requires that suitable connector technology meeting IP67 standards have to be defined for transmission speeds up to 100 Mbps. Two solutions to this problem are emerging. The one is a modified RJ-45 connector (Figure 2.9) while the other is an M12 (micro-style) connector (Figure 2.10).

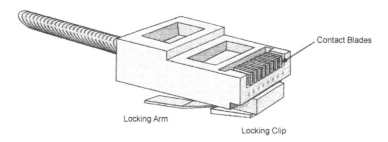

Contact Blades

Locking Arm

Locking Clip

Figure 2.8
RJ-45 connector

Figure 2.9
Modified RJ-45 connector (RJ-LNxx) (Courtesy: AMC Inc)

Standardization groups are addressing the problem both nationally and internationally. User organizations such as IAONA (Industrial Automation Open Networking Alliance), Profibus user organization, and ODVA (Open DeviceNet Vendor Association) are also trying to define standards within their organizations.

Network connectors for IP67 are not easy to implement. Three different approaches can be found. First, there is the RJ-45 connector sealed within an IP67 housing. Then, there is an M12 (micro-style) connector with either four or eight pins. A third option is a hybrid connector based on RJ-45 technology with additional contacts for power distribution. Two of the so-called sealed RJ-45 connectors are in the process of standardization. Initially the 4-pin M12 version will be standardized in Europe. Connectors will be tested against existing standards (e.g. VDE 0110) and provide the corresponding IP67 class protection at 100 Mbps. In the US, the ODVA has standardized a sealed version of the RJ-45 connector for use with Ethernet/IP.

For the use of the standard M12 in Ethernet, systems are covered in standard EN 61076-2-101. The transmission performance of 4-pin M12 connector for Ethernet up to 100 Mbps is comparable, if not better than standardized office grade Ethernet products. In office environments, four-pair UTP cabling is common. For industrial applications, two-pair cables are less expensive and easier to handle. Apart from installation difficulties, 8-pin M12 connectors may not meet all the electrical requirements described in EN 50173 or EIA/TIA-568B (Figure 2.10).

Figure 2.10
M12 connector (EtherMate) (Courtesy: Lumberg Inc.)

2.7   Earthing/grounding

This is a contentious issue and a detailed discussion laying out all the theory and practice is possibly the only way to minimize areas of disagreement. The picture is further complicated by different national codes, which whilst not actively disagreeing with the basic precepts of other countries, tend to lay down different practical techniques in the implementation of a good earthing system. There is also a great deal of confusion between what exactly is meant by earthing and grounding, the two words often (incorrectly) used as synonyms of each other.

'Ground' is defined as a common reference point for all signals in equipment, situated at zero potential. Therefore, the ideal ground is actually the planet Earth since it can source or sink an almost indefinite amount of energy without changing its potential.

There are essentially three forms of grounding for electronic circuits.

The first is the 'circuit ground' or 'circuit common', indicated by a triangular shape. This refers, for example, to the common ground area on a printed circuit board, to which all circuitry on the board is referenced. Generally speaking, this would be the ground reference for the electronics of a data communication system (Figure 2.11).

Figure 2.11
Symbol for common ground

A second type of ground is the 'protective ground' or 'chassis ground', represented by a rectangular shape. This could be, for example, the metal casing of an instrument or rack-mounted device. In the case of a rack-mounted device, it would be bonded to the rack in which the device is mounted. The circuit ground needs to be connected to the chassis ground, either directly or through a resistor (e.g. 100 Ω 1/2 W) to limit any currents that may flow due to potential differences (Figure 2.12).

Finally, there is the 'green wire ground', 'power system ground' or 'earth ground'. This is connected to the actual soil and forms the connection to 'planet Earth'. This connection should always be treated with some caution, as it cannot be automatically assumed that it has been done properly. In fact, the connection to 'earth' could very well only exist at the nearest electrical sub-station (Figure 2.13)!

Figure 2.12
Symbol for chassis ground

Figure 2.13
Symbol for earth ground

The symbols shown so far are not the only ones. ISO 7000 and IEC 60417 define the `
following symbols (Figure 2.14).

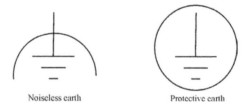

Noiseless earth   Protective earth

Figure 2.14
IEC 60417 symbols

No. 5018, 'noiseless earth' is used to identify a noiseless (clean) earth terminal (e.g. of
a specially designed earthing system to avoid equipment malfunction).

No. 5019, 'protective earth', is used to identify any terminal intended for connection to
an external conductor (for protection against electrical shock in case of a fault) or the
terminal of a protective earth electrode.

For specific examples of when to use these symbols, refer to EN 204, 'Safety of
Machinery-Electrical Equipment of Machines'.

A good grounding system serves to minimize the electrical noise in the system, reduce
the effects of fault or ground loop currents on the instrumentation system and minimize
the hazardous voltages on equipment due to electrical faults.

Below 10 MHz, a single point grounding system is the optimum solution. Two key
concepts to be considered when setting up an effective grounding system are:

1. To minimize the effects of impedance coupling between different circuits
   (i.e. when three different currents, for example, flow through a common impedance) and
2. To ensure that ground loops are not created, for example, by mistakenly tying
   the screen of a cable to earth at two points.

There are three types of grounding systems possible as shown in Figure 2.14. The series
single point is perhaps the most common, while the parallel (multiple) single point is the

preferred approach with a separate grounding system for each of the following groups of signals:

- Safety or power ground
- Low-level signal (or instrumentation) ground
- High-level signal (motor controls) ground
- Building ground.

2.8 Termination

A piece of wire carrying a signal from point A to point B acts as a transmission line. Signals propagate along copper wire at approximately two-thirds the speed of light, i.e. 2×10^8 m/s or 200 m/μs. If the furthest end of the cable is unterminated, the signal is reflected in phase and travels back towards the transmitter. In doing this, it collides with oncoming signals and the two signals become electrically superimposed, thereby corrupting the signal being transmitted. The reflected signal, once it reaches the original point of departure, gets reflected towards the furthest end once more. Fortunately, the wire has some resistance and due to its attenuating effect on the reflected signal, this will eventually stop (Figure 2.15).

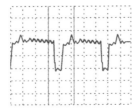 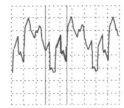

Figure 2.15
Terminated vs unterminated waveforms

The reflections also lead to the formation of standing waves along the transmission line, which create problems if the transmission line is a bus with several receivers attached to it. If a receiver is located at one of the 'troughs' it might not be able to receive anything. If, instead of being open circuit, the furthest end of the cable is short circuited, the signal is simply reflected back inverted (180° out of phase), but the effect is the same.

The only way to eliminate this phenomenon is by making the cable infinitely long, so that the signal travels onwards forever and never gets reflected, or, more realistically, by making the cable appear infinitely long. This is done by terminating the cable with a resistor (R_T) equal to the characteristic impedance of the cable (Z_o). The signal reaching the terminator now gets transformed into heat (Ohm's law: $P = V^2/R_T$) and does not return, creating the impression the cable is infinitely long.

It should be obvious that if the bit rate is relatively low and/or the cable is relatively short, the reflections (although they still exist) will not be much of a problem. In general, if the transient effect due to reflections dies out in less than 10% of the length of a single bit, it should not pose much of a problem.

Assuming the network cable is long enough for transmission-line effects to become relevant, a termination method has to be decided upon. There are quite a few termination methods available and National Semiconductor has published an application note (AN-903) that describes several techniques. Some of the simpler ones are discussed here.

It is, of course, possible that an unterminated network is an option. Unterminated networks are simple to build (no additional terminating components) but the data rates must be quite slow or the cable length must be short for the network to operate reliably.

Parallel termination (termination resistor at the furthest end) works well but it is limited to networks that only have one driver (e.g. RS-422). The driver must be located on one end of the network and the termination resistor must be located at the opposite end. The resistor, R_p, should have the same value as the characteristic impedance (Z_o) of the transmission line. Z_o for various cables are published by manufacturers. The larger the Z_o, the less power R_p must dissipate as heat. A 1/4 W or 1/2 W resistor is usually fine (Figure 2.16).

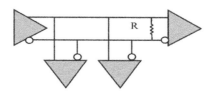

Figure 2.16
Parallel termination

Most twisted-pair cables have a Z_o in the range 100–130 Ω whereas coaxial cables have Z_o in the range 50–100 Ω. The characteristic impedance of a given cable depends on the diameters and spacing of the conductors, as well as the dielectric used.

The third termination technique is a bi-directional termination, which offers excellent signal integrity. With this technique, the line drivers can be anywhere on the network. This technique is probably the most reliable RS-485 termination technique (Figure 2.17).

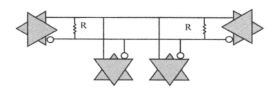

Figure 2.17
Bi-directional termination

The fourth technique is called AC termination. The idea is to use a capacitor as a DC blocking element to reduce power consumption in the terminating resistor. This method is tricky since the RC combination effectively forms a low-pass filter, hence the value of C has to be chosen so that the signal is not affected adversely. The inverse of τ, the time constant = RC, should be at least 10 times higher than the maximum signal frequency component. This type of termination is necessary on buses where the DC power and the signal is carried on the same pair of wires, as is the case with Foundation Fieldbus. Typical component values for RS-485 is 100 nF in series with 120 Ω (Figure 2.18).

Figure 2.18
RC termination

2.9   Transient protection

Electro static discharge (ESD) and capacitively or inductively coupled transients are a fact of life often overlooked when designing communication networks. Quite often the receiver circuits used for data communications (e.g. RS-485) fail for no apparent reason, despite everything apparently being done by the book. Inspection of damaged chips might reveal that often only one of several receivers on a chip is blown; the others remain functional.

This might be caused by transient voltages finding their way onto the data lines, despite no single source or coupling mechanism being apparent. If this is suspected, a method has to be devised to eliminate the problem at the board level. On new systems, this protection should be built in from the start.

There are several *transient voltage suppressant* (TVS) schemes to be used. Figures 2.19 to 2.22 show two specific methods. Both increase the ability of the receivers to tolerate transient events. Figure 2.22 shows the simplest and most effective method. It protects the receiving circuitry to about 8 kV. The tradeoff for good transient voltage protection is, however, a fairly high capacitive loading. The TranZorbs used have an open-circuit capacitance of around 500 pF. This is to be treated with caution as Figure 2.21 shows the effect of the protective devices having too large a capacitance (some devices can have a capacitance of as much as 6000 pF, equivalent to about 400 m of additional cable!). This effect is, of course, relative to the frequency of the incoming signal. Figure 2.21 shows a second circuit, which only protects to about 4 kV. The circuit uses a bridge with a low capacitance (about 13 pF) in series with the TranZorbs. This is a common circuit used to protect high-speed data lines.

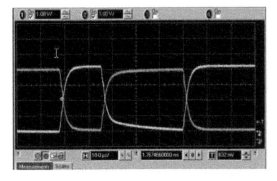

Figure 2.19
Signal at receiving end with capacitance within limits (Courtesy: Rodney Tower)

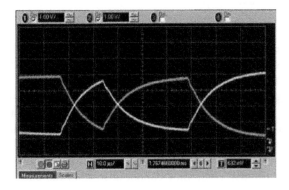

Figure 2.20
Effect of protective devices with too large a capacitance (Courtesy: Rodney Tower)

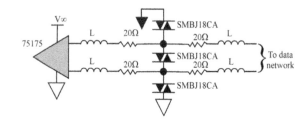

Figure 2.21
TVSs directly on the data line (Courtesy: National Semiconductor)

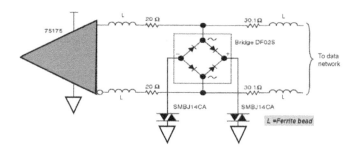

Figure 2.22
Alternative protection scheme (Courtesy: National Semiconductor)

A typical protective device will have a peak power rating of 500 W for 1 ms and a surge current rating of 70 A for 1/120 s. The response time of these devices is almost instantaneous (1×10^{-12} s).

Should it be necessary to test the effectiveness of the protective circuitry in a lab, an ESD gun such as a Shaffner NSG-435 must be used to simulate transient events on the transmission lines. A small network can be built in the lab and energy discharged into the data lines directly. Some devices, e.g. the Texas Instruments TI 75175 quad receiver, a very common device in RS-485 circuits, can often be destroyed with a single 1 to 2 kV air-gap discharge into either or both data lines.

A 1 kV air gap discharge seems a lot, but it is right on the edge of human perception. This means the receiver chips could be destroyed by ESD that may not even be noticeable to a technician.

TVSs directly on the data line provide the highest level of protection and the highest capacitive loading of the transmission line.

The second figure is common circuit for protecting high-speed data lines. Both TVS schemes shown provide significant improvement in the ability of receiver circuits to withstand transient voltage events.

It might also be prudent to specify receiver chips with a high-published resistance against static damage. For example, the datasheet for the Maxim MAX3095 claims a ±15 kV protection using IEC1000-4-2 air-gap discharge, ±8 kV using IEC1000-4-2 contact discharge, and ±15 kV using the Human Body Model.

If there is a possibility of damage by lightning induced transients, the TranZorbs alone are not sufficient since they cannot absorb all the energy. In this case, it is necessary to place *metal oxide varistors* (MOVs) or gas diodes in parallel with the TranZorbs. The TranZorbs are much quicker, and can clamp the input voltage for a few milliseconds until the MOV or gas diode fires. Care should be taken to supply a solid ground return for the large currents involved. Please note that the larger protective devices usually have a large capacitance that can lead to unacceptable signal degradation. The effect of the protective circuitry should be verified by means of a signal generator, line driver and oscilloscope before installation.

3

Fiber optics

3.1   Introduction

Fiber-optic communication uses light signals guided through a fiber core. Fiber-optic cables act as wave-guides for light, with all the energy guided through the central core of the cable. The light is guided due to the presence of a lower refractive index cladding surrounding the central core. None of the energy in the signal is able to escape into the cladding and no energy is able to enter the core from any external sources. Therefore the transmissions are not subject to electromagnetic interference.

The core and the cladding will trap the light ray in the core, provided the light ray enters the core at an angle greater than the critical angle. The light ray will then travel through the core of the fiber, with minimal loss in power, by a series of total internal reflections. Figure 3.1 illustrates this process.

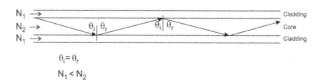

Figure 3.1
Light ray traveling through an optical fiber

Little of the light signal is absorbed in the glass core, so fiber-optic cables can be used for longer distances before the signal must be amplified, or repeated. Some fiber-optic segments can be many kilometers long before a repeater is needed. Data transmission using a fiber-optic cable is many times faster than with electrical methods, and speeds of over 10 Gbps are possible. Fiber-optic cables deliver more reliable transmissions over greater distances, although at a somewhat greater cost. Cables of this type differ in their physical dimensions and composition and in the wavelength(s) of light with which the cable transmits.

Fiber-optic cables offer the following advantages over other types of transmission media:

- Light signals are impervious to interference from EMI or electrical crosstalk.
- Light signals do not interfere with other signals. As a result, fiber-optic connections can be used in extremely adverse environments, such as in elevator shafts or assembly plants, where powerful motors produce lots of electrical noise.

- Optical fibers have a much wider, flat bandwidth than coaxial cables and equalization of the signals is not required.
- The fiber has a much lower attenuation, so signals can be transmitted much further than with coaxial or twisted-pair cable before amplification is necessary.
- Optical fiber cables do not conduct electricity and so eliminates problems of ground loops, lightning damage and electrical shock when cabling in high-voltage areas.
- Fiber-optic cables are generally much thinner and lighter than copper cable.
- Fiber-optic cables have greater data security than copper cables.
- Licensing is not required, although a right-of-way for laying the cable is needed.

3.2   Fiber-optic cable components

The major components of a fiber-optic cable are the core, cladding, buffer, strength members, and jacket, as shown in Figure 3.2. Some types of fiber-optic cable even include a conductive copper wire that can be used to provide power to a repeater.

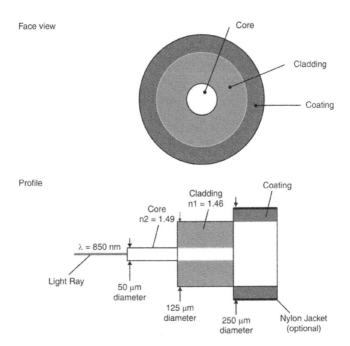

Figure 3.2
Fiber-optic cable components

3.2.1   Fiber core

The core of a fiber-optic telecommunications cable consists of a glass fiber through which the light signal travels. The most common core sizes are 50 and 62.5 μm (microns), which are used in multimode cables. 8.5 micron fibers are used in single-mode systems.

3.2.2   Cladding

The core and cladding are actually manufactured as a single unit. The cladding is a protective layer with a lower index of refraction than the core. The lower index means any light that hits the core walls will be redirected back to continue on its path. The cladding diameter is typically 125 microns.

3.2.3   Fiber-optic buffer

The buffer of a fiber-optic cable is made of one or more layers of plastic surrounding the cladding. The buffer helps strengthen the cable, thereby decreasing the likelihood of micro cracks, which can eventually break the fiber. The buffer also protects the core and cladding from potential invasion by water or other materials in the operating environment. The buffer typically doubles the diameter of the fiber.

A buffer can be tight or loose, as shown in Figure 3.3. A tight buffer fits snugly around the fiber. A tight buffer can protect the fibers from stress due to pressure and impact, but not from changes in temperature. A loose buffer is a rigid tube of plastic with one or more fibers (consisting of core and cladding) running through it. The fibers are longer than the tube so that the tube takes all the stresses applied to the cable, isolating the fiber from these stresses.

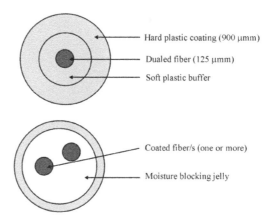

Figure 3.3
Fiber housing types

3.2.4   Strength members

Fiber-optic cable also has strength members, which are strands of very tough material (such as steel, fiberglass, or Kevlar) that provide tensile strength for the cable. Each of these materials has advantages and drawbacks. For example, steel conducts electricity making the cable vulnerable to lightning, which will not disrupt an optical signal but may seriously damage the cable or equipment.

3.2.5   Cable sheath

The sheath of a fiber-optic cable is an outer casing that provides primary mechanical protection, as with electrical cable.

3.3   Fiber-optic cable parameters

3.3.1   Attenuation

The attenuation of a multimode fiber depends on the wavelength and the fiber construction, and range from around 3 to 8 dB/km at 850 nm and 1 to 3 dB/km at 1300 nm. The attenuation of single-mode fiber ranges from around 0.4 to 0.6 dB/km at 1300 nm and 0.25 to 0.35 dB/km at 1550 nm.

3.3.2   Diameter

The fiber diameter is either 50 or 62.5 microns for multimode fiber or 8.5 microns for single mode.

- *Multimode fibers (50 or 62.5 micron)*:   In multimode fibers, a beam of light has room to follow multiple paths through the core. Multiple modes in a transmission produce signal distortion at the receiving end, due to the difference in arrival time between the fastest and slowest of the alternate light paths.
- *Single mode fibers (8.5 micron)*:   In a single-mode fiber, the core is so narrow that the light can take only a single path through it. Single-mode fiber has the least signal attenuation, usually less than 0.5 dB/km. This type of cable is the most difficult to install, because it requires precise alignment of the system components and the light sources and detectors are very expensive. However, transmission speeds of 50 Gbps and higher is possible.

3.3.3   Wavelength

Fiber-optic systems today operate in one of the three-wavelength bands viz. 850 nm, 1300 nm, or 1550 nm. The shorter wavelengths have a greater attenuation than the longer wavelengths. Short-haul systems tend to use the 850 or 1300 nm wavelengths with the multimode cable and light emitting diode (LED) light sources. The 1550 nm fibers are used almost exclusively with the long-distance systems using single-mode fiber and laser light sources.

3.3.4   Bandwidth

The bandwidth of a fiber is given as the range of frequencies across which the output power is maintained within 3 dB of the nominal output. It is quoted as the product of the frequencies of bandwidth multiplied by distance, for example, 500 MHz km. This means that 500 MHz of bandwidth is available over a distance of one kilometer, or 100 MHz of bandwidth over 5 km.

3.3.5   Dispersion

Modal dispersion is measured as nanoseconds of pulse spread per kilometer (ns/km). The value also imposes an upper limit on the bandwidth, since the duration of a signal must be larger than the nanoseconds of a tail value. With step-index fiber, expect between 15 and 30 ns/km. Note that a modal dispersion of 20 ns/km yields a bandwidth of less than 50 Mbps. There is no modal dispersion in single-mode fibers, because only one mode is involved.

Chromatic dispersion occurs in single-mode cables and is measured as the spread of the pulses in picoseconds for each nanometer of spectral spread of the pulse and for each kilometer traveled. This is the only dispersion effect in single-mode cables and typical values are in the order of 3.5 ps/nm km at 1300 nm and 20 ps/nm km at 1550 nm.

3.4   Types of optical fiber

One reason optical fiber makes such a good transmission medium is because the different indices of refraction for the cladding and core help to contain the light signal within the core, producing a waveguide for the light. Optical fiber can be constructed by changing abruptly from the core refractive index to that of the cladding, or this change can be made gradually (Figure 3.4). The two main types of multimode fiber differ in this respect.

- *Step-index cable*:   Cable with an abrupt change in refraction index is called step-index cable. In step-index cable, the change is made in a single step. Single-step multimode cable uses this method, and it is the simplest, least expensive type of fiber-optic cable. It is also the easiest to install. The core is usually 50 or 62.5 microns in diameter; the cladding is normally 125 microns. The core width gives light quite a bit of room to bounce around in, and the attenuation is high (at least for fiber-optic cable); between 10 and 50 dB/km. Transmission speeds up to 10 Mbps over 1 km are possible.

- *Graded-index cable*:   Cable with a gradual change in refraction index is called graded-index cable, or graded-index multimode. This fiber-optic cable type has a relatively wide core, like single-step multimode cable. The change occurs gradually and involves several layers, each with a slightly lower index of refraction. A gradation of refraction indexes controls the light signal better than the step-index method. As a result, the attenuation is lower, usually less than 15 dB/km. Similarly, the modal dispersion can be 1 ns/km and lower, which allows more than ten times the bandwidth of step-index cable.

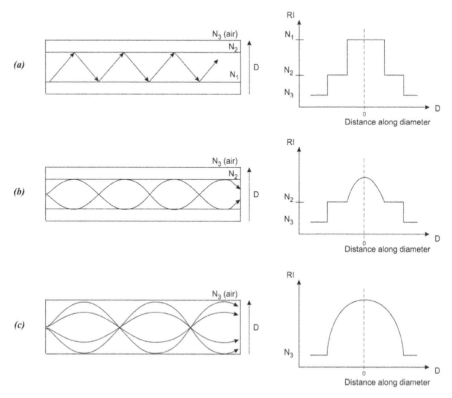

Figure 3.4
Fiber refractive index profiles

- *Fiber designations*: Optical fibers are specified in terms of their core, cladding, and coating diameters. For example, a 62.5/125/250 fiber has a core diameter of 62.5 microns, a cladding of 125 microns and a coating of 250 microns.

3.5 Basic cable types

There are four broad application areas into which fiber-optic cables can be classified: aerial cable, underground cable, sub-aqueous cable, and indoor cable. The special properties required for each of these applications will now be considered. Note that this list is not all encompassing, and that some specialized cables need to combine the features of several of these classes.

3.5.1 Aerial cable

Aerial cables are literally exposed to the elements, more than any other application, and as such are exposed to many external forces and hazards. Aerial cables are installed between poles with the weight of the cable continuously supported by usually a steel messenger wire to which the cable can be directly lashed, or by the strength members integral to the cable construction. Greatly increased tensile forces can be produced by the effects of combined wind and ice loadings. Other considerations are the wide variations in temperature to which the cable may be subjected, affecting the physical properties of the fibers and the attenuation of the fibers. The longitudinal cable profile is important for reducing the wind and ice loadings of such cables. Moisture barriers are essential, with jelly-filled, loose buffered fiber cable configurations being predominant. Any water freezing within the fiber housings would expand and could produce excessive bending of fibers.

The cable sheath material is required to withstand the extremes of temperature and the intense ultraviolet light exposure from continuous exposure to sunlight. UV-stabilized polyethylene is frequently used for this purpose.

The installed span length and sag requirements are important design parameters affecting the maximum cable tension, and which dictates the type of cable construction to be used. Short-span cables have less-stringent tension requirements, which can be met by the use of integral Kevlar layers, whereas long-span cables may need to utilize multiple-stranded FRP rods to meet the required maximum tensions.

Advantages of aerial cable

- Useful in areas where it may be very difficult or too expensive to bury the cable or install it in ducts.
- Also useful where temporary installations are required.

Disadvantages

- System availability is not as high as for underground cables. Storms can disrupt these communication bearers, with cables damaged by falling trees, storm damage, and blown debris. Roadside poles can be hit by vehicles and frustrated shooters seem unable to miss aerial cables!

3.5.2 Underground cable

Underground cables experience less environmental extremes than aerial cables. Cables are usually pulled into ducts or buried directly in the ground, with the cables being placed in deep narrow trenches, which are backfilled with dirt or else ploughed directly into the ground.

Cable type

Loose buffering, using loose tube or slotted core construction, is generally used to isolate fibers from external forces including temperature variations.

Advantages

- Usually the most cost-effective method of installing cables outdoors
- Greater environmental protection than aerial cable
- Usually more secure than aerial cable.

Disadvantages

- Can be disrupted by earthworks, farming, flooding, etc.
- Rodents biting cables can be a problem in some areas. This is overcome with the use of steel tape armor or steel braid, or the use of a plastic duct of more than 38 mm OD for all dielectric cable installations. Also the use of Teflon coatings on the sheath make the cable too slippery for the rodent to grip with its teeth.

3.5.3   Sub-aqueous cables

Sub-aqueous cables are basically outdoor cables designed for continuous immersion in water. While international telecommunications carriers use the most sophisticated cables for deep ocean communications, there are practical applications for sub-aqueous cables for smaller users. These include cabling along or across rivers, lakes, water races, or channels, where alternatives are not cost effective. Sub-aqueous cable is a preferred option for direct buried cabling in areas subjected to flooding or with a high water table, where, for example, if the cable were buried at, say, 1 m depth, it would be permanently immersed in water. These cables are essentially outdoor cable constructions incorporating a hermetically sealed unit, using a welded metallic layer, and encasing the fiber core.

Advantages

- Cheaper installation in some circumstances.

Disadvantages

- Unit cost of cable is higher.

3.5.4   Indoor cables

Indoor cables are used inside buildings and have properties dictated by the fire codes. Such cables need to minimize the spread of fires, and must comply with your relevant local fire codes, such as outlined in the national electrical codes (NEC) in USA. Outdoor cables generally contain oil-based moisture-blocking compounds like petroleum jelly. These support combustion and so, their use inside buildings is strictly controlled. Outdoor cables are frequently spliced to appropriate indoor cables close to the building entry points, to avoid the expense of encasing long runs of outdoor cable inside metallic conduit.

The fiber in indoor cables and the indoor cable itself is usually tightly buffered, as was discussed in Section 3.2. The tight buffer provides adequate water resistance for indoor applications, but such cables should not be used for long outdoor cable runs. The buffered fibers can be given sufficient strength to enable them to be directly connected to equipment from the fiber structure without splicing to patch cords.

3.6   Connecting fibers

This section will identify the main issues involved in connecting fibers together and to optical devices, such as sources and detectors. This can be done using splices or connectors. A splice is a permanent connection used to join two fibers and a connector is used where the connection needs to be connected and disconnected repeatedly, such as at patch panels. A device used to connect three or more fibers or devices is called a coupler.

3.6.1   Connection losses

The main parameter of concern when connecting two optical devices together is the attenuation – that fraction of the optical power lost in the connection process. This attenuation is the sum of losses caused by a number of factors, the main ones being:

- Lateral misalignment of the fiber cores
- Differences in core diameters
- Misalignment of the fiber axes
- Numerical aperture differences of the fibers
- Reflection from the ends of fibers
- Spacing of the ends of the fibers
- End finish and cleanliness of fibers.

The most important of these loss mechanisms involved in connecting multimode fibers is the axial misalignment of the fibers.

With connectors, the minimum loss across the glass/air interface between them will always be about 0.35 dB, unless index-matching gel is used.

3.6.2   Splicing fibers

Two basic techniques are used for splicing of fibers: fusion splicing and mechanical splicing. With the fusion splicing technique, the fibers are welded together, requiring expensive equipment, but will produce consistently lower loss splices with low consumable costs. With mechanical splicing, the fibers are held together in an alignment structure, using an adhesive or mechanical pressure. Mechanical splicers require lower capital cost equipment but have a high consumable cost per splice.

- *Fusion splicing*: Fusion splices are made by melting the end faces of the prepared fibers and fusing the fibers together. Practical field fusion splicing machines use an electric arc to heat the fibers. Factory splicing machines often use a small hydrogen flame. The splicing process needs to precisely pre-align the fibers, then heat their ends to the required temperature and move the softened fiber ends together sufficiently to form the fusion joint, whilst maintaining their precise alignment. Fusion splices have consistently very low losses and are the preferred method for joining fibers, particularly for single-mode systems. Modern single-mode fusion splicers utilize core alignment systems to ensure the cores of the two fibers are precisely aligned before splicing.
- *Mechanical splicing*: Mechanical splicing involves many different approaches for bringing the two ends of the fibers into alignment and then clamping them within a jointing structure or gluing them together. Mechanical splices generally rely on aligning the outer diameters of the fiber cladding and assumes that the cores are concentric with the outside of the cladding. This is not always

the case, particularly with single mode fibers. Various mechanical structures are used to align the fibers, including V grooves, sleeves, 3 rods and various proprietary clamping structures.

3.6.3   Connectors

Connectors are used to make flexible interconnections between optical devices. Connectors have significantly greater losses than splices since it is much more difficult to repeatedly align the fibers with the required degree of precision. Active alignment, as was used to minimize some splice losses, is not possible. Axial misalignment of the fibers contributes most of the losses at any connection, consequently connector loss can be expected to be in the range from 0.2 to over 3 dB.

Most connector designs produce a butt joint with the fiber ends as close together as possible. The fiber is mounted in a ferrule with a central hole sized to closely match the diameter of the fiber cladding. The ferrule is typically made of metal or ceramic and its purpose is to center and align the fiber as well as provide mechanical protection to the end of the fiber. The fiber is normally glued into the ferrule then the end cut and polished to be flush with the face of the ferrule. The two most common connectors are the SC and ST, as detailed below. Many new proprietary connectors are now available for different types of equipment.

- *SC connector*:   This is built with a cylindrical ceramic ferrule which mates with a coupling receptacle. The connector has a square cross section for high packing density on equipment, and has a push–pull latching mechanism. The ISO and TIA have adopted a polarized duplex version as standard and this is now being used as a low-cost FDDI connector. The SC connector has a specified loss of less than 0.6 dB (typically 0.3 dB) for both single mode and multimode fibers and a typical return loss of 45 dB.
- *ST connector*:   The ST connector is shown in Figure 3.5. This is an older standard used for data communications. This is also built with a cylindrical ceramic ferrule which mates with a coupling receptacle. The connector has a round cross section and is secured by twisting to engage it in the spring-loaded bayonet coupling. Since it relies on the internal spring to hold the ferrules together, optical contact can be lost if a force of greater than about 1 kg is applied to the connector.

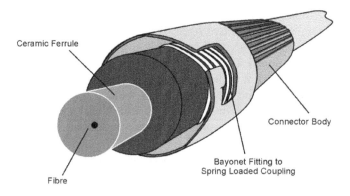

Figure 3.5
ST connector

3.6.4   Connector handling

Most fiber-optic connectors are designed for indoor use. Connectors for outdoor use require to be hermetically sealed. It is very important to protect the optical faces of the connectors from contamination. The optical performance can be badly degraded by the presence of dirt or dust on the fiber ends. A single dust particle could be 10 microns in diameter, which would scatter or absorb the light and could totally disrupt a single-mode system. Connectors and patch panels are normally supplied with protective caps. These should always be fitted whenever the connectors are not mated. These not only protect from dust and dirt, but also provide protection to the vulnerable, polished end of the fiber. Compressed air sprays are available for cleaning connectors and adapters, without needing to physically touch the mating surfaces.

Take care not to touch the end of the connector ferrules as the oil from your fingers can cause dirt to stick to the fiber end. Clean connectors with lint-free wipes and isopropyl alcohol.

Durability of the connectors is important throughout their lifetime. Typical fiber connectors for indoor use are specified for 500 to 1000 mating cycles, and the attenuation is typically specified not to change by more than 0.2 dB throughout that lifetime. Repeated connection and disconnection of the connectors can wear the mechanical components and introduce contamination to the optical path.

3.6.5   Optical couplers

Optical couplers or splitters and combiners are used to connect three or more fibers or other optical devices. These are devices which split the input power to a number of outputs. While the splitting of the light is done passively, active couplers include optical amplifiers, which boost the signal before or after the splitting process. Coupler configuration depends on the number of ports and whether each of these are unidirectional, so called directional couplers, or bi-directional. Most couplers are found within the equipment for monitoring purposes.

3.7   Splicing trays/organizers and termination cabinets

This section looks at the different types of storage units that are used for housing optical fiber splices and end of cable terminations.

3.7.1   Splicing tray

Splices are generally located in units referred to as 'splicing centers', 'splicing trays' or 'splicing organizers'. The splicing tray is designed to provide a convenient location to store and to protect the cable and the splices. They also provide cable strain relief to the splices themselves.

Splicing trays can be located at intermediate points along a route where cables are required to be joined or at the termination and patch panel points at the end of the cable runs.

The incoming cable is brought into the splicing center where the sheath of the cable is stripped away. The fibers are then looped completely around the tray and into a splice holder. Different holders are available for different types of splices. The fibers are then spliced onto the outgoing cable if it is an intermediate point or on to pigtails if it is a termination point. These are also looped completely around the tray and then fed out of the tray. A typical splicing tray is illustrated in Figure 3.6.

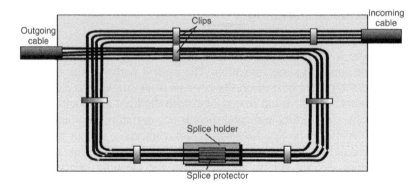

Figure 3.6
A typical splicing tray

The cables are physically attached to the splice tray to provide strain relief. The cables normally enter the tray on one side only to facilitate moving the tray/joint enclosure to a more accessible jointing location. The fibers are looped completely around the tray to provide slack, which may be required to accommodate any changes in the future, and also to provide tension relief on the splices.

Each splice joint is encased in a splice protector (plastic tube) or in heat shrink before it is clipped into the holder.

Splicing trays are available that have patching facilities. This allows different fibers to be cross-connected and to be looped back for testing purposes.

3.7.2   Splicing enclosures

The splicing trays are not designed to be left in the open environment and must be placed in some type of enclosure. The enclosure that is used will depend on the application. The following are examples of some enclosures used for splicing trays.

- *Direct buried cylinders*:   At an intermediate point where two cables are joined to continue a cable run, the splices can be directly buried by placing the splice trays in a tightly sealed cylindrical enclosure that is generally made from heavy duty plastic or aluminum. The container is completely sealed from moisture ingress and contains desiccant packs to remove any moisture that may get in. A typical direct buried cylinder is illustrated in Figure 3.7. Note that the cables normally enter the enclosure at one end only to allow the enclosure to be lifted from the ground for easier splicing access.

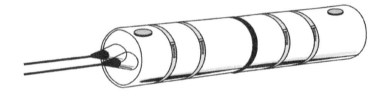

Figure 3.7
Direct buried splicing enclosure

- *Termination cabinets*: At junction points where a lot of cables meet, the splicing trays are stored in a larger wall-mounted cabinet (approximately 500 × 500 × 100 mm) with a hinged door. For outdoor use, the cabinets must be sealed against bad weather conditions. Figure 3.8 illustrates a splicing tray in a termination cabinet.
- *Patch panels and distribution frames*: Splice trays can be installed in the back of patch panels and distribution frames used for connection of patch cords to the main incoming cable.

3.7.3 Termination in patch panels and distribution frames

There are three main methods of connecting an incoming cable into a patch panel or distribution frame. Firstly, if the incoming cable contains fibers that have a large minimum bending radius, then it is recommended to splice each fiber to a fiber patch cord that has a smaller bending radius. This reduces undue stress on the incoming fibers but does introduce small losses into the link. This also replaces the more fragile glass of the incoming cable with the more flexible and stronger glass of the patch cords. This is illustrated in Figure 3.8.

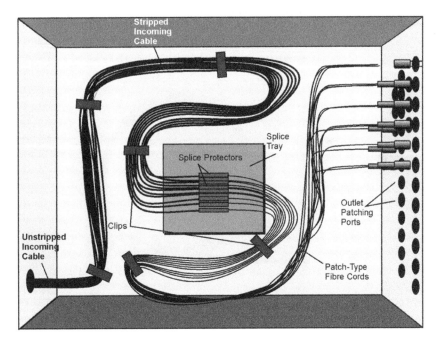

Figure 3.8
Termination cabinet for splicing trays

The second method is to place the fibers from the incoming cable into a breakout unit. The breakout unit separates the fibers and allows a plastic tube to be fitted over the incoming fibers to provide protection and strength as they are fed to the front of the patch panel. Note there are no splices, which therefore keep losses to a minimum. This is illustrated in Figure 3.9.

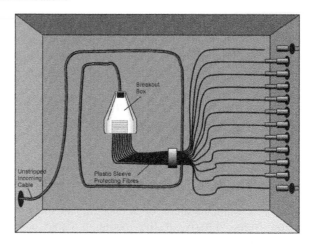

Figure 3.9
Patch panel with break out box

If the incoming cable contains tight buffered fibers that are flexible and strong, then they can be taken directly to the front of the patch panel. This is referred to as direct termination, and is illustrated in Figure 3.10.

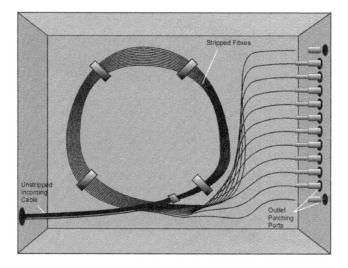

Figure 3.10
Direct termination of cables in a patch panel

3.8   Troubleshooting

3.8.1   Introduction

This section deals with problems of fiber-optic cables. Problems can be caused by poor installation practices, where fibers are subjected to excessive tension or bending forces. This section also deals with the basic methods of testing fibers and how to locate faults on fiber-optic systems.

3.8.2   Standard troubleshooting approach

The standard approach to troubleshooting fiber-optic systems is as follows:

- Observe the system status indicators and determine whether signals are being transmitted and received at both terminals.
- Determine whether the appropriate fibers are functional by either a simple continuity test or a qualitative insertion loss measurement between the patch panels.
- Once the faulty fiber is identified, clean the optical connectors and repeat the test.
- If the fault remains, swap the system onto a spare fiber by rearranging the patch cords on the patch panels at both ends.
- Update the records to indicate the faulty fiber.
- When a link does not have sufficient spare fibers available to maintain system integrity, then attempt fault localization using an OTDR, if appropriate.
- On short lengths of fiber, total replacement may be more cost effective than expensive location and subsequent repair. This is particularly appropriate where a spare duct is available for the cable replacement.

3.8.3   Tools required

Continuity tester

This device has a fiber-optic transmitter with a suitable fiber-optic connector that transmits a visible red light (650 nm). This can transmit visible light over several kilometers and is used for such applications as continuity testing, finding fractures in fibers or bad splices by observing light that may be leaking out and for identifying fibers at the end of a cable that has many fibers in it.

Optical source

This device has a calibrated fiber-optic transmitter with a suitable fiber-optic connector and is used with an optical power meter for insertion loss testing of fibers.

Optical power meter

This device has a fiber-optic receiver with a suitable fiber-optic connector and displays the received optical power levels. It is used with an optical source for insertion loss testing of fibers.

Optical time domain reflectometer (OTDR)

The OTDR sends a short pulse of light down the fiber and measures and records the light energy that is reflected back up the fiber. A reflection may be caused by the presence of a connector, splice, crack, impurity, or break in the fiber. By measuring the time it takes for the reflected light to return to the source, and knowing the refractive index of the fiber, it is possible to calculate the distance to the reflection point.

3.9   Fiber installation rules

The following section provides general installation rules that should be followed when installing fiber-optic cabling systems to avoid long-term reliability problems. Fibers can break at any surface defect if subjected to excessive bending forces while under tension.

3.9.1   Cable bending radius

- The most important consideration when installing fiber-optic cables is to ensure that at all times during an installation the cable radius is not less than the manufacturer's recommended minimum installation bending radius.
- Avoidance of sharp bends along the installation route is absolutely essential. Sharp bends in cable trays or in conduits can cause macrobends or microbends in the fibers. This can lead to fiber breakage or adversely affect signal attenuation.
- Ensure that the conduit or the cable tray is constructed with no sharp edges. Use curved construction components (ducts or cable trays) and not right-angled components.
- Ensure the cables are laid on to a flat surface, and that no heavy objects will be laid on to the cables in the future.
- Avoid putting kinks or twists into the cable. This is best achieved by pulling the cable directly off the reel and having a member of the installation team carefully watch any cable slack for possible formation of kinks.
- Cable manufacturers will specify a minimum bending radius that applies to the long-term final installed cable. The long-term radius is significantly larger than the installation radius. If this long-term radius is exceeded, the macrobending in the cable will produce additional attenuation. While not only damaging the fiber, such unnecessary losses will be detrimental to cable performance. Once the cable has been installed and the tension has been released, ensure that the cable radius is not less than the long-term installed radius at any point along the cable.

3.9.2   Cable tension

When a longitudinal tensile force is applied to an optical fiber, it can cause minute surface defects. These potential weak points can develop into microcracks, which may cause breakage of the fiber, when it is later subjected to an equal or greater tension.

Optical fibers have some elasticity, stretching under light loads before returning to their original length when the load is removed. Under heavier loads, the fiber may theoretically stretch as much as 9% before breaking; however, it is considered advisable to limit this, in practice, to permanent strains of less than 0.2% to avoid promoting premature failures.

Although modern fiber-optic cables are generally stronger than copper cables, failure due to excess cable tension during installation is more catastrophic (i.e. fiber snapping rather than copper stretching). The following guidelines should be observed during installation.

- The maximum allowable installation cable tension is specified by the manufacturer; the cable tension should not exceed that limit at any time. A general rule of thumb that is sometimes used is that the maximum allowable cable tension during installation is approximately the weight of 1 km of the cable itself.
- When pulling the cable during installation, avoid sudden, short sharp jerking. These sudden forces could easily exceed the maximum cable tension. The cable should be pulled in an easy smooth process.
- When pulling cable off a large drum, ensure that the cable drum is smoothly rotated by one team member to feed off the cable. If the cable is allowed to jerk the drum around, the high moment of inertia of the drum can cause excessive tension in the cable.

- It is very important to minimize cable stress after the installation is complete. A slack final resting condition will help to ensure that the fiber-optic cable has a long operating life. It is recommended that slack be left in the junction boxes at the completion of the installation to reduce overall stress in the cable.
- If there are a lot of bends in the cable route, it is recommended to use as many intermediate junction boxes as possible to reduce cable tension. The cable can be pulled through at these points, laid out in a large figure '8' pattern on the ground, and then pulled into the next section. On long cable runs, pulling assistance can also be done at these intermediate access points. Laying the cable in a figure '8' pattern naturally avoids kinking and twisting of the cable. Curved guides or block systems may be used in the junction boxes where the cable changes direction.

3.10   Cleaning optical connectors

With the core of a single mode fiber being only 9 microns in diameter, a lot of dust particles can easily cover much of the core area on the end face of the connector. In addition, connector damage can occur if foreign particles are caught in the end face area of mated connectors.

It is vital to make sure that cleaning of connectors is completed by all staff handling them, and that 'good housekeeping' practices are employed, such as always installing the protective dust caps and never allowing any object other than the approved cleaners to contact the end face.

- The preferred method of connector cleaning is by wiping the end face and ferrule of the connector with some isopropyl alcohol on a lint-free tissue. Cleaning tissues can be obtained in sealed packages already impregnated with alcohol.
- Another method of connector cleaning is the proprietary cassette-type cleaners. These use a dry tape which is advanced every time the cassette is opened, ensuring a clean section of tape is available each time.
- Where proprietary connectors have bare fibers exposed such as Volition or MTRJ, the only acceptable method of cleaning is to use a can of compressed gas.

Adapters are primarily kept clean by always cleaning the connectors prior to insertion, and fitting of dust caps to all unused patch panel ports. A method of cleaning adapters is through the careful use of a can of compressed gas. An alternative is a pipe cleaner moistened with isopropyl alcohol. Remember that most pipe cleaners have a steel wire center and the end will damage any connector if it is inserted into an adapter, which still has a connector inserted in the other side.

3.11   Locating broken fibers

3.11.1   Continuity testing

The most fundamental of all fiber-optic cable tests that can be performed is to carry out a continuity test. The continuity test simply checks that the fiber is continuous from one end to the other. A light beam is inserted from a light source in one end of the fiber and is observed coming out of the other end of the fiber. This test provides little information about the condition of the fiber, other than that there are no complete breaks along the fiber length. This can be performed by shining a powerful torch beam (or laser pointer) into one end of the fiber and observing the light coming out of the other end. This is a cost-effective method for multimode fibers with large core diameters over distances up to approximately 500 m. It is not reliable over longer distances or with single-mode fibers because the small diameter core makes penetration into the fiber difficult for the light.

There is specific test equipment available that can be used as a continuity tester. The device has a fiber-optic transmitter with a suitable fiber-optic connector that transmits a 650 nm visible red light. This will transmit visible light over several kilometers and can be used for such applications as continuity testing, finding fractures in fibers or bad splices by observing light that may be leaking out and for identifying fibers at the end of a cable that has many fibers in it. It can also be used for identifying fibers along the route of a cable (where it is required to break into a cable for a system extension) by bending the fiber and watching the light leaking out of the bend. This type of fiber-optic test has limited application, as it is of no use in finding faults in buried cables or aerial cables.

As a word of warning, the user should not look into fiber groups at the end of cables if any fibers on the system at any location are connected to lasers. The infra-red light from lasers cannot be seen by the human eye but can cause permanent eye damage.

3.11.2   Insertion loss testing

The most common qualitative test that is carried out on a fiber-optic system is to measure the attenuation of a length of fiber. This figure will allow most elements of the system design to be verified.

Most insertion loss testing is carried out with a power source and a power meter. Firstly, the power meter is calibrated to the power source by connecting the two instruments together with a short piece of optic fiber approximately 2 m in length. Generally, the power source is set to transmit a level of –10 dBm and the power meter then adjusted accordingly to read –10 dBm. Ensure that the level used to calibrate the power meter is within the dynamic range of the power meter.

There are four important points to check before commencing insertion loss testing. Firstly, ensure that the optic fiber type used for calibration purposes is the same optic fiber type that is to be tested for insertion loss. Secondly, the power meter and the power source must operate at the same wavelength as the installed system equipment. Thirdly, the power meter and source must also use the same source and detector types (LED or laser) that the transmitter and receiver in the installed system are to use. Fourthly, to avoid possible incorrect calibration, ensure that the same connectors are used for calibration as are used in the installation.

Once the power meter has been calibrated, then the power meter and source are taken into the field and connected to the installed cable. The level that is read at the meter can be used to calculate the insertion loss through the cable section under test. This will include the losses caused by the optic fiber, splices and the connectors. The test procedure is illustrated in Figure 3.11.

If the power source and the power meter are calibrated in milliwatts, then the formula for converting the loss figure to decibels is:

$$\text{Attenuation (dB)} = -10\log\left(\frac{P_\text{o}}{P_\text{i}}\right)$$

Where
  P_o = power out of the fiber
  P_i = power into the fiber.

To calculate the insertion loss, subtract the dBm reading at the power meter from the input power source value. For the example shown in Figure 3.11 the insertion loss is 9.3 dB.

It is recommended that the insertion loss measurement be performed in both directions of an installed cable. The losses measured in each direction tend to vary because connectors and splices sometimes connect unevenly and because the core diameter of fibers tends to vary slightly. For example, if the core diameters of two fibers spliced together are 49.5 mm and 50.5 mm, light waves traveling from the thinner fiber into the thicker fiber will all enter the thicker fiber. For light traveling from the larger diameter fiber into the smaller diameter fiber, a small amount will be lost around the edges of the interface between the two cores. A mismatch of this type could account for a difference in insertion loss in the two directions of 0.2 dB. If the fiber losses are different in each direction, then that fiber can be used in whichever direction gives the best system performance.

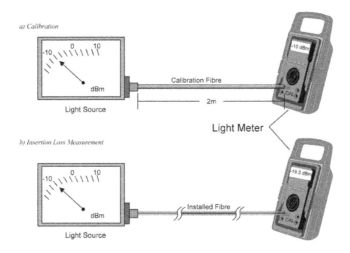

Figure 3.11
Insertion loss measurement

3.11.3 Optical time domain reflectometer

The only method of analyzing the losses along an individual fiber is to test it with an optical time domain reflectometer (OTDR). In particular, this allows the location of a broken fiber to be established. The OTDR sends a short pulse of light down the fiber and measures and records the light energy that is reflected back up the fiber. A reflection may be caused by the presence of a connector, splice, crack, impurity, or break in the fiber. By measuring the time, it takes for the reflected light to return to the source, and knowing the refractive index of the fiber, it is possible to calculate the distance to the reflection point.

Impurities in the glass will cause a continuous low-level reflection as the light travels through the glass fiber. This is due to Rayleigh scattering and is commonly referred to as backscatter. The strength of the backscattered signal received at the source gradually drops as the pulse moves away from the source. This is seen on an OTDR display as a near linear drop in the received reflected signal and the slope of this line is the attenuation of the fiber (dB per km). Figure 3.12 illustrates a typical reflection curve for an OTDR and notes the backscatter.

An OTDR will generally not provide accurate readings of irregularities and losses in the fiber for the first 15 m of the cable. This is because the pulse length and its rise time from the OTDR are comparatively large when compared to the time it takes for the pulse to travel the short distance to the point of reflection within this 15 m and back.

In general, for shorter local cable running less than 200 m, there is not a lot to be gained from carrying out an OTDR test unless there are connectors and splices along the cable route.

With reference to the OTDR plot in Figure 3.12, the *Y*-axis of the plot shows the relative amplitude of the light signal that has reflected back to the source, and the *X*-axis represents time. The time base is directly translated and displayed as distance by the OTDR.

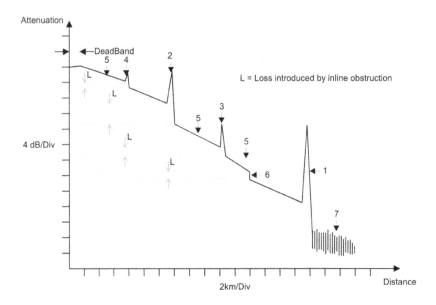

Figure 3.12
Trace from an OTDR

The sudden peaks that appear along the slope are the points where reflections have occurred, and light that has reflected back to the source is stronger than the backscatter. There are four main reflection points illustrated in Figure 3.12.

In their order of decreasing magnitude they are:

- Reflection from the unterminated end of the fiber
- Reflection from a connector
- Reflection from a splice
- Reflection from a hairline crack in the fiber
- Backscatter.

After each of the reflections, the slope of the attenuation curve drops suddenly. This drop represents the loss introduced by the connector, splice, or imperfection in the fiber.

Point (6) noted in Figure 3.12 illustrates a splice where the cores of the fibers are well matched for light traveling in the direction away from the source. This splice has no reflection, just a loss introduced by the splice. The type of drop at point (6) in the attenuation curve could also be caused by a sharp bend in the fiber where light escapes out of the fiber at the bend and is not reflected back. Some types of faults in the fiber will also cause a similar result.

Point (7) noted in Figure 3.12 shows the noise floor of the instrument. This is the lowest sensitivity of received signal that the device can accept. Measurements made close to this level are not very accurate.

OTDR testing can provide very accurate fault analysis over long lengths of fiber. On the better quality instruments, a resolution of 1 m for fault location and 0.01 dB for in line losses is available. Some instruments will operate with a range up to 200 km.

In general, OTDRs are relatively easy to use and special analysis software packages are available for downloading the test results and carrying out detailed analysis if required. The unfortunate downside with OTDR technology is that it is generally very expensive. Even small reduced feature units can be very expensive.

Care should be taken when interpreting the results from an OTDR. Where different fibers are joined together, this connection may represent a change in refractive index, core size, modal properties, and/or material properties of the fiber. For example, after a splice or connector the OTDR may display what appears to be a signal gain on the screen. What has probably occurred is that the light has entered a fiber with greater impurities and there has been an increase in backscatter.

The OTDR test should be carried out on every optical fiber in a cable while it is still on the reel prior to installation to ensure that faulty fibers are not installed. The results of these tests should be stored in memory or as a print out. These pre-installation tests are generally carried out when the custody of the cable is passed from one party to the next; for example, when the cable is handed down from the purchaser to the installation contractor.

Once the cable has been installed, the OTDR tests should be carried out again on every optical fiber. The results of the 'as installed' tests can then be compared to the pre-installation test results to determine if the fibers have been damaged or poorly installed.

The results of the pre-installation and the post-installation tests should be kept as part of the commissioning documentation. If there is a fault with the system at a later date, then the commissioning test results can be used to help determine where the faults are located. For high-integrity longer-distance systems, it is worth carrying out an audit of the system after a number of years of operation and performing the OTDR tests again and comparing them to the commissioning test results to measure any deterioration in the cabling system since installation.

The OTDR can be used for attenuation measurements but it is generally not recommended, as OTDR measurements are a relative measurement rather than an absolute measurement. Also, the OTDR does not account for poor-quality OTDR connector to fiber end-face connections. Therefore the insertion loss measurement procedure that was described above is a more appropriate and accurate technique.

Since the OTDR is not used for accurate attenuation measurements but only for relative measurements, the wavelength at which it operates is not important. Distance readings, splice losses, and connector losses are not affected by the small changes in wavelength associated with lasers and LEDs.

It was noted in the previous section that the loss of a connector or splice might be different when measured from each direction into the optic fiber. For cable sections of greater than 2 km, it is recommended that the OTDR tests be carried out from each end of the optical fiber.

Some fiber-optic cables are constructed so that the fibers are laid in a helical fashion around the center of the cable. In this case, the length of the cable is not going to be the length of the fibers. This difference will make it inherently difficult to determine the distance to faults. To overcome this problem, the manufacturer will generally provide a ratio of fiber length to cable length. The ratio is then used to calculate the exact cable distance to the fault from the OTDR distance reading. If there is not a ratio available, an OTDR measurement is performed on a known length of cable (generally 1 km) and the ratio is calculated.

$$\text{Fiber/cable ratio} = \frac{\text{Length of fiber in 1km of cable}}{1\text{km}}$$

$$\text{Distance to fault} = \frac{\text{OTDR distance reading}}{\text{Fiber/cable ratio}}$$

4a

RS-232 overview

Objectives

When you have completed study of this chapter, you will be able to:

- List the main features of the RS-232 standard
- Fix the following problems:

  - Incorrect RS-232 cabling
  - Male/female D-type connector confusion
  - Wrong DTE/DCE configuration
  - Handshaking
  - Incorrect signaling voltages
  - Excessive electrical noise
  - Isolation.

4a.1 RS-232 interface standard (CCITT V.24 interface standard)

The RS-232 interface standard was developed for the single purpose of interfacing data terminal equipment (DTE) and data circuit terminating equipment (DCE) employing serial binary data interchange. In particular, RS-232 was developed for interfacing data terminals to modems.

The RS-232 interface standard was issued in the USA in 1969 by the engineering department of the EIA. Almost immediately, minor revisions were made and RS-232C was issued. RS-232 was originally named RS-232 (Recommended Standard), which is still in popular usage. The prefix 'RS' was superseded by 'EIA/TIA' in 1988. The current revision is EIA/TIA-232E (1991), which brings it into line with the international standards ITU V.24, ITU V.28, and ISO-2110.

Poor interpretation of RS-232 has been responsible for many problems in interfacing equipment from different manufacturers. This had led some users to dispute as to whether it is a 'standard'. It should be emphasized that RS-232 and other related RS standards define the electrical and mechanical details of the interface (layer 1 of the OSI model) and do not define a protocol.

The RS-232 interface standard specifies the method of connection of two devices – the DTE and DCE. DTE refers to data terminal equipment, for example, a computer or a printer. A DTE device communicates with a DCE device. DCE, on the other hand, refers to data communications equipment such as a modem. DCE equipment is now also called data circuit-terminating equipment in EIA/TIA-232E. A DCE device receives data from the DTE and retransmits to another DCE device via a data communications link such as a telephone link (Figure 4a.1).

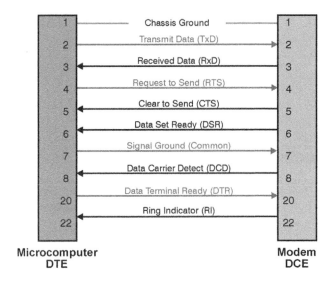

Figure 4a.1
Connections between the DTE and the DCE using DB-25 connectors

4a.1.1   The major elements of RS-232

The RS-232 standard consists of three major parts, which define:

- Electrical signal characteristics
- Mechanical characteristics of the interface
- Functional description of the interchange circuits.

Electrical signal characteristics

RS-232 defines electrical signal characteristics such as the voltage levels and grounding characteristics of the interchange signals and associated circuitry for an unbalanced system.

The RS-232 transmitter is required to produce voltages in the range ±5 to ±25 V as follows:

- Logic 1: –5 to –25 V
- Logic 0: +5 to +25 V
- Undefined logic level: +5 to –5 V.

At the RS-232 receiver, the following voltage levels are defined:

- Logic 1: –3 to –25 V
- Logic 0: +3 to +25 V
- Undefined logic level: –3 to +3 V.

Note: The RS-232 transmitter requires a slightly higher voltage to overcome voltage drop along the line.

The voltage levels associated with a microprocessor are typically 0 to +5 V for transistor–transistor logic (TTL). A line driver is required at the transmitting end to adjust the voltage to the correct level for the communications link. Similarly, a line receiver is required at the receiving end to translate the voltage on the communications link to the correct TTL voltages for interfacing to a microprocessor. Despite the bipolar input voltage, TTL-compatible RS-232 receivers operate on a single +5 V supply (Figure 4a.2).

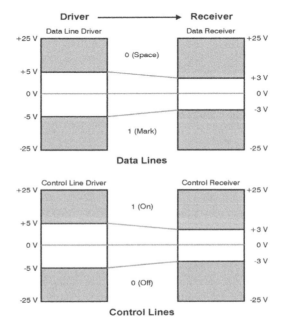

Figure 4a.2
Voltage levels for RS-232

Modern PC power supplies usually have a standard +12 V output that could be used for the line driver.

The control or 'handshaking' lines have the same range of voltages as the transmission of logic 0 and logic 1, except that they are of opposite polarity. This means that:

- A control line asserted or made active by the transmitting device has a voltage range of +5 to +25 V. The receiving device connected to this control line allows a voltage range of +3 to +25 V.
- A control line inhibited or made inactive by the transmitting device has a voltage range of –5 to –25 V. The receiving device of this control line allows a voltage range of –3 to –25 V.

At the receiving end, a line receiver is necessary in each data and control line to reduce the voltage level to the 0 V and +5 V logic levels required by the internal electronics (Figure 4a.3).

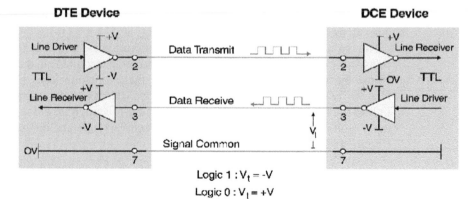

Figure 4a.3
RS-232 transmitters and receivers

The RS-232 standard defines 25 electrical connections. The electrical connections are divided into four groups viz.:

1. Data lines
2. Control lines
3. Timing lines
4. Special secondary functions.

Data lines are used for the transfer of data. Data flow is designated from the perspective of the DTE interface. The transmit line, on which the DTE transmits and the DCE receives, is associated with pin 2 at the DTE end and pin 2 at the DCE end for a DB-25 connector. These allocations are reversed for DB-9 connectors. The receive line, on which the DTE receives, and the DCE transmits, is associated with pin 3 at the DTE end and pin 3 at the DCE end. Pin 7 is the common return line for the transmit and receive data lines.

Control lines are used for interactive device control, which is commonly known as hardware handshaking. They regulate the way in which data flows across the interface.

The four most commonly used control lines are:

1. RTS: Request to send
2. CTS: Clear to send
3. DSR: Data set ready (or DCE ready in RS-232D/E)
4. DTR: Data terminal ready (or DTE ready in RS-232D/E).

It is important to remember that with the handshaking lines, the enabled state means a positive voltage and the disabled state means a negative voltage.

Hardware handshaking is the cause of most interfacing problems. Manufacturers sometimes omit control lines from their RS-232 equipment or assign unusual applications to them. Consequently, many applications do not use hardware handshaking but, instead, use only the three data lines (transmit, receive, and signal common ground) with some form of software handshaking. The control of data flow is then part of the application program. Most of the systems encountered in data communications for instrumentation and control use some sort of software-based protocol in preference to hardware handshaking.

There is a relationship between the allowable speed of data transmission and the length of the cable connecting the two devices on the RS-232 interface. As the speed of data transmission increases, the quality of the signal transition from one voltage level to another, for example, from −25 to +25 V, becomes increasingly dependent on the capacitance and inductance of the cable.

The rate at which voltage can 'slew' from one logic level to another depends mainly on the cable capacitance, and the capacitance increases with cable length. The length of the cable is limited by the number of data errors acceptable during transmission. The RS-232 D&E standard specifies the limit of total cable capacitance to be 2500 pF. With typical cable capacitance having improved from around 160 pF/m to only 50 pF/m in recent years, the maximum cable length has extended from around 15 m (50 ft) to about 50 m (166 ft).

The common data transmission rates used with RS-232 are 110, 300, 600, 1200, 2400, 4800, 9600, and 19 200 bps. For short distances, however, transmission rates of 38 400, 57 600, and 115 200 can also be used. Based on field tests, Table 4a.1 shows the practical relationship between selected baud rates and maximum allowable cable length, indicating that much longer cable lengths are possible at lower baud rates. Note that the achievable speed depends on the transmitter voltages, cable capacitance (as discussed above) as well as the noise environment.

In the context of the NRZ-type of coding used for asynchronous transmission on RS-232 links, 1 baud = 1 bit per second.

Baud Rate	Cable Length (meters)
110	850
300	800
600	700
1200	500
2400	200
4800	100
9600	70
19 200	50
115 k	20

Table 4a.1
Demonstrated maximum cable lengths with RS-232 interface

Mechanical characteristics of the interface

RS-232 defines the mechanical characteristics of the interface between the DTE and the DCE. This dictates that the interface must consist of a plug and socket and that the socket will normally be on the DCE.

Although not specified by RS-232C, the DB-25 connector (25 pin, D-type) is closely associated with RS-232 and is the *de facto* standard with revision D. Revision E formally specifies a new connector in the 26-pin alternative connector (known as the ALT A connector). This connector supports all 25 signals associated with RS-232. ALT A is physically smaller than the DB-25 and satisfies the demand for a smaller connector suitable for modern computers. Pin 26 is not currently used. On some RS-232-compatible equipment, where little or no handshaking is required, the DB-9 connector (9 pin, D-type) is common. This practice originated when IBM decided to make a combined serial/parallel adapter for the AT&T personal computer. A small connector format was needed to allow both interfaces to fit onto the back of a standard ISA interface card. Subsequently, the DB-9 connector has also become an industry standard to reduce the wastage of pins. The pin allocations commonly used with the DB-9 and DB-25 connectors for the RS-232 interface are shown in Table 4a.2. The pin allocation for the DB-9 connector is not the same as the DB-25 and often traps the unwary.

The data pins of DB-9 IBM connector are allocated as follows:

- Data transmit pin 3
- Data receive pin 2
- Signal common pin 5.

Pin No. DTE	DB-9 Connector IBM Assignment	DB-25 Connector RS-232 pin Assignment	DB-25 Connector EIA-530 pin Assignment
1	Received line signal	Shield	Shield
2	Received data	Transmitted data	Transmitted data (A)
3	Transmitted data	Received data	Received data (A)
4	DTE ready	Requeste to send	Requeste to send (A)
5	Signal/common ground	Clear to send	Clear to send (A)
6	DCE ready	DCE ready	DCE ready (A)
7	Request to send	Signal/common ground	Signal/common ground
8	Clear to send	Received line signal	Received line signal (A)
9	Ring indicator	+ Voltage (testing)	Receiver signal DCE element timing (B)
10		– Voltage (testing)	Received line (B)
11		Unassigned	Transmitter signal DTE element timing (B)
12		Sec received line signal Detector/data signal	Transmitter signal DCE element timing
13		Sec clear to send	Clear to send (B)
14		Sec transmitted data	Transmitted data (B)
15		Transmitted signal DCE element timing	Transmitted signal DCE element timing (A)
16		Sec received data	Received data (B)
17		Receiver signal DCE element timing	Receiver signal DCE element timing (A)
18		Local loopback	Local loopback
19		Sec request to send	Request to send (B)
20		DTE ready	DTE ready (A)
21		Remote loopback/signal quality detector	Remote loopback

Pin No. DTE	DB-9 Connector IBM Assignment	DB-25 Connector RS-232 pin Assignment	DB-25 Connector EIA-530 pin Assignment
22		Ring indicator	DCE ready (B)
23		Data signal rate	DTE ready (B)
24		Transmit signal DTE element timing	Transmit signal DTE element timing (A)
25		Test mode	Test mode

Table 4a.2
Common DB-9 and DB-25 pin assignments for RS-232 and EIA/TIA-530 (often used for RS-422 and RS-485)

Functional description of the interchange circuits

RS-232 defines the function of the data, timing, and control signals used at the interface of the DTE and DCE. However, very few of the definitions are relevant to applications for data communications for instrumentation and control (Table 4a.3).

The circuit functions are defined with reference to the DTE as follows:

- *Protective ground (shield)*:   The protective ground ensures that the DTE and DCE chassis are at equal potentials (remember that this protective ground could cause problems with circulating earth currents).
- *Transmitted data (TxD)*:   This line carries serial data from the DTE to the corresponding pin on the DCE. The line is held at a negative voltage during periods of line idle.
- *Received data (RxD)*:   This line carries serial data from the DCE to the corresponding pin on the DTE.
- *Request to send (RTS)*:   RTS is the request to send hardware control line. This line is placed active (+V) when the DTE requests permission to send data. The DCE then activates (+V) the CTS (clear to send) for hardware data flow control.
- *Clear to send (CTS)*:   When a half-duplex modem is receiving, the DTE keeps RTS inhibited. When it is the DTE's turn to transmit, it advises the modem by asserting the RTS pin. When the modem asserts the CTS, it informs the DTE that it is now safe to send data.
- *DCE ready*:   Formerly called data set ready (DSR). The DTE ready line is an indication from the DCE to the DTE that the modem is ready.
- *Signal ground (common)*:   This is the common return line for all the data transmit and receive signals and all other circuits in the interface. The connection between the two ends is always made.
- *Data carrier detect (DCD)*:   This is also called the received line signal detector. It is asserted by the modem when it receives a remote carrier and remains asserted for the duration of the link.
- *DTE ready (data terminal ready)*:   Formerly called data terminal ready (DTR). DTE ready enables-but does not cause, the modem to switch onto the line. In originate mode, DTE ready must be asserted in order to auto dial. In answer mode, DTE ready must be asserted to auto answer.
- *Ring indicator*:   This pin is asserted during a ring voltage on the line.
- *Data signal rate selector (DSRS)*:   When two data rates are possible, the higher is selected by asserting DSRS; however, this line is not used much these days.

Pin No.	CCITT No.	Circuit	Description	Circuit Direction
1	–	–	Shield	To DCE
2	103	BA	Transmitted data	To DCE
3	104	BB	Received data	From DCE
4	105/133	CA/CJ	Request to send/ready for receiving	To DCE
5	106	CB	Clear to send	From DCE
6	107	CC	DCE ready	From DCE
7	102	AB	Signal common	–
8	109	CF	Received line signal detector	From DCE
9	–	–	Reserved for testing	–
10	–	–	Reserved for testing	–
11	126	See Note	Unassigned	–
12	122/112	SCF/CI	Secondary received line signal Detector/data signal rate selected	From DCE
13	121	SCB	Secondary clear to send	From DCE
14	118	SBA	Secondary transmitted data	To DCE
15	114	DB	Transmitter signal element timing (DTE source)	From DCE
16	119	SBB	Secondary received data	From DCE
18	141	LL	Local loopback	To DCE
19	120	SCA	Secondary request to send	To DCE
20	108/112	CD	DTE ready	To DCE
21	140/110	RL/CG	Remote loopback/signal quality Detector	T/F DCE
22	125	CE	Ring indicator	From DCE
23	111/112	CH/CI	Data signal rate selector (DTE/DCE source)	T/F DCE
24	113	DA	Transmit signal element timing (DTE/DCE source)	To DCE
25	142	TM	Test mode	From DCE
26		None	(Alt A connector) No connection at this time	

Table 4a.3
ITU-T V24 pin assignment (ISO 2110)

4a.2   Half-duplex operation of the RS-232 interface

The following description of one particular operation of the RS-232 interface is based on half-duplex data interchange. The description encompasses the more generally used full-duplex operation.

Figure 4a.4 shows the operation with the initiating user terminal, DTE, and its associated modem DCE on the left of the diagram and the remote computer and its modem on the right.

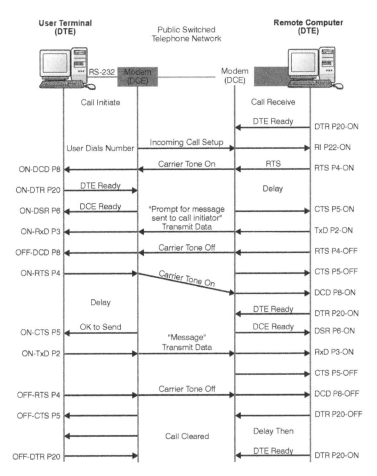

Figure 4a.4
Half-duplex operational sequence of RS-232

The following sequence of steps occurs when a user sends information over a telephone link to a remote modem and computer:

- The initiating user manually dials the number of the remote computer.
- The receiving modem asserts the ring indicator line (RI) in a pulsed ON/OFF fashion reflecting the ringing tone. The remote computer already has its data terminal ready (DTR) line asserted to indicate that it is ready to receive calls. Alternatively, the remote computer may assert the DTR line after a few rings. The remote computer then sets its request to send (RTS) line to ON.
- The receiving modem answers the phone and transmits a carrier signal to the initiating end. It asserts the DCE ready line after a few seconds.
- The initiating modem asserts the data carrier detect (DCD) line. The initiating terminal asserts its DTR, if it is not already high. The modem responds by asserting its DTE ready line.

- The receiving modem asserts its clear to send (CTS) line, which permits the transfer of data from the remote computer to the initiating side.
- Data is transferred from the receiving DTE (transmitted data) to the receiving modem. The receiving remote computer then transmits a short message to indicate to the originating terminal that it can proceed with the data transfer. The originating modem transmits the data to the originating terminal.
- The receiving terminal sets its request to send (RTS) line to OFF The receiving modem then sets its clear to send (CTS) line to OFF.
- The receiving modem switches its carrier signal OFF.
- The originating terminal detects that the data carrier detect (DCD) signal has been switched OFF on the originating modem and switches its RTS line to the ON state. The originating modem indicates that transmission can proceed by setting its CTS line to ON.
- Transmission of data proceeds from the originating terminal to the remote computer.
- When the interchange is complete, both carriers are switched OFF, and in many cases, the DTR is set to OFF. This means that the CTS, RTS, and DCE ready lines are set to OFF.

Full-duplex operation requires that transmission and reception occur simultaneously. In this case, there is no RTS/CTS interaction at either end. The RTS and CTS lines are left ON with a carrier to the remote computer.

4a.3   Summary of EIA/TIA-232 revisions

A summary of the main differences between RS-232 revisions C, D, and E are discussed below.

4a.3.1   Revision D – RS-232D

The 25-pin D-type connector was formally specified. In revision C, reference was made to the D-type connector in the appendices and a disclaimer was included revealing that it was not intended to be part of the standard; however, it was treated as the *de facto* standard.

The voltage ranges for the control and data signals were extended to a maximum limit of 25 V from the previously specified 15 V in revision C.

The 15 m (50 ft) distance constraint, implicitly imposed to comply with circuit capacitance, was replaced by 'circuit capacitance shall not exceed 2500 pF'. (Standard RS-232 cable has a capacitance of 50 pF/ft.)

4a.3.2   Revision E – RS-232E

Revision E formally specifies the new 26-pin alternative connector, the ALT A connector. This connector supports all 25 signals associated with RS-232, unlike the 9-pin connector, which has become associated with RS-232 in recent years. Pin 26 is currently not used. The technical changes implemented by RS-232E do not present compatibility problems with equipment confirming to previous versions of RS-232.

This revision brings the RS-232 standard into line with international standards CCITT V.24, V.28, and ISO 2110.

4a.4   Limitations

In spite of its popularity and extensive use, it should be remembered that the RS-232 interface standard was originally developed for interfacing data terminals to modems. In the context of modern requirements, RS-232 has several weaknesses. Most have arisen as a result of the increased requirements for interfacing other devices such as PCs, digital instrumentation, digital variable speed drives, power system monitors, and other peripheral devices in industrial plants.

The main limitations of RS-232 when used for the communications of instrumentation and control equipment in an industrial environment are:

- The point-to-point restriction, a severe limitation when several 'smart' instruments are used.
- The distance limitation of 15 m (50 ft) end-to-end, too short for most control systems.
- The 20 kbps rate, too slow for many applications.
- The –3 to –25 V and +3 to +25 V signal levels, not directly compatible with modern standard power supplies.

Consequently, a number of other interface standards have been developed by the RS to overcome some of these limitations. The RS-485 interface standards are increasingly being used for instrumentation and control systems.

4b

RS-232 troubleshooting

4b.1   Introduction

Since RS-232 is a point-to-point system, installation is fairly straightforward and simple, and all RS-232 devices use either DB-9 or DB-25 connectors. These connectors are used because they are cheap and allow multiple insertions. None of the 232 standards define which device uses a male or female connector, but traditionally the male (pin) connector is used on the DTE and the female-type connector (socket) is used on DCE equipment. This is only traditional and may vary on different equipment. It is often asked why a 25-pin connector is used when only 9 pins are needed. This was done because RS-232 was used before the advent of computers. It was therefore used for hardware control (RTS/CTS). It was originally thought that, in the future, more hardware control lines would be needed hence the need for more pins.

When doing an initial installation of an RS-232 connection it is important to note the following:

- Is one device a DTE and the other a DCE?
- What is the sex and size of connectors at each end?
- What is the speed of the communication?
- What is the distance between the equipment?
- Is it a noisy environment?
- Is the software set up correctly?

4b.2   Typical approach

When troubleshooting a serial data communications interface, one needs to adopt a logical approach in order to avoid frustration and wasting many hours. A procedure similar to that outlined below is recommended:

- Check the basic parameters. Are the baud rate, stop/start bits and parity set identically for both devices? These are sometimes set on DIP switches in the device. However, the trend is towards using software, configured from a terminal, to set these basic parameters.
- Identify which is DTE or DCE. Examine the documentation to establish what actually happens at pins 2 and 3 of each device. On the 25-pin DTE device, pin 2 is used for transmission of data and should have a negative voltage (mark) in idle state, whilst pin 3 is used for the receipt of data (passive) and should be approximately at 0 V. Conversely, at the DCE device, pin 3 should have a

negative voltage, whilst pin 2 should be around 0 V. If no voltage can be detected on either pin 2 or 3, then the device is probably not RS-232 compatible and could be connected according to another interface standard, such as RS-422, RS-485, etc. (Figure 4b.1).

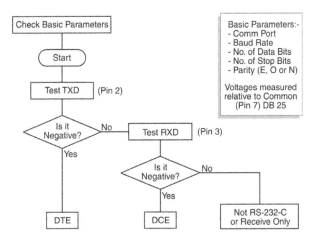

Figure 4b.1
Flowchart to identify an RS-232 device as either a DTE or DCE

- Clarify the needs of the hardware handshaking when used. Hardware handshaking can cause the greatest difficulties and the documentation should be carefully studied to yield some clues about the handshaking sequence. Ensure all the required wires are correctly terminated in the cables.
- Check the actual protocol used. This is seldom a problem but, when the above three points do not yield an answer, it is possible that there are irregularities in the protocol structure between the DCE and DTE devices.
- Alternatively, if software handshaking is utilized, make sure both have compatible application software. In particular, check that the same ASCII character is used for XON and XOFF.

4b.3   Test equipment

From a testing point of view, the RS-232-E interface standard states that: 'The generator on the interchange circuit shall be designed to withstand an open circuit, a short circuit between the conductor carrying that interchange circuit in the interconnecting cable and any other conductor in that cable including signal ground, without sustaining damage to itself or its associated equipment.'

In other words, any pin may be connected to any other pin, or even earth, without damage and, theoretically, one cannot blow up anything! This does not mean that the RS-232 interface cannot be damaged. The incorrect connection of incompatible external voltages can damage the interface, as can static charges.

If a data communication link is inoperable, the following devices may be useful when analyzing the problem:

- A digital multimeter: Any cable breakage can be detected by measuring the continuity of the cable for each line. The voltages at the pins in active and inactive states can also be ascertained by the multimeter to verify its compatibility to the respective standards

- An LED: The use of an LED is to determine which are the asserted lines or whether the interface conforms to a particular standard. This is laborious, and accurate pin descriptions should be available
- A breakout box
- PC-based protocol analyzer (including software)
- Dedicated hardware protocol analyzer (e.g. Hewlett Packard).

4b.3.1   The breakout box

The breakout box is an inexpensive tool that provides most of the information necessary to identify and fix problems on data communications circuits, such as the serial RS-232, RS-422, RS-423, and RS-485 interfaces and also on parallel interfaces (Figure 4b.2).

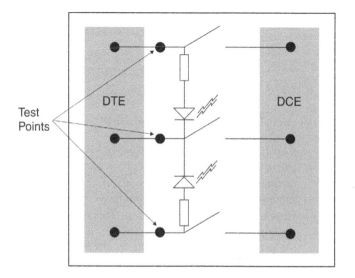

Figure 4b.2
Breakout box showing test points

A breakout box is connected to the data cable, to bring out all conductors in the cable to accessible test points. Many versions of this equipment are available on the market, from the 'homemade' using a back-to-back pair of male and female DB-25 sockets to fairly sophisticated test units with built-in LEDs, switches, and test points.

Breakout boxes usually have a male and a female socket and by using two standard serial cables, the box can be connected in series with the communication link. The 25 test points can be monitored by LEDs, a simple digital multimeter, an oscilloscope, or a protocol analyzer. In addition, a switch in each line can be opened or closed while trying to identify the problem.

The major weakness of the breakout box is that while one can interrupt any of the data lines, it does not help much with the interpretation of the flow of bits on the data communication lines. A protocol analyzer is required for this purpose.

4b.3.2   Null modem

Null modems look like DB-25 'through' connectors and are used when interfacing two devices of the same gender (e.g. DTE to DTE, DCE to DCE) or devices from different manufacturers with different handshaking requirements. A null modem has appropriate internal connections between handshaking pins that 'trick' the terminal into believing conditions are correct for passing data. A similar result can be achieved by soldering extra loops inside the DB-25 plug. Null modems generally cause more problems than they cure and should be used with extreme caution and preferably avoided.

Note that the null modem may inadvertently connect pins 1 together, as in Figure 4b.3. This is an undesirable practice and should be avoided.

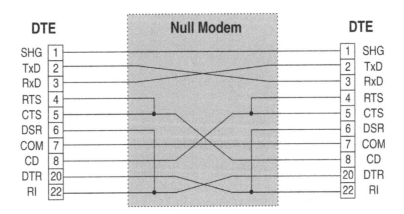

Figure 4b.3
Null modem connections

4b.3.3   Loop back plug

This is a hardware plug which loops back the transmit data pin to receive data pin, and similarly for the hardware handshaking lines. This is another quick way of verifying the operation of the serial interface without connecting to another system.

4b.3.4   Protocol analyzer

A protocol analyzer is used to display the actual bits on the data line, as well as the special control codes, such as STX, DLE, LF, CR, etc. The protocol analyzer can be used to monitor the data bits, as they are sent down the line and compared with what should be on the line. This helps to confirm that the transmitting terminal is sending the correct data and that the receiving device is receiving it. The protocol analyzer is useful in identifying incorrect baud rate, incorrect parity generation method, incorrect number of stop bits, noise, or incorrect wiring and connection. It also makes it possible to analyze the format of the message and look for protocol errors.

When the problem has been shown not to be due to the connections, baud rate, bits, or parity, then the content of the message will have to be analyzed for errors or inconsistencies. Protocol analyzers can quickly identify these problems.

Purpose-built protocol analyzers are expensive devices and it is often difficult to justify the cost when it is unlikely that the unit will be used very often. Fortunately, software has been developed that enables a normal PC to be used as a protocol analyzer. The use of a PC as a test device for many applications is a growing field, and one way of connecting a PC as a protocol analyzer is shown in Figure 4b.4.

Figure 4b.4 has been simplified for clarity and does not show the connections on the control lines (for example, RTS and CTS).

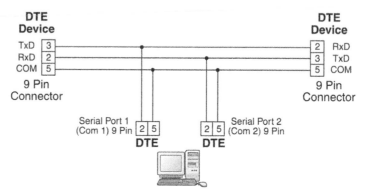

Figure 4b.4
Protocol analyzer connection

4b.4 Typical RS-232 problems

Below is a list of typical RS-232 problems, which can arise because of inadequate interfacing. These problems could equally apply to two PCs connected to each other or to a PC connected to a printer (Table 4b.1).

Problem	Probable Cause of Problem
Garbled or lost data	Baud rates of connecting ports may be different
	Connecting cables could be defective
	Data formats may be inconsistent (Stop bit/parity/number of data bits)
	Flow control may be inadequate
	High error rate due to electrical interference
	Buffer size of receiver inadequate
First characters garbled	The receiving port may not be able to respond quickly enough. Precede the first few characters with the ASCII (DEL) code to ensure frame synchronization
No data communications	Power for both devices may not be on
	Transmit and receive lines of cabling may be incorrect
	Handshaking lines of cabling may be incorrectly connected
	Baud rates mismatch
	Data format may be inconsistent
	Earth loop may have formed for RS-232 line
	Extremely high error rate due to electrical interference for transmitter and receiver

Problem	Probable Cause of Problem
	Protocols may be inconsistent/Intermittent communications
	Intermittent interference on cable
ASCII data has incorrect spacing	Mismatch between 'LF' and 'CR' characters generated by transmitting device and expected by receiving device

Table 4b.1
A list of typical RS-232 problems

To determine whether the devices are DTE or DCE, connect a breakout box at one end and note the condition of the TX light (pin 2 or 3) on the box. If pin 2 is ON, then the device is probably a DTE. If pin 3 is ON, it is probably a DCE. Another clue could be the sex of the connector, males are typically DTEs and females are typically DCEs, but not always (Figure 4b.5).

Figure 4b.5
A 9-pin RS-232 connector on a DTE

When troubleshooting an RS-232 system, it is important to understand that there are two different approaches. One approach is followed if the system is new and never been run before and the other if the system has been operating and for some reason does not communicate at present. New systems that have never worked have more potential problems than a system that has been working before and now has stopped. If a system is new it can have three main problems viz. mechanical, setup, and noise. A previously working system usually has only one problem, viz. mechanical. This assumes that no one has changed the setup, and noise has not been introduced into the system. In all systems, whether having previously worked or not, it is best to check the mechanical parts first.

This is done by:

- Verifying that there is power to the equipment
- Verifying that the connectors are not loose
- Verifying that the wires are correctly connected
- Checking that a part, board or module has not visibly failed.

4b.4.1   Mechanical problems

Often, mechanical problems develop in RS-232 systems because of incorrect installation of wires in the D-type connector or because strain reliefs were not installed correctly.

The following recommendations should be noted when building or installing RS-232 cables:

- Keep the wires short (20 m maximum)
- Stranded wire should be used instead of solid wire (solid wire will not flex)
- Only one wire should be soldered in each pin of the connector
- Bare wire should not be showing out of the pin of the connector
- The back shell should reliably and properly secure the wire.

The speed and distance of the equipment will determine if it is possible to make the connection at all. Most engineers try to stay less than 50 ft or about 16 m at 1 15 200 bps. This is a very subjective measurement and will depend on the cable, voltage of the transmitter, and the amount and noise in the environment. The transmitter voltage can be measured at each end when the cable has been installed. A voltage of at least ±5 V should be measured at each end on both the TX and RX lines (Figure 4b.6).

Figure 4b.6
Measuring the voltage on RS-232

An RS-232 breakout box is placed between the DTE and DCE to monitor the voltages placed on the wires by looking at pin 2 on the breakout box (Figure 4b.7). Be careful here because it is possible that the data is being transmitted so fast that the light on the breakout box does not have time to change. If possible, lower the speed of the communication at both ends to something like 2 bps.

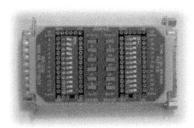

Figure 4b.7
A RS-232 breakout box

Once it has been determined that the wires are connected as DTE to DCE and that the distance and speed are not going to be a problem, the cable can be connected at each end. The breakout box can still be left connected with the cable and both pin 2 and 3 lights on the breakout box should now be on.

The color of the light depends on the breakout box. Some breakout boxes use red for a one and others use green for a one. If only one light is on then that may mean that a wire is broken or there is a DTE to DTE connection. A clue to a possible DTE to DTE connection would be that the light on pin 3 would be off and the one on pin 2 would be on. To correct this problem, first check the wires for continuity then turn switches 2 and 3 off on the breakout box and use jumper wires to swap them. If the TX and RX lights come on, a null modem cable or box will need to be built and inserted in-line with the cable.

If the pin 2 and pin 3 lights are on, one end is transmitting and the control is correct, then the only thing left is the protocol or noise. Either a hardware or software protocol analyzer will be needed to troubleshoot the communications between the devices. On new installations, one common problem is mismatched baud rates. The protocol analyzer will tell exactly what the baud rates are for each device. Another thing to look for with the analyzer is the timing. Often, the transmitter waits some time before expecting a proper response from the receiver. If the receiver takes too long to respond or the response is incorrect, the transmitter will 'time out'. This is usually denoted as a 'communications error or failure'.

4b.4.2   Setup problems

Once it is determined that the cable is connected correctly and the proper voltage is being received at each end, it is time to check the setup. The following circumstances need to be checked before trying to communicate:

- Is the software communications setup at both ends for either 8N1, 7E1, or 7O1?
- Is the baud rate the same at both devices? (1200, 4800, 9600, 19 200, etc.)
- Is the software setup at both ends for binary, hex, or ASCII data transfer?
- Is the software setup for the proper type of control?

Although the 8 data bits, no parity, and 1 stop bit is the most common setup for asynchronous communication, often 7 data bits even parity with 1 stop bit is used in industrial equipment. The most common baud rate used in asynchronous communications is 9600. Hex and ASCII are commonly used as communication codes.

If one device is transmitting but the other receiver is not responding, then the next thing to look for is what type of control the devices are using. The equipment manual may define whether hardware or software control is being used. Both ends should be set up either for hardware control, software control, or none.

4b.4.3   Noise problems

RS-232, being a single-ended (unbalanced) type of circuit, lends itself to receiving noise. There are three ways that noise can be induced into an RS-232 circuit:

- Induced noise on the common ground
- Induced noise on the TX or RX lines
- Induced noise on the indicator or control lines.

Ground-induced noise

Different ground voltage levels on the ground line (pin 7) can cause ground loop noise. Also, varying voltage levels induced on the ground at either end by high-power equipment can cause intermittent noise. This kind of noise can be very difficult to reduce. Sometimes, changing the location of the ground on either the RS-232 equipment or the high-power equipment can help, but this is often not possible. If it is determined that the noise problem is caused by the ground it may be best to replace the RS-232 link with a fiber-optic or RS-422 system. Fiber-optic or RS-422 to RS-232 adapters are relatively cheap, readily available, and easy to install. When the cost of troubleshooting the system is included, replacing the system often is the cheapest option.

Induced noise on the TX or RX lines

Noise from the outside can cause the communication on an RS-232 system to fail, although this voltage must be quite large. Because RS-232 voltages in practice are usually between ±7 and ±12, the noise voltage value must be quite high in order to induce errors. This type of noise induction is noticeable because the voltage on the TX or RX will be outside of the specifications of RS-232. Noise on the TX line can also be induced on the RX line (or vice versa) due to the common ground in the circuit. This type of noise can be detected by comparing the data being transmitted with the received communication at the other end of the wire (assuming no broken wire). The protocol analyzer is plugged into the transmitter at one end and the data monitored. If the data is correct, the protocol analyzer is then plugged into the other end and the received data monitored. If the data is corrupt at the receiving end, then noise on that wire may be the problem. If it is determined that the noise problem is caused by induced noise on the TX or RX lines, it may be best to move the RS-232 line and the offending noise source away from each other. If this does not help, it may be necessary to replace the RS-232 link with a fiber-optic or RS-485 system.

Induced noise on the indicator or control lines

This type of noise is very similar to the previous TX/RX noise. The difference is that noise on these wires may be harder to find. This is because the data is being received at both ends, but there still is a communication problem. The use of a voltmeter or oscilloscope would help to measure the voltage on the control or indicator lines and therefore locate the possible cause of the problem, although this is not always very accurate. This is because the effect of noise on a system is governed by the ratio of the power levels of the signal and the noise, rather than a ratio of their respective voltage levels. If it is determined that the noise is being induced on one of the indicator or control lines, it may be best to move the RS-232 line and the offending noise source away from each other. If this does not help, it may be necessary to replace the RS-232 link with a fiber-optic or RS-485 system.

4b.5   Summary of troubleshooting

4b.5.1   Installation

- Is one device a DTE and the other a DCE?
- What is the sex and size of the connectors at each end?
- What is the speed of the communications?
- What is the distance between the equipments?
- Is it a noisy environment?
- Is the software set up correctly?

4b.5.2   Troubleshooting new and old systems

- Verify that there is power to the equipment
- Verify that the connectors are not loose

- Verify that the wires are correctly connected
- Check that a part, board, or module has not visibly failed.

4b.5.3 Mechanical problems on new systems

- Keep the wires short (20 m maximum)
- Stranded wire should be used instead of solid wire (stranded wire will flex)
- Only one wire should be soldered in each pin of the connector
- Bare wire should not be showing out of the connector pins
- The back shell should reliably and properly secure the wire.

4b.5.4 Setup problems on new systems

- Is the software communications set up at both ends for either 8N1, 7E1, or 7O1?
- Is the baud rate the same for both devices (1200, 4800, 9600, 19 200, etc.)?
- Is the software set up at both ends for binary, hex, or ASCII data transfer?
- Is the software setup for the proper type of control?

4b.5.5 Noise problems on new systems

- Noise from the common ground
- Induced noise on the TX or RX lines
- Induced noise on the indicator or control lines.

5a

RS-485 overview

Objectives

When you have completed study of this chapter, you will be able to:

- Describe the RS-485 standard
- Remedy the following problems:

  - Incorrect RS-485 wiring
  - Excessive common mode voltage
  - Faulty converters
  - Isolation
  - Idle state problems
  - Incorrect or missing terminations
  - RTS control via hardware or software.

5a.1   The RS-485 interface standard

The RS-485-A standard is one of the most versatile of the RS interface standards. It is an extension of RS-422 and allows the same distance and data speed but increases the number of transmitters and receivers permitted on the line. RS-485 permits a 'multidrop' network connection on two wires and allows reliable serial data communication for:

- Distances of up to 1200 m (4000 ft, same as RS-422)
- Data rates of up to 10 Mbps (same as RS-422)
- Up to 32 line drivers on the same line
- Up to 32 line receivers on the same line.

The maximum bit rate and maximum length can, however, not be achieved at the same time. For 24 AWG twisted-pair cable the maximum data rate at 4000 ft (1200 m) is approximately 90 kbps. The maximum cable length at 10 Mbps is less than 20 ft (6 m). Better performance will require a higher-grade cable and possibly the use of active (solid-state) terminators in the place of the 120 Ω resistors.

According to the RS-485 standard, there can be 32 'standard' transceivers on the network. Some manufacturers supply devices that are equivalent to 1/2 or 1/4 standard device, in which case this number can be increased to 64 or 128. If more transceivers are required, repeaters have to be used to extend the network.

The two conductors making up the bus are referred to as A in B in the specification. The A conductor is alternatively known as A−, TxA, and Tx+. The B conductor, in similar fashion, is called B+, TxB, and Tx–. Although this is rather confusing, identifying the A and B wires is not difficult. In the MARK or OFF state (i.e. when the RS-232 TxD pin is LOW (e.g. –8 V), the voltage on the A wire is more negative than that on the B wire.

The differential voltages on the A and B outputs of the driver (transmitter) are similar (although not identical) to those for RS-422, namely:

- –1.5 to –6 V on the A terminal with respect to the B terminal for a binary 1 (MARK or OFF) state
- +1.5 to +6 V on the A terminal with respect to the B terminal for a binary 0 (SPACE or ON state).

As with RS-422, the line driver for the RS-485 interface produces a ±5 V differential voltage on two wires.

The major enhancement of RS-485 is that a line driver can operate in three states called tri-state operation:

- Logic 1
- Logic 0
- High-impedance.

In the high-impedance state, the line driver draws virtually no current and appears not to be present on the line. This is known as the 'disabled' state and can be initiated by a signal on a control pin on the line driver integrated circuit. Tri-state operation allows a multidrop network connection and up to 32 transmitters can be connected on the same line, although only one can be active at any one time. Each terminal in a multidrop system must be allocated a unique address to avoid conflicting with other devices on the system. RS-485 includes current limiting in cases where contention occurs.

The RS-485 interface standard is very useful for systems where several instruments or controllers may be connected on the same line. Special care must be taken with the software to coordinate which devices on the network can become active. In most cases, a master terminal, such as a PC or computer, controls which transmitter/receiver will be active at a given time.

The two-wire data transmission line does not require special termination if the signal transmission time from one end of the line to the other end (at approximately 200 m/μs) is significantly smaller than one quarter of the signal's rise time. This is typical with short lines or low bit rates. At high bit rates or in the case of long lines, proper termination becomes critical. The value of the terminating resistors (one at each end) should be equal to the characteristic impedance of the cable. This is typically 120 Ω for twisted-pair wire.

Figure 5a.1 shows a typical two-wire multidrop network. Note that the transmission line is terminated on both ends of the line but not at drop points in the middle of the line.

An RS-485 network can also be connected in a four-wire configuration as shown in Figure 5a.2. In this type of connection it is necessary that one node is a master node and all others slaves. The master node communicates to all slaves, but a slave node can communicate only to the master. Since the slave nodes never listen to another slave's response to the master, a slave node cannot reply incorrectly to another slave node. This is an advantage in a mixed protocol environment.

During normal operation there are periods when all RS-485 drivers are off, and the communications lines are in the idle, high-impedance state. In this condition the lines are susceptible to noise pick up, which can be interpreted as random characters on the communications line. If a specific RS-485 system has this problem, it should incorporate bias resistors, as indicated in Figure 5a.3. The purpose of the bias resistors is not only to reduce the amount of noise picked up, but to keep the receiver biased in the IDLE state when no input signal is received. For this purpose the voltage drop across the 120 Ω termination resistor must exceed 200 mV AND the A terminal must be more negative than the B terminal. Keeping in mind that the two 120 Ω resistors appear in parallel, the bias resistor values can be calculated using Ohm's Law. For a +5 V supply and 120 Ω terminators, a bias resistor value of 560 Ω is sufficient. This assumes that the bias resistors are only installed on ONE node.

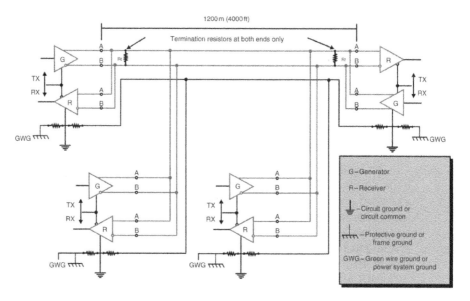

Figure 5a.1
Typical two-wire multidrop network

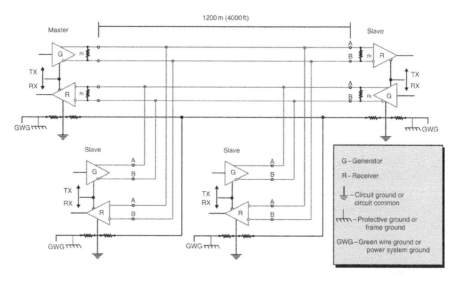

Figure 5a.2
Four-wire network configuration

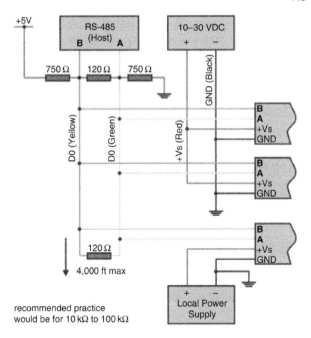

Figure 5a.3
Suggested installation of bias resistors

Some commercial systems use higher values for the bias resistors, but then assume that all or several nodes have bias resistors attached. In this case the value of all the bias resistors in parallel must be small enough to ensure 200 mV across the A and B wires.

RS-485 line drivers are designed to handle 32 nodes. This limitation can be overcome by employing an RS-485 repeater connected to the network. When data occurs on either side of the repeater, it is transmitted to the other side. The RS-485 repeater transmits at full voltage levels, consequently another 31 nodes can be connected to the network. A diagram for the use of RS-485 with a bi-directional repeater is given in Figure 5a.4.

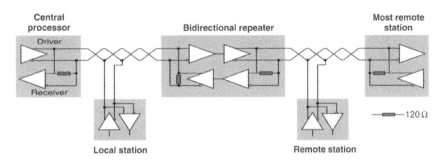

Figure 5a.4
RS-485 used with repeaters

The 'gnd' pin of the RS-485 transceiver should be connected to the logic reference (also known as circuit ground or circuit common), either directly or through a 100 Ω 1/2 W resistor. The purpose of the resistor is to limit the current flow if there is a significant potential difference between the earth points. This is not shown in Figure 5a.2. In addition, the logic reference is to be connected to the chassis reference (protective ground or frame ground) through a 100 Ω 1/2 W resistor. The chassis reference, in turn, is connected directly to the safety reference (green wire ground or power system ground).

If the grounds of the nodes are properly interconnected, then a third wire running in parallel with the A and B wires are, technically speaking, not necessary. However, this is often not the case and thus a third wire is added, as in Figure 5a.2. If the third wire is added, a 100 Ω 1/2 W resistor is to be added at each end, as shown in Figure 5a.2.

The 'drops' or 'spurs' that interconnect the intermediate nodes to the bus need to be as short as possible since a long spur creates an impedance mismatch, which leads to unwanted reflections. The amount of reflection that can be tolerated depends on the bit rate. At 50 kbps a spur of, say, 30 m could be in order, whilst at 10 Mbps the spur might be limited to 30 cm. Generally speaking, spurs on a transmission line are 'bad news' because of the impedance mismatch (and hence the reflections) they create, and should be kept as short as possible.

Some systems employ RS-485 in a so-called 'star' configuration. This is not really a star, since a star topology requires a hub device at its center. The 'star' is in fact a very short bus with extremely long spurs, and is prone to reflections. It can therefore only be used at low bit rates.

The 'decision threshold' of the RS-485 receiver is identical to that of both RS-422 and RS-423 receivers (not discussed as they have been superseded by RS-423) at ±200 mV (±0.2 V), as indicated in Figure 5a.5.

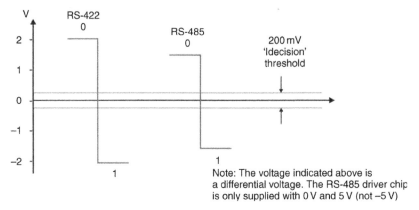

Figure 5a.5
RS-485/422 and 423 receiver sensitivities

5b

RS-485 troubleshooting

5b.1 Introduction

RS-485 is the most common asynchronous voltage standard in use today for multi-drop communication systems since it is very resistant to noise, can send data at high speeds (up to 10 Mbps), can be run for long distances (5 km at 1200 bps, 1200 m at 90 kbps), and is easy and cheap to use.

The RS-485 line drivers/receivers are differential chips. This means that the TX and RX wires are referenced to each other. A one is transmitted, for example, when one of the lines is +5 V and the other is 0 V. A zero is then transmitted when the lines reverse and the line that was +5 V is now 0 V and the line that was 0 V is now +5 V. In working systems the voltages are usually somewhere around ±2 V with reference to each other. The indeterminate voltage levels are ±200 mV. Up to 32 devices can be connected on one system without a repeater. Some systems allow the connection of five legs with four repeaters and get 160 devices on one system (Figure 5b.1).

Figure 5b.1
RS-485 Chip

Resistors are sometimes used on RS-485 systems to reduce noise, common mode voltages and reflections.

Bias resistors of values from 560 Ω to 4 kΩ can sometimes be used to reduce noise. These resistors connect the B+ line to +5 V and the A-line to ground. Higher voltages should not be used because anything over +12 V will cause the system to fail. Unfortunately, sometimes these resistors can increase the noise on the system by allowing a better path for noise from the ground. It is best not to use bias resistors unless required by the manufacturer.

Common mode voltage resistors usually have a value between 100 k and 200 kΩ. The values will depend on the induced voltages on the lines. They should be equal and as high as possible and placed on both lines and connected to ground. The common mode voltages should be kept less than +7 V, measured from each line to ground. Again, sometimes these resistors can increase the noise on the system by allowing a better path for noise from the ground. It is best not to use common mode resistors unless required by the manufacturer or as needed.

The termination resistor value depends on the cable used and is typically 120 Ω. Values less than 110 Ω should not be used since the driver chips are designed to drive a load resistance not less than 54 Ω, being the value of the two termination resistors in parallel plus any other stray resistance in parallel. These resistors are placed between the lines (at the two furthest ends, not on the stubs) and reduce reflections. If the lines are less than 100 m long and speeds are 9600 baud or less, the termination resistor usually becomes redundant, but having said that, you should always follow the manufacturer's recommendations.

5b.2   RS-485 vs RS-422

In practice, RS-485 and RS-422 are very similar to each other and manufacturers often use the same chips for both. The main working difference is that RS-485 is used for two-wire multi-drop half-duplex systems and RS-422 is for four-wire point-to-point full-duplex systems. Manufacturers often use a chip like the 75154 with two RS-485 drivers on board as an RS-422 driver. One driver is used as a transmitter and the other is dedicated as a receiver. Because the RS-485 chips have three states, TX, RX, and high impedance, the driver that is used as a transmitter can be set to high-impedance mode when the driver is not transmitting data. This is often done using the RTS line from the RS-232 port. When the RTS goes high (+voltage) the transmitter is effectively turned off by putting the transmitter in the high-impedance mode. The receiver is left on all the time, so data can be received when it comes in. This method can reduce noise on the line by having a minimum of devices on the line at a time.

5b.3   RS-485 installation

Installation rules for RS-485 vary per manufacturer and since there are no standard connectors for RS-485 systems, it is difficult to define a standard installation procedure. Even so, most manufacture procedures are similar. The most common type of connector used on most RS-485 systems is either a one-part or two-part screw connector. The preferred connector is the two-part screw connector with the sliding box under the screw (phoenix type). Other connectors use a screw on top of a folding tab. Manufacturers sometimes use the DB-9 connector instead of a screw connector to save money. Unfortunately, the DB-9 connector has problems when used for multidrop connections. The problem is that the DB-9 connectors are designed so that only one wire can be inserted per pin. RS-485 multidrop systems require the connection of two wires so that the wire can continue down the line to the next device. This is a simple matter with screw connectors, but it is not so easy with a DB-9 connector. With a screw connector, the two wires are twisted together and inserted in the connector under the screw. The screw is then tightened down and the connection is made. With the DB-9 connector, the two wires must be soldered together with a third wire. The third wire is then soldered to the single pin on the connector.

Note: When using screw connectors, the wires should NOT be soldered together (Figure 5b.2). Either the wires should be just twisted together or a special crimp ferrule should be used to connect the wires before they are inserted in the screw connector.

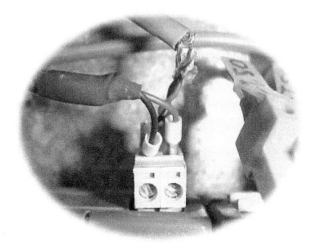

Figure 5b.2
A bad RS-485 connection

Serious problems with RS-485 systems are rare (that is one reason it is used) but having said that, there are some possible problems that can arise in the installation process:

- The wires get reversed (e.g. black to white and white to black)
- Loose or bad connections due to improper installation
- Excessive electrical or electronic noise in the environment
- Common mode voltage problems
- Reflection of the signal due to missing or incorrect terminators
- Shield not grounded, grounded incorrectly, or not connected at each drop
- Starring or tee-ing of devices (i.e. long stubs).

To make sure the wires are not reversed, check that the same color is connected to the same pin on all connectors. Check the manufacturer's manual for proper wire color codes.

Verifying that the installers are informed of the proper installation procedures can reduce loose connections. If the installers are provided with adjustable torque screwdrivers, then the chances of loose or over tightened screw connections can be minimized.

5b.4   Noise problems

RS-485, being a differential type of circuit, is resistant to receiving common mode noise. There are five ways that noise can be induced into an RS-485 circuit.

1. Induced noise on the A/B lines
2. Common mode voltage problems
3. Reflections
4. Unbalancing the line
5. Incorrect shielding.

5b.4.1   Induced noise

Noise from the outside can cause communication on an RS-485 system to fail. Although the voltages on an RS-485 system are small (±5 V), because the output of the receiver is the difference of the two lines, the voltage induced on the two lines must be different. This makes RS-485 very tolerant to noise. The communications will also fail if the voltage level of the noise on the either or both lines is outside of the minimum or maximum RS-485 specification. Noise can be detected by comparing the data communication being transmitted out of one end with the received communication at the other (assuming no broken wire). The protocol analyzer is plugged into the transmitter at one end and the data monitored. If the data is correct, the protocol analyzer is then plugged into the other end and the received data monitored. If the data is corrupt at the received end, then the noise on that wire may be the problem. If it is determined that the noise problem is caused by induced noise on the A or B lines it may be best to move the RS-485 line or the offending noise source away from each other.

Excessive noise is often due to the close proximity of power cables. Another possible noise problem could be caused by an incorrectly installed grounding system for the cable shield. Installation standards should be followed when the RS-485 pairs are installed close to other wires and cables. Some manufacturers suggest biasing resistors to limit noise on the line while others dissuade the use of bias resistors completely. Again, the procedure is to follow the manufacturer's recommendations. Having said that, it is usually found that biasing resistors are of minimal value, and that there are much better methods of reducing noise in an RS-485 system.

5b.4.2   Common mode noise

Common mode noise problems are usually caused by a changing ground level. The ground level can change when a high-current device is turned on or off. This large current draw causes the ground level as referenced to the A and B lines to rise or decrease. If the voltages on the A or B line are raised or lowered outside of the minimum or maximum, as defined by the manufacturer specifications, it can prohibit the line receiver from operating correctly. This can cause a device to float in and out of service. Often, if the common mode voltage gets high enough, it can cause the module or device to be damaged. This voltage can be measured using a differential measurement device like a handheld digital voltmeter. The voltage between A and ground and then B to ground is measured. If the voltage is outside of specifications then resistors of values between 100 and 200 kΩ are placed between A and ground and B and ground. It is best to start with the larger value resistor and then verify the common mode voltage. If it is still too high, try a lower resistor value and recheck the voltage. At idle the voltage on the A line should be close to 0 and the B line should be between 2 and 6 V. It is not uncommon for an RS-485 manufacturer to specify a maximum common voltage value of +12 and –7 V, but it is best to have a system that is not near these levels. It is important to follow the manufacturer's recommendations for the common mode voltage resistor value or whether they are needed at all (Figure 5b.3).

Note: When using bias resistors, neither the A nor the B line on the RS-485 system should ever be raised higher than +12 V or lower than –7 V. Most RS-485 driver chips will fail if this happens. It is important to follow the manufacturer recommendations for bias resistor values or whether they are needed at all.

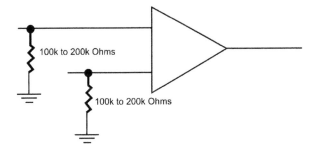

Figure 5b.3
Common mode resistors

5b.4.3 Reflections or ringing

Reflections are caused by the signal reflecting off the end of the wire and corrupting the signal. It usually affects the devices near the end of the line. It can be detected by placing a balanced ungrounded oscilloscope across the A and B lines. The signal will show ringing superimposed on the square wave. A termination resistor of typically 120 Ω is placed at each end of the line to reduce reflections. This is more important at higher speeds and longer distances (Figure 5b.4).

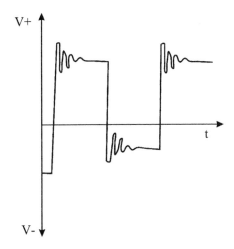

Figure 5b.4
Ringing on an RS-485 signal

5b.4.4 Unbalancing the line

Unbalancing the line does not actually induce noise, but it does make the lines more susceptible to noise. A line that is balanced will more or less have the same resistance, capacitance, and inductance on both conductors. If this balance is disrupted, the lines then become affected by noise more easily. There are a few ways most RS-485 lines become unbalanced:

- Using a star topology
- Using a 'tee' topology

- Using unbalanced cable
- Damaged transmitter or receiver.

There should, ideally, be no stars or tees in the RS-485-bus system. If another device is to be added in the middle, a two-pair cable should be run out and back from the device. The typical RS-485 system would have a topology that would look something as in Figures 5b.5 and 5b.6.

Figure 5b.5
A typical RS-485 multi-drop configuration

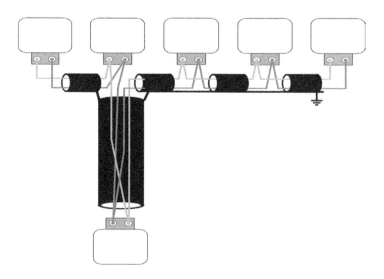

Figure 5b.6
Adding a new device to a RS-485 bus

The distance between the end of the shield and the connection in the device should be no more than 10 mm or 1/2 in. The end of the wires should be stripped only far enough to fit all the way into the connector, with no exposed wire outside the connector. The wire should be twisted tightly before insertion into the screw connector. Often, installers will strip the shield from the wire and connect the shields together at the bottom of the cabinet. This is incorrect, as there would be from 1 to 2 m of exposed cable from the terminal block at the bottom of the cabinet to the device at the top. This exposed cable will invariably receive noise from other devices in the cabinet. The pair of wires should be brought right up to the device and stripped as mentioned above.

5b.4.5   Shielding

The choices of shielding for an RS-485 installation are:

- Braided
- Foil (with drain wire)
- Armored.

From a practical point of view, the noise reduction difference between the first two is minimal. Both the braided and the foil shields will provide the same level of protection against capacitive noise. The third choice, armored cable has the distinction of protecting against magnetic induced noise. Armored cable is much more expensive than the first two and therefore the braided and the foil types of cable are more popular. For most installers, it is a matter of personal choice when deciding to use either braided or foil shielded wire.

With the braided shield, it is possible to pick the A and B wires between the braids of the shield without breaking the shield. If this method is not used, then the shields of the two wires should be soldered or crimped together. A separate wire should be run from the shield at the device down to the ground strip in the bottom of the cabinet, but only one per bus, not per cabinet. It is incorrect in most cases to connect the shield to ground in each cabinet, especially if there are long distances between cabinets.

5b.5   Test equipment

When testing or troubleshooting an RS-485 system, it is important to use the right test equipment. Unfortunately, there is very little in generic test equipment specifically designed for RS-485 testing. The most commonly used are the multimeter, oscilloscope and the protocol analyzer. It is important to remember that both of these types of test equipment must have floating differential inputs. The standard oscilloscope or multimeter each has their specific uses in troubleshooting an RS-485 system.

5b.5.1   Multimeter

The multimeter has three basic functions in troubleshooting or testing an RS-485 system.

1. Continuity verification
2. Idle voltage measurement
3. Common mode voltage measurement.

Continuity verification

The multimeter can be used before start-up to check that the lines are not shorted or open. This is done as follows:

- Verify that the power is off
- Verify that the cable is disconnected from the equipment
- Verify that the cable is connected for the complete distance
- Place the multimeter in the continuity check mode
- Measure the continuity between the A and B lines
- Verify that it is open
- Short the A and B at the end of the line
- Verify that the lines are now shorted
- Un-short the lines when satisfied that the lines are correct.

If the lines are internally shorted before they are manually shorted, then check to see if an A line is connected to a B line. In most installations the A line is kept as one color wire and the B is kept as another. This procedure keeps the wires away from accidentally being crossed.

The multimeter is also used to measure the idle and common mode voltages between the lines.

Idle voltage measurement

At idle the master usually puts out a logical '1' and this can be read at any station in the system. It is read between A and B lines and is usually somewhere between –1.5 and –5 V (A with respect to B). If a positive voltage is measured, it is possible that the leads on the multimeter need to be reversed. The procedure for measuring the idle voltage is as follows:

- Verify that the power is on
- Verify that all stations are connected
- Verify that the master is not polling
- Measure the voltage difference between the A– and B+ lines starting at the master
- Verify and record the idle voltage at each station.

If the voltage is zero, then disconnect the master from the system and check the output of the master alone. If there is idle voltage at the master, then plug in each station one at a time until the voltage drops to or near zero. The last station probably has a problem.

Common mode voltage measurement

Common mode voltage is measured at each station, including the master. It is measured from each of the A and B lines to ground. The purpose of the measurement is to check if the common mode voltage is getting close to maximum tolerance. It is important therefore to know what the maximum common mode voltage is for the system. In most cases, it is +12 and –7 V. A procedure for measuring the common mode voltage is:

- Verify that the system is powered up
- Measure and record the voltage between the A and ground and the B and ground at each station
- Verify that voltages are within the specified limits as set by the manufacturer.

If the voltages are near or out of tolerance, then either contact the manufacturer or install resistors between each line to ground at the station that has the problem. It is usually best to start with a high value such as 200 kΩ 1/4 W and then go lower as needed. Both resistors should be of the same value.

5b.5.2   Oscilloscope

Oscilloscopes are used for:

- Noise identification
- Ringing
- Data transfer.

Noise identification

Although the oscilloscope is not the best device for noise measurement, it is good for detection of some types of noise. The reason the oscilloscope is not that good at noise detection is that it is a two-dimensional voltmeter; whereas the effect of the noise is seen in the ratio of the power of a signal vs the power of the noise. But having said that, the oscilloscope is useful for determining noise that is constant in frequency. This can be a signal such as 50/60 Hz hum, motor-induced noise or relays clicking on and off. The oscilloscope will not show intermittent noise, high-frequency radio waves or the power ratio of the noise vs the signal.

Ringing

Ringing is caused by the reflection of signals at the end of the wires. It happens more often on higher baud rate signals and longer lines. The oscilloscope will show this ringing as a distorted square wave.

As mentioned before, the 'fix' for ringing is a termination resistor at each end of the line. Testing the line for ringing can be done as follows:

- Use a two-channel oscilloscope in differential (A-B) mode.
- Connect the probes of the oscilloscope to the A and B lines. Do NOT use a single-channel oscilloscope, connecting the ground clip to one of the wires will short that wire to ground and prevent the system from operating.
- Set up the oscilloscope for a vertical level of around 2 V per division.
- Set up the oscilloscope for horizontal level that will show one square wave of the signal per division.
- Use an RS-485 driver chip with a TTL signal generator at the appropriate baud rate. Data can be generated by allowing the master to poll, but because of the intermittent nature of the signal, the oscilloscope will not be able to trigger. In this case a storage oscilloscope will be useful.
- Check to see if the waveform is distorted.

Data transfer

Another use for the oscilloscope is to verify that data is being transferred. This is done using the same method as described for observing ringing, and by getting the master to send data to a slave device. The only difference is the adjustment of the horizontal level. It is adjusted so that the screen shows complete packets. Although this is interesting, it is of limited value unless noise is noted or some other aberration is displayed.

5b.5.3 Protocol analyzer

The protocol analyzer is a very useful tool for checking the actual packet information. Protocol analyzers come in two varieties, hardware and software. Hardware protocol analyzers are very versatile and can monitor, log, and interpret many types of protocols.

When the analyzer is hooked-up to the RS-485 system, many problems can be displayed such as:

- Wrong baud rates
- Bad data
- The effects of noise
- Incorrect timing
- Protocol problems.

The main problem with the hardware protocol analyzer is the cost and the relatively rare use of it. The devices can cost from US$5000 to US$10 000 and are often used only once or twice a year.

The software protocol analyzer, on the other hand, is cheap and has most of the features of the hardware type. It is a program that sits on the normal PC and logs data being transmitted down the serial link. Because it uses existing hardware (the PC), it can be a much cheaper but useful tool. The software protocol analyzer can see and log most of the same problems a hardware type can.

The following procedure can be used to analyze the data stream:

- Verify that the system is on and the master is polling
- Set up the protocol analyzer for the correct baud rate and other system parameters
- Connect the protocol analyzer in parallel with the communication bus
- Log the data and analyze the problem.

5b.6   Summary

5b.6.1   Installation

- Are the connections correctly made?
- What is the speed of the communications?
- What is the distance between the equipment?
- Is it a noisy environment?
- Is the software setup correctly?
- Are there any tees or stars in the bus?

5b.6.2   Troubleshooting new and old systems

- Verify that there is power to the equipment
- Verify that the connectors are not loose
- Verify that the wires are correctly connected
- Check that a part, board or module has not visibly failed.

5b.6.3   Mechanical problems on new systems

- Keep the wires short, if possible
- Stranded wire should be used instead of solid wire (stranded wire will flex)
- Only one wire should be soldered in each pin of the connector
- Bare wire should not be showing out of the pin of the connector
- The back shell should reliably and properly secure the wire.

5b.6.4   Setup problems on new systems

- Is the software communications setup at both ends for 8N1, 7E1, or 7O1?
- Is the baud rate the same at both devices (1200, 4800, 9600, 19 200, etc.)?
- Is the software setup at both ends for binary, hex, or ASCII data transfer?
- Is the software setup for the proper type of control?

5b.6.5   Noise problems on new systems

- Induced noise on the A or B lines?
- Common mode voltage noise?
- Reflection or ringing?

6a

Current loop and RS-485 converters overview

Objectives

When you have completed study of this chapter, you will be able to:

- Describe current loop hardware
- Describe RS-232/RS-485 interface converters
- Fix problems with cabling and isolation for interface converters.

6a.1   The 20 mA current loop

Another commonly used interface technique is the current loop. This uses a current signal rather than a voltage signal, employing a separate pair of wires for the transmitter current loop and receiver current loop.

A current level of 20 mA, or up to 60 mA, is used to indicate logic 1 and 0 mA or 4 mA to indicate logic 0. The use of a constant current signal enables a far greater separation distance to be achieved than with a standard RS-232-voltage connection. This is due to the higher noise immunity of the 20 mA current loop, which can drive long lines of up to 1 km, but at reasonably slow bit rates. Current loops are mainly used between printers and terminals in the industrial environment. Figure 6a.1 illustrates the current loop interface.

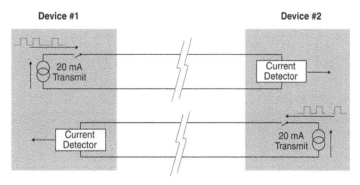

Figure 6a.1
The 20 mA current loop interface

6a.2　Serial interface converters

Serial interface converters are becoming increasingly important with the move away from RS-232C to industrial standards such as RS-422 and RS-485. Since many industrial devices still use RS-232 ports, it is necessary to use converters to interface a device to other physical interface standards. Interface converters can also be used to increase the effective distance between two RS-232 devices.

The most common converters are:

- RS-232/422
- RS-232/485 (Figure 6a.2)
- RS-232/current loop.

Figure 6a.3 is a block diagram of an RS-232/RS-485 converter.

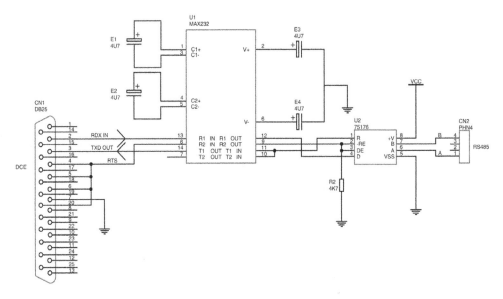

Figure 6a.2
RS-232/485 converter

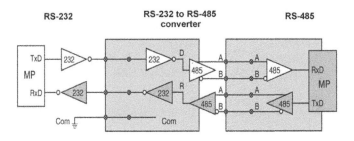

Figure 6a.3
Block structure of RS-232/RS-485 converter

Figure 6a.4 shows a circuit-wiring diagram.

The RS-232/422 and RS-232/485 interface converters are very similar and provide bidirectional full-duplex conversion for synchronous or asynchronous transfer between RS-232 and RS-485 ports. These converters may be powered from an external AC source, such as 240 V, or smaller units can be powered at 12 V DC from pins 9 and 10 of the RS-232 port. For industrial applications, externally powered units are recommended. The RS-232 standard was designed for communications, not as a power supply unit!

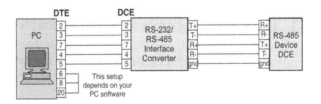

Figure 6a.4
Wiring diagram for RS-232/485 converter

LEDs are provided to show the status of incoming signals from both RS-232 and RS-485.

When operating over long distances, a useful feature of interface converters is optical isolation. This is especially valuable in areas prone to lightning. Even if the equipment is not directly hit by lightning, the earth potential rise (EPR) in the surrounding area may be sufficient to damage the communications equipment at both ends of the link. Some specifications quote over 10 kV isolation, but these figures are seldom backed up with engineering data and should be treated with some caution.

Typical specifications for the RS-232/422 or RS-232/485 converters are:

- Data transfer rate of up to 1 Mbps
- DCE/DTE switch selectable
- Converts all data and control signals
- LEDs for status of data and control signals
- Powered from AC source
- Optically isolated (optional)
- DB-25 connector (male or female)
- DB-37 connector (male or female).

Typical specifications for the RS-232/current loop converters are:

- 20 or 60 mA operation
- DCE/DTE, full/half-duplex selectable
- Active or passive loops supported
- Optically isolated (optional)
- Powered from AC source
- Data rates of up to 19 200 kbps over 3 km (10 000 ft)
- DB-25 connector (male or female)
- Current loop connector – 5 screw.

6b

Current loop and RS-485 converters troubleshooting

6b.1 Troubleshooting converters

The troubleshooting procedure is very similar to that discussed in the RS-232 and RS-485 sections with a few additional considerations. It should be emphasized that care should be taken in using non-isolated converters where there are any possibilities of electrical surges and transients. In addition, loop-powered RS-232/485 converters should also be avoided, as they can be unreliable. Using one of the handshaking pins of the RS-232 port may sound clever and avoid the necessity of providing a separate power supply but RS-232 was never intended to be a power supply.

A few suggestions for troubleshooting and the diagnostic LEDs used are outlined in the following sections.

6b.1.1 Check that the converter is powered up

If there is no power to the converter or the power supply on the converter is damaged the LED on the converter will not light up. Typically, it should be illuminated solid green.

In addition, on some converters there is provision for an isolated power LED, which should also be illuminated solid green.

With all the connections made, the converter should have the power light on, DCD, CTS, RTS LEDs on, and the receive and transmit lights off. If you loop back the transmit and receive pins of the converter, and use a protocol analysis program such as PAT, you should see the transmit and receive lights flickering to indicate data flow and characters transmitted should be received. This will be the quickest test to indicate that all is well with the converter.

6b.1.2 Network transmit

This LED will be lit up to indicate that the RS-485 converter is active and driving the network. In a multi-drop network, only one unit should be driving the line at one time otherwise, there will be contention with no resultant transmission at all.

6b.1.3 Configuration jumpers

Although the configuration jumpers are often set internally, sometimes the user can also set them.

Choose the RTS transmit polarity correctly. Normally assertion of RTS is used to place the RS-485 transmitter in transmit mode.

6b.1.4   Failsafe termination

This jumper determines what happens if the RS-232 host is disconnected from the converter. Conventionally, the RS-485 transmitter should be disabled when the RS-232 host is disconnected. To test this jumper, power up the system and disconnect the RS-232 connection. The network transmit LED should be off.

6b.1.5   DTE/DCE settings

These should be checked that they are correctly set up depending on the application. Note that no damage will occur if a mistake is made in setting them up. The system simply will not work.

6b.1.6   Digital ground/shield

Sometimes, noise rejection performance can be improved by grounding the digital logic. But this is a very rare setting and other issues should be examined first before trying this configuration.

7a

TCP/IP overview

7a.1 Introduction

TCP/IP is the *de facto* global standard for the Internet (network) and host-to-host (transport) layer implementation of internetwork applications because of the popularity of the Internet. The Internet (in its early years known as ARPANet), was part of a military project commissioned by the Advanced Research Projects Agency (ARPA), later known as the Defense Advanced Research Agency or DARPA. The communications model used to construct the system is known as the ARPA (or DoD) model.

Whereas the OSI model was developed in Europe by the International Organization for Standardization (ISO), the ARPA model was developed in the USA by ARPA. Although they were developed by different bodies and at different points in time, both serve as models for a communications infrastructure and hence provide 'abstractions' of the same reality. The remarkable degree of similarity is therefore not surprising.

Whereas the OSI model has seven layers, the ARPA model has four layers. The OSI layers map onto the ARPA model as follows:

- The OSI session, presentation and applications layers are contained in the ARPA process/application layer
- The OSI transport layer maps onto the ARPA host-to-host layer (sometimes referred to as the service layer)
- The OSI network layer maps onto the ARPA Internet layer
- The OSI physical and data-link layers map onto the ARPA network interface layer.

The relationship between the two models is depicted in Figure 7a.1.

TCP/IP, or rather the TCP/IP protocol suite, is not limited to the TCP and IP protocols, but consists of a multitude of interrelated protocols that occupy the upper three layers of the ARPA model. TCP/IP does NOT include the bottom network interface layer, but depends on it for access to the medium.

As depicted in Figure 7a.2, an IP transmission frame originating on a specific host (computer) would contain the local network (for example, Ethernet) header and trailer applicable to that host. As the message proceeds along the internetwork, this header and trailer could be replaced depending on the type of network on which the packet finds itself – be that X.25, frame relay, or ATM. The IP datagram itself would remain untouched, unless it has to be fragmented and reassembled along the way.

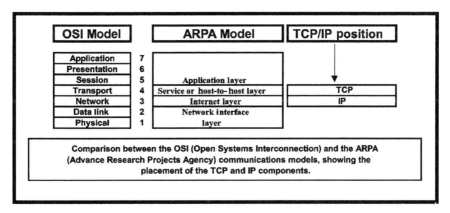

Figure 7a.1
OSI vs ARPA models

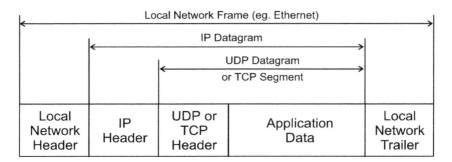

Figure 7a.2
Internet frame

Note: Any Internet-related specification is referenced as a request for comments or RFC, RFCs can be obtained from various sources on the Internet such as www.rfc-editor.org.

7a.1.1 The Internet layer

This layer is primarily responsible for the routing of packets from one host to another. Each packet contains the address information needed for its routing through the internetwork to the destination host. The dominant protocol at this level is the Internet protocol (IP). There are, however, several other additional protocols required at this level such as:

- *Address resolution protocol (ARP), RFC 826*: This is used for the translation of an IP address to a hardware (MAC) address, such as required by Ethernet.
- *Reverse address resolution protocol (RARP), RFC 903*: This is the complement of ARP and translates a hardware address to an IP address.
- *Internet control message protocol (ICMP), RFC 792*: This is a protocol used for exchanging control or error messages between routers or hosts.

7a.1.2   The host-to-host layer

This layer is primarily responsible for data integrity between the sender host and the receiver host regardless of the path or distance used to convey the message. It has two protocols associated with it, namely:

1. *User data protocol* (UDP), a connectionless (unreliable) protocol used for higher layer port addressing with minimal protocol overhead (RFC 768).
2. *Transmission control protocol* (TCP), a connection-oriented protocol that offers a very reliable method of transferring a stream of data in byte format between applications (RFC 793).

7a.1.3   The process/application layer

This layer provides the user or application programs with interfaces to the TCP/IP stack. These include (but are not limited to) file transfer protocol (FTP), trivial file transfer protocol (TFTP), simple mail transfer protocol (SMTP), telecommunications network (TELNET), post office protocol (POP3), remote procedure calls (RPC), remote login (RLOGIN), hypertext transfer protocol (HTTP), and network time protocol (NTP). Users can also develop their own application layer protocols.

7a.2   Internet layer protocols (packet transport)

This section will deal with the Internet protocol (IP), the Internet control message protocol (ICMP) and the address resolution protocol (ARP). IPv4 is officially in the process of being replaced by IPv6 but it will still be some time before IPv6 makes its appearance. This section will therefore, for the sake of simplicity, only deal with IPv4 and its associated protocols.

7a.2.1   IP version 4 (IPv4)

IP (RFC 791) is responsible for the delivery of packets ('datagrams') between hosts. It is analogous to the postal system, in that it forwards (routes) and delivers datagrams on the basis of IP addresses attached to the datagrams, in the same way the postal service would process a letter based on the postal address. The IP address is a 32-bit entity containing both the network address (the 'zip code') and the host address (the 'street address').

IP also breaks up (fragments) datagrams that are too large. This is often necessary because with LANs and WANs, a datagram may have to traverse on its way to its destination that may have different frame size limitations. For example, Ethernet can handle 1500 bytes but X.25 can handle only 576 bytes. IP on the sending side will fragment a datagram if necessary, attach an IP header to each fragment, and send them off consecutively. On the receiving side, IP will again rebuild the original datagram.

The IPv4 header

The IP header is appended to the information that IP accepts from higher-level protocols, before passing it around the network. This information could, within itself, contain the headers appended by higher-level protocols such as TCP. The header consists of at least five 32-bit (4 byte) 'long words', i.e. 20 bytes total and is made up as in Figure 7a.3.

The ver (version) field is 4 bits long and indicates the version of the IP protocol in use. For IPv4, it is 4.

```
0   3 4  7 8           15  16              31   bits
```

Ver	IHL	Type of Service	Total Length	
Identifier			Flags	Fragment Offset
Time to Live		Protocol	Checksum Header	
Source Address				
Destination Address				
Options + Padding				

Figure 7a.3
IPv4 header

This is followed by the 4-bit IHL (Internet header length) field that indicates the length of the IP header in 32 bit 'long words'. This is necessary since the IP header can contain options and therefore does not have a fixed length.

The 8-bit type of service (ToS) field informs the network about the quality of service required for this datagram. The ToS field is composed of a 3-bit precedence field (which is often ignored) and an unused (LSB) bit that must be 0. The remaining 4 bits may only be turned on (set = 1) one at a time, and are allocated as follows:

Bit 3: minimize delay
Bit 4: maximize throughput
Bit 5: maximize reliability
Bit 6: minimize monetary cost.

Total length (16 bits) is the length of the entire datagram, measured in bytes. Using this field and the IHL length, it can be determined where the data starts and ends. This field allows the length of a datagram to be up to $2^{16} = 65\,536$ bytes, although such long datagrams are impractical. All hosts must at least be prepared to accept datagrams of up to 576 octets.

The 16-bit identifier uniquely identifies each datagram sent by a host. It is normally incremented by one for each successive datagram sent. In the case of fragmentation, it is appended to all fragments of the same datagram for the sake of reconstructing the datagram at the receiving end. It can be compared to the 'tracking' number of an item delivered by registered mail or UPS.

The 3-bit flag field contains two flags, used in the fragmentation process, viz. DF and MF. The DF (don't fragment) flag is set (=1) by the higher-level protocol (for example, TCP) if IP is NOT allowed to fragment a datagram. If such a situation occurs, IP will not fragment and forward the datagram, but simply return an appropriate ICMP error message to the sending host. If fragmentation does occur, MF = 1 will indicate that there are more fragments to follow, whilst MF = 0 indicates that it is the last fragment to be sent.

The 13-bit fragment offset field indicates where in the original datagram a particular fragment belongs, for example, how far the beginning of the fragment is removed from the end of the header. The first fragment has offset zero. The fragment offset is measured in units of 8 bytes (64 bits); i.e. the transmitted offset is equal to the actual offset divided by eight.

The TTL (time to live) field ensures that undeliverable datagrams are eventually discarded. Every router that processes a datagram must decrease the TTL by one and if this field contains the value zero, then the datagram must be destroyed. Typically, a datagram can be delivered anywhere in the world by traversing no more than 30 routers.

The 8-bit protocol field indicates the next (higher) level protocol header present in the data portion of the IP datagram, in other words the protocol that resides above IP in the protocol stack and which has passed the datagram down to IP. Typical values are 1 for ICMP, 6 for TCP, and 17 for UDP. A more detailed listing is contained in RFC1700.

The checksum is a 16-bit mathematical checksum on the header only. Since some header fields change all the time (for example, TTL), this checksum is recomputed and verified at each point that the IP header is processed. It is not necessary to cover the data portion of the datagram, as the protocols making use of IP, such as ICMP, IGMP, UDP, and TCP, all have a checksum in their headers to cover their own header and data.

Finally, the source and destination addresses are the 32-bit IP addresses of the origin and the destination hosts of the datagram.

IPv4 addressing

The ultimate responsibility for the issuing of IP addresses is vested in the Internet assigned numbers authority (IANA). This responsibility is, in turn, delegated to the three regional Internet registries (RIRs) viz. APNIC (Asia-Pacific network information center), ARIN (American registry for Internet numbers), and RIPE NCC (Reseau IP Europeans). RIRs allocate blocks of IP addresses to Internet service providers (ISPs) under their jurisdiction, for subsequent issuing to users or sub-ISPs.

The IPv4 address consists of 32 bits, e.g. 11000000011001000110010 0000000001. Since this number is fine for computers but a little difficult for human beings, it is divided into four octets w, x, y and z. Each octet is converted to its decimal equivalent. The result of the conversion is written in the format 192.100.100.1. This is known as the 'dotted decimal' or 'dotted quad' notation. As mentioned earlier, one part of the IP address is known as the network ID or 'NetID' while the rest is known as the 'HostID'.

Originally, IP addresses were allocated in so-called address classes. Although the system proved to be problematic, and IP addresses are currently issued 'classless', the legacy of IP address classes remains and has to be understood.

To provide for flexibility in assigning addresses to networks, the interpretation of the address field was coded to specify either a small number of networks with a large number of hosts (class A), or a moderate number of networks with a moderate number of hosts (class B), or a large number of networks with a small number of hosts (class C). There was also provision for extended addressing modes, class D was intended for multicasting whilst E was reserved for future use (Figure 7a.4).

For class A, the first bit is fixed at 0. The values for 'w' can therefore only vary between 0 and 127_{10}. 0 is not allowed and 127 is a reserved number used for testing. This allows for 126 class A NetIDs. The number of HostIDs is determined by octets 'x', 'y' and 'z'. From these 24 bits, $2^{24} = 16\,777\,218$ combinations are available. All zeros and all ones are not permissible, which leaves 16 777 216 usable combinations.

For class B, the first two bits are fixed at 10. The binary values for 'w' can therefore only vary between 128_{10} and 191_{10}. The number of NetIDs is determined by octets 'w' and 'x'. The first 2 bits are used to indicate class B and hence cannot be used. This leaves fourteen usable bits. Fourteen bits allow $2^{14} = 16\,384$ NetIDs. The number of HostIDs is determined by octets 'y' and 'z'. From these 16 bits, $2^{16} = 65\,536$ combinations are available. All zeros and all ones are not permissible, which leaves 65 534 usable combinations.

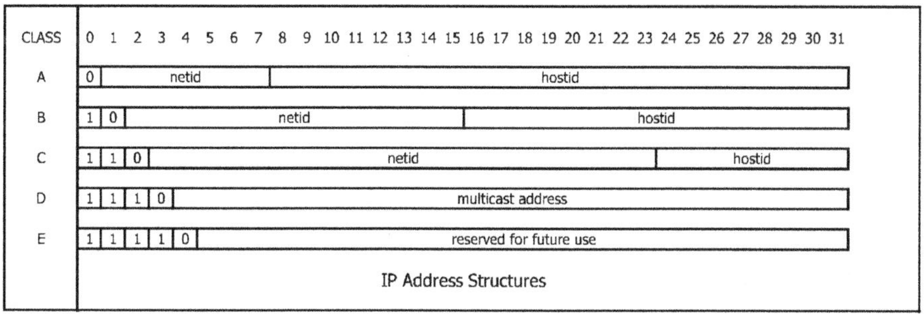

Figure 7a.4
Address structure for IPv4

For class C, the first three bits are fixed at 110. The binary values for 'w' can therefore only vary between 192_{10} and 223_{10}. The number of NetIDs is determined by octets 'w', 'x' and 'y'. The first three bits (110) are used to indicate class C and hence cannot be used. This leaves 22 usable bits. Twenty-two bits allow $2^{22} = 2\,097\,152$ combinations for NetIDs. The number of HostIDs is determined by octet 'z'. From these 8 bits, $2^8 = 256$ combinations are available. Once again, all zeros and all ones are not permissible which leaves 254 usable combinations.

In order to determine where the NetID ends and the HostID begins, each IP address is associated with a subnet mask, or, technically more correct, a netmask. This mask starts with a row of contiguous ones from the left; one for each bit that forms part of the NetID. This is followed by zeroes, one for each bit comprising the HostID.

7a.2.2   Address resolution protocol (ARP)

Some network technologies make address resolution difficult. Ethernet interface boards, for example, come with built-in 48-bit hardware addresses. This creates several difficulties:

- No simple correlation, applicable to the whole network, can be created between physical (MAC) addresses and IP addresses.
- When the interface board fails and has to be replaced the IP address then has to be remapped to a different MAC address.
- The MAC address is too long to be encoded into the 32-bit IP address.

To overcome these problems in an efficient manner, and eliminate the need for applications to know about MAC addresses, TCP/IP designers developed the address resolution protocol (ARP), which resolves addresses dynamically.

When a host wishes to communicate with another host on the same physical network, it needs the destination MAC address in order to compose the basic frame. If it does not know what the destination MAC address is, but has its IP address, it broadcasts a special type of datagram in order to resolve the problem. This is called an address resolution protocol (ARP) request. This datagram requests the owner of the unresolved Internet protocol (IP) address to reply with its MAC address. All hosts on the network will receive the broadcast, but only the one that recognizes its own IP address will respond.

While the sender could, of course, just broadcast the original datagram to all hosts on the network, this would impose an unnecessary load on the network, especially if the datagram was large. A small address resolution protocol (ARP) request, followed by a small address resolution protocol (ARP) reply, followed by a direct transmission of the original datagram, is a much more efficient way of resolving the problem.

Address resolution cache

Because communication between two computers usually involves transfer of a succession of datagrams, it is prudent for the sender to 'remember' the MAC information it receives, at least for a while. Thus, when the sender receives an ARP reply, it stores the MAC address it receives as well as the corresponding IP address in its ARP cache. Before sending any message to a specific IP address, it checks first to see if the relevant address binding is in the cache. This saves it from repeatedly broadcasting identical ARP requests.

To further reduce communication overheads, when a host broadcasts an ARP request it includes its own IP address and MAC address, and these are stored in the ARP caches of all other hosts that receive the broadcast. When a new host is added to a network, it can be made to send an ARP broadcast to inform all other hosts on that network of its address.

Some very small networks do not use ARP caches, but the continual traffic of ARP requests and replies on a larger network would have a serious negative impact on the network's performance.

The ARP cache holds four fields of information for each device:

1. *IF Index*:   The physical port
2. *Physical address*:   The MAC address of the device
3. *Internet protocol (IP) address*:   The corresponding IP address
4. *Type*:   The type of entry in the ARP cache; there are four possible types:

  - 4 = static – the entry will not change
  - 3 = dynamic – the entry can change
  - 2 = the entry is invalid
  - 1 = none of the above.

ARP datagram

The layout of an ARP request or reply datagram is as in Figure 7a.5.

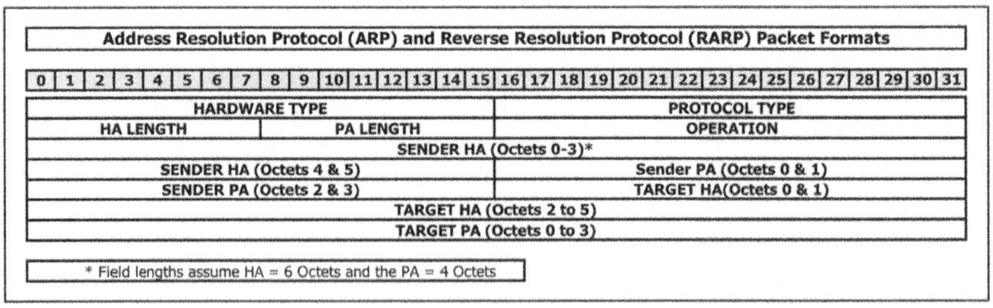

Figure 7a.5
Address resolution protocol

Hardware type

Specifies the hardware interface type of the target:

1 = Ethernet
3 = X.25
7 = ARCnet.

Protocol type

Specifies the type of high-level protocol address the sending device is using. For example,

2048 = Internet Protocol (IP)
2054 = Address Resolution Protocol (ARP)
3282 = Reverse ARP (reverse address resolution protocol (RARP)).

Hardware address length

The length, in bytes, of the MAC address.

Protocol address length

The length, in bytes, of the IP address.

Operation code

Indicates the type of ARP datagram:

1 = Address resolution protocol (ARP) request
2 = Address resolution protocol (ARP) reply
3 = Reverse address resolution protocol (RARP) request
4 = Reverse address resolution protocol (RARP) reply.

Sender hardware address

The MAC address of the sender.

Sender protocol address

The IP address of the sender.

Target hardware address

The MAC address of the target host.

Target protocol address

The IP address of the target host.

Because of the use of fields to indicate the lengths of the hardware and protocol addresses, the address fields can be used to carry a variety of address types, making ARP useful for a number of different types of network.

The broadcasting of ARP requests presents some potential problems. Networks such as Ethernet are 'best-effort' delivery systems, i.e. the sender does not receive any feedback whether datagrams it has transmitted were received by the target device. If the target is not available, the ARP request destined for it will be lost without trace and no ARP response will be generated. Thus the sender must be programed to retransmit its ARP request after a certain time period and must be able to store the datagram it is attempting to transmit in the interim. It must also remember what requests it has sent out so that it does not send out multiple ARP requests for the same address. If it does not receive an ARP reply, it will eventually have to discard the outgoing datagrams.

Because it is possible for a machine's hardware address to change, as happens when an Ethernet interface fails and has to be replaced, entries in an ARP cache have a limited life span after which they are deleted. Every time a machine with an ARP cache receives an ARP message, it uses the information to update its own ARP cache. If the incoming address binding already exists, it overwrites the existing entry with the fresh information and resets the timer for that entry.

If a machine is the target of an incoming ARP request, its own ARP software must organize a reply. It must swap the target and sender address pairs in the ARP datagram, insert its physical address into the relevant field, change the operation code to 2 (ARP reply), and send it back to the requester.

7a.2.3   ICMP

When nodes fail, or become temporarily unavailable, or when certain routes become overloaded with traffic, a message mechanism called the Internet control message protocol (ICMP) reports errors and other useful information about the performance and operation of the network.

ICMP communicates between the Internet layers on two nodes and is used by routers as well as individual hosts. Although ICMP is viewed as residing within the Internet layer, its messages travel across the network encapsulated in IP datagrams in the same way as higher-layer protocol (such as TCP or UDP) datagrams. The ICMP message, consisting of an ICMP header and ICMP data, is encapsulated as 'data' within an IP datagram that is, in turn, carried as 'payload' by the lower network interface layer (for example, Ethernet).

7a.2.4   ICMP datagrams

There are a variety of ICMP messages, each with a different format, yet the first three fields as contained in the first 4 bytes or 'Long word' is the same for all.

The various ICMP messages are shown in Figure 7a.6.

The three common fields are:

1. An ICMP message type (4 bits) which is a code that identifies the type of ICMP message
2. A code (4 bits) in which interpretation depends on the type of ICMP message
3. A checksum (16 bits) that is calculated on the entire ICMP datagram.

Table 7a.1 lists the different types of ICMP messages.

ICMP messages can be further sub-divided into two broad groups viz. ICMP error messages (destination unreachable, time exceeded, invalid parameters, source quench or redirect) and ICMP query messages (echo request and reply messages, timestamp request and reply messages, and subnet mask request and reply messages).

```
0           7 8          15 16                    31  bits
 ┌─────────────┬─────────────┬────────────────────────┐
 │    Type     │    Code     │       Checksum         │
 ├─────────────┴─────────────┼────────────────────────┤
 │       Identifier          │    Sequence Number     │
 ├───────────────────────────┴────────────────────────┤
 │                                                     │
 │                      Data                           │
 └─────────────────────────────────────────────────────┘
```

Echo and Echo Reply Messages

```
0           7 8          15 16                    31  bits
 ┌─────────────┬─────────────┬────────────────────────┐
 │    Type     │    Code     │       Checksum         │
 ├─────────────┴─────────────┴────────────────────────┤
 │                     Unused                          │
 ├─────────────────────────────────────────────────────┤
 │   Internet Header + 64 bits of Original Datagram Data │
 └─────────────────────────────────────────────────────┘
```

Destination Unreachable, Source Quench and Time Exceeded Messages

```
0           7 8          15 16                    31  bits
 ┌─────────────┬─────────────┬────────────────────────┐
 │    Type     │    Code     │       Checksum         │
 ├─────────────┼─────────────┴────────────────────────┤
 │   Pointer   │              Unused                  │
 ├─────────────┴────────────────────────────────────────┤
 │   Internet Header + 64 bits of Original Datagram Data │
 └─────────────────────────────────────────────────────┘
```

Parameter Problem Message

```
0           7 8          15 16                    31  bits
 ┌─────────────┬─────────────┬────────────────────────┐
 │    Type     │    Code     │       Checksum         │
 ├─────────────┴─────────────┴────────────────────────┤
 │              Gateway Internet Address               │
 ├─────────────────────────────────────────────────────┤
 │   Internet header + 64 bits of Original Data Stream │
 └─────────────────────────────────────────────────────┘
```

Redirect Message

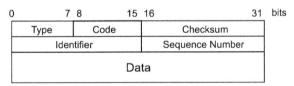

```
0           7 8          15 16                    31  bits
 ┌─────────────┬─────────────┬────────────────────────┐
 │    Type     │    Code     │       Checksum         │
 ├─────────────┴─────────────┼────────────────────────┤
 │       Identifier          │    Sequence Number     │
 ├───────────────────────────┴────────────────────────┤
 │              Originate Timestamp                    │
 ├─────────────────────────────────────────────────────┤
 │               Receive Timestamp                     │
 ├─────────────────────────────────────────────────────┤
 │               Transit Timestamp                     │
 └─────────────────────────────────────────────────────┘
```

Timestamp and Timestamp Reply Messages

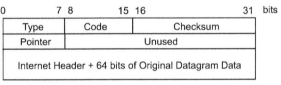

```
0           7 8          15 16                    31  bits
 ┌─────────────┬─────────────┬────────────────────────┐
 │    Type     │    Code     │       Checksum         │
 ├─────────────┴─────────────┼────────────────────────┤
 │       Identifier          │    Sequence Number     │
 ├───────────────────────────┴────────────────────────┤
 │                  Address Mask                       │
 └─────────────────────────────────────────────────────┘
```

Address mask Request and Address Mask Reply Messages

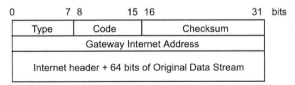

Figure 7a.6
ICMP message formats

Type Field	Description
0	Echo reply
3	Destination unreachable
4	Source quench
5	Redirect (change a route)
8	Echo request
11	Time exceeded (datagram)
12	Parameter problem (datagram)
13	Time stamp request
14	Time stamp reply
15	Address mark request
16	Address mark reply

Table 7a.1
ICMP message types

7a.2.5   Routing

Unlike the host-to-host layer protocols (for example, TCP), which control end-to-end communications, IP is rather 'shortsighted'. Any given IP node (host or router) is only concerned with routing (switching) the datagram to the next node, where the process is repeated. Very few routers have knowledge about the entire internetwork, and often the datagrams are forwarded based on default information without any knowledge of where the destination actually is.

Direct vs indirect delivery

When the source host prepares to send a message to another host, a fundamental decision has to be made; namely, is the destination host also resident on the local network or not? If the NetID portions of the source and destination IP addresses match, the source host will assume that the destination host is resident on the same network, and will attempt to forward it locally. This is called direct delivery. If not, the message will be forwarded to the default gateway (a router on the local network), which will forward it. This is called indirect delivery. If the router can deliver it directly, i.e. the destination host resides on a network directly connected to the router, it will. If not, it will consult its routing tables and forward it to the next appropriate router. This process will repeat itself until the packet is delivered to its final destination.

Static vs dynamic routing

Each router maintains a table with the format presented in Table 7a.2.

It basically reads as follows: 'If a packet is destined for network 200.0.0.0 with a netmask of 255.255.255.0, then forward it to the router IP address 207.194.66.100', etc. It is logical that a given router cannot contain the whereabouts of each and every network in the world in its routing tables, hence it will contain default routes as well. If a packet cannot be specifically routed, it will be forwarded on a default route, which should (it is hoped) move it closer to its intended destination.

These routing tables can be maintained in two ways. In most cases, the routing protocols will do this automatically. The routing protocols are implemented in software that runs on the routers, enabling them to communicate on a regular basis and allowing them to share their 'knowledge' about the network with each other. In this way they continuously 'learn' about the topology of the system, and upgrade their routing tables accordingly. This process is called dynamic routing. If, for example, a particular router is removed from the system, the routing tables of all routers containing a reference to that router will change. However, because of the interdependence of the routing tables, a change in any given table will initiate a change in many other routers and it will be a while before the tables stabilize. This process is known as convergence.

Network Address	Net Mask	Gateway Address	Interface	Metric
127.0.0.0	255.0.0.0	127.0.0.1	127.0.0.1	1
207.194.66.0	255.255.255.224	207.194.66.100	207.194.66.100	1
207.194.66.0	255.255.255.255	127.0.0.1	127.0.0.1	1
200.0.0.0	255.255.255.0	207.194.66.100	207.194.66.100	1
224.0.0.0	224.0.0.0	207.194.66.100	207.194.66.100	1
255.255.255.255	255.255.255.255	207.194.66.100	0.0.0.0	1

Table 7a.2
Active routes

Dynamic routing can be further sub-classified as distance vector, link-state, or hybrid, depending on the method by which the routers calculate the optimum path.

In distance vector dynamic routing, the 'metric' or yardstick used for calculating the optimum routes is simply based on distance, i.e. which route results in the least number of 'hops' to the destination. Each router constructs a table, which indicates the number of hops to each known network. It then periodically passes copies of its tables to its immediate neighbors. Each recipient of the message then simply adjusts its own tables based on the information received from its neighbor.

It is also possible for a network administrator to make static entries into routing tables. These entries will not change, even if a router that they point to is not operational.

Autonomous systems

For the purpose of routing, a TCP/IP-based internetwork can be divided into several autonomous systems (ASs) or domains. An autonomous system consists of hosts, routers, and data links that form several physical networks and are administered by a single authority such as a service provider, university, corporation, or government agency.

Routing decisions that are made within an AS are totally under the control of the administering organization. Any routing protocol, using any type of routing algorithm, can be used within an autonomous system since the routing between two hosts in the system are completely isolated from any routing that occurs in other autonomous systems. Only if a host within one autonomous system communicates with a host outside the system, will another autonomous system (or systems) and possibly the Internet backbone be involved (Figure 7a.7).

There are three categories of TCP/IP routing protocols namely Interior gateway protocols, exterior gateway protocols, and gateway-to-gateway protocols.

Two routers that communicate directly with one another and are both part of the same autonomous system are said to be interior neighbors and are called interior gateways. They communicate with each other using interior gateway protocols such as RIP, HELLO, IS-IS, or OSPF.

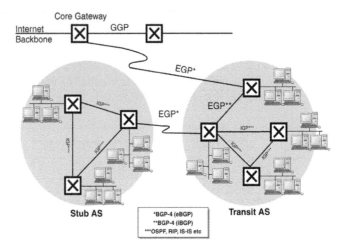

Figure 7a.7
Autonomous systems and routing protocols

Routers in different ASs, however, cannot use IGPs for communication for more than one reason. Firstly, IGPs are not optimized for long-distance path determination. Secondly, the owners of ASs (particularly Internet service providers) would find it unacceptable for their routing metrics (which include sensitive information such as error rates and network traffic) to be visible to their competitors. For this reason, routers that communicate with each other and are resident in different ASs communicate with each other using exterior gateway protocols such as BGP-4.

7a.3 Host-to-host layer: end to end reliability

7a.3.1 TCP

Transmission control protocol (TCP) is a connection-oriented protocol and is said to be 'reliable', although this word is used in a data communications context. TCP establishes a session between two machines before data is transmitted. Because a connection is set up beforehand, it is possible to verify that all packets are received on the other end and to arrange retransmission in case of lost packets. Because of all these built-in functions, TCP involves significant additional overhead in terms of processing time and header size.

TCP fragments large chunks of data into smaller segments if necessary, reconstructs the data stream from packets received, issues acknowledgments of data received, provides socket services for multiple connections to ports on remote hosts, performs packet verification and error control, and performs flow control.

TCP header

The TCP header is structured as in Figure 7a.8.

The source and destination ports (16 bits each) identify the host processes at each side of the connection. Examples are post office protocol (POP3) at port 110 and simple mail transfer protocol (SMTP) at port 25. Whereas a destination host is identified by its IP address, the process on that host is identified by its port number. A combination of port number and IP address is called a socket.

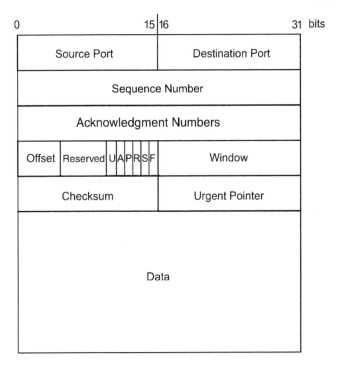

Figure 7a.8
TCP header format

The sequence number (32 bits) ensures the sequential of the data stream. TCP, by implication, associates a 32-bit number with every byte it transmits. The sequence number is the number of the first byte in every segment (or 'chunk') of data sent by TCP. If the SYN flag is set, however, it indicates that the sender wants to establish a connection and the number in the sequence number field becomes the initial sequence number or ISN. The receiver acknowledges this, and the sender then labels the first byte of the transmitted data with a sequence number of ISN + 1. The ISN (initial sequence number) is a pseudo-random number with values between 0 and 2^{32}.

The acknowledgments number (32 bits) is used to verify correct receipt of the transmitted data. The receiver checks the incoming data, and if the verification is positive, acknowledges it by placing the number of the next byte expected in the acknowledgments number field and setting the ACK flag. The sender, when transmitting, sets a timer and if an acknowledgment is not received within a specific time, an error is assumed and the data is retransmitted.

Data offset (4 bits) is the number of 32-bit words in the TCP header. This indicates where the data begins. It is necessary since the header can contain options and thus does not have a fixed length.

Six flags control the connection and data transfer. They are:

1. URG: Urgent pointer field significant
2. ACK: Acknowledgments field significant
3. PSH: Push function
4. RST: Reset the connection
5. SYN: Synchronize sequence numbers
6. FIN: No more data from sender.

The window field (16 bits) provides flow control. Whenever a host sends an acknowledgment to the other party in the bidirectional communication, it also sends a window advertisement by placing a number in the window field. The window size indicates the number of bytes, starting with the one in the acknowledgments field that the host is able accept.

The checksum field (16 bits) is used for error control. The urgent pointer field (16 bits) is used in conjunction with the URG flag and allows for the insertion of a block of 'urgent' data in the beginning of a particular segment. The pointer points to the first byte of the non-urgent data following the urgent data.

7a.3.2   UDP

User datagram protocol (UDP) is a 'connectionless' protocol and does not require a connection to be established between two machines prior to data transmission. It is therefore said to be 'unreliable' – the word 'unreliable' used here as opposed to 'reliable' in the case of TCP and should not be interpreted against its everyday context.

Sending a UDP datagram involves very little overhead in that there are no synchronization parameters, no priority options, no sequence numbers, no timers, and no retransmission of packets. The header is small, the protocol is streamlined functionally. The only major drawback is that delivery is not guaranteed. UDP is therefore used for communications that involve broadcasts, for general network announcements, or for real-time data.

The UDP header

The UDP header is significantly smaller than the TCP header and only contains four fields (Figure 7a.9).

Figure 7a.9
UDP header format

UDP source port (16 bits) is an optional field. When meaningful, it indicates the port of the sending process, and may be assumed to be the port to which a reply should be addressed in the absence of any other information. If not used, a value of zero is inserted. UDP destination port has the same meaning as for the TCP header, and indicates the process on the destination host to which the data is to be sent.

UDP message length is the length in bytes of the datagram including the header and the data.

The 16-bit UDP checksum is used for validation purposes.

7b

TCP/IP troubleshooting

7b.1   Introduction

This section deals with problems related to the TCP/IP protocol suite. The TCP/IP protocols are implemented in software and cover the second (Internet), the third (host-to-host), and the upper (application) layers of the ARPA model. These protocols need a network infrastructure as well as a medium in order to communicate. This infrastructure is typically Ethernet, as dealt with in the previous section.

7b.2   Common problems

TCP/IP is a complex topic and this section cannot really do justice to it. This section will therefore try to show some common approaches that do not necessarily require an in-depth knowledge of the protocols involved.

7b.3   Tools of the trade

7b.3.1   TCP/IP utilities

These utilities are DOS programs that form part of the TCP/IP software. They are not protocols, but simply executable DOS programs that utilize some of the protocols. The utilities that will be shown here are ping, arp, and tracert. This is not the complete list, but it is sufficient for the purposes of this chapter.

7b.3.2   Third party utilities

Most of the TCP/IP utilities are included in more recent third-party software packages. The advantage of these packages such as TJPingPro is that they are windows based and hence much easier to use.

7b.3.3   Software protocol analyzers

These have already been discussed in the section on Ethernet.

7b.3.4   Hardware-assisted protocol analyzers

These have also been discussed in the section on Ethernet.

7b.4   Typical network layer problems

7b.4.1   TCP/IP protocol stack not properly installed on local host (host unable to access the network)

The easiest way to confirm this, apart from checking the network configuration via the control panel and visually confirming that TCP/IP is installed for the particular NIC used on the host, is to perform a loop-back test by pinging the host itself. This is done by executing `ping localhost` or `ping 127.0.0.1`. If a response is received, it means that the stack is correctly installed.

7b.4.2   Remote host (e.g. a web server) not reachable

If it needs to be confirmed that a remote host is available, the particular machine can be checked by pinging it. The format of the command is:

- `Ping 193.7.7.3` (for example), where 193.7.7.3 is the IP address of the remote machine, or
- `Ping www.idc-online.com` where www.idconline.com is the domain name of the remote host, or
- `Ping john` where john (in this example) has been equated to the IP address of the remote machine in the hosts file of the local machine.

This is an extremely powerful test, since a positive acknowledgment means that the bottom three layers (OSI) of the local and the remote hosts as well as all routers and all communication links between the two hosts are operational.

7b.4.3   A host is unable to obtain an automatically assigned IP addresses

When TCP/IP is configured and the upper radio button is highlighted (indicating that an IP address has to be obtained automatically) the host, upon booting up, will broadcast a request for the benefit of the local dynamic host configuration protocol (DHCP) server. Upon hearing the request, the DHCP server will offer an IP address to the requesting host. If the host is unable to obtain such IP address, it can mean one of two things:

1. The DHCP server is down. If this is suspected, it can be confirmed by pinging the DHCP server. If the local host supports automatic IP address allocation, it will temporarily assume an IP address in the range 169.254.x.x. As soon as the DHCP server is on line again, it will obtain an address from the server.
2. There are no spare IP addresses available. Nothing can be done about this and the user will have to wait until one of the other logged-in machines are switched off which will cause it to relinquish it IP address and make it available for reissue.

7b.4.4   Reserved IP addresses

Reserved IP addresses are IP addresses in the ranges 10.0.0.0/8–10.255.255.255/8, 172.16.0.0/12–172.16.255.255/12, and 192.168.0.0/16–192.168.255.255/16. These IP addresses are only allocated to networks that will never have access to the Internet. All Internet routers are pre-programed to ignore these addresses. If a user therefore tries to access such an IP address over the Internet, the message will not be transported across the Internet and hence the desired network cannot be reached.

7b.4.5   Duplicate IP addresses

Since an IP address is the Internet equivalent of a postal address, it is obvious that duplicate IP addresses cannot be tolerated. If a host is booted up, it tries to establish if any other host with the same IP address is available on the local network. If this is found to be true, the booting up machine will not proceed with logging on to the network and both machines with the duplicate IP address will display error messages in this regard.

7b.4.6   Incorrect network ID – different NetIDs on the same physical network

As explained in the chapter on TCP/IP, an IP address consists of two parts, namely, a network ID (NetID), which is the equivalent of a postal zip code and a HostID, which is the equivalent of a street, address. If two machines on the same network have different NetIDs, their 'zip codes' will differ and hence the system will not recognize them as coexisting on the same network. Even if they are physically connected to the same Ethernet network, they will not be able to communicate directly with each other using TCP/IP.

7b.4.7   Incorrect subnet mask

As explained in the chapter on TCP/IP, the subnet mask indicates the boundary between the NetID and the HostID. A faulty subnet mask, when applied to an IP address, could result in a NetID (zip code) that includes bits from the adjacent HostID and hence looks different than the NetID of the machine wishing to send a message. The sending host will therefore erroneously believe that the destination host exists on another network and that the packets have to be forwarded to the local router for delivery to the remote network.

If the local router is not present (no default gateway specified) the sender will give up and not even try to deliver the packet. If, on the other hand, a router is present (default gateway specified), the sender will deliver the packet to the router. The router will then realize that there is nothing to forward since the recipient does in fact, live on the local network, and it will try to deliver the packet to the intended recipient. Although the packet eventually gets delivered, it leads to a lot of unnecessary packets transmitted as well as unnecessary time delays.

7b.4.8   Incorrect or absent default gateway(s)

An incorrect or absent default gateway in the TCP configuration screen means that a host, wishing to send a message to another host on a different network, is not able to do so. The following is an example:

Assuming that a host with IP address 192.168.0.1 wishes to ping a non-existent host on IP address 192.168.0.2. The subnet mask is 255.255.255.0. The pinging host applies the mask to both IP addresses and comes up with a result of 192.168.0.0 in both cases. Realizing that the destination host resides on the same network as the sender, it proceeds to ping 192.168.0.2. Obviously, there will be no response from the missing machine and hence a time-out will occur. The sending host will issue a time-out message in this regard.

Now consider a scenario where the destination host is 193.168.0.2 and there is no valid default gateway entry. After applying the subnet mask, the sending host realizes that the destination resides on another network and that it therefore needs a valid default gateway. Not being able to find one, it does not even try to ping but simply issues a message to the effect that the destination host is unreachable.

The reason for describing these scenarios is that the user can often figure out the problem by simply observing the error messages returned by the ping utility.

7b.4.9   MAC address of a device not known to user

The MAC address of a device, such as a PLC, is normally displayed on a sticker attached to the body. If the MAC address of the device is not known, it can be pinged by its IP address (for example, ping 101.3.4.5) whereafter the MAC address can be obtained by displaying the ARP cache on the machine that did the ping. This is done by means of the arp – a command.

7b.4.10   IP address of a device not known to user

On a computer, this is not a problem since the IP address can simply be looked up in the TCP/IP configuration screen. Alternatively, the IP address can be displayed by commands such as winipcfg (Windows 95/98) or ipconfig /all (Windows 98/NT).

On a PLC, this might not be so easy unless the user knows how to attach a terminal to the COM (serial) port on the PLC and has the configuration software handy. An easier approach to confirm the IP address setup on the PLC (if any) is to attach it to a network and run a utility such as WebBoy or EtherBoy. The software will pick up the device on the network, regardless of its NetID, and display the IP address.

7b.4.11   Wrong IP address

It is possible that all devices on a network could have valid and correct IP addresses but that a specific host fails to respond to a message sent to it by a client program residing on another host. A typical scenario could be a supervisory computer sending a command to a PLC. Before assuming that the PLC is defective, one has to ascertain that the supervisory computer is in fact using the correct IP address when trying to communicate with the PLC. This can only be ascertained by using a protocol analyzer and capturing the communication or attempt at communication between the computer and the PLC. The packets exchanged between the computer and the PLC can be identified by means of the MAC addresses in the appropriate Ethernet headers. It then has to be confirmed that the IP headers carried within these frames do in fact contain the correct IP addresses.

7b.5   Transport layer problems

A detailed treatment of the TCP protocol is completely beyond the scope of this course but there are a few simple things that even a relatively inexperienced user can check.

7b.5.1   No connection established

Before any two devices can communicate using TCP/IP, they need to establish a so-called triple handshake. This will be clearly indicated as a SYN, ACK / SYN, ACK sequence to the relevant port. Without a triple handshake the devices cannot communicate at all.

To confirm this, simply try to establish a connection (for example, by using an FTP client to log into an FTP server) and use a protocol analyzer to capture the handshake.

7b.5.2   Incorrect port number

TCP identifies different programs (processes) on a host by means of so-called port numbers. For example, an FTP server uses ports 21 and 22, a POP3 server (for e-mail) uses port 110 and a web server (HTTP) uses port 80. Any other process wishing to communicate with one of these has to use the correct port number. The port number used is visible right at the beginning of the TCP header that can be captured with a protocol analyzer. Port numbers 1–1023 are referred to as 'well known' ports. Port numbers are administered by the Internet Assigned Numbers Authority (IANA). These are detailed in RFC 1700.

8a

Modbus overview

Objectives

When you have completed study of this chapter, you will be able to:

- List the main Modbus structures and frames used
- Identify and correct problems with:
    - No reponse to protocol messages
    - Exception reports
    - Noise.

8a.1   General overview

MODBUS is an application layer (OSI layer 7) messaging protocol that provides client/server communication between devices connected to different types of buses of networks. The MODBUS protocol implements a client/server architecture and operates essentially in a 'request/ response' mode, irrespective of the media access control used at layer 2. This client/server model is based on four types of message namely:

- MODBUS requests, the messages sent on the network by the clients to initiate transactions
- MODBUS confirmations, the response messages received on the client side
- MODBUS indications, the request messages received on the server side and
- MODBUS responses, the response messages sent by the servers.

These messaging services of the client/server model are used to exchange real-time information between two device applications, between device applications and devices, or between devices and HMI/SCADA applications (Figure 8a.1).

Figure 8a.1
MODBUS client/server interaction
[Note: Use Figure 19.1 from FE manual]

In an error-free scenario, the exchange of information between client and server can be illustrated as follows. The client (on the master device) initiates a request. The MODBUS messaging protocol (layer 7) then generates a protocol data unit or PDU, consisting of a function code and a data request. At layer 2, this PDU is converted to an application data unit (ADU) by the addition of some bus or network related fields, such as a slave address and a checksum for error detection purposes. This process is depicted in Figure 8a.2.

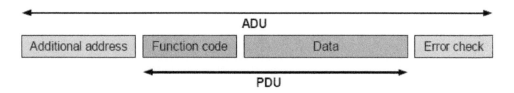

Figure 8a.2
Generic MODBUS frame
[Note: Use Figure 19.2 from FE manual]

The server (on the slave device) then performs the required action and initiates a response. The interaction between client and server is shown in Figure 8a.3.

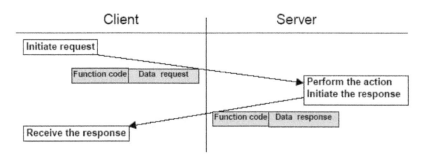

Figure 8a.3
MODBUS transaction
[Note: Use Figure 19.3 from FE manual]

The various types of function codes, with their associated requests and responses, are described in detail in this chapter.

The MODBUS Messaging Protocol (layer 7) needs additional support at the lower layers in order to get the message across. A popular method is the use of a master/slave (half-duplex) layer 2 protocol, transmitting the data in serial format over RS-232, RS-485 or Bell 202 type modem links. Other methods include MODBUS+ (half-duplex over RS-485), or MAP. A recent addition is the use of TCP/IP and Ethernet to convey data from client to server. The TCP/IP approach enables client/server interaction over routed networks, albeit at the cost of additional overheads (processing time, headers, etc.). An additional sub-layer is required to map the MODBUS application layer on to TCP. The function of this sub-layer is to encapsulate the MODBUS PDU so that it can be transported as a packet of data by TCP/IP (Figure 8a.4).

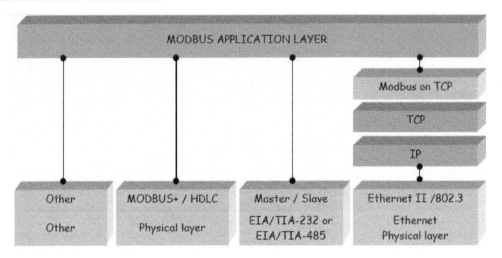

Figure 8a.4
MODBUS communication stack
[Note: Use Figure 19.4 from FE manual]

8a.2   Modbus protocol structure

Table 8a.1 illustrates a typical Modbus message frame format.

Address Field	Function Field	Data Field	Error Check Field
1 byte	1 byte	Variable	2 bytes

Table 8a.1
Format of Modbus message frame

The first field in each message frame is the address field, which consists of a single byte of information. In request frames, this byte identifies the controller to which the request is being directed. The resulting response frame begins with the address of the responding device. Each slave can have an address field between 1 and 247, although practical limitations will limit the maximum number of slaves. A typical Modbus installation will have one master and two or three slaves.

The second field in each message is the function field, which also consists of a single byte of information. In a host request, this byte identifies the function that the target PLC is to perform.

If the target PLC is able to perform the requested function, the function field of its response will echo that of the original request. Otherwise, the function field of the request will be echoed with its most significant bit set to one, thus signaling an exception response. Table 8a.1 summarizes the typical functions used.

The third field in a message frame is the data field, which varies in length according to which function is specified in the function field. In a host request, this field contains information the PLC may need to complete the requested function. In a PLC response, this field contains any data requested by that host.

The last two bytes in a message frame comprise the error-check field. The numeric value of this field is calculated by performing a cyclic redundancy check (CRC-16) on the message frame. This error checking assures that devices do not react to messages that may have been damaged during transmission.

Table 8a.2 lists the address range and offsets for these four data types, as well as the function codes that apply to each. The diagram Table 8a.1 also gives an easy reference to the Modbus data types.

Data Type	Absolute Addresses	Relative Addresses	Function Codes	Description
Coils	00001–09999	0–9998	01	Read coil status
Coils	00001–09999	0–9998	05	Force single coil
Coils	00001–09999	0–9998	15	Force multiple coils
Discrete inputs	10001–19999	0–9998	02	Read input status
Input registers	30001–39999	0–9998	04	Read input registers
Holding registers	40001–49999	0–9998	03	Read holding register
Holding registers	40001–49999	0–9998	06	Preset single register
Holding registers	40001–49999	0–9998	16	Preset multiple registers
–	–	–	07	Read exception status
–	–	–	08	Loopback diagnostic test

Table 8a.2
Modicon addresses and function codes

8a.3 Function codes

Each request frame contains a function code that defines the action expected for the target controller. The meaning of the request data fields is dependent on the function code specified.

The following paragraphs define and illustrate most of the popular function codes supported. In these examples, the contents of the message-frame fields are shown as hexadecimal bytes.

8a.3.1 Read coil or digital output status (function code 01)

This function allows the host to obtain the ON/OFF status of one or more logic coils in the target device.

The data field of the request consists of the relative address of the first coil followed by the number of coils to be read. The data field of the response frame consists of a count of the coil bytes followed by that many bytes of coil data.

The coil data bytes are packed with one bit for the status of each consecutive coil (1 = ON, 0 = OFF). The least significant bit of the first coil data byte conveys the status of the first coil read. If the number of coils read is not an even multiple of eight, the last data byte will be padded with zeros on the high end. Note that if multiple data bytes are requested, the low order bit of the first data byte in the response of the slave contains the first addressed coil.

In Figure 8a.5, the host requests the status of coils 000A (decimal 00011) and 000B (decimal 00012). The target device's response indicates both coils are ON.

Request Message

Address	Function Code	Initial Coil Offset		Number of Points		CRC
		Hi	Lo	Hi	Lo	
01	01	00	0A	00	02	9D C9

Response Frame

Address	Function Code	Byte Count	Coil Data	CRC
01	01	01	03	11 89

Figure 8a.5
Example of read coil status

8a.3.2   Read digital input status (function code 02)

This function enables the host to read one or more discrete inputs in the target device.

The data field of the request frame consists of the relative address of the first discrete input followed by the number of discrete inputs to be read. The data field of the response frame consists of a count of the discrete input data bytes followed by that many bytes of discrete input data.

The discrete-input data bytes are packed with one bit for the status of each consecutive discrete input (1 = ON, 0 = OFF). The least significant bit of the first discrete input data byte conveys the status of the first input read. If the number of discrete inputs read is not an even multiple of eight, the last data byte will be padded with zeros on the high end. The low order bit of the first byte of the response from the slave contains the first addressed digital input.

In Figure 8a.6, the host requests the status of discrete inputs with offsets 0000 and 0001 hex, i.e. decimal 10001 and 10002. The target device's response indicates that discrete input 10001 is OFF and 10002 are ON.

Request Message

Address	Function Code	Initial Coil Offset		Number of Points		CRC
		Hi	Lo	Hi	Lo	
01	02	00	00	00	02	F9 CB

Response Frame

Address	Function Code	Byte Count	Input Data	CRC
01	02	01	02	20 49

Figure 8a.6
Example of read input status

8a.3.3   Read holding registers (function code 03)

This function allows the host to obtain the contents of one or more holding registers in the target device.

The data field of the request frame consists of the relative address of the first holding register followed by the number of registers to be read. The data field of the response time consists of a count of the register data bytes followed by that many bytes of holding register data.

The contents of each requested register (16 bits) are returned in two consecutive data bytes (most significant byte first).

In Figure 8a.7, the host requests the contents of holding register hexadecimal offset 0002 or decimal 40003. The controller's response indicates that the numerical value of the register's contents is hexadecimal 07FF or decimal 2047. The first byte of the response register data is the high order byte of the first addressed register.

Request Message

Address	Function Code	Starting Register		Register Count		CRC
		Hi	Lo	Hi	Lo	
01	03	00	02	00	01	25 CA

Response Frame

Address	Function Code	Byte Count	Register Data		CRC
			Hi	Lo	
01	03	02	07	FF	FA 34

Figure 8a.7
Example of reading holding register

8a.3.4   Reading input registers (function code 04)

This function allows the host to obtain the contents of one or more input registers in the target device.

The data field of the request frame consists of the relative address of the first input register followed by the number of registers to be read. The data field of the response frame consists of a count of the register-data bytes followed by that many bytes of input-register data.

The contents of each requested register are returned in two consecutive register-databytes (most significant byte first). The range for register variables is 0–4095.

In Figure 8a.8, the host requests the contents of input register hexadecimal offset 000 or decimal 30001. The PLC's response indicates that the numerical value of that register's contents is 03FFH, which would correspond to a data value of 25% (if the scaling of 0–100% is adopted) and a 12-bit D to A converter with a maximum reading of 0FFFH is used.

8a.3.5   Force single coil (function code 05)

This function allows the host to alter the ON/OFF status of a single logic coil in the target device.

Request Message

Address	Function Code	Starting Register		Register Count		CRC	
		Hi	Lo	Hi	Lo		
01	04	00	00	00	01	31	CA

Response Frame

Address	Function Code	Byte Count	Register Data		CRC	
			Hi	Lo		
01	04	02	03	FF	F9	80

Figure 8a.8
Example of reading input register

The data field of the request frame consists of the relative address of the coil followed by the desired status for that coil. A hexadecimal status value of FF00 will activate the coil, while a status value of 0000H will deactivate it. Any other status value is illegal.

If the controller is able to force the specified coil to the requested state, the response frame will be identical to the request. Otherwise, an exception response will be returned.

If the address 00 is used to indicate broadcast mode, all attached slaves will modify the specified coil address to the state required.

Figure 8a.9 illustrates a successful attempt to force coil 11 (decimal) OFF.

Request Message

Address	Function Code	Coil Offset		New Coil Status		CRC	
		Hi	Lo	Hi	Lo		
01	05	00	0A	00	00	ED	C8

Response Frame

Address	Function Code	Coil Offset		New Coil Status		CRC	
		Hi	Lo	Hi	Lo		
01	05	00	0A	00	00	ED	C8

Figure 8a.9
Example of forcing a single coil

8a.3.6   Preset single register (function code 06)

This function enables the host to alter the contents of a single holding register in the target device.

The data field of the request frame consists of the relative address of the holding register followed by the new value to be written to that register (most significant byte first).

If the controller is able to write the requested new value to the specified register, the response frame will be identical to the request. Otherwise, an exception response will be returned.

Figure 8a.10 illustrates a successful attempt to change the contents of holding register 40003 to 3072 (0C00 Hex).

When slave address is set to 00 (broadcast mode), all slaves will load the specified register with the value specified.

Request Message

Address	Function Code	Register Offset		Register Value		CRC
		Hi	Lo	Hi	Lo	
01	06	00	02	0C	00	2D 0A

Response Frame

Address	Function Code	Register Offset		Register Value		CRC
		Hi	Lo	Hi	Lo	
01	06	00	02	0C	00	2D 0A

Figure 8a.10
Example of presetting a single register

8a.3.7 Read exception status (function code 07)

This is a short message requesting the status of eight digital points within the slave device.

This will provide the status of eight predefined digital points in the slave. For example, this could be items such as the status of the battery, whether memory protect has been enabled, or the status of the remote input/output racks connected to the system (Figure 8a.11).

Request Message

Address	Function Code	CRC
11	07	.. ..

Response Frame

Address	Function Code	Coil Station	CRC
11	07	02	.. ..

Figure 8a.11
Read exception status query message

8a.3.8 Loopback test (function code 08)

The objective of this function code is to test the operation of the communications system without affecting the memory tables of the slave device. It is also possible to implement additional diagnostic features in a slave device (should this be considered necessary) such as number of CRC errors, number of exception reports, etc.

The most common implementation will only be considered in this section; namely, a simple return of the query messages (Figure 8a.12).

Request Frame

Address	Function Code	Data Diagnostic Code		Data		CRC
		Hi	Lo	Hi	Lo	
11	08	00	00	A5	37	.. ..

Response Frame

Address	Function Code	Data Diagnostic Code		Data		CRC
		Hi	Lo	Hi	Lo	
11	08	00	00	A5	37	.. ..

Figure 8a.12
Loopback test message

8a.3.9   Force multiple coils or digital outputs (function code 0F)

This forces a contiguous (or adjacent) group of coils to an ON or OFF state. The following example sets 10 coils starting at address 01 Hex (at slave address 01) to the ON state. If slave address 00 is used in the request frame, broadcast mode will be implemented resulting in all slaves changing their coils at the defined addresses (Figure 8a.13).

Request Frame

Address	Function Code	Address		Byte Count	Data Coil Status		CRC
		Hi	Lo		Hi	Lo	
01	0F	00	01	0F	FF	03	.. ..

Response Frame

Address	Function Code	Address		Number of Coils		CRC
		Hi	Lo	Hi	Lo	
01	0F	00	01	00	0A	.. ..

Figure 8a.13
Example of forcing multiple coils

8a.3.10   Force multiple registers (function code 10)

This is similar to the preset a single register and the forcing of multiple coils. In Figure 8a.14, a slave address 01 has 2 registers changed commencing at address 10.

Table 8a.3 lists the most important exception codes that may be returned.

Request Frame

Address	Function Code	Address		Quantity		Byte Count	First Register		Second Register		CRC
		Hi	Lo	Hi	Lo		Hi	Lo	Hi	Lo	
01	10	00	0A	00	02	04	00	0A	01	02	.. ..

Response Frame

Address	Function Code	Address		Quality		CRC
		Hi	Lo	Hi	Lo	
01	10	00	0A	00	02	.. ..

Figure 8a.14
Example of presetting multiple registers

Code	Name	Description
01	Illegal function	Requested function is not supported
02	Illegal data address	Requested data address is not supported
03	Illegal data value	Specified data value is not supported
04	Failure in associated device	Slave PLC has failed to respond to a message
05	Acknowledge	Slave PLC is processing the command
06	Busy, rejected message	Slave PLC is busy

Table 8a.3
Abbreviated list of exception codes returned

An example of an illegal request and the corresponding exception response is shown in Figure 8a.15. The request in this example is to READ COIL STATUS of points 514 to 521 (eight coils beginning with an offset 0201H). These points are not supported in this PLC, so an exception report is generated indicating code 02 (illegal address).

Request Message

Address	Function Code	Starting Point	Number of Points	CRC
01	01	02 01	00 08	6D B4

Exception Response Message

Address	Function Code	Exception Code	CRC
01	81	02	C1 91

Figure 8a.15
Example of an illegal request

8b

Modbus troubleshooting

8b.1   Common problems and faults

No matter what extremes of care you may have taken, there is hardly ever an installation that boasts of trouble-free setup and configuration. Some of the commonly faced problems and faults that one comes across in the industry are listed below. This list is broken into two distinct groups:

1. *Hardware-related*: This includes mis-wired communication cabling and faulty communication interfaces.
2. *Software-related*: Software-related issues arise when the master application tries to access non-existent nodes or use invalid function codes, address non-existent memory locations in the slaves, or specify illegal data format types, which obviously the slave devices do not understand. These issues will be dealt with in detail under the Modbus plus protocol, as these issues are common to both the traditional Modbus protocol and the Modbus plus protocol. They are summarized under software-related problems. These issues are also applicable to the latest Modbus/TCP protocol.

8b.2   Description of tools used

In order to troubleshoot the problems listed above, one would require the use of a few tools, hardware and software, to try and decipher the errors. The most important tool of all would always be the instruction manuals of the various components involved.

The hardware tools that may be required include RS-232 break-out boxes, RS-232 to RS-485 converters, continuity testers, voltmeters, screw drivers, pliers, crimping tools, spare cabling, and other similar tools and tackle. These would generally be used to ensure that the cabling and terminations are proper and have been installed as per the recommended procedures detailed in the instruction manuals.

On the software front, one would need some form of protocol analyzer that is in a position to eavesdrop on the communications link between the master and the slave modules. This could be either a dedicated hardware protocol analyzer, that is very expensive, or a software-based protocol analyzer that could reside on a computer (Figure 8b.1).

Obviously, this second option is more economical and also requires the relevant hardware component support in order to connect to the network.

```
Display File Config                                                      406288
╔══════════════════════════════════════ Status. ═══════════════════════════════╗
║  Serial Port Setup. (ISR: Normal)                                             ║
║      Format                    Address    IRQ                                 ║
║  Con 1: 9600     .None.  8.1    03F8       4     RTS CTS DSR DCD DTR RI    I   ║
║  Con 2: 9600     .None.  8.1    02F8       3     RTS CTS DSR DCD DTR RI    I   ║
╟───────────────────────────────────────────────────────────────────────────────╢
║  Code.                                                                        ║
║  Table. ASCII_xlt                                                             ║
╟───────────────────────────────────────────────────────────────────────────────╢
║  Trapping.                                                                    ║
║  Port.       Pattern.                            Matches.                     ║
║  Con 1       Con 1 Pattern.                          0           Disabled     ║
║  Con 2       Con 2 Pattern.                          0           Disabled     ║
║  Buffer length    →  8192          Chunk length  →  512                       ║
║  Time Stamping    →  Enabled    File Open Mode  →  Create                     ║
╟───────────────────────────────────────────────────────────────────────────────╢
║  Files.                                                                       ║
║  Configuration File  :  Default.cfg                                          ║
║  Logging File        :  LogFile.log                                          ║
║  Path To Data Files :  C:\PAT\DATA\                                          ║
║  Transnit File       :  ASCII.DOC                                            ║
╚═══════════════════════════════════════════════════════════════════════════════╝
  F1 Help.     Alt-x Exit.
```

Figure 8b.1
Screen shot of the protocol analysis tool

8b.3   Detailed troubleshooting

8b.3.1   Mis-wired communication cabling

RS-232 wiring for three-wire point-to-point mode

There are various wiring scenarios such as point-to-point, multi-drop two-wire, multi-drop four-wire, etc. In a point-to-point configuration, the physical standard used is usually RS-232 on a 25-pin D connector, which means a minimum of three wires are used. They are: on the DTE (master) side: transmit (TxD – pin 2), receive (RxD – pin 3), and signal ground (common – pin 7); and on the DCE (slave) side: receive (RxD – pin 2), transmit (TxD – pin 3), and signal ground (common – pin 7).

The other pins were primarily used for handshaking between the two devices for data flow control. Nowadays, these pins are rarely used as the flow control is done via software handshaking protocols.

With the advent of VLSI technology, the footprint of the various devices have a tendency to shrink; thereby even the physical connections of communications have been now been standardized on 9-pin D connectors. The pin assignment that has been adopted is the IBM standard in which the pin configurations are: on the DTE (master) side: transmit (TxD – pin 3), receive (RxD – pin 2), and signal ground (common – pin 5); and on the DCE (slave) side: receive (RxD – pin 3), transmit (TxD – pin 2), and signal ground (common – pin 5).

It follows that the cabling between the two devices must be straight-through pin-for-pin. In this manner, the transmit pin of the master is directly connected to the receive pin of the slave and vice-versa. These cables are standard off-the-shelf products available in standard predetermined lengths. They can also be fabricated to custom lengths, with ease.

Master devices are usually the present day IBM compatible computers, with a Modbus application enabled on it, and therefore have the standard IBM RS-232 port provided. The slave devices usually have a user-selectable option to have either an RS-232 or RS-485 port for communication. Unfortunately some manufacturers, in order to force the customers to return to them time-and-again, employ a strategy of modifying these standards to their own advantage.

Figure 8b.2 illustrates a couple of these combinations.

Case I

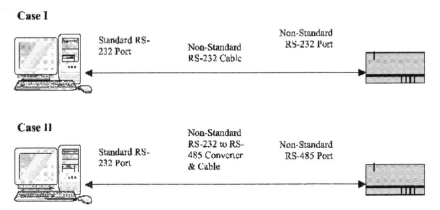

Case II

Figure 8b.2
Typical customizations in RS-232 cabling

As can be seen in case I, the manufacturer has modified the standard pin-out of the RS-232 connection or has totally replaced the standard IBM RS-232 9-pin DIN connector with his own standard. In situations like these, it is then imperative to possess the manufacturer's manuals of the device being used.

With the aid of the continuity checker, and the use of the RS-232 breakout box, you can determine the non-standard pin-out of the cable, and fabricate a spare cable to the required lengths without having to revert to the supplier.

As in case II, the manufacturer has embedded an RS-232 to RS-485 converter into the cable itself and this would mimic a standard off-the-shelf RS-232 serial cable. This obviously would not be clearly evident if you were not aware of the modification. With the aid of the voltage tester, you can determine the operating voltages and therefore be in a position to decipher the type of standard being employed.

In other implementations, where multi-dropped RS-485 is used, the installations usually cater for both configurations of two-wire and four-wire communications. In the case of single-master configurations, either of the two wiring modes could be used. In the case of multi-master configurations, only the two-wire communication can be used.

RS-485/RS-422 wiring for four-wire, repeat or multi-drop modes

The four-wire configuration is, in actual fact, the RS-422 standard where there is one line driver connected to multiple receivers, or multiple line drivers connected to one line receiver. When using four-wire RS-422 communications, messages are transmitted on one pair of shielded, twisted wires and received on another (Belden part number 9729, 9829, or equivalent). Both multi-drop and repeat configurations are possible when RS-422 is used.

This is the classic case where the one line driver is the one that belongs to the master and the remaining receivers belong to the multiple slaves. The slaves receive their commands via this link and respond via their line drivers that are all connected to each other and finally connected to the master's receiver (Figure 8b.3).

RS-485 wiring for two-wire, multi-drop mode only

The two-wire configuration is the actual RS-485 standard where both the line drivers and the receivers are connected to the same pair of communication cables. When using two-wire RS-485 communications, messages are transmitted and received on the same pair of shielded, twisted wires (Figure 8b.4). Care must be taken to turn the host driver IC on when sending messages and off when receiving messages. This can be accomplished using software or hardware. Only multi-drop wiring configuration is possible when RS-485 is used.

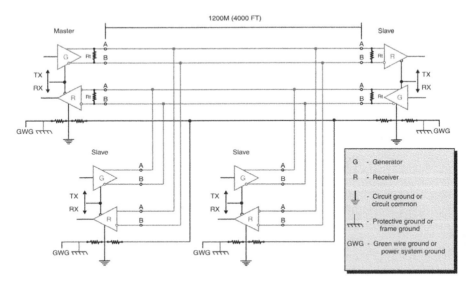

Figure 8b.3
Typical four-wire RS-485 multi-drop cabling

Typically, the maximum number of physical RS-485 nodes on a network is 32. If more physical nodes are placed on the network an RS-485 repeater must be used.

This system works inherently similar to the four-wire system, except that the master transmits requests to the various slaves and the slaves respond to the master over the same pair of wires.

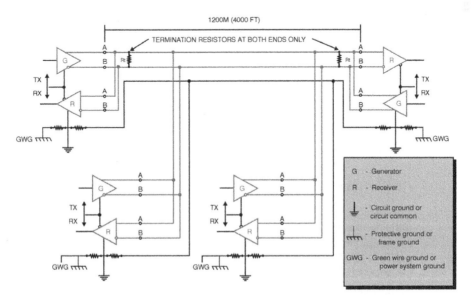

Figure 8b.4
Typical two-wire RS-422/485 cabling

Note: The shield grounds should be connected to system ground at one point only. This will eliminate the possibility of ground loops causing erroneous operation.

Grounding

The logic ground of all controllers and any other communication device on the same network must reference the same ground. If one power supply is used for all controllers, then they will be referenced to the same ground. When multiple supplies are used, there are a couple of options to consider:

- Connect the supply output ground to a solid earth ground on all power supplies. If the grounding system is good, all controllers will be referenced to the same ground. (Note that the typical PC follows this practice.)

  In some older buildings, the earth ground could vary by several volts within the building. In this case, option 2 should be considered.
- Use the GND position on each controller to tie all controllers to the same potential. Note that each power supply output must be isolated from the input lines, otherwise irreparable damage may result if two power supplies are powered from different phases of an electrical distribution system. It is not recommended that the shield of a cable be used for this purpose, use a separate conductor.
- Where it is not possible to get all controllers referenced to the same ground, use an isolated RS-485 repeater between controllers that are located at different ground potentials. Isolated repeaters are also an excellent way to clean up signals and extend distances in noisy environments.

8b.3.2   Faulty communication interfaces

RS-232 driver failed

The RS-232 driver may be tested with a good high-impedance voltmeter. Place the meter in the DC voltage range. Place the RED probe on the transmit pin (TxD) and the BLACK probe on the signal ground (common). While the node is not transmitting (TX light off), there should be a voltage between -5 and -25 V DC across these pins. This is referred to as the idle state of the RS-232 driver. When the node is transmitting, the voltage will oscillate through between ±5 and ±25 V DC. It may be difficult to see the deflection at the higher baud rates and an oscilloscope is suggested for advanced troubleshooting. If the voltage is fixed at anywhere between -25 and $+25$ V DC and does not oscillate as the TX light blinks, then the transmitter is probably damaged and must be returned to the factory for repair or replacement.

RS-232 receiver failed

This requires the use of an RS-232 loop back plug or an RS-232 breakout box with a jumper installed between the transmit and the receive pins. After connecting this to the communication port of the node to be tested, the node is made to transmit data, and when the TxD light of the node flashes, the RxD light must also flash, then it can be said that the RS-232 receiver of that node is good. If the RxD light does not flash at the same time as the TxD, then the RS-232 receiver may be bad.

Alternatively, two nodes may be connected to each other with a tested and working communication cable and both their RS-232 drivers working. If one of the nodes is transmitting to the other, the second node indicates a good reception by flashing its RxD light as the first node transmits, then the RS-232 receiver on the second node is good. The same is true when the second node transmits and the first flashes its RxD light.

RS-485 driver failed

The RS-485 driver too may be tested with a good high-impedance voltmeter. Place the meter in the DC voltage range. Place the RED probe on the non-inverted transmit terminal (TX+) and the BLACK probe on the inverted transmit terminal (TX–). While the node is not transmitting (TX light off), there should be approximately –4 V DC across these wires. When the node is transmitting, the voltage will oscillate through ±4 V DC. It may be difficult to see the deflection at the higher baud rates and an oscilloscope is suggested for advanced troubleshooting. The minimum voltage obtained during a full 1200 baud to 19 200 baud sweep will be around –1.6 V DC. If the voltage is fixed at around +4, 0, or –4 V, and does not oscillate as the TX light blinks, then the transmitter is probably damaged and must be returned to the factory for repair or replacement.

RS-485 receiver failed

This requires two nodes connected to each other with a tested and working communication cable, and both their RS-485 drivers working. If one of the nodes is transmitting to the other, the second node indicates a good reception by flashing its RX light as the first node transmits, then the RS-485 receiver on the second node is good. If the RX light flashes when the first node polls at other baud rates then most likely, the polarity is reversed between the OUT of the first node and the second node. Reverse the TX+ and TX– wires at the first node.

8b.3.3 Software-related problems

See the suggestions under Modbus Plus. But the important issues to consider are:

No response to message from master to slave This could mean that either the slave does not exist or there are CRC errors in the transmitted message due to noise (or incorrectly formatted message).

Exception responses See the list of potential problems reported by the exception responses. This could vary from slave address problems to I/O addresses being illegal.

8b.4 Conclusion

We have seen that the master computer sends commands to the various slave units to determine the status of its various process inputs or to change the status of its outputs using the Modbus protocol. The commands are transmitted over a single pair of twisted wires (RS-485) or two pairs of twisted wires (RS-422) at speeds of 9600, 19 200, 38 400, or 57 600 baud. The addressed slave decodes the commands and returns the appropriate response. If the master computer is an IBM PC or compatible, inexpensive interface driver software is available. This software dramatically simplifies sending and receiving these messages. If you prefer, you can use one of the off-the-shelf graphics-based data acquisition and control software packages. Many of these packages offer a Modbus compatible driver.

If you were to follow the recommended installation and startup procedure and took extra precaution while setting up the following items, then you would achieve trouble-free startup:

- Setting the base address
- Setting the protocol and baud rate
- Serial communications wiring
- Communication wiring termination.

9

Fundamentals of DNP3

9.1 Fundamental concepts

9.1.1 The OSI seven-layer model

The open systems interconnection model, as defined by the International Standards Organization (ISO), was a significant step in the development of standardization of data communications systems. The OSI model presents data communications in a hierarchical manner, starting at the bottom with the physical layer (layer 1), and moving to the application layer (layer 7) at the top (Figure 9.1).

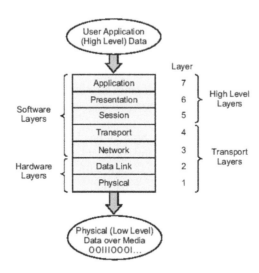

Figure 9.1
ISO open systems interconnection (OSI) model

In the arena of SCADA and IED communications, there was a need for a simplified model. Such a model was created by the International Electro Technical Commission (IEC) that defined a three-layer model. This is known as the enhanced performance architecture (EPA) model and it is this model on which DNP3 is based. The functions of each of the layers used by DNP3 are discussed in the next section.

Before moving to the EPA model, we will use the general OSI reference model to illustrate message build-up (Figure 9.2). This will demonstrate the general principle and introduce the idea of message headers. These concepts will assist us in understanding the details of message construction under DNP3.

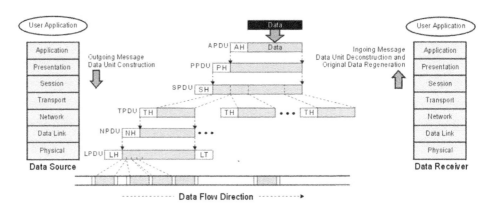

Figure 9.2
Generic message build-up using the OSI seven-layer model

Some of the features and terminology illustrated by the message build-up are now discussed.

Data flow during message construction is from the application level down to the physical level, then across the physical medium, then at the receiving device up through the model layers until the original message is regenerated.

The application data is given an application header by the application layer. This forms the application protocol data unit or APDU. The APDU is the data unit used by the next layer, the presentation layer. This adds its own header and so on.

The data may be split into smaller size units during the process of message construction. In this example, the session protocol data unit (SPDU) is broken into multiple data units at the transport level.

The data-link layer adds both a header, and a trailer section containing an error detection code, forming the link protocol data unit (LPDU). At the physical layer this is broken down into 8-bit blocks, each with start and stop bits appended for asynchronous transmission.

Figure 9.3 shows a distinction in terminology between the service data unit and the protocol data unit, which is worth being aware of because it will assist in understanding of terms like TSDU and TPDU when used in relation to DNP3. The TSDU is the data unit used to communicate with the higher level, that is, to provide the service to the higher level. The TPDU is the data unit exchanged with the level below.

Figure 9.3 illustrates in this case the transport level breaking down the higher-level data unit into multiple data units to be passed down to the next level.

9.1.2   Enhance performance architecture (EPA)

The enhanced performance architecture model developed by IEC Technical Committee 57 is a three-layer sub-set of the OSI seven-layer model. The layers used in this model are the two hardware layers and the top software layer, the application layer (Figure 9.4).

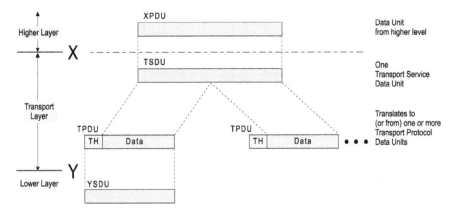

Figure 9.3
Definition of service data unit vs protocol data unit

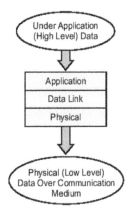

Figure 9.4
Enhanced performance architecture (EPA) model

As for the OSI seven-layer model, during transmission high-level data is passed from the user application to the application level, and from there down through the hierarchy to produce a stream of data over the physical communications medium. In the process, the data may be converted from a single user application data unit into smaller chunks and ultimately to a bit stream. On reception at its destination, the reverse process is applied, and leading to regeneration of the original application level data unit.

DNP3 uses these three layers, but adds some transport functions. These are often referred to as the pseudo-transport layer, and are sometimes depicted as corresponding to the transport and network layers in a limited manner. This relationship is shown in Figure 9.5.

This drawing shows the relationship between the three-layer enhanced performance architecture (EPA), as implemented by DNP3, and the OSI reference model.

In the following section the message, structure will be analyzed in terms of the EPA model. Before looking at that, a brief review of the general functions of each of the layers will be made.

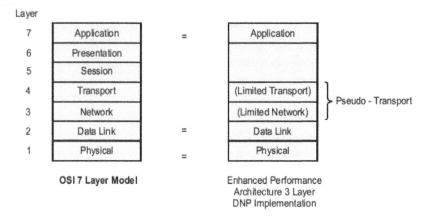

Figure 9.5
Relationship of EPA model to OSI seven-layer model

9.1.3   Functions of the model layers

The functions of each layer of the EPA model are described briefly in the following paragraphs. The network and transport layer functions have included as the pseudo-transport layer, as limited transport and network functions are supported by the DNP3 protocol.

Physical layer

The physical layer is the physical media over which the protocol is transmitted. The definition of this, the physical interface characteristics, in terms of electrical specifications, timing, pin-outs and so on. The data element at this level is essentially the bit, i.e. it is concerned with how to pass one bit of data at a time across the physical media.

Definition of the physical layer also includes the functions for controlling the media, such as details required to establish and maintain the physical link, and to control data flow.

The actual specification of this layer is normally a separate standard such as ITU-T X.21, or V.24, RS-232 or others.

The physical layer specification for DNP3 is covered in greater detail later in this text, but it is noted here that RS-232C was originally specified for voltage levels and control signals, and ITU-T (formerly CCITT) V.24 for DTE–DCE signaling.

Other communications media such as over Ethernet are in the process of being defined for use by the DNP3 user group technical committee.

Data-link layer

The data-link layer provides for reliable transmission of data across the physical medium. While the physical layer is concerned with the passage of a signal, or a bit of data, the data-link layer is concerned with the passage of groups of data. These groups may be referred to as a frame. Functions provided by the data-link layer include flow control and error detection.

The pseudo-transport layer

This layer is included in DNP3 to allow for the transmission of larger blocks of data than could otherwise be handled. Some writers have described this in terms of both network and transport services, although these are usually simply referred to as pseudo-transport services. Network functions are concerned with routing and flow control of data packets over networks. Transport functions provide network transparent end-to-end delivery of whole messages, including disassembly and reassembly, and error correction.

Application layer

The application layer is the level where the data is generated for sending, or requested to be sent. The layer interfaces to the lower levels in order to transmit the required information. In turn, the DNP3 application layer provides its services to the user application programs, such as an HMI system, an RTU, or other system.

9.2 Understanding the DNP3 message structure

In the preceding sections, the build-up of a generic OSI seven-layer model message was shown, and the Enhanced Performance Architecture was introduced. In this section, the build-up of a DNP3 message will be examined. This will provide an introduction to the overall structure of the DNP3 message. At this point we need not be concerned with the detailed meaning of each part of the message. Detailed descriptions of the meaning of the data added at each layer will be given in later sections.

9.2.1 DNP3 message build-up

Figure 9.6 shows how the transmitted message is built up in DNP3. Each layer of the model takes the information passed from the higher layer, and adds information connected with the services performed by that layer. The additional information is usually added as a header, that is, in front of the original message.

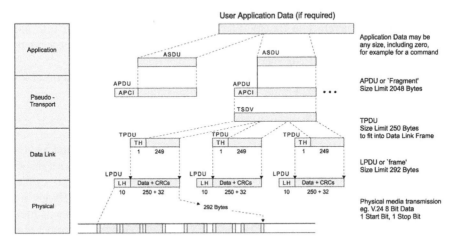

Figure 9.6
Build-up of DNP3 message

Thus during message assembly, the message will grow in size with each layer that it passes down through. It is also disassembled in this process into smaller units of data.

The message build-up illustrated in Figure 9.6 is now briefly described for each layer. It is described here from the highest level, the application level, downwards. This reflects the sequence of message building during sending. Of course, the sequence at the other end is in reverse, as the message is passed over the physical medium, into the data-link layer, and up to the application layer.

9.2.2 Application layer

The user data is the data arising from the user application. The user application can be visualized as a layer above the application layer, and could for example be a human machine interface (HMI) program such as 'Citect' or 'Intellution Fix', or it could be an embedded program, such as a C+ application program. The data could be alarm and event data, digital status data, or even a data file such as a configuration file being passed from a master station to an RTU or an IED. On the other hand, in the case of many types of command being issued by a master station, there may be no data at all. A key point is that this data can be of any size. The total data size is not limited by the protocol.

The application layer initially forms the data into manageable sized blocks. These are called application service data units or ASDUs. The application layer then creates the application protocol data unit APDU by combining a header with the ASDU data. The application header is referred to as the application protocol control information, or APCI. This is either 2 bytes or 4 bytes in length, depending on whether the message is a request or a response. In the case of a command or other user request requiring no additional data, there is only a header, and no ASDU.

Depending on the total size of the data to be transmitted (the size of the ASDU), one or more APDUs are created. In the case that multiple APDUs are required, these are each termed fragments. Whilst the number of fragments required representing an ASDU is not limited, the size of each fragment is limited to a maximum of 2048 bytes.

9.2.3 The pseudo-transport layer

The APDU from the application layer may be referred to as the transport service data unit within the pseudo-transport layer. It is interpreted purely as data to be transported by the transport layer. The transport layer breaks the TSDU down into smaller units termed transport protocol data units or TPDUs. These are made up of a 1-byte header, followed by a maximum of 249 bytes of data.

The overall size of the TPDUs, which is 250 bytes, was determined so that each TPDU will fit within one 'Frame' or LPDU at the data-link layer.

9.2.4 The data-link layer

This layer takes the TPDUs from the pseudo-transport layer and adds a 10-byte header to each. As the data-link layer is also responsible for providing error detection and correction functions, error-checking codes are introduced here. A 16-bit cyclic redundancy code (CRC) is used. Each TPDU is converted to a frame of up to 292 bytes in length.

It is worth noting at this point that the frame format is known as the FT3 frame format, which was originally described by IEC 870-5-1. This frame format represents a historical point of common ground between DNP3 and IEC 870-5. This frame format will be returned to in the next section.

9.2.5 The physical layer

The physical layer converts each frame into a bit stream over the physical media. In the original DNP3 documentation, a bit-serial asynchronous physical layer is specified. It calls for 8-bit data, one start bit, one stop bit, no parity, and RS-232C voltage levels and control signals.

9.2.6   Summary of message build-up

The build-up of DNP3 messages has been shown from a top-down perspective to have the following features:

- Application functions may or may not require the passage of data
- Commands will often require no data
- The application layer parses the data into APDUs
- The APDU maximum size is 2048 bytes
- The pseudo-transport layer parses the APDU into smaller TPDUs
- TPDU maximum size is 250 bytes
- The data-link layer adds headers and CRCs to form the LPDU
- LPDU maximum size is 292 bytes, of which 250 bytes are data.

In the following sections, the detailed functioning of each of the model layers will be examined. Looking at the functionality of each layer it will be necessary to examine and understand the message header sections applied at each layer, and to see how the functions of the layer are performed using them.

9.3   Physical layer

The physical layer may be described in terms of the network topology as well as the characteristics of the communication paths.

As previously noted, the physical layer defines the physical interface characteristics in terms of electrical specifications, timing, pin-outs and so on. This includes details required to establish and maintain the physical link. The data element at this level is essentially the bit, i.e. it is concerned with how to pass one bit of data at a time.

9.3.1   Description of physical layer

The physical layer originally recommended for DNP3 has the following specification:

- Bit serial asynchronous
- Eight data bits
- One start bit, one stop bit
- No parity
- RS-232C voltage levels and control signals
- CCIT V.24 hardware protocol for DTE/DCE communications.

The DNP3 Users Group Technical Committee subsequently produced a standard for transmission of DNP3 over networks. This provides an alternative definition of the physical layer for that situation.

9.3.2   Services provided by physical layer

The physical layer must provide these functions:

- Connect
- Disconnect
- Send
- Receive
- Status.

9.3.3   Topologies

As previously described, DNP3 supports either master–slave or peer-to-peer communications, with either one-on-one or multi-drop topologies.

- Point-to-point
- Multi-drop from one master
- Hierarchical with intermediate data concentrators
- Multiple master.

Point-to-point or direct topology refers to the case of two DNP3 devices connected together, either directly with a cable, or via modems and a communications path. This could be via a leased line, via radios, or via the public switched telephone network (PSTN).

A serial bus topology is the alternative to a direct topology. This may also be referred to as multi-drop. In this case, multiple devices are connected to the same communications path.

9.3.4   Physical layer procedures

Procedures must be provided to support both half-duplex and full-duplex communications. The specific procedures used will depend on the topology as well as whether half- or full-duplex transmission is available. One particular role of the procedures is to manage the event of message collision, where it can occur. Because DNP3 supports peer–peer communications, any station can act as a primary, or message initiator. Because of this, messages can be sent from two stations simultaneously, causing a collision.

Before discussing the physical layer procedures, a brief review of the terminology is given in the following table.

Simplex	Communications are in one direction only
Half-duplex	Two-way communication is possible, but only in one direction at a time. This is because only one communication path or channel is used. To effect communication a protocol for handing over the channel is required
Full-duplex	Simultaneous two-way communication is possible. Two channels are provided to do this
Two-wire	A two-wire connection will provide one communication channel. A PSTN line is an example of this. Therefore, half-duplex communications only are possible via this channel
Four-wire	A four-wire connection will provide two channels, and is capable of supporting duplex communications

In the following procedures, the data carrier detect (DCD) indication is used to determine if the communications medium is free. Generally, a time delay must be used to prioritize access to the channel once it has become free.

Half-duplex procedures

Direct link

With a direct, or point-to-point link, the delay from DCD clear needs to be just sufficient to allow the master station to detect loss of DCD and begin transmission. Note that if a dial-up connection is being used, the DCD signal indicates the establishment of a link rather than the presence of data. In this case the RTS and CTS signals must be used.

DNP3 must assert the RTS signal and await the CTS signal before transmitting each frame.

Multi-drop link

In the case of a multi-drop link, time delays must be used to ensure that stations get access to the medium. This is accomplished by providing a back-off time made of a fixed delay plus a variable delay. These delay times are configurable by the user. Normally the master station will be given a zero fixed delay time, so that it can always gain access in a half-duplex environment. Prioritization of slave stations can be accomplished by this method. Again, the minimum delay must be long enough for the master station to be able to gain control of the medium before any outstation.

Full-duplex procedures

Direct link

No collision can occur as both master and slave have their own channel to each other.

Multi-drop link

Time delays are used as for half-duplex multi-drop, except that the fixed time delay may be reduced, as it is not necessary to provide this for the master. In the full-duplex multi-drop environment, the master has its own channel to all receivers.

9.4 Data-link layer

9.4.1 Description of data-link layer

The purpose of the data-link layer is to establish and maintain reliable communication of data over the physical link.

Link establishment involves setting up the logical communications link between sender and receiver. DNP3 is capable of supporting either connection-oriented or connectionless operation. Thus, if a channel operates over a PSTN line and requires connection by dialing before communication can commence, the data-link layer manages this without any direction from higher levels.

As seen previously, the data unit at the link layer level may be called the frame. The frame has a maximum size of 292 bytes including CRC codes, and carries a total of 250 bytes of information from the higher levels. The frame includes 16-bit source and destination addresses in its header. These provide for 65 536 different addresses. The address range FFF0–FFFF is reserved for broadcast messages, which are intended to be processed by all receivers. Note that addresses are logical in the sense that it is possible for one physical device to have more than one logical address. In such a case, the different addresses would appear as separate devices to the master station.

The frame header also contains a function code. The functions supported by this are those required to initialize and test the operation of each logical link between sender and receiver. As an additional security feature, every frame transmitted can request a confirmation of receipt. This is termed link layer confirmation.

These services and functions are expanded upon in the following sections.

9.4.2 Services provided

The following services are all provided by the data-link layer. Understanding how these are provided begins with examining the frame format. The frame format includes necessary control bits for controlling message flow, functions, error detection, and correction.

Services provided by the data-link layer:

- Establish and maintain the communication channel
- Report on link status to higher layers
- Detect and correct errors that may occur during transmission
- Conversion of data between LSDUs and LPDUs
- Error notification to higher levels
- Sequencing and prioritized delivery of LSDUs.

9.4.3   Some terminology

Communications in a SCADA system will generally have a structure where some stations may be identified as master stations, and others as slave stations, sub-master stations, or outstations. In a hierarchical structure, there may be some devices that act both as slave stations and master stations.

At the data-link level, the terms balanced and unbalanced are used to describe whether all stations may initiate communications or not. In 'unbalanced' systems, only master stations will initiate communications. That is, only a master station will be a primary, or originating, station, and slave stations will always be secondary, or responding, stations. In these systems when a slave station has data that it needs to transmit to the master, it must wait until the master station polls it.

The DNP3 protocol supports balanced communications at the data-link level. This provides greater flexibility by allowing non-master stations to initiate communications. In DNP3 any station can be an originator or primary station.

The terminology 'balanced' and 'unbalanced' can be confused with the terms 'master' and 'slave'. This confusion can arise because it is easy to imagine that in a balanced system, all stations must be equal. This is not the case, however. The reason is that the terms balanced and unbalanced apply only to the lower data-link level communications, whereas the master/slave distinction applies at the application level. In DNP3 the terms master and slave have real meaning, and a station is configured as one or the other. The key to understanding is that only a master station can issue a request, and only a slave can provide a response. These are each application level messages.

In the case of an outstation (a slave station) having unsolicited data to send to the master station, it issues an unsolicited response to the master. At the application level this is different type of message to a request. At the data-link level, however, the message frame appears no different from any other message frame whether issued by a master or a slave. These concepts are illustrated in Figure 9.7.

Figure 9.7 shows how these terms relate to the communication process. It illustrates a request for data from a master station to a non-master station. This could be a poll for current data, a 'static' poll. It illustrates the communication sequence by showing the parties on each side, with message directions shown between them. The time sequence is shown from top to bottom.

In the diagram, the designated master station initiates a communication with a non-master station. The request message itself is contained in the application layer information within the message. The designated master station has initiated this communication and is therefore the primary station. A response is required to this message at the data-link level, i.e. a confirmation of receipt is expected. The non-master station sends an acknowledgment. This is a secondary message, i.e. a data-link response to the primary message. Note that at the data-link level, this transaction is now completed.

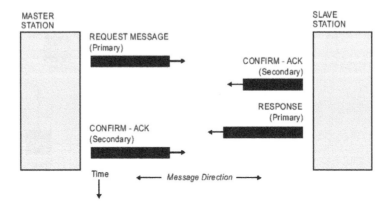

Figure 9.7
Example communication sequence diagram

Because the last transaction contained an application level request for the transmission of data, the non-master station then initiates a communication with the requested data. Now the non-master station is initiating the communication, and it is the primary station for this transaction. This is a new communication sequence, or transaction, at the data-link level. Although it is related to the prior transaction at the application level, it is unrelated at this level.

It can be seen from this example that the terms primary and secondary relate to the station initiating a transaction at the data-link level, and not to whether the stations are master or non-master.

Although the communications are balanced, and therefore any station can be a primary station and initiate messages, it is incorrect to believe that the terms master and non-master have no meaning. In DNP3 stations may be defined as either master or non-master.

This information is used at the link level to determine the setting of a message direction bit, the DIR bit. The direction bit is set for messages from a master, and cleared for messages from a non-master station.

A final definition that is important to understand is the 'data link' or just 'link'. The link refers to the logical connection between a primary station and a secondary station. It is therefore a one-way communication path. To establish two-way communications between two devices, it is necessary to establish the links in each direction. The logic in this may be better understood by recognizing that a communication channel between two devices can be duplex, using two entirely separate physical media, one in each direction. The simplest example of this is of course a four-wire connection.

Figure 9.8 shows two communication channels between the master and non-master stations. The first channel uses a data radio, and is full-duplex. The second channel is a back-up using modems and the public switched telephone network. The second channel is half-duplex, although parts of it are in fact full-duplex.

In this example, there are four links, as follows:

1. Channel 1 A to B
2. Channel 1 B to A

3. Channel 2 A to B
4. Channel 2 B to A.

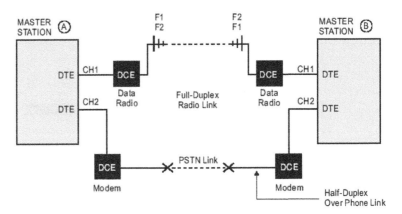

Figure 9.8
Example of communication channels

9.4.4　How it does it

DNP3 controls transmission at the link layer level by using defined transmission procedures. These procedures make use of a control byte contained within the message frame to control transmission. It is important to realize that neither the control byte nor the procedures can by themselves do this. The procedures define what actions are taken at each end, and the control byte provides the coordination between them. It defines what type of transmission is being sent, i.e. the frame type, and where in the process the frame fits.

In order to understand how the overall process works, it is necessary to examine the structure of the frame, the meaning of the information in the control byte, and finally the procedures themselves.

The FT3 frame format

The LPDU or frame format was based on the FT3 format specified by IEC 870-5-1. This was one of the four possible frame formats specified by IEC 870-5-1. The others are FT1.1, FT1.2, and FT2. These will be discussed further when comparing DNP3 with IEC 870.

The format specifies a 10-byte header, followed optionally by up to 16 data blocks. The overall message size is limited to 292 bytes, which provides for a maximum data capacity of 250 bytes. Thus a fully packed frame will comprise the header plus 16 data blocks, with the last block containing 10 data bytes (Figure 9.9).

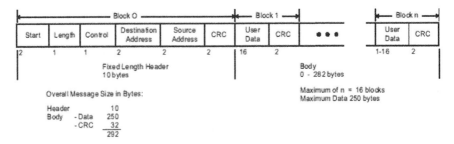

Figure 9.9
FT3 frame format

Start: 2 bytes: 0564 (Hex)

Length: Count of user data in bytes, plus 5, not counting CRC bytes. This represents all data; excluding CRC codes following the LENGTH count byte. Its range is 0–255. This is convenient as it is the largest length count that may be represented by 1 byte (=FF Hex)

Control: Frame control byte. See later section

Destination: Two-byte destination address (LSB, MSB)

Source: Two-byte source address (LSB, MSB)

CRC: Two-byte cyclic redundancy check code

User data: Each block has 16 bytes of user data. Last block has 1–16 as required. In case of a full frame the last block will have 10 bytes of user data.

Control byte

The control byte follows the start and length bytes in the frame format. It provides for control of data flow over the physical link, identifies the type, and indicates the direction. The interpretation of most of the control byte is dependent on whether the communication is a primary or a secondary message (Figure 9.10).

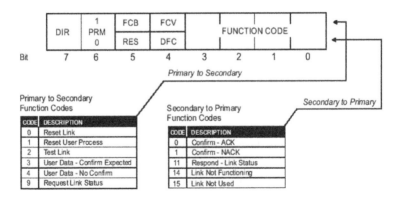

Figure 9.10
Control byte

DIR   Direction
        1 = A to B
        0 = B to A

PRM Primary message
        1 = frame from primary (initiating station)
        0 = frame from secondary (responding station)

FCB   Frame count bit

FCV   Frame count bit valid
        0 = ignore FCB
        1 = FCV is valid

RES   Reserved = 0

DFC   Data flow control bit. Set to 1 by secondary station if further send of user data will cause buffer overflow.

FC   Function code

Direction bit

The DIR bit indicates the message direction between master and non-master stations. If a message is from a designated master station, this bit is set. Otherwise it is cleared.

Primary bit

The PRM bit is set if the frame is primary (initiating) or a secondary (responding). This is used directly in interpreting the function code. There are six valid function codes for primary frames, and five valid function codes for secondary frames.

Frame count bits

These are the frame count bit (FCB) and the frame count valid bit (FCV). These bits are only used for primary messages. The frame count bit is used to detect losses or duplication of frames to a secondary station. The frame count valid bit enables the use of the FCB. When the FCV bit is true, the FCB is toggled for each successful SEND–CONFIRM transaction between the same primary and secondary stations.

How they work is like this:

- Following data-link start-up or a failed transaction, a secondary station will not accept any primary SEND–CONFIRM frames with FCV = 1 until a reset transaction is completed. This means it will only accept either a RESET Link or a RESET user process command.
- After a secondary station receives a RESET link frame from a primary and it responds with a CONFIRM, that link will be operational until a frame transmission error occurs.
- The secondary station will expect the next frame to contain FCV = 1 and FCB = 1.
- The next primary SEND–CONFIRM message will have FCV = 1 and FCB = 1. The secondary station will accept this as the FCB is valid and is set, as expected.
- Each subsequent primary SEND–CONFIRM message will have the FCB cleared or set in turn.

Data-flow control bit

The data flow control bit (DFC) is included in secondary frames. The secondary station will set DFC = 1 if a further SEND of user data will cause its buffer to overflow. On receipt of a frame with DFC = 1 a primary station will cease to send data, but will request link status until DFC = 0.

Data-link function codes

The tables below show the detailed meanings for different values of the function code byte. The meanings are different depending on whether the message is a primary or a secondary transmission.

Function Codes from Primary Station

Function Code	Frame Type	Service Function	FCY Bit
0	SEND–CONFIRM expected	Reset of remote link	0
1	SEND–CONFIRM expected	Reset of user process	0
2	SEND–CONFIRM expected	Test function for link	1
3	SEND–CONFIRM expected	User data	1
4	SEND–NO REPLY expected	Unconfirmed user data	0
9	REQUEST–RESPOND expected	Request link status	0

Codes 5–8, 10–15 are not used.

Function Codes from Secondary Station

Function Code	Frame Type	Service Function
0	CONFIRM	ACK – positive acknowledgment
1	CONFIRM	NACK – Message not accepted, link busy
11	RESPOND	Status of link (DFC = 0 or 1)
14		Link service not functioning
15		Link service not used or implemented

Codes 2–10, 12–13 are not used.

The following shortened version of the function codes is included in the sequence diagrams. The codes are preceded with a P or and S, representing primary or secondary codes.

Function Code Key

P0	Reset link	S0	Confirm–ACK
P1	Reset user process	S1	Confirm–NACK
P2	Test link	S11	Link status
P3	User data – confirm	S14	Not functioning
P4	User data – no confirm	S15	Not implemented
P9	Request link status		

The use of the function codes by the transmission procedures is described in the following sections.

Error control

Error control is effected by the use of an error detection code and by the transmission procedures.

The first part of error control is detecting when an error has occurred in a message. DNP3 uses a 16-bit cyclic redundancy code or CRC to do this. The CRC is transmitted once in the frame header, and thereafter once for every block of up to 128 bits of user data being transmitted. By calculating a CRC for each block of data received, and comparing it to the transmitted CRC for that block, errors will be detected if they occur. If the CRCs do not agree, then an error is indicated. This technique is not foolproof, as it is possible to obtain equal CRCs for different data blocks, but the probability of this is very low.

The second part of error control is the action performed when an error is detected. In every case where there is an error detected in any part of a frame, the frame is rejected by the receiving data-link layer.

For all primary frame types except for SEND–NO REPLY, an error will result in a negative acknowledgment and subsequent resending of the frame by the primary. The SEND–NO REPLY frame type is used for sending low-priority user data, which does not require confirmations. This type of data will simply be lost in the event of error.

The calculation of the CRC and processing on sending and receipt is a moderately complex operation using binary modulo-2 division. Although tricky for people to actually do, it is accomplished readily by computational devices. The algorithm for CRC processing is presented as a separate section.

9.4.5   Transmission procedures

Link reset

A link reset is required to enable communications between a primary and secondary station. A primary station must send the reset frame on power-up, or after a link is placed on-line.

Main points

- Must be used after a start, restart, or any link failure.
- It is the responsibility of the primary station to perform the reset (of its link to a secondary station).
- Initiates the primary and secondary stations for further SEND–CONFIRM transactions.
- Synchronizes the FCB so that FCB = 1 is expected by the secondary for the transaction following the reset.

In the communication sequence diagram in Figure 9.11 the link reset transaction is represented. Blocks are shown representing the actual frames transmitted. The primary station is shown on the left and the secondary station is on the right. States are shown for the FCB (frame control bit) at the primary, and the expected value of the FCB, at the secondary station. User indications are noted for each station also. These are indications on link status provided to service users.

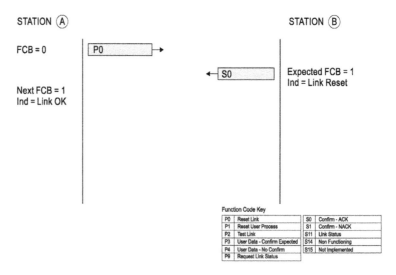

Figure 9.11
Reset link

In Figure 9.12, the same example is presented showing the actual byte pattern that would be seen if the transaction was captured by a protocol analyzer.

Primary to Secondary (A to B)
```
<05 64 05 C0 01 00 0C 00 CF A0>
Link Header              0564
Length                   05
Control Byte         C0    ; Dir=1, PRI=1, FCV=0, FC=RESET
Destination Address      0001
Source Address           000C
CRC value                CFA0
```

Secondary to Primary (B to A)
```
<05 64 05 00 0C 00 01 00 FD E9>
Link Header              0564
Length                   05
Control Byte         00    ; Dir=1, PRI=0, FC=ACK
Destination Address      000C
Source Address           0001
CRC value                FDE9
```

Figure 9.12
Data-link transaction detail – reset

It may be noticed that the primary DIR bit is set in the primary frame, and cleared in the secondary frame. This shows that this transaction is between a master and a non-master. This is coincidental, as it could equally have been the other way (e.g. as for the return link between B and A.

Reset user process

The reset user process (Figure 9.13) function code has been discontinued. The original DNP3 documentation defined the following functionality:

- Used to reset the link user process
- An ACK is sent if accepted by the user process
- Otherwise a NACK response is sent.

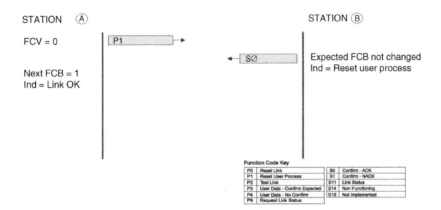

Figure 9.13
Reset user process

Test

The test procedure is used by the primary station to test the link. If the FCBs do not match, the secondary station should resend the last secondary confirm frame.

If the FCBs do match, it should send a CONFIRM–ACK frame and toggle the FCB. The data flow control bit DFC should be set accordingly in the return frame (Figure 9.14).

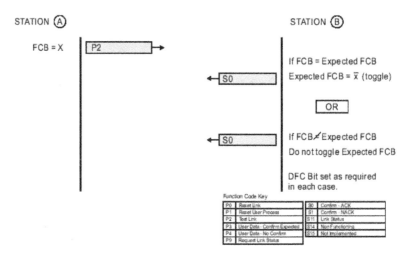

Figure 9.14
Test

Summary

- Used to test the link
- Secondary station checks FCB to expected FCB
- If FCBs match it sends ACK and toggles expected FCB
- If FCB does not match it resends the last confirm frame.

Confirmed send user data

This procedure is used for sending frames with user data that require confirmation of receipt. The link must be initially reset before the user data function may be used.

Summary

- The user data function is the most common message.
- Link must be reset prior to use.
- It carries the user data.
- Provides reliable transfer of user data by resending frames with errors.

Figure 9.15 shows the transmission of two consecutive user data frames by the primary station. On the successful receipt of the first user data frame an ACK (confirm-acknowledge) response is sent by the secondary station. The station also indicates the receipt of user data and toggles the expected FCB. On receipt of the confirmation by the primary, the FCB flag is toggled and another user data frame is sent.

In the event of an error in the received message, the frame is ignored and therefore no confirmation is sent. In this case, the primary will resend the message after an appropriate retry delay time.

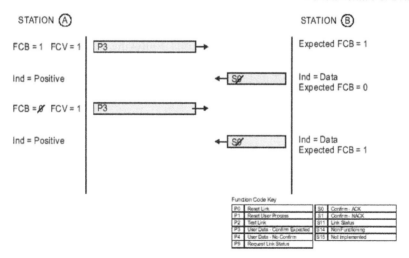

Figure 9.15
User data

Unconfirmed send user data

This procedure is used for sending user data without requiring confirmation from the secondary station. It may be used where the data is of low priority. The advantage is that data can be transmitted at a greater rate, thus providing a better use of bandwidth.

However, the disadvantage is that errors in transmission will result in lost frames. A frame found to have an error (by CRC checking) will be rejected by the secondary station, but as no confirmation was expected by the primary there will be no way for the primary to know that the message was unsuccessful (Figure 9.16).

Summary

- Used for low-priority user data
- No confirmations are sent by secondary
- More efficient use of bandwidth.

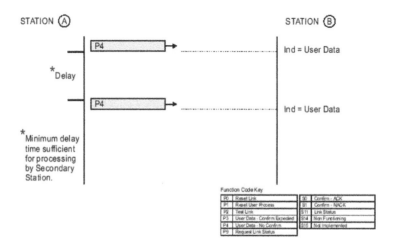

Figure 9.16
Unconfirmed send user data

Request link status

The request link status frame is used following receipt of a NACK or and ACK with DFC = 1 is received during transmission. The DFC (data flow control) bit is set by the secondary station if its buffers are full or if for any other reason it cannot process further data. The request link status is then used to determine when the link can again accept data.

Summary

- Sent to request the status of the secondary station
- Used after a NACK or an ACK with DFC = 1 is received
- Response frame will have DFC either set or cleared to give status.

In Figure 9.17, the secondary station's buffer is full after the second user data frame. The secondary responds with an ACK containing the data flow control DFC bit set to 1. The primary station now waits and at intervals sends a request link status frame. When this is acknowledged with DFC = 0 the user data transmission is resumed.

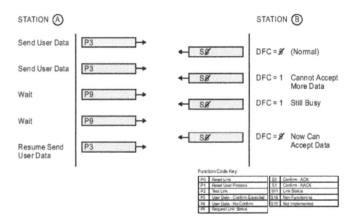

Figure 9.17
Request link status

9.4.6   CRC error code

The use of the cyclic redundancy code for detection of errors within transmitted frames has been introduced in terms of its function. This section examines the detail of the CRC processing.

DNP3 defines a 16-bit cyclic redundancy check code (or CRC) for error detection. The 16-bit CRC is provided for the 64-bit header data, and for each 128-bit (16-byte) block of user data transmitted.

The CRC code is generated by the following simple algorithm illustrated in Figure 9.18, and described following.

Generation of message:

- Start with user data block M of k bits (k = 64 for header, 8–128 for blocks in body)
- Multiply by 2^{16} (i.e. append 16 zeros to end to form k + 16 bit number)
- Divide by generator polynomial P to obtain quotient Q and remainder R (module-2 division is used)

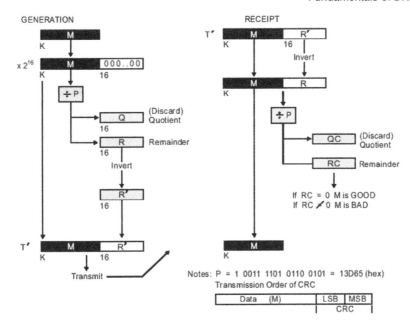

Figure 9.18
CRC code processing

- Discard Q, keep R
- Invert R to obtain R^1
- Append R^1 to M forming message T^1 to be transmitted.

Where generator polynomial:

$$P = X^{16} + X^{13} + X^{12} + X^{10} + X^8 + X^5 + X^2 + 1$$

This forms a 17-bit number, which is 13D65 (in Hex).
Processing on receipt of message

- Receive $T' = M$ followed by R'
- Invert R' and form $T = M$ appended with R
- Divide T by P (using modulo-2 division)
- Discard quotient QC, keep calculated remainder RC
- If $RC = 0$, result is GOOD, copy M to data output
- If RC not $= 0$, result is BAD, reject message.

It is noted that this CRC has a 'Hamming distance' of 6. This means that at least 6 bits must have been received in error to obtain a false GOOD DATA result.

9.4.7   Summary of data-link operation

Summary of data-link layer

- Receives link service data units from higher layer
- Forms the LPDU by including addresses, the control byte, and CRC codes
- Uses procedures to deliver the frame across the physical layer
- Function codes provide for link initialization and error recovery
- Reassembles LSDU at secondary station
- Provides status indications to higher levels.

9.5   Transport layer (pseudo-transport)

9.5.1   Description of transport layer

The primary function of the transport layer in DNP3 is to implement message disassembly and reassembly. This allows for the transmission of larger blocks of data than can be handled by the data-link layer. Because this functionality is fairly limited compared to the wider OSI definition of the transport layer, the prefix 'pseudo' is often used. For simplicity, the layer is referred to in this text as the transport layer.

9.5.2   The transport protocol data unit

The transport layer takes the user data, the transport service data unit (TSDU) and breaks it down into one or more transport protocol data units (TPDUs) and sends each to the data-link layer for sending. The TPDUs become the user data within the data-link layer, that is the LSDUs.

Recalling that the LSDUs can be a maximum of 250 bytes of user data, this defines the maximum size of the LPDU, including any transport layer overheads. In fact the transport functions are accomplished with a single-header byte, leaving 249 bytes for carrying data. This is pictured in Figure 9.19.

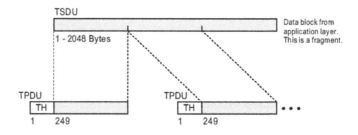

Figure 9.19
Transport protocol data unit

In a receiving, or secondary station, the incoming TPDUs are reformed into the TSDU for use by the application layer. The transport header bytes are stripped off and the TSDU is reformed from the multiple TPDMs. The transport layer is responsible for ensuring that the TSDU is reassembled in the correct sequence.

9.5.3   The transport header

The single byte transport header contains two bits that identify the start and end of a sequence of frames (TPDUs), plus a six-bit sequence counter (Figure 9.20).

Rules

- If a secondary station receives a frame with the FIR bit set, any previous incomplete sequence of frames is discarded.
- If a frame is received without the FIR bit set, and no sequence is in progress, then this frame is ignored.

- Sequence number may be any value 0–63 for first frame, and must increment for each frame in the sequence thereafter.
- Sequence number rolls over from 63 to 0.

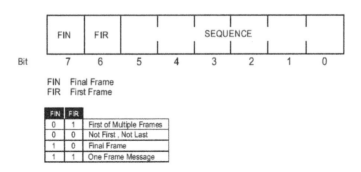

Figure 9.20
Transport header byte

9.5.4 Summary of transport layer

Summary

- Takes TSDU Fragments up to 2048 bytes and breaks them multiple TPDUs
- Includes a one-byte header
- TPDU can carry 249 bytes of user data
- The TPDU can fit into one FT3 frame format (LSDU)
- Header has FIR and FIN bits and six-bit sequence number
- Passes TPDUs to and from data-link layer
- Assembles incoming TPDUs into TSDU.

9.6 Application layer message handling

9.6.1 Description the application layer

The application layer is the highest level of the protocol, and communicates directly with the user application program. Master stations generate application level request messages for transmission to outstations, and outstations generate application level responses for transmission to the master station. These messages may contain commands, or requests for provision of data, or they may perform other functions such as time synchronization.

Summary

- Forms request messages to outstations
- Request messages may be commands, send data, or request data
- Accepts data from user application to send to master or to outstation
- Breaks user data down into multiple ASDUs
- Adds control information (APCI) to form APDUs
- Multiple APDUs are called fragments
- Fragments do not exceed 2048 bytes
- Fragments contain data objects
- Each fragment must be processable on its own.

The fragment size and data content requirements have been specified so that a fragment is always processable on its own. This means that a fragment buffer size of 2048 bytes should be sufficient to allow receipt of a fully processable piece of information. The buffer can then be left empty for receipt of the next fragment.

9.6.2   Application message sequences

At the application level, there are two basic message types in DNP3. These are requests and responses. Only a master station can send a request, and only an outstation can send a response. However, there is a special class of response called an 'unsolicited response'. This allows an outstation to send information to a master station or to a peer (another non-master station).

The message sequences are shown in Figures 9.21 and 9.22.

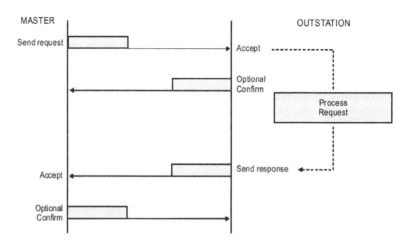

Figure 9.21
Application message sequences

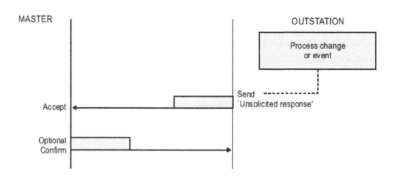

Figure 9.22
Unsolicited response message

In the sequence in Figure 9.21, the outstation receives a request from the master station. If the master station has set a 'confirm' bit, the outstation will send a confirm message. It will at the same time commence processing the request. Once it has assembled the necessary information, it will send its response. The master station will send a confirmation if the confirm bit is set in the response.

The case of an unsolicited response is shown in Figure 9.22. An event or defined process change is detected, causing the generation of a message by the outstation.

Whilst the message sequences appear simple enough, complexities arise from various causes. This includes the need to generate multi-fragment messages, and the need to handle crossovers in communications such as might arise if both a master and an outstation send messages simultaneously. These complexities are catered for by 'flow control' and the APCI, discussed in the following sections.

9.6.3   Application message formats

As noted previously, application messages are of two types, request and response. Each of these appears as one or more APDUs. Each APDU is made up of a header, which is termed the application protocol control information, and optional data, the ASDU.

The request and response headers differ by one field. The response header includes an additional two-byte field designated internal indications (IIN). The content of the ASDU is not depicted in Figure 9.23, but it is made up of data objects, each with an object header. These will be presented in detail later. For now the ASDU may be thought of merely as data.

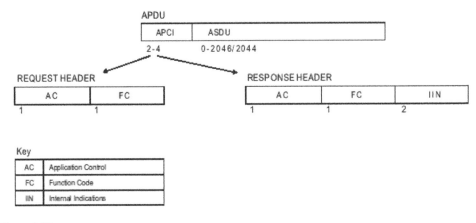

Figure 9.23
Application message format

9.6.4   Application control field

The application control field (Figure 9.24) is the first byte of the control information, or APCI. It is used to control the communication flow. It has three bits or flags, plus a sequence number that is used to sequentially number fragments.

Key
FIR   First fragment of multi-fragment message
FIN   Final fragment of multi-fragment message
CON   Confirmation required
          Sequence fragment sequence number
0–15   Master station requests and outstation responses
16–31 Outstation unsolicited responses.

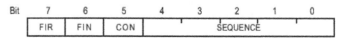

Bit	7	6	5	4	3	2	1	0
	FIR	FIN	CON		SEQUENCE			

Key

FIR	First fragment of multi-fragment message
FIN	Final fragment of multi-fragment message
CON	Confirmation required
Sequence	Fragment sequence number 0 - 15 Master station requests and outstation respones (solicited) 16 - 31 Outstation unsolicited responses

Figure 9.24
Application control field

Flow control is implemented by:

- The FIR and FIN bits
- The CON bit
- Master and outstation response timeouts
- Master and outstation retry counts (optional).

Using the following rules:

- If CON = 1 a confirmation must be sent.
- Sequence number is incremented for each fragment.
- Sequence number rolls over from 15 to 0, or 31 to 16.
- Response fragment has same sequence number as request fragment.
- If multiple request fragments, response starts at last request fragment number.
- Increment sequence number for each extra response fragment.
- A retransmitted response uses the original sequence number.
- Outstation must process one request before starting a second request.

These are further detailed in the following sub-sections.

Message confirmations

- If the CON bit is set, then a confirmation is required.
- A confirmation response to a request has the same sequence number as the request.
- If two confirmation messages are received with same sequence number, ignore the second.

Sequence numbers

- Sequence number is 0–15 for requests, outstation responses, and the associated confirmations.
- Number rolls over from 15 to 0.
- Sequence number is 16–31 for unsolicited responses and confirmations.
- Confirmations have same sequence number as request or response.
- The first fragment of a response has the same sequence number as the request, or as the last fragment of a multi-fragment request.

- For a single-fragment request retry, the retry has the same sequence number as the original request.
- For a multi-fragment request retry, the retry commences with the sequence number of the last fragment of the previous request.

Identical sequence numbers

- If two messages are received with the same sequence number, it usually means that the response message was not received by the other station. Retransmit response.
- If two confirmation responses are received with the same sequence number, ignore the second response.

9.6.5 Message transaction flow diagrams

The DNP3 basic four documentation includes a number of diagrams illustrating typical message transactions. These are very useful in understanding the transaction sequences. These are represented in the following diagrams, although the layout has been altered.

In these diagrams, the transaction sequence is represented by showing the application control (AC) information in each message passing between master station and outstation. The time sequence in the diagrams is from top to bottom.

The AC information is shown in the form:

[FIR FIN CON SEQ Number]

Receipt of a message fragment is depicted by an equals sign (=) in the diagrams, indicating the received message was as sent. Where a message is not received, a timeout may subsequently occur.

It should be remembered that at this point the diagrams are concentrating on only the AC part of the message, which is the first byte of the message, as this is the part that is controlling the message flow. Of course, in the whole message the AC byte is followed by the function code FC, the internal indications for response messages, and the data if present. Nevertheless, it is only the AC information that is of importance to the flow control.

Typical message transaction

Case One shows an initial master request without the confirmation bit set. The outstation responds without a prior confirmation. As the outstation's response has CON set, the master sends a confirmation on receipt. Later, the outstation makes an unsolicited response. It uses a sequence number in the range 16–31. The master station responds using the same sequence number.

Case One: Typical Message Transaction

Master AC	Outstation AC	Description
[110 7]	=	Request, no confirm required
=	[111 7]	Response to master request
[110 7]	=	Confirm
=	[111 24]	Unsoliciated response
[110 24]	=	Confirm

[FIR FIN CON SEQ]

Case Two shows a typical request–response with confirmation sequence. Notice that the sequence number is unchanged for the whole transaction.

Case Two: Request with Confirm

Master AC	Outstation AC	Description
[111 2]	=	Request
=	[110 2]	Confirm
=	[111 2]	Response to master request
[110 2]	=	Confirm

[FIR FIN CON SEQ]

Multi-fragment response

Case Three shows a single-fragment request, without confirmation, requiring a multi-fragment response. Two response fragments were required. The master station increments it sequence number for the subsequent transaction, shown as the 'new request'.

Case Three: Multi-fragment Response

Master AC	Outstation AC	Description
[110 2]	=	Request, no confirm required
=	[101 2]	Response, fragment 1, first
[110 2]	=	Confirm
=	[011 3]	Response, fragment 2, last
[110 3]	=	Confirm
[110 4]	=	Request (new request)

[FIR FIN CON SEQ]

Confirmation timeouts

In Case Four the outstation response was not received by the master station and so no confirmation was issued by the master. After the confirmation timeout period at the outstation, it resends its response. Note that it has used the same sequence number.

Case Four: Outstation Confirmation Timeout

Master AC	Outstation AC	Description
[110 3]	=	Request
	[111 3]	Response to master request, not received by master
	Timeout	Confirmation not received
=	[111 3]	Resend response
[110 3]	=	Confirm

[FIR FIN CON SEQ]

Case Five appears identical to Case Four at the outstation. In this case the master station did receive its response, but the confirmation it sent was garbled and lost. After its confirmation timeout operates, the outstation resends its response. The master station on receiving a second response with the same sequence number just resends the confirmation. It does not reprocess the information as it already has that.

Case Five: Confirmation Lost

Master AC	Outstation AC	Description
[110 5]	=	Request
=	[111 5]	Response to master request
[110 5]		Confirm sent, not received
	Timeout	Confirmation timeout
=	[111 5]	Resend response
[110 5]	=	Confirm

[FIR FIN CON SEQ]

Case Six shows the loss of a master station request. After a request timeout period, the master station resends its request using the same sequence number.

Case Six: Master Request Timeout

Master AC	Outstation AC	Description
[110 8]		Request, not received
Timeout		Master station timeout
[110 8]	=	Request resent by master
=	[101 8]	Response sent
[110 8]	=	Confirm
=	[011 9]	Second fragment
[110 9]	=	Confirm

[FIR FIN CON SEQ]

Effects of network delays

In the following cases delays in the network cause transmissions to arrive after timeouts have operated. Such cases might occur for example when a store and forward device becomes heavily loaded.

In Case Seven the outstation response has been delayed in the network. The master station times out and then resends its request using the same sequence number. The outstation resends its response. The first response is received by the master and a confirmation is sent. When the master receives a second response it does not process the data, but sends a confirmation. The outstation receives the second confirmation and discards it.

Case Seven: Master Station Timeout

Master AC	Outstation AC	Description
[110 12]	=	Request
	[111 12]	Response to master delayed
Timeout		Master station timeout
[110 12]	=	Request resent
	[111 12]	Resend response
=(1st)		First response received
[110 12]	=	Confirm
=(2nd)		Second response received
[110 12]	=	Confirmation resent
		Confirmation ignored by RTU

[FIR FIN CON SEQ]

In general, message delays lead to timeouts and resending of either requests or messages. When the delayed message subsequently arrives it is recognized as being part of the current transaction because of its sequence number. If it is a repeat message requiring a confirmation, the confirmation is sent but the message itself is not acted on further. If it is a delayed confirmation that is received, this is simply discarded.

Case Eight shows a repeat message being sent by the master after the confirmation is delayed. When the confirmation to the first request is received it is discarded by the master station.

Case Eight: Delayed Confirmation from Outstation

Master AC	Outstation AC	Description
[111 12]	=	Request, No Response Expected e.g. freeze command
	[110 12]	Confirm sent, delayed in network
Timeout		
[111 12]	=	Request resent and received
=	[110 12]	Confirm
=(1st)		Delayed first confirm received, ignored by master

[FIR FIN CON SEQ]

In Case Nine the unsolicited message is delayed in the network. After confirmation timeout, the outstation resends the message. This time it is received directly and a confirmation is sent. If the master subsequently receives the original message it ignores it but sends a confirmation. This confirmation is ignored by the outstation. The situation is no different if the messages are received in the opposite order, i.e. the delayed 1st message arrives first, but after the outstation confirmation timeout.

Case Nine: Master Request Timeout

Master AC	Outstation AC	Description
	[111 28]	Unsolicited message sent, but delayed in network
	Timeout	Confirmation timeout
=	[110 28]	Message resent
[110 28]	=	Confirm
=(1st)		Delayed first message received
[110 28]	=	Confirm, outstation ignores this

[FIR FIN CON SEQ]

Collision with unsolicited response

If outstations are configured and enabled to provide unsolicited responses, then there will be the possibility of these occurring at the same time as a master station request. Special features are provided to handle the cases of these transactions becoming intermingled. The first feature is the use of different sequence numbers for unsolicited response transactions. Because these use only the numbers 16–31, these transactions are differentiated by the sequence number.

A second feature is provided to ensure that data is not lost or duplicated arising from an inappropriate sequence of actions. This feature is termed process mode, for which two modes are defined. These are the 'immediate mode', and the 'process after confirm' mode. Immediate mode is used for all transactions except for a master station read request to an outstation, when an unsolicited response transaction is in progress. When an outstation is waiting for confirmation for an unsolicited response, it will delay processing a read request until the confirmation is received. This is the process after confirm mode.

Rules for unsolicited message transactions

- Master station always processes an unsolicited response immediately, even if waiting for a response to a previous message.
- If a confirmation for the unsolicited response is requested it is issued immediately by master.
- Outstation will process most requests immediately, even if waiting for a response to a previous unsolicited response. This is 'immediate mode'.
- Outstation will not process a master station read request if it is waiting for confirmation of a previous unsolicited response.
- This is 'process after confirm' mode.

These rules are illustrated in the following transactions.

In Case Ten both master and outstation transmits messages at the same time. The outstation responds immediately to the master station. Because it responded immediately, it may be deduced that this was an immediate mode request, that is, the master station had not made a read request.

Case Ten: Simultaneous Transactions

Master AC	Outstation AC	Description
[110 7]	[110 24]	Both master and outstations transmit simultaneously
=	=	
=	[111 7]	Response to master station
[110 7]	=	Confirmation to outstation response
[110 24]	=	Confirmation to unsolicited message

[FIR FIN CON SEQ]

Note that the order of receipt of confirmations at the outstation is unimportant.

In Case Eleven a normal message sequence is shown in which an unsolicited message does not require a confirmation. A simultaneous master station request is serviced by the outstation.

Case Eleven: Unsolicited Response without Confirm

Master AC	Outstation AC	Description
[111 2]	[110 22]	Both master and outstations transmit simultaneously
=	=	
		Master stores and processes unsolicited response. No confirm was requested
=	[110 2]	Confirmation to master station request
=	[111 2]	Response to master station request
[110 2]		Confirm

[FIR FIN CON SEQ]

Note that sending unsolicited responses without requesting confirmation is not recommended, as this may lead to data loss. Considering this situation leads to understanding when the use of non-confirmed messages is appropriate. This is when timeouts will function to ensure that a missed transaction is reattempted. For example, requests from the master station requiring responses will be repeated if a response is not received. In this case the message response timeout will cause resending of the message when a response is not obtained.

In Case Twelve the unsolicited response is confirmed during the course of a multi-fragment transaction.

Case Twelve: Simultaneous Transactions Multi-fragment

Master AC	Outstation AC	Description
[110 2]	[111 18]	Master and outstation send messages simultaneously
=	=	
=	[101 2]	Fragment 1 of response
[110 2]	=	Confirm for fragment 1
=	[011 3]	Fragment 2 of response
[110 18]	=	Confirm for unsolicited response
[110 3]	=	Confirm for fragment 2

[FIR FIN CON SEQ]

In Case Thirteen an unsolicited response from the outstation is lost or garbled. The outstation responds to a separate transaction from the master station, but resends the unsolicited response after its confirmation timeout expires.

Case Thirteen: Simultaneous Transactions

Master AC	Outstation AC	Description
[110 3]	[111 28]	Master and outstation send messages simultaneously
	=	Unsolicited response not received
=	[111 3]	Response to request from master
[110 3]	=	Confirm
	Timeout	Confirmation timeout
=	[111 28]	Unsolicited message resent
[110 28]	=	Confirm

[FIR FIN CON SEQ]

Case Fourteen shows the process after confirm mode. The outstation receives a master station read request after it has commenced an unsolicited response. It waits until it has received a confirmation for its unsolicited response before proceeding.

Case Fourteen: Process After Confirm Mode (1)

Master AC	Outstation AC	Description
[110 2]	[111 18]	Master and outstation send messages simultaneously
=	=	Request is for read data
		Outstation waits for confirmation
[110 18]	=	Confirm for unsolicited response
		RTU now processes master request
=	[111 2]	Response
[110 2]	=	Confirm

[FIR FIN CON SEQ]

Case Fifteen is similar to Case Fourteen except that the unsolicited response is not received. Again the outstation completes the unsolicited response transaction prior to responding to the master station's read request.

Case Fifteen: Process After Confirm Mode (2)

Master AC	Outstation AC	Description
[110 3]	[111 28]	Master and outstation send messages simultaneously
	=	Request is for read data. Master does not receive unsolicited response
		Outstation waits for confirmation
	Timeout	Outstation confirmation timeout
=	[111 28]	Resends unsolicited response
[110 28]	=	Confirm for unsolicited response
		RTU now processes master request
=	[111 3]	Response
[110 3]	=	Confirm

[FIR FIN CON SEQ]

9.7 Application layer message functions

9.7.1 General introduction

In the previous section entitled 'Application layer message handling', we have been concerned purely with the flow control of application layer messages. We have seen how the first byte of the application protocol control information (APCI) is used in managing the sequence of application level messages between master and outstation.

In doing this, almost no reference has been made to the actual content of the messages. In this and the following sections, we turn the focus on to the actual messages and the information they carry.

In general terms, as we are dealing with SCADA systems, we expect that messages will be capable of sometimes carrying commands, and other times carrying data, which may be generated in response to commands. This is, after all, the high-level functionality provided by a SCADA system – control and data acquisition. Not surprisingly then, the messages contain both function codes and data objects. Function codes define exactly what the meaning and purpose of a message is. They may, for example, tell an outstation to perform a particular operation, like freeze some counters, or to send some data. The data objects define the structure and interpretation of the data itself.

The reader might at this point wonder why the data should need any predefined formats, that is to have any specific 'data object' definition. Why cannot the outstation simply send data in any format that will be understood by the particular user application? The answer to this lies in the purpose of the protocol in the first place. The protocol is not just intended to provide a means for communication between devices from different manufacturers, but it is intended to make that data meaningful across different platforms. The data is not just unspecified data therefore, but it is specific data types like digital inputs, analog values and so on, each of which has a defined type under DNP3. For all this to work therefore, very specific definitions of the purposes and meaning of the message content are necessary.

We will examine these now. We will begin with the function codes, and then look at the data objects defined under DNP3.

9.7.2 Application function codes

The function code is the second byte of the application protocol control information. It follows the application control byte in both request headers from master stations, and response headers from outstations. The function code indicates what function is required to be performed.

Overview of function codes

The specific actions required for each function code is included in the following tables. The information in these is reproduced directly from that presented in the DNP3 basic four documentation, DNP3 application layer, Section 3.5 Function codes.

Many of the functions need identify specific data on which they operate. They do this with data object references that are included in the data within the ASDU, which follows the APCI header. In this section only the function codes themselves will be examined, with the referencing of the data objects being presented in following sections. In the function descriptions these data objects are referred to as 'specified data objects'.

Request Function Codes

Code	General Type	Function
0	Transfer function	Confirm
1		Read
2		Write
3–6	Control function	
7–2	Freeze function	
13–8	Application control function	
19–22	Configuration function	
23	Time synchronization	
24–128	Reserved	

Response Function Codes

Code	General Type	Function
0	Response function	Confirm
129		Read
130		Write

Request function codes

Transfer functions are those concerned with transferring defined data objects. These are the functions that acquire data from the outstation, or write control information to it.

Transfer Functions			
Code	Function	Action	Response
0	Confirm	Message fragment confirmation used by both requests and responses	No further response required
1	Read		Respond with requested data objects
2	Write	Store specified data objects in outstation	Respond with status of operation

The control functions are used to operate or change control points in an outstation. These may be control relay outputs, i.e. digital points, or analog setpoint values. These may be operated directly, with or without acknowledgment, or with the select before operate sequence.

Control Functions			
Code	**Function**	**Action**	**Response**
3	Select	Select or arm points, but do not produce any control action, or change of set point. The operate function code must be subsequently received to activate these outputs	Respond with the status of the selected control points
4	Operate	Set or produce the output actions on the points previously selected by the Select function	Respond with the status of the control points following action
5	Direct operate	Select and operate the specified outputs or control points	Respond with the status of the control points following action
6	Direct operate, no acknowledgment	Select and operate the specified outputs or control points	No response message to be sent

The select before operate sequence is a security feature that is well known in the electrical supply industry. It provides an additional level of security to ensure against miss-operation arising from a corrupted message, or a human error such as selecting the wrong device from a group of similar devices shown on an HMI screen.

Select before operate sequence requires the following to occur:

- Selection of the control points is made.
- The outstation responds with the identity and status of the selected points.
- The outstation starts a select-operate timer.
- The HMI displays the selected points differently, showing they have been selected.
- The operate function is sent for the selected points.
- The outstation will reject the operate message if the point identities do not match those of the previously selected points.
- The outstation will de-select the points if the select-operate timer expires before the operate function is received.

Freeze functions are typically used for the following:

- Record system-wide state data at a common time (e.g. midnight)
- Record status or value of specific point at regular intervals (e.g. for trending a flow rate).

The application control functions are coded in order of decreasing effect. The cold restart is a complete restart of the outstation, as if it had been de-powered and then repowered up. The warm restart may be used to reset the DNP3 application, but not necessarily do reset other application programs. Typically the warm restart is used to initialize its configuration and clear events stored in its buffers. Once either a cold or warm restart has been initiated, the master station should not attempt to communicate with the outstation until the restart time interval returned in the outstation's response has elapsed.

Freeze Functions			
Code	**Function**	**Action**	**Response**
7	Immediate freeze	Copy specified objects to a freeze buffer	Respond with status of operation. Note that the data themselves are not returned
8	Immediate freeze – no acknowledgment	Copy specified objects to a freeze buffer	No response to be sent
9	Freeze and clear	Copy specified objects to a freeze buffer, then clear the objects	Respond with status of operation. Note that the data themselves are not returned
10	Freeze and clear – no acknowledgment	Copy specified objects to a freeze buffer, then clear the objects	No response to be sent
11	Freeze with time	Copy specified objects to a freeze buffer at the specified time and thereafter at intervals (if) specified	Respond with status of operation. Note that the data themselves are not returned
12	Freeze with time – no acknowledgment	Copy specified objects to a freeze buffer at the specified time and thereafter at intervals (if) specified	No response to be sent

Application Control Functions			
Code	**Function**	**Action**	**Response**
13	Cold restart	Restart application on completion of communication sequence	Respond with time until outstation availability following restart
14	Warm restart	Partial restart on completion of communication sequence	Respond with time until outstation availability following restart
15	Initialize data to defaults	Initialize specified data to initial of default settings	Respond with status of operation
16	Initialize application	Initialize specified applications	Respond with status of operation
17	Start application	Start specified applications	Respond with status of operation
18	Stop application	Stop specified applications	Respond with status of operation

The 'initialize data to defaults' could, for example, set up standard set points, and clear counters. The specific data objects to be initialized are identified in the request, but not the default values themselves. These are stored locally in the outstation, as fixed read-only data, or as parameters in non-volatile memory, for example.

The configuration referred to by these functions is the state of the parameters and settings that collectively determine the behavior of the outstation. It is not referring to a complete program or 'configuration' download. The save configuration function causes storing in a specified non-volatile memory location the settings that define the system's configuration.

Configuration Functions			
Code	Function	Action	Response
19	Save configuration	Save the specified configuration to non-volatile memory	Respond with time outstation availability
20	Enable unsolicited messages	Enable spontaneous reporting of the specified data objects	Respond with status of operation
21	Disable unsolicited messages	Disable spontaneous reporting of the specified data objects	Respond with status of operation
22	Assign class	Assign specified data objects to a particular class	Respond with status of operation

The enable and disable of unsolicited messages allows for a live change to this configuration aspect.

The assign class function allows for live assignment of data objects to classes. These are discussed later in the text. The effect of classes is to provide a broad means of referencing data, for example, by allowing a read of all data in a particular class.

Time Synchronization Function			
Code	Function	Action	Response
23	Delay measurement	Allows measurement of the path delay between the master and the outstation. The value determined is used as an offset when setting the system time at the outstation	Response message with time delay between receipt and response, i.e. outstation processing delay time
24	Record current time	Causes outstation to record the time of its clock on completion of receipt of this command message	Respond with status (internal indications bits)

The delay measurement function is used immediately prior to performing a time setting by writing to the outstation clock. It is used over asynchronous serial links, for which the message transmission time is significant in comparison to the 1 ms clock resolution. The outstation measures the time in milliseconds that it takes to turnaround the message, that is, the time from message receipt to sending the response to the master. The master station subtracts this time from the turnaround time it sees, to determine the time the messages spent in the communication system. It then divides that time by two to obtain an approximation of the one-way message delay from master station to outstation.

The record current time function is used when performing a time setting over a LAN. In this case the transmission occurs essentially instantaneously, so no turnaround time measurement is needed. Both the master station and the outstation record the current values of their own clocks at the time this message is sent. Subsequently, the master sends its recorded time to the outstation, which calculates the its time error from the difference between the recorded values.

The file function codes provide for file operations with configuration and other files in outstation devices. Some devices may implement security features to control file access. Where required, these make use of an authentication step, where the master station submits a user name and password with the authenticate function. The outstation responds with a one-time use key, which is then used by the master in conjunction with file change operations.

File Functions			
Code	**Function**	**Action**	**Response**
25	Open file	The required file is locked to prevent use by other processes, and opened	Respond with File Command Status (Object Group 70, Variation 4)
26	Close file	The file is closed and released for use by other processes	Respond with File Command Status (Object Group 70, Variation 4)
27	Delete file	The required file is deleted, provided that it is not open. If it is open the command is not executed	Respond with File Command Status (Object Group 70, Variation 4)
28	Get file information	Provide file information: type, size, time of creation, permissions	Respond with File Descriptor Object (Object Group 70, Variation 7)
29	Authenticate	Requests an authentication key from the outstation, if required, to allow file change operations	Respond with Authentication Object (Object Group 70, Variation 2)
30	Abort	Immediately abort a file transfer operation in progress, and close the associated file without saving changes	Respond with File Command Status (Object Group 70, Variation 4)

Response functions

The response function codes apply for all messages from outstations, i.e. stations that are not designated as master stations. The only response these messages require (of the master station) is an optional confirmation on receipt by the master station.

Response Functions			
Code	**Function**	**Action**	**Response**
0	Confirm	Message fragment confirmation Used by both requests and responses	No further response required
129	Response	Respond to request	Master station will respond with confirm if CON bit set
130	Unsolicited message	Unsolicited message from outstation	Master station will respond with confirm if CON bit set

9.7.3 Internal indications

The internal indications (IIN) field (Figure 9.25) is a two-byte field that follows the function code in all responses. It is by using the internal indications that the outstation status is reported to the master following a request. Each bit in the field has a specific meaning, in accordance with the table. An outstation would have defined flags within its dynamic memory to correspond to the IIN field bits. These flags would then be copied in each response message. Descriptions of the detailed meaning of each bit are included in the following table.

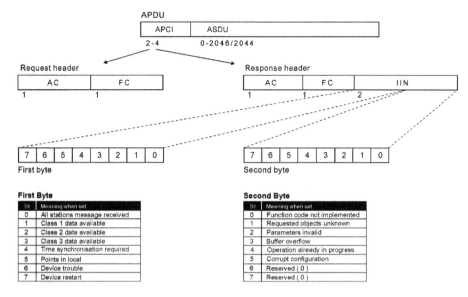

Figure 9.25
Internal indications

First Byte

Bite	Meaning When Set	Notes
0	All stations message received	Set when an address of FFFF is received. Cleared after next response. Used to confirm that a broadcast message was received by this station
1	Class 1 data available	Indicates that date of specified class is available. Master should request this data
2	Class 2 data available	
3	Class 3 data available	
4	Time synchronization required	After a restart this will be set. It is cleared during time synchronization, or by a direct write to the outstation II object
5	Points in local	Set when one or more points are inaccessible to DNP
6	Device trouble	Used when an abnormal condition is present, and this cannot be described by the other II bits
7	Device restart	Set when the user application restarts. Will be cleared when the master writes a 0 directly to this bit of the outstation II object

Second Byte

Bit	Meaning When Set	Notes
0	Function code not implemented	This function code is not available at this outstation
1	Requested objects unknown	There are no objects as specified or in the specified class
2	Parameters invalid	Parameters in the qualifier, range, or data fields are not valid or are out of range
3	Buffer overflow	Event or other application buffers have overflowed
4	Operation already in progress	This operation is already executing
5	Corrupt configuration	This is a specific problem indication showing that the master will have to download a new configuration
6	Reserved (0)	Always to return 0
7	Reserved (0)	Always to return 0

9.7.4   The object header

In DNP3, the data is always comprised of two parts, object headers and data objects. The object headers identify the data object types, and specific instances of those data that are being referenced by the message. These data may not necessarily be contained in the message; for example, a read request carries only the references identifying which data is required. The response to the read request will contain both the data identification and the data itself. The position of the object headers and data objects within the application protocol data unit, or message frame, is shown in Figure 9.26.

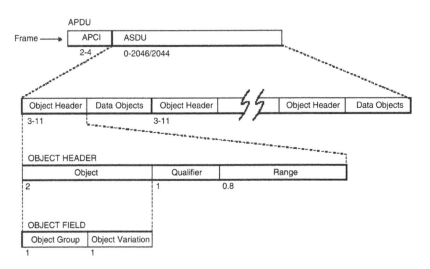

Figure 9.26
The object header

The ASDU is made up of one or more object header and data object fields, up to a maximum frame size of 2048 bytes including the frame header (the APCI).

The object header is between three and eleven bytes in length, and is made up of the object, qualifier and range fields. The object field is further sub-divided into two bytes, which are the object group and object variation respectively. The range is between 0 and 8 bytes.

The object field

The object field (Figure 9.27) is made up of the object group and the object variation bytes. The group specifies the general type of data, such as analog inputs. The variation specifies a particular variation of that type of data. A list of the object groups is shown in the table below. Full details of these and the object variations for each group is included under Section 5.8 Data object library.

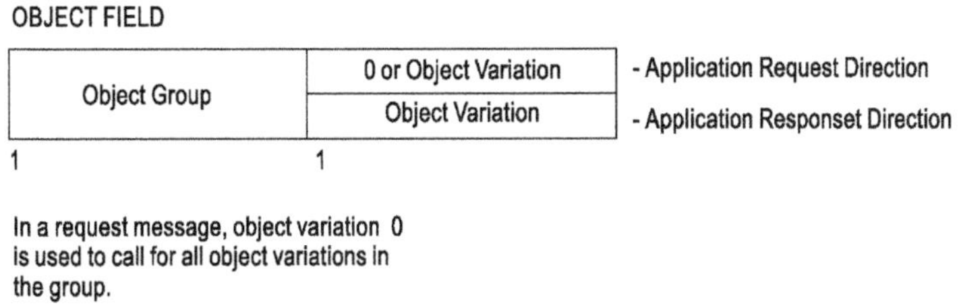

OBJECT FIELD

| Object Group | 0 or Object Variation | - Application Request Direction |
| | Object Variation | - Application Responset Direction |

1   1

In a request message, object variation 0
is used to call for all object variations in
the group.

Figure 9.27
The object field

Table of Object Groups

Group Range	Object Group Description
0–9	Binary input objects
10–19	Binary output objects
20–29	Counter objects
30–39	Analog input objects
40–49	Analog output objects
50–59	Time objects
60–69	Class objects
70–79	File objects
80–89	Device objects
90–99	Application objects
100+	Alternate numeric objects

It can be seen from the table that the object groups are organized into decade ranges. Within each decade, there may be more than one object group. Each of these groups has its variations, making altogether a substantial number individual objects.

Object variation zero

Object variation zero (0) is not used within any group, because this is reserved for a special purpose. When a master station specifies object variation zero in a request message, this defined to mean all variations of that particular object group. This allows the master station to obtain all object variations without identifying each one.

9.7.5 The qualifier and range fields

In the following sub-sections the operation of the qualifier and range fields are presented. After looking at the structure of these fields, and the meaning of the codes they contain, the different means of referencing data are presented. In the discussion, use is made of referencing 'modes'. It is noted that the mode labels used here are not included within the DNP3 documentation, but are applied here to assist understanding of this complicated area.

It is noted that the reader may find point referencing in DNP3 somewhat difficult to grasp. This arises from the flexibility of referencing that has been provided for by the protocol. At the same time, it may be observed that although a number of different referencing modes and variations for each are defined in DNP3, in practice only a small number are generally used.

Purpose and structure

The qualifier and range fields follow the object field in the object header. These fields are used to identify the specific data points of each object group and variation that are being referred to. For example, this may simply be a range of consecutive points, in which case the start and stop point indexes will be included in the range field. Alternatively, a list of non-consecutive points may be required, and in this case the list of points must be provided separately. These cases, and others are all handled by the qualifier and range field values.

The qualifier and range fields are used both in request messages from master stations, and in response messages from outstations. For request messages, only identification of the data may be required. In response messages the data objects themselves may be included in the message.

The structure of the qualifier field is shown in Figure 9.28.

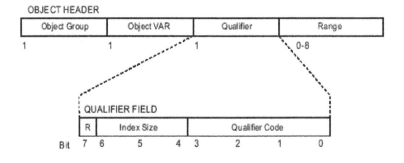

Figure 9.28
The qualifier field

The qualifier field is made up of two sub-fields. These are the qualifier code (or Q-code) and the index size (or I-size). The primary meaning of the qualifier field is provided by the qualifier code value. The index-size sub-field provides additional information required for some qualifier code values. These sub-fields, together with the following range field, act to fully identify the data object that follows each object header.

Qualifier codes

In the following table, a summary of the qualifier codes is presented. Understanding the meaning of the table hinges on understanding the different modes of referencing that are used. These are explained in the sub-sections following the table.

From the qualifier code table it may be seen that there are five different referencing modes, or ways of referencing or identifying the data objects contained within messages. Also, for some of the referencing modes there are three Q-codes applicable. These allow for three different bit-sizes for the numbers in the range field.

Qualifier Code Table

Q Code	Interpretation of Qualifier Code		
	Range Value Size (Bits)	Referencing Mode	Notes
0	8	Range-index mode	The range field contains start and stop indexes points are I1 to I2. I-size = 0, or 4–6 for individual object size prefixes
1	16		
2	32		
3	8	Range-absolute mode	The Range field contains start and stop absolute memory addresses in outstation. Data are Bytes B1 to B2. I-size = 0, or 4–6 for individual object size prefixes (response messages only)
4	16		
5	32		
6	–	All object mode	Specifies all objects in the referenced group/variation. Only used for requests. There is no range field with this mode. I-size must = 0
7 8 9	8 16 32	Non-ranged mode	Specifies a list of unrelated points. The Range field contains the number of points referenced I-size = 0: No indexes, points only I-size = 1: Indexes are 8 bit I-size = 2: Indexes are 16 bit I-size = 3: Indexes are 32 bit
11	As for I-size	Object identifier mode	The Range field contains the number of Object Identifiers following. Each Object Identifier is preceded by a 'Size' field. The size of the Size and Range fields depends on I-size: I-size = 1: Fields are 8 bit I-size = 2: Fields are 16 bit I-size = 3: Fields are 32 bit

The index-size sub-field

For most of the referencing modes, additional information is provided by the I-size sub-field. The specific meaning of the sub-field is dependent on the referencing mode. In each case where the I-size sub-field is used (i.e. is non-zero), it gives the size of additional fields that are given for each data object. Depending on the referencing mode, these extra fields contain either an identifier, an index, or a number giving the object size in bytes.

The I-size codes are shown in the table below. The use of these is demonstrated in the following sub-sections for each referencing mode.

Table of Index-Size Codes

I-size Code	Size in Bits	Meaning in Request with Q-code = 11	Meaning in Request or Response Containing Data Objects
0	No index		No indexing. Objects are packed directly
1	8	Identifier field size	Objects are prefixed with an index of this length
2	16		
3	32		
4	8		Objects are prefixed with an object size field of this length
5	16		
6	32		

Range-index mode

The range-index mode is indicated by Q-codes 0, 1, and 2.

In this mode the range field contains two numbers. These are the start and stop index values for the data objects.

Index values imply that in the outstation there is an index giving a one-to-one correspondence between the value of the index, and the actual locations within the device memory of the data objects. The use of indexes simplifies referencing of data objects because regardless of the object's size, each consecutive number represents successive data objects. If the start and stop numbers are I1 and I2, then there are a total of $I2 - I1 + 1$ data objects being referenced.

In the diagrams following, Q-code 0 is used, defining the range-index mode with eight-bit indexes. These can reference a maximum of 256 data objects. In the request message only the header is present. In the response message, the data objects follow the message.

In the response message only, it is possible to prefix each data object returned with an object size identifier. When this is desired, the I-size field is used to specify the size of the object size fields. This would only be required if the object sizes were variable within an object variation group. When object size fields are not required, the I-size field is set to zero, meaning the objects are packed in sequence without size fields. The diagrams following show the structure of the messages for each of these cases.

REQUEST MESSAGE OBJECT GROUP

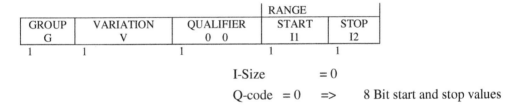

GROUP G	VARIATION V	QUALIFIER 0 0	RANGE START I1	STOP I2
1	1	1	1	1

$$I\text{-Size} \qquad = 0$$

$$Q\text{-code} \ = 0 \quad => \qquad 8 \text{ Bit start and stop values}$$

RESPONSE MESSAGE OBJECT GROUP

GROUP G	VARIATION V	QUALIFIER 0 0	RANGE START I1	STOP I2	DATA OBJECTS DO I1+1	DO I1+1	DO I1+2	...
1	1	1	1	1	x	x	x	

Note: Size of data objects x = determined by object group/variation definition

Qualifier Codes for Range-Index Mode

Q Code	Interpretation of Qualifier Code		
	Range Value Size (Bits)	Referencing Mode	Notes
0	8	Range-index mode	The Range field contains start and stop indexes. Points are I1 to I2. I-size = 0, or 4–6 for individual object size prefixes
1	16		
2	32		

- Non-zero index-size is valid only with response messages (for this mode)
- It is used when object size prefixes are required before each data object
- The I-size codes 4, 5, and 6 are valid
- They define 8-, 16-, and 32-bit object size fields respectively.

RESPONSE MESSAGE OBJECT GROUP

GROUP G	VARIATION V	QUALIFIER 4 0	RANGE START I1	STOP I2	DATA OBJECT SIZE I1	DO I1	SIZE I1+1	DO I1+1	...	SIZE I2	
1	1	1	1	1	1	x	x	x		1	

Note: Size of data objects is determined individually by each object size prefix

Qualifier Codes for Range-Index Mode

Q Code	Interpretation of Qualifier Code		
	Range Value Size (Bits)	Referencing Mode	Notes
0	8	Range-index mode	The Range field contains start and stop Indexes. Points are I1 to I2. I-size = 0, or 4–6 for individual object size prefixes (response messages only)
1	16		
2	32		

Range-absolute mode

The range-absolute mode is indicated by Q-codes 3, 4, and 5.

This mode is similar to the range-index mode in that the range field contains start and stop values. However, these values represent absolute memory addresses rather than index numbers. This mode is intended for use as a diagnostic tool during manufacturing. This is because use of this mode requires detailed knowledge of the memory structure to interpret the information returned.

In the example following, Q-code 4 is used, defining the absolute-index mode with 16-bit indexes. These can reference a maximum of 65 536 data objects. It is noted when multi-byte indexes are used, they are given in order of lowest significant byte to highest significant byte, i.e. LSB, MSB.

As for the range-index mode, it is also possible to use object size prefixes in the response message. To do this the I-size code is set to 4, 5, or 6 to select 6-, 16-, or 32-bit object size prefixes. These have not been illustrated, as the concept has already been demonstrated for the range-index mode.

10

Fundamentals of IEC 60870-5

10.1 The IEC 60870-5 standard

10.1.1 Overall structure of the standard

The standard IEC 60870-5 was produced by the International Electrotechnical Commission Technical Committee 57, Working Group 03, and published progressively from 1988.

The structure of IEC 60870-5 was introduced in the preview Section 8.1. This showed how the standard is structured in a hierarchical manner, and illustrated how the companion standards relate to the other sections making up Part 5. Table 10.1 extends the preview information by showing the full structure of IEC 60870, together with the years of publication of the component parts and sections.

The sections IEC 60870-5-1 to IEC 60870-5-5 are the core specification documents for Part 5, the Transmission Protocols part of the standard. The companion standard sections, or simply companion standards, IEC 60870-5-101 to IEC 60870-5-104, are each separate application protocols intended for specific purposes. They provide the definitions of application level data objects and functions to completely define a working protocol. They are also referred to as profiles, and may sometimes be given the shorthand references T101, T102, T103, and T104, the T standing for telecontrol.

As shown in the preview, IEC 60870-5-101 provided the first complete working SCADA protocol under IEC 60870-5. This defines all the necessary application level functions and data objects to provide for telecontrol applications operating over geographically wide areas, using low bandwidth bit-serial communications. It covers general communications with RTUs, including data types and services that are suitable for electrical and substation systems. The data types are generic and suitable for wider SCADA applications.

The IEC 60870-5-102 and IEC 60870-5-103 companion standards provide data types and functions to support electrical protection systems. These include distance protection, line differential protection, and transformer differential protection.

As explained in the preview, the IEC 60870-5-104 companion standard has special significance. This defines operation of the transmission protocol over networks using standard transport profiles specifying the TCP and IP protocols. This companion standard is not really independent of IEC 60870-5-101, but replaces the message transport sections with a network version, leaving the application level functions largely unaltered.

Main Parts

Reference	Description	Year
IEC 60870-1	General considerations	1988
IEC 60870-2	Operating conditions	1995
IEC 60870-3	Interfaces (electrical characteristics)	1989
IEC 60870-4	Performance requirements	1990
IEC 60870-5	Transmission protocols	1990
IEC 60870-6	Telecontrol protocols compatible with ISO and ITU-T recommendations	1995

Sections of IEC 60870-5

Reference	Description	Year
IEC 60870-5-1	Transmission frame formats	1990
IEC 60870-5-2	Link transmission procedures	1992
IEC 60870-5-3	General structure of application data	1992
IEC 60870-5-4	Definition and coding of application information elements	1993
IEC 60870-5-5	Basic application functions	1995

Companion Standards of IEC 60870-5

Reference	Description	Year
IEC 60870-5-101	Companion standard for basic telecontrol tasks	1995
IEC 60870-5-102	Companion standard for transmission of integrated totals	1996
IEC 60870-5-103	Companion standard for protection communication	1997
IEC 60870-5-104	Network access using standard transport profiles	2000

Table 10.1
Full structure of IEC 60870 standard

10.1.2 Development of standards

IEC standards are subject to review and the issue of amendments from time to time, and since the publication of IEC 60870-5-101, this profile has had two amendments issued. The first amendment added a small number of information object definitions. The second amendment added a significant amount of clarifying detail, the purpose of which was to remove ambiguities and so better provide for interoperability. It is anticipated that during 2002 the standard will be reissued as one document including the two amendments.

The complete version of this profile with amendments is as shown in Table 10.2.

10.1.3 Obtaining standards

Should access to the standards be required, they may be purchased on-line from the IEC (at www.iec.ch). As an alternative that may be less expensive, it is worth checking if they have been published as a national standard, as is often the case. In Australia, IEC 60870-5 sections 1 to 5 are available as AS 60870.5.1 to AS 60870.5.5 and are available online (at www.standards.com.au). However, the companion standards are not presently available and must be obtained from the IEC.

Reference	Description	Year-Month
IEC 60870-5-101	Companion standard for basic telecontrol tasks	1995–11
IEC 60870-5-101-am1	Companion standard for basic telecontrol tasks amendment 1	2000–04
IEC 60870-5-101-am2	Companion standard for basic telecontrol tasks amendment 2	2001–10

Table 10.2
IEC 60870-5-101 including amendments

An alternative to purchase of the standards is to view them at a public or university library.

10.1.4   Description of contents

In this section the contents of each section of IEC 60870-5 are briefly described. This is intended to provide a guide to assist the reader should it be necessary to refer to them.

IEC 60870-5-1 1990: transmission frame formats

This describes the operation of the physical and data-link layers in terms of the services provided to higher layers. It provides a choice of four data-link frame types identified as FT1.1, FT1.2, FT2, and FT3, each with a different level of security against data errors. Fixed- and variable-length versions of the frames are described, and a set of transmission rules is provided for each. Two single-control character transmissions are provided as an efficient means of transmitting control information such as acknowledgments.

IEC 60870-5-1 1990: link transmission procedures

This section represents the four frame formats from IEC 60870-5-1 and then describes the internal processes in terms of the service primitives and transmission procedures. The service primitives are the control indications passed between the link layer and its higher level user, and the transmission procedures describe the sequence of events occurring over the physical communications link. A control field is described that is transmitted over the link and is used by the link layer procedures of each side of the link in controlling the transmission process. The terms unbalanced and balanced transmissions are presented and used to describe whether transmission can be initiated only by a master station or by any station. Services and transmission procedures are presented in detail for both unbalanced and balanced transmissions.

IEC 60870-5-3 1992: general structure of application data

This section presents two models of the structure of data at the application level. The reference model 2 version shows how application user data, for example, point information to be transmitted, is encapsulated within an application protocol data unit, with or without application protocol control information added, and then passed to the underlying link layer for transmission. It also describes a general structure for application data, and rules for forming application data units in general.

IEC 60870-5-4 1993: definition and coding of application information elements

This section provides rules for the definition of information elements, and defines a common set of information elements that may be used for transmission of information in telecontrol applications. These include generic elements such as signed and unsigned integers, fixed and floating-point numbers, bit-strings, and time elements. The intention of this section is to provide a set of information building blocks from which a companion standard, or profile can utilize selectively to build a complete set of application level information objects. No such set of information objects is selected by this section, however.

IEC 60870-5-5 1995: basic application functions

This section describes the highest level functions of the transmission protocol, which are those application functions above layer 7 of the OSI model. Application service primitives are the request and response indications passed between the application layer and the application user. Application functions are described.

A set of basic application functions and associated service primitives, or requests and indications, are presented. These cover the highest level functions that would be required to carry out telecontrol operations. They include station initialization, methods of acquiring data, clock synchronization, transmission of commands, totaliser counts, and file transfer. Again, it is stated in this section that it would be the role of a specific companion standard to select from these functions and possibly add to them in defining a complete working protocol.

IEC 60870-5-101 1995: companion standard for basic telecontrol tasks (including amendments 1 and 2)

The companion standard defines a complete telecontrol protocol by detailing selections from options described in sections 1 to 5 of IEC 60870 Part 5, and by defining a complete set of application service data units (ASDUs). Its main subsections are listed below, and a short description of the contents of these follows this list.

- General rules
- Physical layer
- Link layer
- Application layer and user process
- Interoperability.

General rules

This is really an introduction that states the main selections made for the physical layer, link layer, application layer, and user process. They in effect provide a brief overview of each of the following sections.

Physical layer

This describes the requirements for the interface with external data communication equipment using standard ITU-T V.24/V.28 (RS-232) or balanced X.24/X.27 (RS-485) signals. The types of fixed network configurations such as point-to-point, and multi-point, are described.

Link layer

Selections of the frame format F1.2, and the fixed and variable frame lengths are made. The detailed operation of the link layer is specified, making selections from IEC 60870-5-2. Operation of the link is described for both unbalanced and balanced operations, which corresponds to whether only the master station, or any station, may initiate message transmissions. Amendment 2 contains significant additional information clarifying the procedures with the use of state transition diagrams.

Application layer and user process

This defines the overall structure of the application level data, the ASDU, defines the set of ASDUs available, and makes selections of application functions from IEC 60870-5-5. The definition of ASDUs is carried out in two subsections. The first subsection defines the available information elements. These are used in the second subsection as building blocks in constructing the full set of ASDUs. The user process subsection makes selections from IEC 60870-5-5 and includes additional detail for some of the functions.

Interoperability

This provides a check-box method for specifying the particular features supported by a specific product, under the following type headers:

- System or device
- Network configuration
- Physical layer
- Link layer
- Application layer.

10.2   Protocol architecture

10.2.1   EPA and OSI reference models

As for DNP3, IEC 60870-5 is based on the three-layer enhanced performance architecture or EPA model for data communications. These models are described in detail in Section 2 of this text, which shows how the EPA model is a simplified form of the OSI seven-layer reference model to provide optimum performance for telecontrol applications.

In Figure 10.1, the relationship between the OSI model and the EPA model is represented. This shows that the EPA model basically omits the presentation, session, and transport layers of the OSI model.

The structure of the EPA model is appropriate for a continuously operating system that operates over a single network. One layer normally added to the top of the basic EPA model representation is identified as the user layer. This is included to represent the various functions or processes that must be defined to provide telecontrol system operations. These must be defined to provide for the interoperability between equipment that will result in a fully operable telecontrol system, rather than merely a data communication system.

For the first defined companion standard IEC 60870-5-101 or T101 profile, a four-layer model, as illustrated at the right-hand side of Figure 10.1, provides an accurate representation of the architecture of the protocol. In the case of the networked version IEC 60870-5-104, or the T104 profile, additional layers of the OSI model must be included to provide for transport of messages over networks using standard network protocols. These are the transport and network layers corresponding to the use of the TCP and IP protocols.

The two architectures are shown in Figure 10.2.

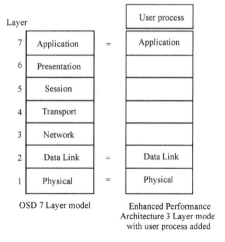

Figure 10.1
Relationship of EPA model to OSI seven-layer model

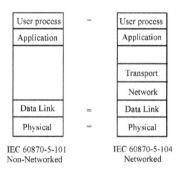

Figure 10.2
Architectures for T101 and T104

As is clear from Figure 10.2, the operation of the lower layers of the networked version, IEC 60870-5-104 is completely different from that of the non-networked version, IEC 60870-5-101. These layers correspond to all the layers below the application layer, which for these architectures are the layers concerned with message transport.

10.2.2   Selections from standards

The benefit of the OSI reference model, and the EPA models derived from it and shown in Figure 10.2, is that they provide a framework for description of protocol operation. Describing the operation of the protocol is a matter of specifying the functions of each layer, and specifying the structure of information passing between the layers.

Under the IEC standard, it is the companion standard IEC 60870-5-101 that completely specifies the protocol. It does this by referring to the main sections of the IEC 60870-5 standard, and by making particular selections from options that may be available within those sections.

Table 10.3 shows how the different sections of the IEC 60870-5 set of standards correspond with the layers of the model.

Layer	Source	Selections
User process	IEC 60870-5-5	Application functions
Application	IEC 60870-5-4	Application information elements
	IEC 60870-5-3	ASDUs
Link	IEC 60870-5-2	Transmission procedures
	IEC 60870-5-1	Frame formats
Physical	ITU-T	Interface specification

Table 10.3
Standards selections for IEC 60870-5-101

For comparison the corresponding information for the networked version IEC 60870-5-104 is shown in Table 10.4. This illustrates how the lower layers of the IEC 60870-5-101 companion standard have been completely replaced by the standard TCP/IP transport profiles.

Layer	Source	Selections
User process	IEC 60870-5-101	Application functions
Application	IEC 60870-5-101	ASDUs and application information elements
Transport		
Network	TCP/IP transport and network protocol suite	
Link		
Physical		

Table 10.4
Standards selection for IEC 60870-5-104

10.3   Physical layer

The physical layer is concerned with the transmission and reception of data over the physical medium. This level is concerned with the transmission of bits and bytes, but not with the meaning of those bytes. The physical interface is defined in terms of the electrical characteristics, and individual signals passing over the interface.

The definition of the physical layer includes specification of the signal interface between the IEC 60870-5 and the communications devices to external world, and the network configurations that are attached to these. These are illustrated in Figure 10.3. This shows a SCADA master station server connected to a radio modem via a serial port operating at 9.6 kB/s. The radio modems form a multipoint-star configuration in which the master communicates with both outstations simultaneously, and either outstation can communicate back to the master.

10.3.1   Communications interface

To allow the use of standard data communications equipment, the standard utilizes existing widely used standards covering the exchange of between data terminal equipment (DTE) and data communication equipment (DCE). These communication interface standards are the ITU-T equivalents to the well-known Electrical Industries Association RS-232 and RS-485 standards. These provide for unbalanced and balanced full-duplex serial data transmission between the data device and communications equipment such as a modem.

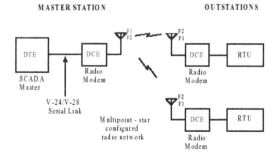

Figure 10.3
Interfacing to communications network

The use of this interface is illustrated in Figure 10.3, at the connection between the server of a SCADA master station, and a radio modem. The DTE–DCE interface is simply an RS-232 cable between a serial port of the computer, and a similar port on the radio modem. It is also used between the RTUs and their radio modems.

The data transmission speeds are defined as follows (Table 10.5):

Interface Type	Transmission Speed (bits/s)
V.24/V.28 FSK interface V.24/V.28 Modern interface X.24/X.27 Synchronous	100, 200, 300, 600, 1200 300, 600, 1200, 2400, 4800, 9600 2400, 4800, 9600, 19200, 38400 56000,64000

Table 10.5
DTE–DCE interface transmission speeds

In addition to interfaces using the specified standards, it should be noted that the T101 profile does allow the use of other physical interfaces by agreement between vendor and user.

10.3.2   Network configurations

The T101 profile specifies support for the following network configurations or topology:

- Point-to-point
- Multiple point-to-point
- Multipoint-star
- Multipoint-party line
- Multipoint-ring.

These are defined by IEC 60870-1-1, and are depicted in Figure 10.4. In the figure the square symbols represent controlling or master stations, and the triangles represent controlled, or outstations. The small circles at the points of connection are the ports.

From the diagram it may be seen that these fall into two basic types: point-to-point and multi-point. A point-to-point link has one master station and one outstation. A multi-point network has a master station connected to a number of outstations. The ring configuration is only different in that it incorporates redundancy by providing a second port on the master station that can be used for communications should the ring be broken.

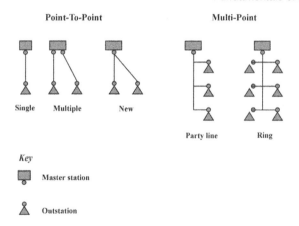

Figure 10.4
Network configurations

In the point-to-point configurations either the master or the outstation(s) can transmit messages, provided that a full-duplex channel is used. In the multi-point configurations the master communicates in parallel to all connected outstations. The outstations share a return communications channel, and therefore only one may transmit at a time.

Note that combinations of links may form a hierarchical network where intermediate RTUs may act as local master stations to RTUs connected to them. These are sometimes referred to as sub-master stations.

10.4   Data-link layer

The data-link layer is responsible for the passing of data across the communications channel, and ensuring that the data is received in full and uncorrupted by errors. It does this using a unit of data known as a frame, combined with procedures to govern its transmission and reception. The frame is made up of an amount of data that is large enough to carry control information such as a destination address, checking information used to detect errors, and a payload of data, if required. It is also an amount of data that is not too large, so that a transmission error will not cause the loss of too much data, or so that timing discrepancies between transmitter and receiver can lead to loss of synchronism.

IEC 60870-5-101, or T101, specifies the operation of the data-link layer by referring to and making selections from the standards identified in Table 10.1, repeated in the following extract:

Link Layer	IEC 60870-5-2	Transmission procedures
	IEC 60870-5-1	Frame formats

In this section the operation of the data-link layer is explained in detail, commencing with the data frame structure and then looking at the transmission procedures.

10.4.1   Frame format

The frame format used by T101 is referred to as the FT1.2 format. There are two forms of this, one of fixed length and the other of variable length. The fixed-length frame is restricted to use for frames carrying no user data, and therefore is used only for data-link control command and acknowledgment frames. In addition to the fixed- and variable-length frames, there is a 'single control character' frame, which consists of a single byte. This may be used for acknowledgment only.

These frames are shown in Figures 10.5 and 10.6. Figure 10.5 shows the actual bit pattern that would be seen on the physical channel, interpreted from left to right. This representation includes the start and stop bits that are transmitted with every byte or octet of the frame. The overall frame construction is shown in Figure 10.6. This does not represent the bit pattern, but shows only the information content down to the octet level. For consistency with the applicable standards, these are presented vertically in octet order. Thus, the first octet is shown at the top, and following octets are shown below. Clarification of the order of bits and octets is included in the following section.

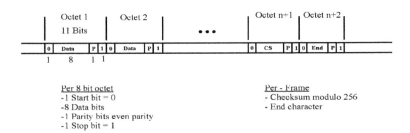

Per 8 bit octet
-1 Start bit = 0
-8 Data bits
-1 Parity bits even parity
-1 Stop bit = 1

Per - Frame
- Checksum modulo 256
- End character

Figure 10.5
Bit-sequence representation of FT1.2 frame

Variable Length Frame	Fixed Length Frame	Single Control Character
Start 0x68	Start 0x10	0xE5
L	C	
L	A	
Start 0x68	A	
C	Checksum	
A	End 0x16	
A		
Link user data		
Checksum		
End 0x16		

Key:

L = Length 0..255
C = Control field
A = Address field

Figure 10.6
FT1.2 frame options under IEC 60870-5-101

From the bit-sequence representation in Figure 10.5, it is possible to see that the maximum data rate of the frame is approximately eight-elevenths of the bit transmission rate. This is reduced further when the frame overheads such as addressing, start and stop characters, checksum, and control information are accounted for. These overheads can be seen in Figure 10.6, which shows the overall frame structure.

The following points are noted about the data-link frames:

- Only the variable length frame can carry user data.
- The variable length frame can carry up to 253 octets of link user data.
- The length L is repeated twice, and the two values of L must be equal for the frame to be accepted as valid.

- The maximum frame length is 261 octets. However, a lower maximum frame length may be specified by a manufacturer or by the system user as a system parameter.
- The fixed length frame is 5 or 6 octets long.
- Address field A may be 1 or 2 octets, determined by a fixed system parameter.
- A broadcast address is defined as 0xFF or 0xFFFF for 1 and 2 octet addresses, respectively.
- The checksum is the modulo-256 sum of the frame user data (not the link user data). This is the data between the last start character and the checksum, *L* octets for the variable frame.
- Rules state that no more than one bit-time idle interval is allowed between characters within the frame, and that an idle interval of 33 bit-times must be allowed after detection of a frame error by the receiver.

10.4.2   Order of information

One technical detail that can be difficult to find in the standards is the ordering of bits and bytes. Under IEC 60870-5, as for DNP3, the following ordering is standard.

Bits are transmitted starting with the least significant byte (LSB) and ending with the most significant byte (MSB). When a bit-sequence representation as in Figure 10.5 is given, the bits are shown in this order. However, when the structure of a message in terms of bytes or octets is depicted, the msb is at the left, and the lsb is at the right, which is consistent with the numerical weighting of the bits. A good way to mentally resolve this is to envisage the octet being right-shifted out of a UART register onto the communication channel.

Similarly, for bytes, the least significant byte (LSB) is transmitted first, and the most significant byte (MSB) is transmitted last. The ordering of bits and bytes is illustrated in Figure 10.7.

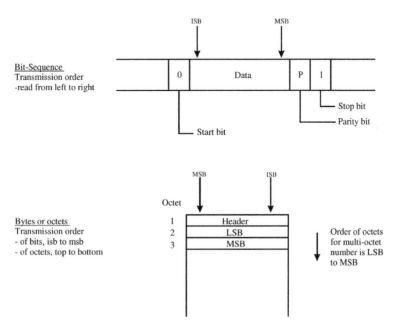

Figure 10.7
Order of information

10.4.3 Link layer concepts

This section presents some concepts that are important for understanding the operation of the link layer transmission procedures. The detailed operation of link layer is then discussed in terms of these concepts.

These are:

- Primary and secondary
- Unbalanced and balanced
- Service procedures
- Service primitives
- Transmission procedures.

Primary and secondary

The terms primary and secondary refer to the ability of a station to initiate communications on a communication channel. Only a primary station can initiate communications. Secondary stations must wait until they are polled by the primary station before they can transmit data. More accurately these terms are applied to individual communications ports of stations, because in a hierarchical system, an intermediate station will be both a controlled and a controlling station. This is illustrated in Figure 10.8. This shows a hierarchical network configuration with primary and secondary ports marked P and S.

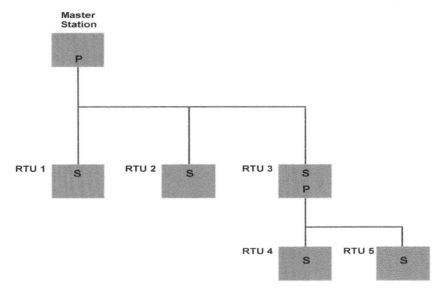

Figure 10.8
Primary and secondary stations

In Figure 10.8 RTU 3 is both a controlling and controlled station. Note that each of the two communications links has only one primary station.

Unbalanced and balanced transmission

The terms 'unbalanced transmission' and 'balanced transmission' are related to the terms 'primary' and 'secondary'. Unbalanced transmission refers to the configuration where the controlling station acts as a primary on the link, and one or more controlled stations act as secondary stations. The stations are not peer-to-peer at the link level, and so are unbalanced in their functionality.

This is the situation in Figure 10.8 for each of the two communications links. In this configuration the controlling station must acquire data from the controlled stations by polling each in turn for data. This is because they cannot initiate transmissions on their own. The advantage of unbalanced communication is that there is no possibility of collisions between controlled stations attempting to transmit information at the same time.

Balanced transmission refers to the configuration where any station on a link may act as a primary, which means it can initiate communications. This configuration is also known as peer-to-peer communications.

Under IEC 60870-5-101, only point-to-point (that is two station) links can be balanced. Multi-point links must be unbalanced. This is in contrast to DNP3, which uses balanced transmission only, and therefore has to have procedures to overcome collisions which can occur when more than one outstation commences communications simultaneously.

A balanced communications link is shown in Figure 10.9. In this case a master station is connected via a point-to-point link to a sub-master station. Note that each station can act as a primary and a secondary at the ports for this link. These may in fact be thought of as two separate processes within each station, which in fact is how they are logically within the stations. Station A has a primary process and a secondary process operating simultaneously for that link, and Station B has the same.

Figure 10.9
Balanced communications

Figure 10.10 shows the primary and secondary processes for unbalanced transmission. The processes are represented by circles identified as primary (P) or secondary (S). The primary station implements the primary process only, and the secondary stations each implement a secondary process only. Note that in effect there is a separate logical link for each secondary station and it is necessary for the primary to keep a record of the state of each link.

Figure 10.11 shows the processes for balanced transmission. In this case there is a primary and secondary process for each station.

Service procedures

The term 'services' is descriptive of the function of the link layer, it provides specific services to the user, which is the application layer, to carry out the transmission of data.

There are three main types of services provided by the data-link layer, which have the following names:

1. Send/No Reply
2. Send/Confirm
3. Request/Respond.

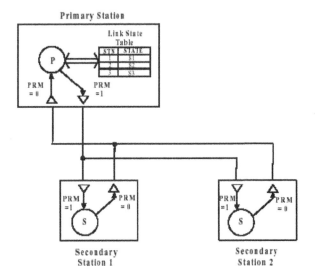

Figure 10.10
Balanced transmission processes

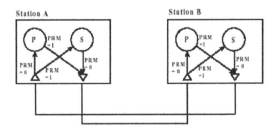

Figure 10.11
Balanced transmission processes

The Send/No Reply service is used to send a message or command for which no reply is required from the addressed station. It is used for sending broadcast messages and for messages for which receipt confirmation is not important. The Send/Confirm service is used to send a command or data which must be reliably transmitted. For this service a confirmation response is required. The Request/Respond service is used to obtain data from the controlled station. In this case the controlled station responds not with a confirmation, but with the required data.

These services are illustrated in Figure 10.12. This shows the link layer of two stations on a communication channel, and a time-sequence diagram of the service interactions. At each side are shown the commands, data, and responses that are passed between the link layer and the service user, which is the application layer. These are termed the 'service primitives'. In the center the message transmission is labeled with the transmission procedure name.

The transmission procedures are a set of rules that ensure that transmissions are successfully carried out in response to link user requests. They must be able to cope with errors on the transmission channel that may introduce errors, or cause information to be lost. The transmission procedures are different for unbalanced and balanced links, and described for each in the following sections.

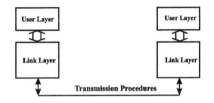

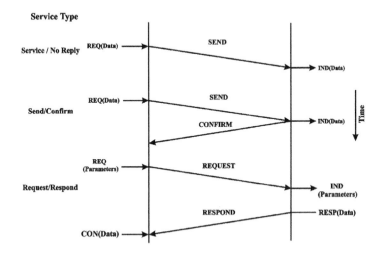

Figure 10.12
Link layer services

Link initialization

Link initialization is a data-link service carried out after a station has been off-line and first becomes available again. While the slave station is off-line the master periodically sends link status request functions until a status of link response is obtained. The sequences are shown following for both unbalanced and balanced modes.

Station/link initialization, unbalanced mode:

- Master sends link status request until status of link received
- Master sends link reset
- Link is active on receipt of ACK
- Slave generates station initialization complete event.

Station/link initialization, balanced mode:

- Each station sends link status request until status of link is received
- Each station sends link reset
- Link is active on receipt of ACK at each station
- One or both may generate station initialization complete event.

10.4.4   Unbalanced transmission procedures

Unbalanced transmission procedures are required for links other than point-to-point, that is multi-point links. For these links the controlling station must control the data traffic by polling the outstations for data. Only when the controlling or primary station on a link polls a particular secondary station may that station respond.

The control field

The control field of the data frame is central to the operation of the transmission procedures. This field is almost identical to that used by the DNP3 protocol because it was derived from the same source document, IEC 60870-5-2 1992. The interpretation of the control field is dependent on whether the communication is a primary or secondary message. Figure 10.13 shows the control field for unbalanced transmission procedures, including the short descriptions of the meanings of the function codes for primary and secondary messages.

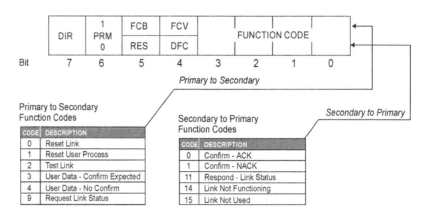

Figure 10.13
Control field – unbalanced transmission

Code	Meaning	Description
PRM	Primary message	1 => Frame from primary or initiating station
PCB	Frame count bit	Alternates between 0 and 1 for sequential frames
FCV	Frame count valid	1 => FCB is valid
		0 => ignore FCB
RES	Reserved	= 0
DFC	Data flow control bit	Set to 1 by secondary station if further send of user data will cause buffer overflow
ACD	Access demand bit	Set to 1 if there is Class 1 data available

Table 10.6
Control field bit meanings – unbalanced transmission

Table 10.7 shows the detailed meanings for the function codes in the control field (Table 10.6). The function codes are also shown in short form in Figure 10.11. The meanings are different depending on whether the message is a primary or a secondary transmission. The frame count bit is used in the primary direction only, and is only valid for certain functions. This is indicated by the state of the frame count valid bit.

Function Codes from Primary Station

Function Codes	Frame Type	Service Function	FCY Bit
0	SEND–CONFIRM expected	Reset of remote link	0
1	SEND–CONFIRM expected	Reset of user process	0

Function Codes	Frame Type	Service Function	FCY Bit
2	SEND–CONFIRM expected	Reserved	–
3	SEND–CONFIRM expected	User data	1
4	SEND–NO REPLY expected	User data (unconfirmed)	0
8	REQUEST–RESPOND expected	Request for access demand	0
9	REQUEST–RESPOND expected	Request status of link	0
10	REQUEST–RESPOND expected	Request user data class 1	1
11	REQUEST–RESPOND expected	Request user data class 2	1

Codes 5–7, 12–15 are reserved.

Function Codes from Secondary Station

Function Code*	Frame Type	Service Function
0	CONFIRM	ACK – positive acknowledgment**
1	CONFIRM	NACK – Message not accepted, link busy
8	RESPOND	User data
9	RESPOND	NACK – Requested data not available
11	RESPOND	Status of link (DFC = 0 or 1) or access demand
14		Link service not functioning
15		Link service not used or implemented

*Codes 2–7, 10, 12–13 are reserved.
**Note that control code 0 x E5 may be used in place of the FC0 or FC9 frames.

Table 10.7
Function codes – unbalanced transmission

The functions of the control bits are explained in more detail in the following paragraphs.

Primary bit

The PRM bit is set if the frame is primary (initiating) or a secondary (responding). This is used directly by the link layer in interpreting the function code.

Frame count bits

These are the frame count bit (FCB) and the frame count valid bit (FCV). These bits are only used for primary messages. The frame count bit is used to detect losses or duplication of frames to a secondary station. The frame count valid bit enables the use of the FCB. When the FCV bit is true, the FCB is toggled for each successful SEND–CONFIRM transaction between the same primary and secondary stations.

How they work is like this:

- Following data-link start-up or a failed transaction, a secondary station will not accept any primary SEND–CONFIRM frames with FCV = 1 until a reset transaction is completed. This means it will only accept either a RESET link or a RESET user process command.
- After a secondary station receives a RESET link frame from a primary and it responds with a CONFIRM, that link will be operational until a frame transmission error occurs.

- The secondary station will expect the next frame to contain FCV = 1 and FCB = 1.
- The next primary SEND–CONFIRM message will have FCV = 1 and FCB = 1. The secondary station will accept this as the FCB is valid and is set, as expected.
- Each subsequent primary SEND–CONFIRM message will have the FCB cleared or set in turn.

Data flow control bit

The data flow control bit (DFC) is included in secondary frames. The secondary station will set DFC = 1 if a further SEND of user data will cause its buffer to overflow. On receipt of a frame with DFC = 1 a primary station will cease to send data, but will request link status until DFC = 0.

Access demand bit

There are two classes of data defined, class 1 and class 2. Class 1 data has higher priority than class 2 data. The ACD bit is a means for the secondary station to indicate to the primary that there is class 1 data available.

Address field

The address field of the link layer frame is one or two octets in length, set as a fixed system parameter. This field contains the link address of the secondary station. A frame transmitted by the primary station on a link contains the link address of the secondary station to which the message is directed. A frame transmitted by a secondary station to the primary contains its own link address. By this means the primary station can identify which secondary station the message is from.

Transmission procedures

In this section the procedures are discussed briefly. The procedures are very similar to those used by the DNP3 protocol. This may be referred to for further illustration of the concepts presented.

Note that in the following procedures, no new procedure is commenced until the previous procedure is terminated. It is for this reason that a single-bit frame count bit is sufficient for protection against frame sequence number errors; there is a frame window of exactly one.

SEND/NO REPLY procedures

The frame is transmitted, and a minimum line-idle time of 33 bit-times is required before any further transmissions by the primary. On receipt of the message at the secondary, it is checked for error by comparison with the checksum octet, and if valid it is notified to the service user.

SEND/CONFIRM procedures

The primary station will transmit the message. If a confirmation is not received from the secondary station within a configured time-out period, it will re-transmit the message up until a configured number of retries.

If the secondary station receives the message, it will respond with either a positive or negative confirmation, function code 0 or 1. FC = 0 means the message is correctly received and accepted, and in this case the procedure terminates. FC = 1 means the secondary cannot accept the message, because its buffer is full or some other reason. In this case the primary will retry, up until a configured number of retries.

This procedure makes use of the frame count bit (FCB) to ensure that the message sequence is not disturbed. The FCB is toggled with each SEND/CONFIRM transmission from the primary station, and an expected FCB flag is maintained by the secondary station. If a message sent by the primary is not confirmed by the secondary, it is retransmitted with the FCB unchanged. Thus a message lost or corrupted in the primary to secondary transmission direction would when retransmitted still have the expected FCB value. Alternatively, if the problem were that the confirmation from the secondary station was lost or corrupted, the secondary station would be able to recognize receipt of a retransmitted message from the primary by the unchanged FCB bit. In this case it retransmits the original confirmation message.

As an alternative to sending a confirmation frame, which is a minimum of six octets in length (that is if single-octet address is used), the single-control character response (hexadecimal $0 \times E5$) is allowed. This option may be used to improve transmission efficiency when there is no need to transmit any other information back to the primary station.

REQUEST/RESPOND procedures

This procedure is similar to the SEND/CONFIRM except instead of receiving a confirmation back from the secondary station, a frame containing data is returned, or a negative response is returned indicating that no data is available. In the case of a negative response, either a frame with FC = 9, or the single-control character ($0'$ E5) may be returned.

As for the SEND/CONFIRM procedures, the frame count bit is toggled at each end for each message transmission, and this is used to detect errors in the transmission in either direction. Basically, when both primary and secondary have incremented their frame count bits and they agree, the procedure is complete.

Philosophy of transmission

For unbalanced transmission only the controlling or primary station on a link can initiate transmissions. Because of this it is necessary that a polling system is implemented by the primary station in order to determine if there is change data available at each secondary station.

To accomplish this the controlling station will poll each secondary station on a cyclic basis for data. It will typically poll for class 2 user data using the Request–Respond function code 10. The secondary station will then return any class 2 data that it has available, and at the same time it will indicate if there is any class 1 data available by setting the access demand bit (ACD). Typically analog values will be assigned to class 2 and be updated during the cyclic scan, and all other data such as events will be assigned to class 1.

Note that although the polling operation is carried out by the link layer, the polling sequence itself is implemented by a higher level of the protocol, the user process level. The higher level generates services requests using service primitives to specify the polling actions to be carried out by the link layer.

10.4.5   Balanced transmission procedures

Balanced transmission procedures may only be used for point-to-point links equipped with duplex channel communication. Under balanced transmission each station can act as both a primary and a secondary station simultaneously. The control field and transmission procedures are modified slightly from the unbalanced case to accommodate this operation.

The control field

There are two modifications to the data-link control field for balanced transmission. The first is that the access demand (ACD) bit is not required, because the either station can initiate transmissions. The second is the inclusion of a direction bit (DIR). This indicates the direction of transmission of a message between the two stations. The control field for balanced transmission is shown in Figure 10.14 (see also Table 10.8).

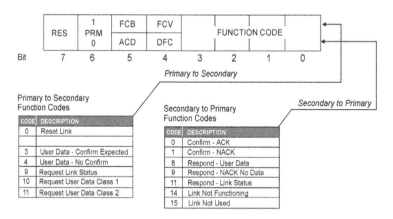

Figure 10.14
Control field – balanced transmission

Code	Meaning	Description
DIR	Direction of message	1 => A to B 0 => B to A
PRM	Primary message	1 => Frame from primary or initiating station
FCB	Frame count bit	Alternates between 0 and 1 for sequential frames
FCV	Frame count valid	1 => FCB is valid 0 => Ignore FCB
RES	Reserved	= 0
DFC	Data flow control bit	Set to 1 by secondary station if further send of user data will cause buffer overflow

Table 10.8
Control field bit meanings – balanced transmission

Table 10.9 shows the detailed meanings for the function codes in the control field. The changes from the codes for unbalanced transmission are shown in italics.

Function Codes from Primary Station

Function Code	Frame Type	Service Function	FCV Bit
0	SEND–CONFIRM expected	Reset of remote link	0
1	SEND–CONFIRM expected	Reset of user process	0
2	SEND–CONFIRM expected	Test for function of link	1
3	SEND–CONFIRM expected	User data	1
4	SEND–NO REPLY expected	User data (unconfirmed)	0

Function Code	Frame Type	Service Function	FCV Bit
8		User by unbalanced only	–
9	REQUEST–RESPOND expected	Request status of link	0
10		Used by unbalanced only	1
11		Used by unbalanced only	1

Codes 5–7, 12–15 are reserved

Table 10.9
Function codes – balanced transmission

The changes in functions from unbalanced transmission are:

- A test link primary function code FC = 2 has been added.
- Requests for access demand and for user data class 1 or 2 have been removed (primary function codes FC = 8, 10, 11).
- Secondary respond function codes FC = 8, 9 have been removed.

These changes reflect the changes to the way data is transmitted. Under balanced transmission the request/respond service is not used for transmission of user data, but only for checking the status of the link. User data is transmitted directly by the link layer using the send service.

Address field

The address field for balanced communications may be zero, one, or two octets. Thus there is the option of having no address field under balanced communications. This is the case because as there is only one station at each end of the link, there is no need for the secondary process at either end to verify the address.

In effect, for a balanced link, the direction (DIR) bit substitutes for the address, making the inclusion of the link address redundant.

Transmission procedures

The transmission procedures for balanced transmission are the same as those for unbalanced transmission. The only difference is that there are both primary and secondary processes operating simultaneously at each station. This is similar to two unbalanced links operating in parallel. These processes maintain a separate frame count bit sequence for each primary–secondary link and use these to detect and recover from errors in the same way as a single unbalanced primary–secondary link operates.

Philosophy of transmission

For balanced transmission either station on the link can initiate transmission. Therefore there is no need for a station to be polled for data as it can send it directly when it is available. This changes the services used at the link layer from the case for unbalanced transmission. Where unbalanced transmission makes use of the request/respond service to obtain user data from the secondary station, for balanced transmission the station with the data just uses the send/confirm service directly. Comparison of Figures 10.13 and 10.14 shows that the secondary codes for responding with user data FC8 and FC9 are not available for balanced transmission. Instead, primary function codes FC3 or FC4 are used to send the data directly.

10.4.6   Data-link security

IEC 60870-5-101 and DNP3 utilize the FT1.2 and FT3 frame formats specified by IEC 60780-5-1, respectively. These formats differ in their security provisions as shown in Table 10.10. IEC 60870-5-101 uses an 8-bit checksum and a maximum frame size of 255 bytes. DNP uses a 16-bit cyclic redundancy code (CRC) for every 16 bytes of user data contained in the body of its frame.

Comparison of Security Features

Protocol	IEC 60870-5 Frame Type	Security Method	Hamming Distance Error Bits	Maximum Secured Length in Bytes
IEC 60870-5-101	FT1.2	8-bit checksum	4	255
DNP 3.0	FT3	16-bit CRC	6	16

Table 10.10
Link layer error security

The effect of these differences in security is often quoted in terms of the 'hamming distance'. This is equal to the minimum number of single bit errors that are required to allow an incorrect message to be mistakenly accepted as a good message that is for the security system to fail. These are 4 and 6 for methods used by FT1.2 and FT3. However, these figures ignore the effect of the ratio of security code bits to message bits, which in the case of DNP is higher due to the inclusion of CRC codes within the body section of the FT3 frame format.

10.4.7   Link vs application data

There is a distinction between link data and application level data that is subtle and can be difficult to grasp at first sight. It derives from the fact that the application level messages are treated simply as data at the link layer level, and may be best illustrated by example.

Take the case where an unbalanced link is operating between primary station A and secondary station D. Suppose that the application level of station D requires some particular data from A. This is in the reverse direction to most data traffic, which is generally from the secondary station to the primary. In this case the application level request from D will generate a class 1 access demand at the link level. This will have to wait until that station is polled for data by the primary station A. At this point, if class 2 data has been polled for it will respond with any class 2 data, or with an FC9 'NACK – no data' frame, but in either case with the ACD (access demand) bit set. The primary station A will then poll for the class 1 data from station D, and at this point D will be able to transmit its class 1 data. This will contain the application level request by D, for the primary station to send the application level data that it requires.

The link layer frame that was requested by polling from primary A, carried an application level request from station D. This resulted in the application layer of A using the send service to return the requested data to station D. Note that a link layer request in direction A to D (the poll) has resulted in an application level request from D to A.

In the following sections dealing with the application layer and above, the operation of the link layer can be generally seen as a message transport mechanism that can be assumed to just transport the application level messages as required. However, awareness of the transport mechanism is important to understanding the response times, as these will depend on the transmission mode and polling frequency for the unbalanced mode.

10.5 Application layer

The remaining sections of Chapter 11 describe the operation of the application layer and above of the IEC 60870-5 protocol. Most of this section is applicable to both the non-networked and networked versions of the protocol, IEC 60870-5-101 and IEC 60870-5-104. The areas that are different are discussed in the following chapter under Advanced considerations of IEC 60870-5.

This information is presented in the following sequence:

- Overall message structure
- ASDU structure
- Message addressing and routing
- Information elements
- Set of ASDUs.

10.5.1 Overall message structure

In the preview, the overall message structure under IEC 60870-5 was presented. This is represented in Figure 10.15. This shows the application layer ASDU, and shows how this is carried as link user data by the data-link layer under IEC 60870-5-101. For the networked version IEC 60870-5-104 the ASDU is carried by the TCP/IP protocols instead of the T101 link layer and so the link frame shown in Figure 10.15 does not apply to this case.

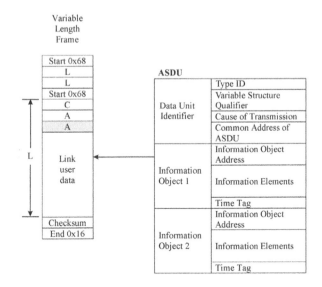

Figure 10.15
Message structure under IEC 60870-5-101

The only important point to note about the relationship between the ASDU and the link layer frame is that a maximum of just one ASDU is allowed per frame. This sets an upper limit for the size of the ASDU at 255 octets, minus 2–3 octets for the link control and address fields.

10.5.2 ASDU structure

The structure of the ASDU is in two main sections. These are the data unit identifier, and the data itself, made up of one or more information objects. The data unit identifier defines the specific type of data, provides addressing to identify the specific identity of the data, and it includes additional information in the cause of transmission field. The fields of the ASDU are now discussed in turn.

Type identification

The type identification field is a single-octet unsigned integer field. Its content is interpreted as a code in the ranges shown in Figure 10.16.

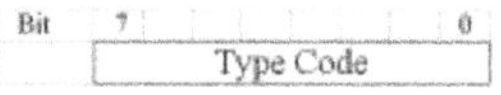

Code Range	Purpose
<1..127>	Standard type definitions
<128..135>	Reserved for message routing – private
<136..255>	For special use - private

Figure 10.16
Type identification field

The following notes apply to these codes:

- The value <0> is not used.
- The range <128..255> is not defined by the standard, and may be used by particular vendors for system specific roles. However this has implications for interoperability.

In the range of the standard type definitions, there are presently 58 specific types defined. These are grouped as shown in Table 10.11, which shows the overall groups and numbers of type identification codes that are defined.

Defined Type Codes	Group
<1..40>	Process information in monitor direction
<45..51>	Process information in control direction
<70>	System information in monitor direction
<100..106>	System information in control direction
<110..113>	Parameter in control direction
<120..126>	File transfer

Table 10.11
Defined type code groups

It is important to note that the type identification applies to the whole ASDU, therefore if there are multiple information objects contained in the ASDU, they are all of the same type.

Table 10.13(a–g) provides a full list of the ASDU types. The table is broken into the code groups shown in Table 10.11. Full details of each individual ASDU type are given under 'Set of ASDUs' later in this text.

Table 10.13 also includes information code references that may be encountered. These references are defined by IEC 60870-5-5. They provide a hierarchical reference system using the following structure (Table 10.12).

Level	Symbol	Description
1	M_ C_ P_ F_	Monitored information Control information Parameter File transfer
2	Various	See actual usages
3	_Nx _Tx _xA _xB _xC _xD	Not time tagged Time tagged Type A: status and normalized, with quality Type B: scaled, with quality Type C: short floating point, with quality Type D: normalized without quality

Table 10.12
Reference information code structure

For example, M_ME_TA_1 is monitored information, a measured value, with time tag, and type A, which is a normalized value with quality.

Type No.	Description	Reference
<0>	Not defined	
<1>	Single-point information	M_SP_NA_1
<2>	Single-point information with time tag	M_SP_TA_1
<3>	Double-point information	M_DP_NA_1
<4>	Double-point information with time tag	M_DP_TA_1
<5>	Step position information	M_ST_NA_1
<6>	Step position information with time tag	M_ST_TA_1
<7>	Bitstring of 32 bit	M_BO_NA_1
<8>	Bitstring of 32 bit with time tag	M_BO_TA_1
<9>	Measured value, normalized value	M_ME_NA_1
<10>	Measured value, normalized value with time tag	M_ME_TA_1
<11>	Measured value, scaled value	M_ME_NB_1
<12>	Measured value, scaled value with time tag	M_ME_TB_1
<13>	Measured value, short floating point number	M_ME_NC_1
<14>	Measured value, short floating point number with time tag	M_ME_TC_1
<15>	Integrated totals	M_IT_NA_1
<16>	Integrated totals with time tag	M_IT_TA_1
<17>	Event of protection equipment with time tag	M_EP_TA_1
<18>	Packed start events of protection equipment with time tag	M_EP_TB_1
<19>	Packed output circuit information of protection equipment with time tag	M_EP_TC_1
<20>	Packed single-point information with status change detection	M_PS_NA_1

(continued)

Type No.	Description	Reference
<21>	Measured value, normalized value without quality descriptor	M_ME_ND_1
<22..29>	Reserved for further compatible definitions	

Table 10.13a
ASDU types – process information in monitoring direction

Table 10.13b shows types that were added to this category with amendment 2 of IEC 60870-5-101. These provide for a longer time tag format.

Type No.	Description	Reference
<30>	Single-point information with time tag CP56Time2a	M_SP_TB_1
<31>	Double-point information with time tag CP56Time2a	M_DP_TB_1
<32>	Step position information with time tag CP56Time2a	M_ST_TB_1
<33>	Bitstring of 32 bits with time tag CP56Time2a	M_BO_TB_1
<34>	Measured value, normalized value with time tag CP56Time2a	M_ME_TD_1
<35>	Measured value, scaled value with time tag CP56Time2a	M_ME_TE_1
<36>	Measured value, short floating point number with time tag CP56Time2a	M_ME_TF_1
<37>	Integrated totals with time tag CP56Time2a	M_IT_TB_1
<38>	Event of protection equipment with time tag CP56Time2a	M_EP_TD_1
<39>	Packed start events of protection equipment with time tag CP56Time2a	M_EP_TE_1
<40>	Packed output circuit information of protection equipment with time tag CP56Time2a	M_EP_TF_1
<30>	Single-point information with time tag CP56Time2a	M_SP_TB_1
<31>	Double-point information with time tag CP56Time2a	M_DP_TB_1
<32>	Step position information with time tag CP56Time2a	M_ST_TB_1
<33>	Bitstring of 32 bits with time tag CP56Time2a	M_BO_TB_1
<34>	Measured value, normalized value with time tag CP56Time2a	M_ME_TD_1
<35>	Measured value, scaled value with time tag CP56Time2a	M_ME_TE_1
<36>	Measured value, short floating point number with time tag CP56Time2a	M_ME_TF_1

Type No.	Description	Reference
<37>	Integrated totals with time tag CP56Time2a	M_IT_TB_1
<38>	Event of protection equipment with time tag CP56Time2a	M_EP_TD_1
<39>	Packed start events of protection equipment with time tag CP56Time2a	M_EP_TE_1
<40>	Packed output circuit information of protection equipment with time tag CP56Time2a	M_EP_TF_1
<41..44>	Reserved for further compatible definitions	

Table 10.13b
ASDU types – process information in monitoring direction cont'd

Type No.	Description	Reference
<45>	Single command	C_SC_NA_1
<46>	Double command	C_DC_NA_1
<47>	Regulating step command	C_RC_NA_1
<48>	Set point command, normalized value	C_SE_NA_1
<49>	Set point command, scaled value	C_SE_NB_1
<50>	Set point command, short floating point number	C_SE_NC_1
<51>	Bitstring of 32 bits	C_BO_NA_1

Table 10.13c
ASDU types – process information in control direction

Type No.	Description	Reference
<70>	End of initialization	M_EI_NA_1
<70..99>	Reserved for further compatible definitions	

Table 10.13d
ASDU types – system information in monitor direction

Type No.	Description	Reference
<100>	Interrogation command	C_IC_NA_1
<101>	Counter interrogation command	C_CI_NA_1
<102>	Read command	C_RD_NA_1
<103>	Clock synchronization command	C_CS_NA_1
<104>	Test command	C_TS_NA_1
<105>	Reset process command	C_RP_NA_1
<106>	Delay acquisition command	C_CD_NA_1
<107..109>	Reserved for further compatible definitions	

Table 10.13e
ASDU types – system information in control direction

Type No.	Description	Reference
<110>	Parameter of measured value, normalized value	P_ME_NA_1
<111>	Parameter of measured value, scaled value	P_ME_NB_1
<112>	Parameter of measured value, short floating point number	P_ME_NC_1
<113>	Parameter activation	P_AC_NA_1
<114..119>	Reserved for further compatible definitions	

Table 10.13f
ASDU types – parameter in control direction

Type No.	Description	Reference
<120>	File ready	F_FR_NA_1
<121>	Section ready	F_SR_NA_1
<122>	Call directory, select File, call File, call section	F_SC_NA_1
<123>	Last section, last segment	F_LS_NA_1
<124>	Ack File, ack section	F_AF_NA_1
<125>	Segment	F_SG_NA_1
<126>	Directory	F_DR_TA_1
<127>	Reserved for further compatible definitions	

Table 10.13g
ASDU types – file transfer

Variable structure qualifier

The variable structure qualifier is a single-octet that specifies the number of information objects or information elements, and how they are addressed. It contains a seven-bit binary number, and a one-bit field that indicates which of two different possible information structures is used. Figure 10.17 shows the variable structure qualifier field, followed by a detail of the two information structures.

It may be seen from Figure 10.17 that there are two different structures, depending on the state of the most significant bit of the variable structure qualifier. This is termed the SQ bit, which may be thought of as the structure qualifier bit.

When SQ = 0, the structure is a sequence of information objects. Each information object carries its own address, and therefore the information elements contained do not need to have sequential addresses. The number of information objects is given by the seven-bit value N. Therefore there can be up to 127 information objects in this ASDU.

When SQ = 1, the structure contains just one information object, but this may contain multiple information elements, all of the same format, such as a measured value. In this case there is only one information object address, and only one time tag (if used).

The effect of the SQ bit is that for each type identification number, there may effectively be two ASDUs. This is seen in the sub-section presenting the set of ASDUs, where it will be seen that some types have both variations (SQ = 0 and SQ = 1), and others have only one of these.

Cause of transmission

The cause of transmission (COT) field is used to control the routing of messages both on the communications network, and within a station, by directing the ASDU to the correct program or task for processing. This sub-section will initially look at the structure and meaning of the sub-fields within the COT, and then look at how these are used (Figure 10.18).

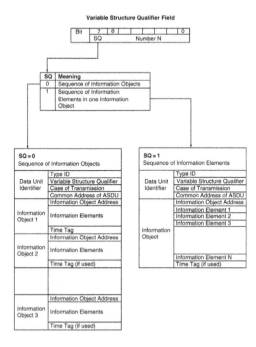

Figure 10.17
Variable structure qualifier and structures

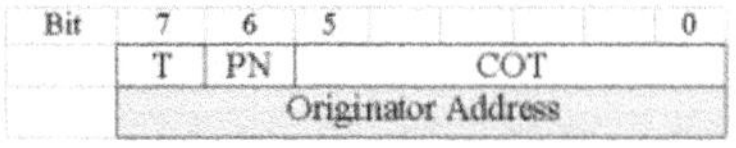

Figure 10.18
Cause of transmission field

The cause of transmission or COT is a six-bit code that is used in interpreting the information at the destination station. The codes are shown in Table 10.14. Each defined ASDU type has a defined sub-set of the codes that are meaningful with it, and these are given in the section presenting the set of ASDUs.

The PN bit is the positive/negative confirmation bit. This is meaningful when used with control commands. This bit is used when the control command is mirrored in the monitor direction, and it provides indication of whether the command was executed or not. When the PN bit is not relevant it is cleared to zero.

The T or test bit is set when ASDUs are generated for test purposes and are not intended to control the process or change the system state. It is used for testing of transmission and equipment.

COT Code	Cause of Transmission
0	Not used
1	Periodic, cyclic
2	Background scan
3	Spontaneous
4	Initialized
5	Request or requested
6	Activation
7	Activation confirmation
8	Deactivation
9	Deactivation confirmation
10	Activation termination
11	Return information caused by a remote command
12	Return information caused by a local command
13	File transfer
14–19	Reserved for future definitions
20	Interrogated by station interrogation
21–36	Interrogated by group (1–16) interrogation
37	Requested by general counter request
38–41	Requested by group (1–4) counter request
42–43	Reserved for future definitions
44	Unknown type identification
45	Unknown cause of transmission
46	Unknown common address of ASDU
47	Unknown information object address

Table 10.14
Cause of transmission codes (COT)

The originator address is optional on a system basis. It provides a means for a controlling station to explicitly identify itself. This is not necessary when there is only one controlling station in a system, but is required when there is more than one controlling station, or some stations are dual-mode stations. These are stations that act both as controlled and controlling stations. In these circumstances the originator address can be used to direct command confirmations back to the particular controlling station that issued the command, rather than to the whole system. The one exception to this is the originator address of zero <0>. This has the same effect as if there was no originator address. It is termed the default address and its effect is that the message is transmitted to all stations. The use of the originator address is discussed in greater detail under message addressing and routing.

Common address of ASDU

The common address of the ASDU (Figure 10.19) is either one or two octets in length, fixed on a per-system basis. The address is called a common address because it is in common to all of the data contained within the ASDU. This is normally interpreted as a station address, however it can be structured to form a station/sector address where individual stations are broken up into multiple logical units. The address <0> is not used.

Single-octet Address

Bit   7   0

Two-octet Address

Bit   7   0
| LSB |
| MSB |

Address Range	Purpose
<0>	Not used
<1..254> or <1..65534>	Station Address
<255> or <65535>	Global Address

Figure 10.19
Common address of ASDU

The highest address 0xFF or 0xFFFF is global. This means that an ASDU with this address will be interpreted by all stations. Use of the global address is restricted to the ASDUs listed below. These are used when the same application function must be initiated simultaneously.

Type	Description	Purpose
100	Interrogation command	Reply with particular system data snapshot at common time
101	Counter interrogation command	Freeze totals at common time
103	Clock synchronization command	Synchronize clocks to common time
105	Reset process command	Simultaneous reset

Information object address

The information object address is the first field of the information object. It identifies the particular data within a defined station. The information object address may be one, two, or three octets in length. However, the case of three octets is provided only to allow for structured address systems, and one station is allowed only 65 536 different information object addresses, as for two-octet addressing. The information object address of zero is reserved for the case when the address is not relevant. The information object address is shown in Figure 10.20.

On a system basis, specific data is uniquely identified by the combination of the common address and the information object address.

| Type ID |
| Variable Structure Qualifier |
| Cause of Transmission |
| Common Address of ASDU |
| Information Object Address |
| Information Elements |
| Time Tag |

Bit 7 6 5   0
| Octet 1 |
| Octet 2 |
| Octet 3 |

Figure 10.20
Information object address

An example of how this might work in practice is where there are a number of identical intelligent electronic devices IEDs connected to a sub-master RTU, which is in turn connected to a master station. These could be re-closers on a distribution system. Each IED will have an identical data structure internally, as determined by the device manufacturer. Most likely this will be some tens of information elements or data points, which could be addressed by a one-octet information object address. However, as the system includes RTUs that have many more data points, two-octet addressing is used across the system. At a system configuration level, there will be a single model for that type of re-closer, and configuration of each device into the system database will be a matter of using the standard point-mapping for that device type and adding the station number to form unique point references.

10.5.3   Message addressing and routing

Control and monitor directions

An important concept in understanding addressing under IEC 60870-5 is the difference between control and monitor directions. It is an assumption that the overall system has a hierarchical structure involving centralized control. Under the protocol, every station is either a controlling station or a controlled station. The communications network structure will normally be aligned with this, and for unbalanced communications links the controlling stations will be primaries, and the controlled stations will be secondaries at the link level.

This follows naturally from the fact that a hierarchical structure involves multiple controlled stations, controlled by one or at least few controlling stations.

In such a system, control messages such as commands or interrogations are transmitted by the controlling station, and these results in actions and return information transmitted by the controlled station.

Addressing of ASDUs

Messages are addressed in the control direction by the common address field of the ASDU. This address field is one or two octets, and defines the station (or logical station) to which the ASDU is being addressed. In the monitor direction, however, the common address field contains the address of the station returning the data. This is required so that the data can be uniquely identified and mapped to the right points in system data images.

In some cases a station that is generally a controlled station may itself act as a controlling station, perhaps to interrogate the master station for data, or to initiate an action in another controlled station. This is called reverse direction operation. A station that can act in both the forward and the reverse direction is called a dual-mode or combined station. When a dual-mode station issues a control ASDU to another station, it must set the controlled station's address as the common address of the ASDU. This is necessary, as for any control direction ASDU, so that the intended station can recognize the message as being directed at it (Figure 10.21).

When the action is carried out, further communication will be necessary with the controlling station to send an action confirmation message, and possibly an execute message if two-phase operation is being used. But as monitor direction messages carry the address of the controlled station, this cannot be used to route the communications back to the controlling station. Instead, the originator address octet of the cause of transmission field is used for this purpose. Its operation is described in the following paragraphs and in Figures 10.22 and 10.23.

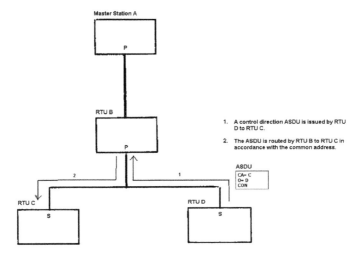

Figure 10.21
Control command issued from dual-mode RTU

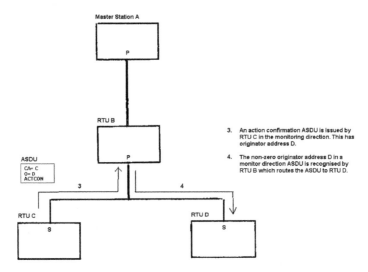

Figure 10.22
Activation confirmation ASDU returned to dual-mode RTU

When a control direction ASDU is transmitted by a dual-mode station that is not the system master station, that station must include a non-zero value in the originator address octet of the cause of transmission field. This has no effect in the control direction of the ASDU, but is used in the monitoring direction to route action confirmation and action termination messages back to the originator. When the controlled station returns an action confirmation or other message arising from this control ASDU, it includes the originator address from the control direction ASDU in the monitoring direction response. It is the responsibility of any intermediate routing devices to recognize a non-zero originator address in a monitor direction ASDU, and to route it back to that originator.

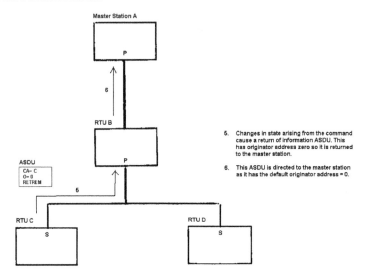

Figure 10.23
Monitoring information returned to SCADA master

As the originator address sub-field is only one octet in length, and common addresses may be two octets, it is clear that either any dual-mode stations on a system must either be numbered within the range <1..256>, or a mapping must be used between originator addresses and common addresses if these are not in that range.

It should be noted that also arising from the control action may be some changes within the controlled station that need to be conveyed to the master station rather than the dual-mode station that initiated the control action. These would typically be to convey the changed system state, and might also include time-tagged events. The monitor direction ASDUs that carry this information need to be directed to the master station, and possibly to other areas of the network if required. These ASDUs are given an originator address value of zero. Thus, in a system which contains dual-mode stations, it is necessary to use the originator address sub-field, and all monitor direction messages going back to the master station will have this field set to zero.

These concepts are illustrated in Figure 10.21. This shows a system with intermediate RTUs acting as controllers and data concentrators, and multiple controlled stations linked to these. One of these issues a command to a peer station. Both action confirmation and change data messages are generated, and are routed to their correct destinations by the use of the originator address field.

10.6   Information elements

As has been shown in the preceding sections on ASDU structure, application data is carried within the ASDU within one or more information objects. Depending on the variable structure flag there may be multiple information objects each containing a defined set of one or more information elements, or there may be just one information object containing a number of identical information elements. In either case, the information element is the fundamental component used to convey information under the protocol. The information elements are used as building blocks in the definition of the set of ASDUs under the protocol.

In this section this set of information building blocks is presented. These are referred to in the following section when the set of ASDUs are defined.

In the following definitions, these interpretation rules should be noted:

- Key descriptions give the logical state for a set bit, i.e. bit = 1.
- Blank bit positions are reserved and must be cleared, i.e. bit = 0.
- Bit positions have been numbered <0..7> for consistency within this text and the powers of 2 the positions represent. Note that the IEC documents actually use <1..8>. This is a matter of definition only and does not change the meaning.

The set of information elements is listed in Table 10.15. This is followed by representations of each of the data elements, grouped by general type.

General Type Symbol	Description
Process	
SIQ	Single-point information with quality descriptor
DIQ	Double-point information with quality descriptor
BSI	Binary state information
SCD	Status and change detection
QDS	Quality descriptor
VTI	Value with transient state indication
NVA	Normalized value
SVA	Scaled value
R32-IEEE STD 754	Short floating point number
BCR	Binary counter reading
Protection	
SEP	Single event of protection equipment
SPE	Start events of protection equipment
OCI	Output circuit information of protection equipment
QDP	Quality descriptor for events of protection equipment
Commands	
SCO	Single command
DCO	Double command
RCO	Regulating step command
Time	
CP56Time2a	Seven octet binary time
CP24Time 2a	Three octet binary time
CP16Time2a	Two octet binary time
Qualifiers	
QOI	Qualifier of interrogation
QCC	Qualifier of counter interrogation command
QPM	Qualifier of parameter of measured values
QPA	Qualifier of parameter activation
QRP	Qualifier of rest process command
QOC	Qualifier of command
QOS	Qualifier of set-point command
File Transfer	
FRQ	File ready qualifier
SRQ	Section ready qualifier
SCQ	Select and call qualifier

(continued)

General Type Symbol	Description
LSQ	Last section or segment qualifier
AFQ	Acknowledge file or section qualifier
NOF	Name of file
NOS	Name of section
LOF	Length of file or section
LOS	Length of segment
CHS	Checksum
SOF	Status of file
Miscellaneous	
COI	Cause of initialization
FBP	Fixed test bit pattern, two octets

Table 10.15
Information elements

10.6.1   Quality bits

Quality bits are not information elements in themselves, but appear as individual bits within information elements. These are defined in this section.

Note that quality bits are set or cleared independently of each other. Examination of these shows that these may be used to differentiate between different types of situation or problem that may be affecting the data. Whether all are used will depend on the system. A simple approach would be to interpret any of the quality bits being set as 'bad value', whereas more sophisticated approaches may differentiate based on the actual bit(s) set. Their individual meanings are explained further below.

Blocked (BL)

This means that the value of the point is as it was prior to being blocked. Blocking prevents updating of the value of the point.

Substituted (SB)

This is where a value has been substituted or forced by manual entry or otherwise. It means that the value is not derived from the normal measurement.

Not topical (NT)

This is means that the value was not updated successfully at the last time it was due to be updated.

Invalid (IV)

This indicates that the value cannot be used because it may be incorrect due to a fault or other abnormal condition.

11a

Industrial Ethernet overview

Objectives

When you have completed study of this chapter, you will be able to:

- Describe how industrial Ethernet systems operate
- Identify, troubleshoot, and fix problems such as:
    - Thin and thick coax cable and connectors
    - UTP cabling
    - Incorrect media selection
    - Jabber
    - Too many nodes
    - Excessive broadcasting
    - Bad frames
    - Faulty auto-negotiation
    - 10/100 Mbps mismatch
    - Full-/half-duplex mismatch
    - Faulty hubs
    - Switched networks
    - Loading.

11a.1   Introduction

During the mid-seventies, Xerox Corporation (Palo Alto) developed the Ethernet network concept, based on work done by researchers at the University of Hawaii. The University's ALOHA network was set up using radio broadcasts to connect sites on the islands. This was colloquially known as their 'Ethernet' since it used the 'ether' as the transmission medium and created a network between the sites. The philosophy was straightforward. Any station wanting to broadcast would do so immediately. The receiving station then had a responsibility to acknowledge the message, advising the original transmitting station of a successful reception of the original message. This primitive system did not rely on any detection of collisions (two radio stations transmitting at the same time) but depended on an acknowledgment within a predefined time.

The initial Xerox system was so successful that it was soon applied to other sites, typically connecting office equipment to shared resources such as printers and large computers acting as repositories of large databases.

In 1980, the Ethernet Consortium consisting of Xerox, Digital Equipment Corporation and Intel (a.k.a. the DIX consortium) issued a joint specification, based on the Ethernet concepts, known as the Ethernet Blue Book 1 specification. This was later superseded by the Ethernet Blue Book 2 (Ethernet V2) specification, which was offered to the IEEE for ratification as a standard. In 1983, the IEEE issued the IEEE 802.3 standard for carrier sense multiple access/collision detect (CSMA/CD) LANs based on the DIX Ethernet standard.

As a result of this, there are two standards in existence viz. Ethernet V2 (Bluebook) and IEEE 802.3. The differences between these two later standards are minor, yet they are nonetheless significant. Despite the generic term 'Ethernet' being applied to all CSMA/CD networks, it should, technically speaking, be reserved for the original DIX standard. This chapter will continue with popular use and refer to all the LANs of this type as Ethernet, unless it is important to distinguish between them.

Early Ethernet (of the 10 Mbps variety) uses the CSMA/CD access method. This results in a system that can operate with little delay, if lightly loaded, but access to the medium can become very slow if the network is heavily loaded. Ethernet network interface cards are relatively cheap and produced in vast quantities. Ethernet has, in fact, become the most widely used networking standard. However, because of its probabilistic access mechanism, there is no guarantee of message transfer and messages cannot be prioritized.

Modern Ethernet systems are a far cry from the original design. From 100BASE-T onwards they are capable of full-duplex (sending and receiving at the same time via switches, without collisions) and the Ethernet frame has been modified to make provision for prioritization and virtual LANs.

Ten Gigabit Ethernet became commercially available in 2002. Ethernet has also been modified for industrial use and as such, has made vast inroads into the process control environment.

As an introduction to Ethernet, the next section will deal with systems based on the original IEEE 802.3 (CSMA/CD) standard.

11a.2   10 Mbps Ethernet

11a.2.1   Media systems

The IEEE 802.3 standard (also known as ISO 8802.3) defines a range of media types that can be used for a network based on this standard such as coaxial cable, twisted-pair cable and fiber-optic cable. It supports various cable media and transmission rates at 10 Mbps, such as:

- *10BASE-2*: Thin wire coaxial cable (6.3 mm/0.25 in. diameter), 10 Mbps baseband operation, bus topology
- *10BASE-5*: Thick wire coaxial cable (13 mm/0.5 in. diameter), 10 Mbps baseband operation, bus topology
- *10BASE-T*: Unscreened twisted-pair cable (0.4–0.6 mm conductor diameter), 10 Mbps baseband operation, hub topology
- *10BASE-F*: Optical fiber cables, 10 Mbps baseband operation, point-to-point topology.

Other variations include 1BASE-5, 10BASE-FB, 10BASE-FP, and 10Broad36 but these versions never became commercially viable.

10BASE-5

This is the original coaxial cable system and is also called 'thicknet'. The coaxial cable (50 Ω characteristic impedance) is yellow or orange in color. The naming convention 10BASE-5 means 10 Mbps, baseband signaling on a cable that will support 500 m (1640 ft) segment lengths. The cable is difficult to work with, and cannot normally be taken to the node directly. Instead, it is laid in a cabling tray and the transceiver electronics (medium attachment unit or MAU) is installed directly on the cable. From there, an intermediate cable, known as an attachment unit interface (AUI) cable, is used to connect to the NIC. This cable can be a maximum of 50 m (164 ft) long, compensating for the lack of flexibility of placement of the coaxial cable. The AUI cable consists of five individually shielded pairs – two each (control and data) for both transmit and receive, plus one for power.

Cutting the cable and inserting N-connectors and a coaxial T or more commonly by using a 'bee sting' or 'vampire' tap can make the MAU connection to the cable. The vampire tap is a mechanical connection that clamps directly over the cable. Electrical connection is made via a probe that connects to the center conductor, and sharp teeth that physically puncture the cable sheath to connect to the braid. These hardware components are shown in Figure 11a.1.

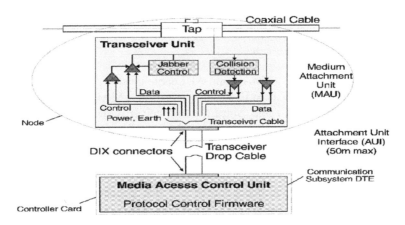

Figure 11a.1
10BASE-5 components

The location of the connection is important to avoid multiple electrical reflections on the cable, and the cable is marked every 2.5 m (8 ft) with a black or brown ring to indicate where a tap should be placed. Fan-out boxes can be used if there are a number of nodes for connection, allowing a single tap to feed each node as though it was individually connected. The connection at either end of the AUI cable is made through a 25 pin-D connector, with a slide latch, often called a DIX connector after the original consortium.

There are certain requirements if this cable architecture is used in a network. These include:

- Segments must be less than 500 m (1640 ft) in length to avoid signal attenuation problems
- Not more than 100 taps on each segment
- Taps must be placed at integer multiples of 2.5 m (8 ft)
- The cable must be terminated with a 50 Ω terminator at each end

- It must not be bent at a radius exceeding 25.4 cm or 10 in.
- One end of the cable shield must be earthed.

The physical layout of a 10BASE-5 Ethernet segment is shown in Figure 11a.2.

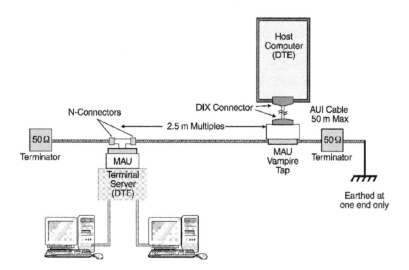

Figure 11a.2
10BASE-5 Ethernet segment

Note that when an MAU and AUI cable is used, the on-board transceiver on the NIC is not used. Rather, there is a transceiver in the MAU and this is fed with power from the NIC via the AUI cable. Since the transceiver is remote from the NIC, the node needs to be aware that the termination can detect collisions if they occur. A signal quality error (SQE), or heartbeat test function in the MAU performs this confirmation. The SQE signal is sent from the MAU to the node on detecting a collision on the bus. However, on completion of every frame transmission by the MAU, the SQE signal is asserted to ensure that the circuitry remains active, and that collisions can be detected. The SQE pulses occur during the 96-bit inter-frame gap between packets, but is recognized by the NIC and is not confused with a collision. Not all components support SQE test, and mixing those that do with those that do not could cause problems. If, for example, an MAU is connected to a repeater, the SQE function on that MAU needs to be turned off. If not, the repeater will mistakenly see the SQE signal as a collision, and respond with a jam signal. This is not easily detectable, but can radically slow down a network.

10BASE-2

The other type of coax-based Ethernet network is 10BASE-2, often referred to as 'thinnet' or 'thinwire Ethernet'. It uses type RG-58 A/U or C/U cable with a 50 Ω characteristic impedance and 5 mm diameter. The cable is normally connected to the NICs in the nodes by means of a BNC T-piece connector. Connectivity requirements include:

- It must be terminated at each end with a 50 Ω terminator.
- The maximum length of a cable segment is 185 m (600 ft) and not 200 m (650 ft).
- Not more than 30 transceivers can be connected to any one segment.
- There must be a minimum spacing of 0.5 m (1.6 ft) between nodes.
- It may not be used as a link segment between two 'thicknet' segments.

- The minimum bend radius is 5 cm (2 in.).
- The maximum distance between the medium and the transceiver is 4 in.; this is taken up by the dimensions of the T-connector and the PCB tracks, which means that no drop cable may be used – the BNC T-piece has to be located on the front panel of the NIC.

The physical layout of a 10BASE-2 Ethernet segment is shown in Figure 11a.3.

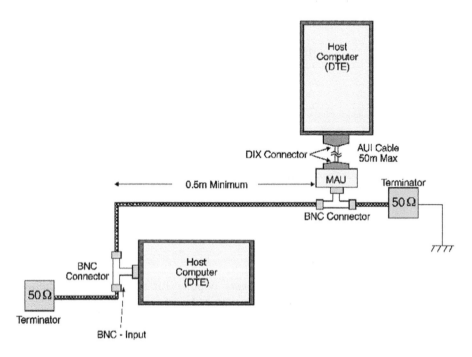

Figure 11a.3
10BASE-2 Ethernet segment

At one stage the use of thinnet cable was very popular as a cheap and relatively easy way to set up a network. However, there are disadvantages with this approach as a cable fault can bring the whole system down.

10BASE-T

10BASE-T uses AWG24 unshielded twisted-pair (UTP) cable for connection to the node. The physical topology of the standard is a star, with nodes connected to a hub. The cable can be Category 3 (Cat3) or Cat5 UTP, although Cat3 does not support the faster versions of Ethernet.

The node cable (hub to node):

- Has a maximum length of 100 m (328 ft)
- Consists of four pairs of which only two pairs are used (one for receiving and one for transmitting)
- Is connected via RJ-45 plugs.

The hub can be considered as a bus internally (any signal input on a given port are reflected as outputs on all other ports), and so the topology is a logical bus topology although it physically resembles a star (hub) topology. Figure11a.4 shows schematically how the hub interconnects the 10BASE-T nodes.

Collisions are detected by the NIC and so the hub must retransmit an input signal on all output pairs, so that each NIC can also receive its own transmitted signal. The electronics in the hub must ensure that the stronger retransmitted signal does not interfere with the weaker input signal. The effect is known as far-end crosstalk (FEXT), and is handled by special adaptive crosstalk echo cancellation circuits.

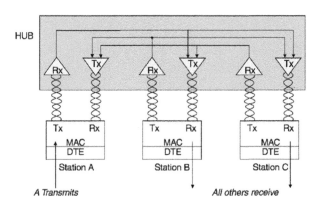

Figure 11a.4
10BASE-T hub concept

The standard has become very popular for new networks, although there are some disadvantages that should be recognized:

- The unshielded cable is not very resistant to electrostatic electrical noise, and may not be suitable for some industrial environments.
- Whilst the cable is inexpensive, there is the additional cost of the associated wiring hubs to be considered.
- The cable length is limited to 100 m (328 ft).

Advantages of the system include:

- The twisted-pair cable provides good electromagnetic noise immunity.
- Intelligent hubs can monitor traffic on each port. This improves on the security of the network – a feature that has often been lacking in a broadcast, common media network such as Ethernet.
- Because of the cheap wire used, flood wiring can be installed in a new building, providing many more wiring points than are initially needed, but giving great flexibility for future expansion. When this is done, patch panels – or punch down blocks – are often installed for even greater flexibility.
- The star-wiring configuration improves physical reliability. A cut cable only affects one node.

10BASE-F

This standard makes provision for three architectures viz. 10BASE-FL, 10BASE-FP, and 10BASE-FB. The latter two have never gained commercial acceptance and are not currently manufactured by any vendor.

10BASE-FL

The fiber link segment standard is basically a 2 km (1.2 miles) upgrade to the existing fiber-optic inter repeater link (FOIRL) standard. The original FOIRL as specified in the IEEE 802.3 standard was limited to a 1 km (0.6 mile) fiber link between two repeaters, with a maximum length of 2.5 km (1.5 miles) if there are five segments in the link. Note that this is a link between two repeaters in a network, and cannot have any nodes connected to it (Figure 11a.5).

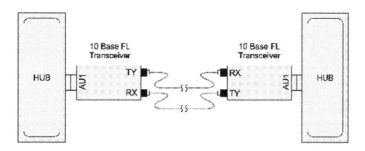

Figure 11a.5
10BASE-FL segment

11a.2.2   Signaling methods

10 Mbps Ethernet signals are encoded using the Manchester encoding scheme. This method allows a clock to be extracted at the receiver end to synchronize the transmission/reception process. The encoding is performed by an exclusive or between a 20 MHz clock signal and the data stream. In the resulting signal, a 0 is represented by a high to low change at the center of the bit cell, whilst a 1 is represented by a low to high change at the center of the bit cell. There may or may not be transitions at the beginning of a cell as well, but these are ignored at the receiver. The transitions in every cell allow the clock to be extracted and synchronized with the transmitter. This method is very wasteful of bandwidth (it requires a cable bandwidth of well above twice the bit rate) and is therefore not used on the faster Ethernet versions.

In the IEEE 802.3 standard, voltages swing between 0 and –2.05 V on coax, or between –2.5 and +2.5 V on twisted pair.

11a.2.3   Medium access control

10 Mbps Ethernet operates in half-duplex mode, so that a station can either receive or transmit, but not both at the same time. The method used to achieve this is called CSMA/CD, or carrier sense multiple access with collision detection.

Essentially, the method used is one of contention. Each node has a connection via a transceiver to the common bus. As a transceiver, it can both transmit and receive at the same time. Each node can be in any one of three states at any time. These states are:

- Idle, or listen
- Transmit
- Contention.

In the idle state, the node merely listens to the bus, monitoring all traffic that passes. If a node then wishes to transmit information, it will defer whilst there is any activity on the bus, since this is the 'carrier sense' component of the architecture. At some stage, the bus will become silent, and the node, sensing this, will then commence its transmission. It is now in the transmit mode, and will both transmit and listen at the same time. This is because there is no guarantee that another node at some other point on the bus has not also started transmitting, having recognized the absence of traffic.

After a short delay as the two signals propagate towards each other on the cable, there will be a collision of signals. Obviously the two transmissions cannot coexist on the common bus, since there is no mechanism for the mixed analog signals to be 'unscrambled'. The transceiver quickly detects this collision, since it is monitoring both its input and output and recognizes the difference. The node now goes into the third state viz. contention. The node will continue to transmit for a short time – the jam signal – to ensure the other transmitting node detects the contention, and then performs a back-off algorithm to determine when it should again attempt to transmit its waiting frames.

11a.2.4 Frame transmission

When a frame is to be transmitted, the medium access control monitors the bus and defers to any passing traffic. After a period of 96 bit times, known as the inter-frame gap (to allow the passing frame to be received and processed by the destination node) the transmission process commences. Since there is a finite time for this transmission to propagate to the ends of the bus cable, and thus ensure that all nodes recognize that the medium is busy, the transceiver turns on a collision detect circuit whilst the transmission takes place. Once a certain number of bits (512) have been transmitted, provided that the network cable segment specifications have been complied with, the collision detection circuitry can be disabled. If a collision should take place after this, it will be the responsibility of higher protocols to request retransmission – a far slower process than the hardware collision detection process.

This is a good reason to comply with cable segment specifications! This initial 'danger' period is known as the collision window, and is effectively twice the time interval for the first bit of a transmission to propagate to all parts of the network. The slot time for the network is then defined as the worst case time delay that a node must wait before it can reliably know that a collision has occurred. It is defined as:

Slot time = 2 $'$ (transmission path delay) + safety margin

For a 10 Mbps system the slot time is fixed at 512 bits or 51.2 µs.

11a.2.5 Frame reception

The transceiver of each node is constantly monitoring the bus for a transmission signal. As soon as one is recognized, the NIC activates a carrier sense signal to indicate that transmissions cannot be made. The first bits of the MAC frame are a preamble and consist of alternating bits of 1010, etc. On recognizing these, the receiver synchronizes its clock, and converts the Manchester-encoded signal back into binary form. The eighth octet is a start of frame delimiter, and this is used to indicate to the receiver that it should strip off the first eight octets and commence frame reception into a frame buffer within the NIC.

Further processing then takes place, including the calculation and comparison of the frame CRC with the transmitted CRC. In valid frames, the destination hardware address is checked. If this matches the MAC address in the card firmware, or a broadcast address, then the message is passed up the protocol stack, otherwise the frame is discarded. It also checks that the frame contains an integral number of octets and is either too short or too long. Provided all is correct, the frame is passed to the data-link layer for further processing.

11a.2.6 MAC frame format

The basic frame format for an IEEE 802.3 network is shown in Figure 11a.6. There are eight fields in each frame, and they are described in detail.

DIX Frame

64 bits	48 bits	48 bits	16 bits	46 to 1500 bytes	32 bits
Preamble	Destination Address	Source Address	Type	Data	Frame Check Sequence

IEEE 802.3 Frame

56 bits	8 bits	48 bits	48 bits	16 bits	46 to 1500 bytes	32 bits
Preamble	SFD	Destination Address	Source Address	Length or Type	LLC/Data	Frame Check Sequence

Figure 11a.6
Ethernet V2/IEEE 802.3 MAC frame formats

Preamble

This field consists of seven octets of the data pattern 10101010. The receiver uses this to synchronize its clock to the transmitter.

Start frame delimiter

This single octet field consists of the data 10101011. It enables the receiver to recognize where the address fields commence.

Source and destination address

These are the physical addresses of both the source and the destination nodes. The fields are six octets long. Assignment of addresses is controlled by the IEEE standards association (IEEE-SA), which administers the allocation of the first three bytes. When assigning blocks of addresses to manufacturers, the IEEE-SA provides a 24 bit organizationally unique identifier (OUI). The OUI (the first three bytes of the hardware address) identifies the manufacturer of the card and is the same for all cards made by it. The second half is the device identifier, and these numbers are assigned sequentially during the manufacturing process so that each card will have a unique address.

The addressing modes according to IEEE 802.3 include:

- *Broadcast*: The destination address is set to all 1s or FF-FF-FF-FF-FF-FF, and all nodes on the network will respond to the message.
- *Unicast (individual, or point-to-point)*: If the first bit of the address is 0, the frame is sent to one specific node. An example of a unicast address is 06-C1-B2-12-56-23.

The addresses allocated by a factory are referred to as globally administered addresses. The standard also makes provision for a locally administered address (in which the second bit is set to one), but in practice this is rarely used as cards are invariably bought with preset MAC addresses.

Length

For IEEE 802.3, this two-octet field contains a number representing the length of the data field. For Bluebook Ethernet this field represents 'type' rather than 'length'. 'Type' is a number bigger than 1500 decimal representing the protocol that has submitted the data for delivery.

Data

The information that has been handed down from the layer above, between 0 and 1500 bytes.

Pad

Since there is a minimum frame length of 64 octets (512 bits) that must be transmitted to ensure that the collision mechanism works, the pad field will pad out any frame that does not meet this minimum specification by adding up to 46 bytes of 'padding'. This pad, if incorporated, is normally random data. The CRC is calculated over the data in the pad field. Once the CRC checks OK, the receiving node discards the pad data, which it recognizes by the value in the length field.

FCS

A 32 bit CRC value is computed in hardware at the transmitter and appended to the frame. It is the same algorithm used in the IEEE 802.4 and IEEE 802.5 standards.

Difference between IEEE 802.3 and Ethernet V2

As mentioned before, there is a difference between IEEE 802.3 and Blue Book Ethernet. These differences are primarily in the frame structure and are shown in Table 11a.1.

802.3 Network	Ethernet Network
Star topology supported using UTP, fiber etc., or bus	Only supports bus topology
Baseband and broadband signaling	Baseband only
Data-link layer divided into LLC and MAC	No subdivision of DLL
Seven octets of preamble plus SFD	8 bytes of preamble with no separate SFD
Length field in data frame	Field used to indicate the higher level protocol using the data-link service

Table 11a.1
Differences between IEEE 802.3 and Blue Book Ethernet (V2)

11a.2.7   IEEE 802.2 LLC

Ethernet V2 implements both the physical and the data-link layer. The frame then contains the detail of the higher-layer protocol being carried in the frame. This information is required for correctly multiplexing and de-multiplexing the packets carried by the network, i.e. ensuring that they get delivered to the same type of protocol that sent them (Figure 11a.7).

In the case of IEEE 802.3, however, it was decided to split the data-link layer into two, namely, a lower half that controls access to the medium (medium access control, or MAC) and an upper half that performs the link control between the two NICs involved (the logical link control or LLC). The MAC part is included together with the physical layer in the IEEE 802.3 specifications, but the LLC is implemented separately in the IEEE 802.2 specification. This was done since the LLC functionality is not unique to IEEE 802.3, but is used by many other IEEE 802 network standards as well.

Since not all LANs necessarily have a 'type' field in their frames, the protocol information required for multiplexing is now carried in the SSAP (source service access point) and DSAP (destination service access point) within the IEEE 802.2 LLC header. The entire LLC header is only 3–4 bytes and is carried within the 'Data' field of the IEEE 802.3 frame, just after the header.

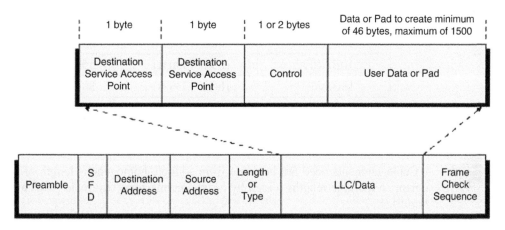

Figure 11a.7
LLC PDU carried in an Ethernet frame

11a.2.8   Reducing collisions

The main contributors to collisions on an Ethernet network are:

- The number of packets per second
- The signal propagation delay between transmitting nodes
- The number of stations initiating packets
- The bandwidth utilization.

A few suggestions on reducing collisions in an Ethernet network are:

- Keep all cables as short as possible
- Keep all high activity sources and their destinations as close as possible. Possibly, isolate these nodes from the main network backbone with bridges/routers to reduce backbone traffic

- Separate segments with bridges and switches rather than with repeaters, which do not truncate the collision domain
- Check for unnecessary broadcast packets
- Remember that the monitoring equipment to check out network traffic can contribute to the traffic (and the collision rate).

11a.2.9   Design rules

The following design rules on length of cable segment, node placement, and hardware usage should be strictly observed.

Length of the cable segments

It is important to maintain the overall Ethernet requirements as far as length of the cable is concerned. Each segment has a particular maximum length allowable (Table 11a.2). For example, 10BASE-2 allows 185 m maximum length. The recommended maximum length is 80% of this figure. Some manufacturers advise that you can disregard this limit with their equipment. This can be a risky strategy and should be carefully considered.

System	Maximum	Recommended
10BASE-5	500 m (1640 ft)	400 m (1310 ft)
10BASE-2	185 m (600 ft)	150 m (500 ft)
10BASE-T	100 m (330 ft)	80 m (260 ft)

Table 11a.2
Suggested maximum lengths

Cable segments need not be made from a single homogenous length of cable and may comprise multiple lengths joined by coaxial connectors (two male plugs and a connector barrel).

To achieve maximum performance on 10BASE-5 cable segments, it is preferable that the total segment be made from one length of cable or from sections of the same drum of cable. If multiple sections of cable from different manufacturers are used, then these should be standard lengths of 23.4 m (76.8 ft), 70.2 m (230.3 ft), or 117 m (383.9 ft) (±0.5 m/1 ft), which are odd multiples of 23.4 m/76.8 ft (half wavelength in the cable at 5 MHz). These lengths ensure that reflections from the cable-to-cable impedance discontinuities are unlikely to add in phase. Using these lengths exclusively a mix of cable sections should be able to be made up to the full 500 m (1640 ft) segment length.

If the cable is from different manufacturers and you suspect potential mismatch problems, you should check that signal reflections, as impedance mismatches do not exceed 7% of the incident wave.

Maximum transceiver cable length

In 10BASE-5 systems, the maximum length of the transceiver cables is 50 m (164 ft) but it should be noted that this only applies to specified IEEE 802.3 compliant cables. Other AUI cables using ribbon or office grade cables can only be used for short distances (less than 12.5 m/41 ft), so check the manufacturer specifications for these.

Node placement rules

Connection of the transceiver media access units (MAU) to the cable causes signal reflections due to their bridging impedance. Placement of the MAUs must therefore be controlled to ensure that reflections from them do not significantly add in phase.

In 10BASE-5 systems, the MAUs are spaced at multiples of 2.5 m (8.2 ft), coinciding with the cable markings.

In 10BASE-2 systems, the minimum MAU spacing is 0.5 m (1.6 ft).

Maximum transmission path

The maximum transmission path is made of five segments connected by four repeaters. The total number of segments can be made up of a maximum of three coax segments containing station nodes and two link segments. The link segments are defined as point-to-point full-duplex links that connect 2 (and only 2) MAUs. This is summarized as the 5–4–3–2 rule (Table 11a.3).

5 segments 4 repeaters 3 coax segments 2 link segments	OR	5 segments 4 repeaters 3 link segments 2 coax segments

Table 11a.3
The 5–4–3–2 rule

It is important to verify that the above transmission rules are met by all paths between any two nodes on the network.

Note that the maximum sized network of four repeaters supported by IEEE 802.3 can be susceptible to timing problems. The maximum configuration is limited by propagation delay.

Note that 10BASE-2 segments should not be used to link 10BASE-5 segments.

Repeater rules

Repeaters are connected to transceivers that count as one node on the segments.

Special transceivers are used to connect repeaters and these do not implement the signal quality error test (SQE).

Fiber-optic repeaters are available giving up to 3000 m links at 10 MB/s. Check the vendor's specifications for adherence with IEEE 802.3 repeater performance and compliance with the fiber-optic inter repeater link (FOIRL) standard.

Cable system grounding

Grounding has safety and noise connotations. IEEE 802.3 states that the shield conductor of each coaxial cable shall make electrical contact with an effective earth reference at one point only.

The single point earth reference for an Ethernet system is usually located at one of the terminators. Most terminators for Ethernet have a screw terminal to which a ground lug can be attached using a braided cable, preferably to ensure good earthing.

Ensure that all other splices taps or terminators are jacketed so that no contact can be made with any metal objects. Insulating boots or sleeves should be used on all in-line coaxial connectors to avoid unintended earth contacts.

Round trip delay time

The maximum round trip propagation delay is 51.2 μs because of the minimum frame size of 64 bytes (512 bits). This time is determined by adding the propagation delays in all of the electronic components and cables that make up the longest signal path and then doubling this figure to obtain the round trip delay time.

Note that this calculation needs to be done for all components within a collision domain, store-and-forward devices such as bridges, routers, or switches terminate collision domains.

Tables 11a.4 and 11a.5 give typical maximum one-way delay times for various components and cables. Repeater and NIC delays for specific components can be obtained from the manufacturers.

Component	Maximum Delay (μs)
Standard transceiver	0.86
Twisted-pair transceiver	0.27
Fiber-optic transceiver	0.20
Multiport transceiver	0.10
10BASE-T concentrator	1.90
Local repeater	0.65
Fiber-optic repeater	1.55
Multiport repeater	1.55

Table 11a.4
Maximum one-way Ethernet component delays

Cable Medium	Maximum Delay per meter (μs)
UTP	0.0057
Coax (10BASE-5)	0.00433
Coax (10BASE-2)	0.00514
Fiber optic	0.005
AUI	0.00514

Table 11a.5
Maximum one-way Ethernet cable delays

11a.3   100 Mbps Ethernet

11a.3.1   Introduction

100BASE-T is the shorthand identifier for all 100 Mbps Ethernet systems, including twisted-pair copper and fiber versions. These include 100BASE-TX, 100BASE-FX, 100BASE-T4, and 100BASE-T2.

100BASE-X is the designator for the 100BASE-TX (copper) and 100BASE-FX (fiber) systems based on the same 4B/5B block encoding system used for FDDI (ANSI X3T9.5) fiber distributed interface system. 100BASE-TX, the most widely used version, is a 100 Mbps baseband system operating over two pairs of Cat5 UTP (Figure 11a.8) while 100BASE-FX operates at 100 Mbps in baseband mode over two multi-mode optic fibers.

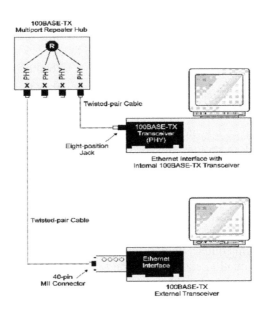

Figure 11a.8
100BASE-TX connection

100BASE-T4 was designed to operate at 100 Mbps over four pairs of Cat3 cable, but this option never gained widespread acceptance. Yet another version, 100BASE-T2, was supposed to operate over just two pairs of Cat3 cable but was never implemented by any vendor.

One of the limitations of the 100BASE-T systems is the size of the collision domain, which is 250 m or 5.12 μs. This is the maximum size of a network segment in which collisions can be detected, being one-tenth of the size of the maximum-size 10 Mbps network. This effectively limits the distance between a workstation and a hub to 100 m, the same as for 10BASE-T. This means that networks larger than 200 m must be logically connected together by store-and-forward type devices such as bridges, routers, or switches. This is not a bad thing, since it segregates the traffic within each collision domain, reducing the number of collisions on the network. The use of bridges and routers for traffic segregation, in this manner, is often done on industrial Ethernet networks.

The format of the frame has been left unchanged. The only difference is that it is transmitted 10 times faster than in 10 Mbps Ethernet, hence its length (in time) is 10 times less.

11a.3.2 Media access: full-duplex

The original Ethernet could only operate in half-duplex mode using CSMA/CD. Later versions of Ethernet (100BASE-T and up) can also operate in full-duplex mode, in which case the CSMA/CD mechanism is switched off. Full-duplex means a node can transmit and receive simultaneously and whenever it wants, since there is no possibility of contention. Full-duplex operation is specified in IEEE 802.3x.

The IEEE 802.3x supplement also describes an optional set of mechanisms used for flow control over full-duplex links, called MAC control and PAUSE. These are unfortunately beyond the scope of this document.

The following requirements must be met for full-duplex operation.

- The media must have separate transmit and receive paths. This is typically true for twisted-pair and fiber-optic links.
- There must only two stations on a segment. As a result of this, there can never be any collisions as the two stations can talk and listen simultaneously, with their transmit and receive ports cross connected (as in a null modem). Each port of a switching hub exists in its own segment, so if only one station is connected to each switch port, this condition is satisfied.
- Both stations must be capable of, and must be set up for, full-duplex operation.

11a.3.3   Auto-negotiation

The specifications for auto-negotiation were published in 1995 as part of the 802.3u Fast Ethernet supplement to the IEEE standard, based on the nWay system developed by National Semiconductor.

Auto-negotiation can be supported on all Ethernet systems using twisted-pair cabling, as well as the Gigabit Ethernet fiber-optic system. It enables devices to set to a mutually acceptable speed and operating mode (full-duplex/half-duplex). Auto-negotiation includes the following concepts.

11a.3.4   Fiber-optic cable distances 100BASE-FX

The following maximum cable distances apply:

- *Node to hub*:   Maximum distance of multi-mode cable (62.5/125) is 160 m (for connections using a single Class II hub).
- *Node to switch*:   Maximum multi-mode cable distance is 210 m.
- *Switch to switch*:   Maximum distance of multi-mode cable for a backbone connection between two 100BASE-FX switch ports is 412 m.
- *Switch to switch full-duplex*:   Maximum distance of multi-mode cable for a full-duplex connection between two 100BASE-FX switch ports is 2000 m.

The IEEE has not included the use of single-mode fiber in the 802.3u standard. However numerous vendors have products available enabling switch-to-switch distances of up to 10–20 km (6–12 miles) using single-mode fiber.

11a.3.5   100BASE-T repeater rules

The cable distance and the number of repeaters (hubs), which can be used in a 100BASE-T collision domain, depends on the delay in the cable and the time delay in the repeaters and NIC delays. The maximum round-trip delay for 100BASE-T systems is the time to transmit 64 bytes or 512 bits, and equals 5.12 µs. A frame has to go from the transmitter to the most remote node then back to the transmitter for collision detection within this round trip time. Therefore the one-way time delay will be half of this.

The maximum sized collision domain can then be determined by the following calculation:

Repeater delays + Cable delays + NIC delays + Safety factor (5 bits minimum) <2.048 µs

Table 11a.6 gives typical maximum one-way delays for various components. Repeater and NIC delays for specific components can be obtained from the manufacturer.

Component	Maximum Delay (µs)
Fast Ethernet NIC	0.25
Fast Ethernet switch port	0.25
Class I hub	0.7 max.
Class II hub	0.46 max.
UTP cable (per 100 m/330 ft)	0.55
Multi-mode fiber (per 100 m/330 ft)	0.50

Table 11a.6
Maximum one-way fast Ethernet component delays

Notes

- If the desired distance is too great it is possible to create a new collision domain by using a switch instead of a repeater.
- Most 100BASE-T repeaters are stackable, which means multiple units can be placed on top of one another and connected together by means of a fast backplane bus, such connections do not count as a repeater hop and make the ensemble function as a single repeater.

Sample calculation

The following calculation is made to confirm whether it is possible to connect two fast Ethernet nodes together using two Class II hubs connected by 50 m fiber. One node is connected to the first repeater with 50 m UTP while the other has a 100 m fiber connection.
Calculation: Using the time delays in Table 11a.6.
The total one-way delay of 2.445 µs is within the required interval (2.56 µs) and allows at least 5 bits safety factor, so this connection is permissible.

11a.4   Gigabit Ethernet

11a.4.1   Introduction

1000BASE-X is the shorthand identifier for the Gigabit Ethernet system based on the 8B/10B block encoding scheme adapted from the Fiber Channel networking standard, developed by ANSI. 1000BASE-X includes 1000BASE-SX, 1000BASE-LX, and 1000BASE-CX.

- 1000BASE-SX is the short wavelength fiber version.
- 1000BASE-LX is the long wavelength fiber version.
- 1000BASE-CX is a short copper cable version, based on the Fiber Channel standard.

1000BASE-T, on the other hand, is a 1000 Mbps version capable of operating over Cat5 (or better, such as Cat5e) UTP. This system is based on a different encoding scheme.

As with fast Ethernet, Gigabit Ethernet supports full-duplex and auto-negotiation. It uses the same IEEE 802.3 frame format as 10 and 100 Mbps Ethernet systems. This operates at ten times the clock speed of Fast Ethernet at 1 Gbps. By retaining the same frame format as the earlier versions of Ethernet, backward compatibility is assured. Despite the similar frame format, the system had to undergo a small change to enable it to function effectively at 1 Gbps. The slot time of 64 bytes used with both 10 and 100 Mbps systems has been increased to 512 bytes. Without this increased slot time the network would have been impracticably small at one-tenth of the size of fast Ethernet – only 20 m! The slot time defines the time during which the transmitting node retains control of the medium, and in particular is responsible for collision detection. With Gigabit Ethernet it was necessary to increase this time by a factor of eight to 4.096 µs to compensate for the tenfold speed increase. This then gives a collision domain of about 200 m (660 ft).

If the transmitted frame is less than 512 bytes the transmitter continues transmitting to fill the 512 byte window. A carrier extension symbol is used to mark frames that are shorter than 512 bytes and to fill the remainder of the frame.

11a.4.2 Gigabit Ethernet full-duplex repeaters

Gigabit Ethernet nodes are connected to full-duplex repeaters, also known as non-buffered switches or buffered distributors. These devices have a basic MAC function in each port, which enables them to verify that a complete frame is received and compute its frame check sequence (CRC) to verify the frame validity. Then the frame is buffered in the internal memory of the port before being forwarded to the other ports of the repeater. It is therefore combining the functions of a repeater with some features of a switch.

All ports on the repeater operate at the same speed of 1 Gbps, and operate in full-duplex so it can simultaneously send and receive from any port. The repeater uses IEEE 802.3x flow control to ensure the small internal buffers associated with each port do not overflow. When the buffers are filled to a critical level, the repeater tells the transmitting node to stop sending until the buffers have been sufficiently emptied. The repeater does not analyze the packet address fields to determine where to send the packet, like a switch does, but simply sends out all valid packets to all the other ports on the repeater.

The IEEE does allow for half-duplex Gigabit repeaters – however none exist at this time.

11a.4.3 Gigabit Ethernet design considerations

Fiber-optic cable distances

The maximum cable distances that can be used between the node and a full-duplex 1000BASE-SX and LX repeater depend mainly on the chosen wavelength, the type of cable, and its bandwidth. The maximum transmission distances on multi-mode cable are limited by the differential mode delay (DMD). The very narrow beam of laser light injected into the multi-mode fiber results in a relatively small number of rays going through the fiber core. These rays each have different propagation times because they are going through differing lengths of glass by zigzagging through the core to a greater or lesser extent. These pulses of light can cause jitter and interference at the receiver. This is overcome by using a conditioned launch of the laser into the multi-mode fiber. This spreads the laser light evenly over the core of the multimedia fiber so that the laser source looks more like a light emitting diode (LED) source. This spreads the light in a large number of rays across the fiber resulting in smoother spreading of the pulses, so less interference. This conditioned launch is done in the 1000BASE-SX transceivers.

Table 11a.7 gives the maximum distances for full-duplex 1000BASE-X repeaters.

NIC	0.25 μs
50 m (165 ft) UTP	0.275 μs
Repeater class II	0.46 μs
50 m (165 ft) fiber	0.25 μs
Repeater class II	0.46 μs
100 m (330 ft) fiber	0.50 μs
NIC	0.25 μs
Total delay	**2.445 μs**

Table 11a.7
Maximum fiber distances for 1000BASE-X (full-duplex)

Gigabit repeater rules

The cable distance and the number of repeaters, which can be used in a half-duplex 1000BASE-T collision domain depends on the delay in the cable and the time delay in the repeaters and NIC delays. The maximum round-trip delay for 1000BASE-T systems is the time to transmit 512 bytes or 4096 bits and equals 4.096 μs. A frame has to go from the transmitter to the most remote node then back to the transmitter for collision detection within this round trip time. Therefore the one-way time delay will be half this.

The maximum sized collision domain can then be determined by the following calculation:

Repeater delays + Cable delays + NIC delays

+ Safety factor (5 bits minimum) <2.048 μs

Table 11a.8 gives typical maximum one-way delays for various components. Repeater and NIC delays for your specific components can be obtained from the manufacturer.

Wavelength (nm)	Cable Type	Bandwidth (MHz/km)	Attenuation (dB/km)	Maximum Distance (m)
850	50/125 multi-mode	400	3.25	500
850	50/125 multi-mode	500	3.43	550
850	62.5/125 multi-mode	160	160	220
850	62.5/125 multi-mode	200	200	275
1300	50/125 multi-mode	500	2.32	550
1300	62.5/125 multi-mode	500	1.0	550
1300	9/125 single-mode	Infinite	0.4	5000

Table 11a.8
Maximum one-way Gigabit Ethernet component delays

These calculations give the maximum collision diameter for IEEE 802.3z half-duplex Gigabit Ethernet systems. The maximum Gigabit Ethernet network diameters specified by the IEEE are shown in Table 11a.9.

Component	Maximum Delay (µs)
Gigabit NIC	0.432
Gigabit repeater	0.488
UTP cable (per 100 m)	0.55
Multi-mode fiber (per 100 m)	0.50

Table 11a.9
Maximum half-duplex Gigabit Ethernet network diameters

Note half-duplex Gigabit Ethernet repeaters are not available for sale. Use full-duplex repeaters with the point-to-point cable distances between node and repeater or node and switch as listed in Table 11a.7.

11a.5   Industrial Ethernet

11a.5.1   Introduction

Early Ethernet was not entirely suitable for control functions as it was primarily developed for office-type environments. The Ethernet technology has, however, made rapid advances over the past few years. It has gained such widespread acceptance in industry that it is becoming the *de facto* field bus technology. An indication of this trend is the inclusion of Ethernet as the Levels 1 and 2 infrastructure for Modbus/TCP (Schneider), Ethernet/IP (Rockwell Automation and ODVA), ProfiNet (PNO), and Foundation Fieldbus HSE (Fieldbus Foundation).

The following sections will deal with problems related to early Ethernet, and how they have been addressed in subsequent upgrades.

11a.5.2   Connectors and cabling

Earlier industrial Ethernet systems such as the first-generation Siemens SimaticNet (Sinec-H1) are based on the 10BASE-5 configuration, and thus the connectors involved include the screw-type N-connectors and the D-type connectors, which are both fairly rugged. The heavy-gage twin-screen (braided) RG-8 coaxial cable is also quite impervious to electrostatic interference.

Most modern industrial Ethernet systems are, however, based on a 10BASE-T/100BASE-X configuration and thus have to contend with RJ-45 connectors and (typically) Cat5 twisted-pair cable. Despite its inherent resistance to electromagnetically induced interference, the UTP cable is not really suited to industrial applications and therefore the trend is towards screened or shielded twisted pair such as Cat5i, or optic fiber. The connectors are problematic as well. The RJ-45 connectors are everything but rugged and are suspect when subjected to great temperature extremes, contact with oils and other fluids, dirt, UV radiation, EMI as well as shock, vibration, and mechanical loading.

As in interim measure, some manufacturers started using D-type (known also as DB or D-Submin) connectors, but currently there is a strong movement towards the M12-based series of connectors. The M12 form factor, governed by IEC 61076, is widely accepted in field bus and automation applications, and is supplied by vendors such as Lumberg, Turck, Escha, InterlinkBT, and Hirschmann. Typical M12 connectors for Ethernet are of the 8-pole variety, with threaded connectors. They can accept various types of Cat5/5e twisted-pair wiring such as braided or shielded wire (solid or stranded), and offer excellent protection against moisture, dust, corrosion, EMI, RFI, mechanical vibration and shock, UV radiation, and extreme temperatures (–40 to 75 °C).

As far as the media is concerned, several manufacturers are producing Cat5 and Cat5e wiring systems using braided or shielded twisted pairs. An example of an integrated approach to Industrial Ethernet cabling is Lumberg's EtherMATE system, which also includes both the cabling and an M12 connector system.

11a.5.3   Deterministic vs stochastic operation

One of the most common complaints with early Ethernet was that it uses CSMA/CD (a probabilistic or stochastic method) as opposed to other automation technologies such as Fieldbus that uses deterministic access methods such as token passing or the publisher–subscriber model. CSMA/CD essentially means that it is impossible to guarantee delivery of a possibly critical message within a certain time. This could be due either to congestion on the network (often due to other less critical traffic) or to collisions with other frames. In office applications there is not much difference between 5 s and 500 ms, but in industrial applications a millisecond counts. Industrial processes often require scans in a 5–20 ms range, and some demanding processes could even require 2–5 ms. On 10BASE-T Ethernet, for example, the access time on a moderately loaded 100-station network could range from 10 to 100 ms, which is acceptable for office applications but not for processes.

With Ethernet, the loading or traffic needs to be carefully analyzed to ensure that the network is not overwhelmed at critical or peak operational times. While a typical utilization factor on a commercial Ethernet LAN of 25–30% is acceptable, figures of less than 10% utilization on an industrial Ethernet LAN are required. Most industrial networks run at 3 or 4% utilization with a fairly large number of I/O points being transferred across the system.

The advent of fast and Gigabit Ethernet, switching hubs, VLAN technology, full-duplex operation, and deterministic Ethernet has effectively put this concern to rest for most applications.

11a.5.4   Size and overhead of Ethernet frame

Data-link encoding efficiency is another problem, with the Ethernet frames taking up far more space than for an equivalent Fieldbus frame. If the TCP/IP protocol is used in addition to the Ethernet frame, the overhead increases dramatically. The efficiency of the overall system is, however, more complex than simply the number of bytes on the transmitting cable and issues such as raw speed on the cable and the overall traffic need to be examined carefully. For example, if 2 bytes of data from an instrument had to be packaged in a 60 byte message (because of TCP/IP and Ethernet protocols being used) this would result in an enormous overhead compared to a Fieldbus protocol. However if the communications link was running at 100 Mbps or 1 Gbps with full-duplex communications this would put a different light on the problem and make the overhead issue almost irrelevant.

11a.5.5   Noise and interference

Due to higher electrical noise near to the industrial LANs some form of electrical shielding and protection is useful to minimize errors in the communication. A good choice of cable is fiber optic (or sometimes coaxial cable). Twisted pair can be used but care should be taken to route the cables far away from any potential sources of noise. If twisted-pair cable is selected, a good decision is to use screened twisted-pair cable (ScTP) rather than the standard UTP.

In saying the above, it should be noted that Ethernet-based networks are installed in a wide variety of systems and rarely have problems reported due to reliability issues. The use of fiber ensures that there are minimal problems due to earth loops or electrical noise and interference.

11a.5.6   Partitioning of the network

It is very important that the industrial network operates separately from that of the commercial network, as speed of response and real-time operation are often critical attributes of an industrial network. An office type network may not have the same response requirements. In addition, security is another concern where the industrial network is split off from the commercial networks so any problems in the commercial network will not affect the industrial side.

Industrial networks are also often partitioned into individual sub-networks for reasons of security and speed of response, by means of bridges and switches.

In order to reduce network traffic, some PLC manufacturers use exception reporting. This requires only changes in the various digital and analog parameters to be transmitted on the network. For example, if a digital point changes state (from on to off or off to on), this change would be reported. Similarly, an analog value could have associated with it a specified change of span before reporting the new analog value to the master station.

11a.5.7   Switching technology

Both the repeating hub and bridge technologies are being superseded by switching technology. This allows traffic between two nodes on the network to be directly connected in a full-duplex fashion. The nodes are connected through a switch with extremely low levels of latency. Furthermore, the switch is capable of handling all the ports communicating simultaneously with one another without any collisions. This means that the overall speed of the switch backplane is considerably greater than the sum of the speeds of the individual Ethernet ports.

Most switches operate at the data-link layer and are also referred to as switching hubs and Layer 2 switches. Some switches can interpret the network layer addresses (e.g. the IP address) and make routing decisions on that. These are known as Layer 3 switches.

Advanced switches can be configured to support virtual LANs. This allows the user to configure a switch so that all the ports on the switch are subdivided into predefined groups. These groups of ports are referred to as virtual LANs (VLANs) – a concept that is very useful for industrial networks. Only switch ports allocated to the same VLAN can communicate with each other.

Switches do have performance limitations that could affect a critical industrial application. If there is traffic on a switch from multiple input ports aimed at one particular output port, the switch may drop some of the packets. Depending on the vendor implementation it may force a collision back to the transmitting device so that the transmitting node backs off long enough for the congestion to clear. This means that the transmitting node does not have a guarantee on the transmission between two nodes – something that could impact a critical industrial application.

In addition, although switches do not create separate broadcast domains, each virtual LAN effectively forms one (if this is enabled on the switch). An Ethernet broadcast message received on one port is retransmitted onto all ports in the VLAN. Hence a switch will not eliminate the problem of excessive broadcast traffic that can cause severe performance degradation in the operation of the network. TCP/IP uses the Ethernet broadcast frame to obtain MAC addresses and hence broadcasts are fairly prevalent here.

A problem with a switched network is that duplicate paths between two given nodes could cause a frame to be passed around and around the 'ring' caused by the two alternative paths. This possibility is eliminated by the 'Spanning Tree' algorithm, the IEEE 802.1d standard for Layer 2 recovery. However, this method is quite slow and could take from 2 to 5 s to detect and bypass a path failure and could leave all networked devices isolated during the process. This is obviously unacceptable for industrial applications.

A solution to the problem is to connect the switches in a dual redundant ring topology, using copper or fiber. This poses a new problem since an Ethernet broadcast message will be sent around the loop indefinitely. One vendor, Hirschmann, has solved this problem by developing a switch with added redundancy management capabilities. The redundancy manager allows a physical 200 Mbps ring to be created, by terminating both ends of the traditional Ethernet bus in itself. Although the bus is now looped back to itself, the redundancy manager logically breaks the loop, preventing broadcast messages from wreaking havoc. Logically the redundancy manager behaves like two nodes, sitting back to back, transmitting and receiving messages to the other around the ring using IEEE 802.1p/Q frames. This creates a deterministic path through any IEEE 802.1p/Q compliant switches (up to 50) in the ring, which results in a real-time 'awareness' of the state of the ring.

When a network failure is detected (i.e. the loop is broken), the redundancy manager interconnects the two segments attached to it, thereby restoring the loop. This takes place in between 20 and 500 ms, depending on the size of the ring.

11a.5.8 Active electronics

With the hub-based Ethernet topologies (e.g. 10BASE-T, 100BASE-TX) the hub (be that a repeating hub or a switching hub) is an active electronic device that requires power to operate. If it fails this will terminate any communications occurring between nodes connected.

To address this problem, some vendors have introduced the concept of dual-redundant switch rings with the ability to reconfigure itself in a very short time (30 ms for small networks to 600 ms for large networks) after a switch failure.

In addition, the power requirements for an Ethernet card (and other hardware components) are often significantly more than an equivalent Fieldbus card (such as from Foundation Fieldbus). There is limited provision within Ethernet for loop powering the instrument through the Ethernet cable. This is called power over Ethernet (PoE) and is often used to power wireless hubs on a network.

11a.5.9 Fast and Gigabit Ethernet

The recent developments in Ethernet technology are making it even more relevant in the industrial market. Fast Ethernet as defined in the IEEE specification 802.3u is essentially Ethernet running at 100 Mbps. The same frame structure, addressing scheme and CSMA/CD access method are used as with the 10 Mbps standard. In addition, Fast Ethernet can also operate in full-duplex mode as opposed to CSMA/CD, which means that there are no collisions. Fast Ethernet operates at ten times the speed of that of standard IEEE 802.3 Ethernet. Video and audio applications can enjoy substantial improvements in performance using Fast Ethernet. Smart instruments that require far smaller frame sizes will not see such an improvement in performance. One area, however, where there may be significant throughput improvements is in the area of collision recovery. The back-off times for 100 Mbps Ethernet will be a tenth that of standard Ethernet. Hence a heavily loaded network with considerable individual messages and nodes would see performance improvements. If loading and collisions are not really an issue on the slower 10 Mbps network then there will not be many tangible improvements in the higher LAN speed of 100 Mbps.

Note that with the auto-negotiation feature built into standard switches and many Ethernet cards, the device can operate at either the 10 or 100 Mbps speeds. In addition the category 5 wiring installed for 10BASE-T Ethernet would be adequate for the 100 Mbps standard as well.

Gigabit Ethernet is another technology that could be used to connect instruments and PLCs. However its speed would probably not be fully exploited by the instruments for the reasons indicated above.

11a.5.10   TCP/IP and industrial systems

The TCP/IP suite of protocols provides for a common open protocol. In combination with Ethernet this can be considered to be a truly open standard available to all users and vendors. However, there are some problems at the application layer area. Although TCP/IP implements four layers which are all open (network interface, Internet, host–host and application layers), most industrial vendors still implement their own specific application layer. Hence equipment from different vendors can coexists on the factory shop floor but cannot inter-operate. Protocols such as MMS (manufacturing messaging service) have been promoted as truly 'open' automation application layer protocols but with limited acceptance to date.

11a.5.11   Industrial Ethernet architectures for high availability

There are several key technology areas involved in the design of Ethernet-based industrial automation architecture. These include available switching technologies, *quality of service* (QOS) issues, the integration of existing (legacy) field buses, sensor bus integration, high availability and resiliency, security issues, long-distance communication and network management – to name but a few.

For high availability systems a single network interface represents a *single point of Failure* (SPOF) that can bring the system down. There are several approaches that can be used on their own or in combination, depending on the amount of resilience required (and hence the cost). The cost of the additional investment in the system has to be weighed against the costs of any downtime.

For a start, the network topology could be changed to represent a switched ring. This necessitates the use of a special controlling switch (redundancy manager) and protects the system against a single failure on the network. It does not, however, guard against a failure of the network interface on one of the network devices.

The next level of resiliency would necessitate two network interfaces on the controller (i.e. changing it to a dual-homed system), each one connected to a different switch. This setup would be able to tolerate both a single network failure AND a network interface failure.

Ultimately one could protect the system against a total failure by duplicating the switched ring, connecting each port of the dual-homed system to a different ring.

Other factors supporting a high degree of resilience would include hot swappable switches and NICs, dual redundant power supplies, and on-line diagnostic software.

11b

Industrial Ethernet troubleshooting

11b.1 Introduction

This section deals with addressing common faults on Ethernet networks. Ethernet encompasses layers 1 and 2, namely the physical and data-link layers of the OSI model. This is equivalent to the bottom layer (the network interface layer) in the ARPA (DoD) model. This section will focus on those layers only, as well as on the actual medium over which the communication takes place.

11b.2 Common problems and faults

Ethernet hardware is fairly simple and robust, and once a network has been commissioned, providing the cabling has been done professionally and certified, the network should be fairly trouble-free.

Most problems will be experienced at the commissioning phase, and could theoretically be attributed to either the cabling, the LAN devices (such as hubs and switches), the *network interface cards* (NICs) or the protocol stack configuration on the hosts.

The wiring system should be installed and commissioned by a certified installer (the suppliers of high-speed Ethernet cabling systems, such as ITT, will not guarantee their wiring if not installed by a certified installer). This effectively rules out wiring problems for new installations.

If the LAN devices such as hubs and switches are from reputable vendors, it is highly unlikely that they will malfunction in the beginning. Care should nevertheless be taken to ensure that intelligent (managed) hubs and switches are correctly set up.

The same applies to NICs. NICs rarely fail and nine times out of ten the problem lies with a faulty setup or incorrect driver installation, or an incorrect configuration of the higher level protocols such as IP.

11b.3 Tools of the trade

Apart from a fundamental understanding of the technologies involved the following tools are helpful in isolating Ethernet-related problems, sufficient time, a pair of eyes, patience, and many cups of coffee/tea.

11b.3.1 Multimeters

A simple multimeter can be used to check for continuity and cable resistance, as will be explained in this section.

11b.3.2   Handheld cable testers

There are many versions on the market, ranging from simple devices that basically check for wiring continuity to sophisticated devices that comply with all the prerequisites for 1000BASE-T wiring infrastructure tests (see Figure 11b.1). Testers are available from several vendors such as MicroTest, Fluke, and Scope.

Figure 11b.1
OMNIscanner2 cable tester

11b.3.3   Fiber-optic cable testers

Fiber-optic testers are simpler than UDP testers, since they basically only have to measure continuity and attenuation loss. Some UDP testers can be turned into fiber-optic testers by purchasing an attachment that fits onto the existing tester. For more complex problems such as finding the location of a damaged section on a fiber-optic cable, an alternative is to use a proper *optical time domain reflectometer* (OTDR) but these are expensive instruments and it is often cheaper to employ the services of a professional wire installer (with his own OTDR) if this is required.

11b.3.4   Traffic generators

A traffic generator is a device that can generate a pre-programed data pattern on the network. Although they are not strictly speaking used for fault finding, they can be used to predict network behavior due to increased traffic, for example, when planning network changes or upgrades. Traffic generators can be stand-alone devices or they can be integrated into hardware LAN analyzers such as the Hewlett Packard 3217.

11b.3.5   RMON probes

An RMON (Remote MONitoring) probe is a device that can examine a network at a given point and keep track of captured information at a detailed level. The advantage of a RMON probe is that it can monitor a network at a remote location. The data captured by the RMON probe can then be uploaded and remotely displayed by the appropriate RMON management software. RMON probes and the associated management software are available from several vendors such as 3COM, Bay Networks and NetScout. It is also possible to create an RMON probe by running commercially available RMON software on a normal PC, although the data collection capability will not be as good as that of a dedicated RMON probe.

11b.3.6 Handheld frame analyzers

Handheld frame analyzers are manufactured by several vendors such as Fluke, Scope, Finisar and PsiberNet, for up to Gigabit Ethernet speeds. These little devices can perform link testing, traffic statistics gathering, etc. and can even break down frames by protocol type. The drawback of these testers is the small display and the lack of memory, which results in a lack of historical or logging functions on these devices.

An interesting feature of some probes is that they are non-intrusive, that is, they simply clamp on to the wire and do not have to be attached to a hub port (see Figure 11b.2).

Figure 11b.2
Clamp-on Gigabit Ethernet probe

11b.3.7 Software protocol analyzers

Software protocol analyzers are software packages running on PCs and using either a general purpose or a specialized NIC to capture frames from the network. The NIC is controlled by a so-called promiscuous driver, which enables the NIC to capture all packets on the medium and not only those addressed to it in broadcast or unicast mode.

There are excellent freeware protocol analyzers such as Ethereal or Analyzer, the latter being developed at the Polytechnic of Torino in Italy. Top range software products such as Network Associates' 'Sniffer' or WaveTek Wandel Goltemann's 'Domino' suite have sophisticated expert systems that can aid in the analysis of the captured software, but unfortunately these products come at a higher price.

11b.3.8 Hardware BASE-d protocol analyzers

Several manufacturers such as Hewlett Packard, Network Associates and WaveTek Wandel Goltemann also supply hardware BASE-d protocol analyzers using their protocol analysis software running on a proprietary hardware infrastructure. This makes them very expensive but dramatically increases the power of the analyzer. For fast and Gigabit Ethernet, this is probably the better approach.

11b.4 Problems and solutions

11b.4.1 Noise

If excessive noise is suspected on a coax or UTP cable, an oscilloscope can be connected between the signal conductor(s) and ground. This method will show up noise on the conductor, but will not necessarily give a true indication of the amount of power in the noise. A simple and cheap method to pick up noise on the wire is to connect a small loudspeaker between the conductor and ground. A small operational amplifier can be used as an input buffer, so as not to 'load' the wire under observation. The noise will be heard as an audible signal.

The quickest way to get rid of a noise problem, apart from using screened UTP (ScTP), is to change to a fiber-BASE-d instead of a copper-BASE-d network, for example, by using 100BASE-FX instead of 100BASE-TX.

Noise can to some extent be counteracted on a coax-BASE-d network by earthing the screen AT ONE END ONLY. Earthing it on both sides will create an earth loop. This is normally accomplished by means of an earthing chain or an earthing screw on one of the terminators. Care should also be taken not to allow contact between any of the other connectors on the segment and ground.

11b.4.2   Thin coax problems

Incorrect cable type

The correct cable for thin Ethernet is RG58-A/U or RG-58C/U. This is a 5 mm diameter coaxial cable with 50 Ω characteristic impedance and a stranded center conductor. Incorrect cable used in a thin Ethernet system can cause reflections, resulting in CRC errors, and hence many retransmitted frames.

The characteristic impedance of coaxial cable is a function of the ratio between the center conductor diameter and the screen diameter. Hence other types of coax may closely resemble RG-58, but may have different characteristic impedance.

Loose connectors

The BNC coaxial connectors used on RG-58 should be of the correct diameter, and should be properly crimped onto the cable. An incorrect size connector or a poor crimp could lead to intermittent contact problems, which are very hard to locate. Even worse is the 'Radio Shack' hobbyist type screw-on BNC connector that can be used to quickly make up a cable without the use of a crimping tool. These more often not lead to very poor connections. A good test is to grip the cable in one hand, and the connector in another, and pull very hard. If the connector comes off, the connector mounting procedures need to be seriously reviewed.

Excessive number of connectors

The total length of a thin Ethernet segment is 185 m and the total number of stations on the segment should not exceed 30. However, each station involves a BNC T-piece plus two coax connectors and there could be additional BNC barrel connectors joining the cable. Although the resistance of each BNC connector is small, they are still finite and can add up. The total resistance of the segment (cable plus connectors) should not exceed 10 Ω otherwise problems can surface.

An easy method of checking the loop resistance (the resistance to the other end of the cable and back) is to remove the terminator on one end of the cable and measure the resistance between the connector body and the center contact. The total resistance equals the resistance of the cable plus connectors plus the terminator on the far side. This should be between 50 and 60 Ω. Anything more than this is indicative of a problem.

Overlong cable segments

The maximum length of a thin net segment is 185 m. This constraint is not imposed by collision domain considerations, but rather by the attenuation characteristics of the cable.

If it is suspected that the cable is too long, its length should be confirmed. Usually, the cable is within a cable trench and hence it cannot be visually measured. In this case, a *time domain reflectometer* (TDR) can be used to confirm its length.

Stub cables

For thin Ethernet (10BASE-2), the maximum distance between the bus and the transceiver electronics is 4 cm. In practice, this is taken up by the physical connector plus the PC board tracks leading to the transceiver, which means that there is no scope for a drop cable or 'stub' between the NIC and the bus. The BNC T-piece has to be mounted directly on to the NIC.

Users might occasionally get away with putting a short stub between the T-piece and the NIC, but this invariably leads to problems in the long run.

Incorrect terminations

10BASE-2 is designed around 50 Ω coax and hence requires a 50 Ω terminator at each end. Without the terminators in place, there would be so many reflections from each end that the network would collapse. A slightly incorrect terminator is better than no terminator, yet may still create reflections of such magnitude that it affects the operation of the network.

A 93 Ω terminator looks no different than a 50 Ω terminator; therefore it should not be automatically assumed that a terminator is of the correct value.

If two 10BASE-2 segments are joined with a repeater, the internal termination on the repeater can be mistakenly left enabled. This leads to three terminators on the segment, creating reflections and hence affecting the network performance.

The easiest way to check for proper termination is by alternatively removing the terminators at each end, and measuring the resistance between connector body and center pin. In each case, the result should be 50–60 Ω. Alternatively, one of the T-pieces in the middle of the segment can be removed from its NIC and the resistance between the connector body and the center pin measured. The result should be the value of the two half cable segments (including terminators) in parallel, that is, 25–30 Ω.

Invisible insulation damage

If the internal insulation of coax is inadvertently damaged, for example, by placing a heavy point load on the cable, the outer cover could return to its original shape whilst leaving the internal dielectric deformed. This leads to a change of characteristic impedance at the damaged point resulting, in reflections. This, in turn, could lead to standing waves being formed on the cable.

An indication of this problem is when a work station experiences problems when attached to a specific point on a cable, yet functions normally when moved a few meters to either side. The only solution is to remove the offending section of the cable. Because of the nature of the damage, it cannot be seen by the naked eye and the position of the damage has to be located with a TDR. Alternatively, the whole cable segment has to be replaced.

Invisible cable break

This problem is similar to the previous one, with the difference that the conductor has been completely severed at a specific point. Despite the terminators at both ends of the cable, the cable break effectively creates two half segments, each with an un-terminated end, and hence nothing will work.

The only way to discover the location of the break is by using a TDR.

11b.4.3   Thick coax problems

Thick coax (RG-8), as used for 10BASE-5 or thick Ethernet, will basically exhibit the same problems as thin coax yet there are a few additional complications.

Loose connectors

10BASE-5 use N-type male screw on connectors on the cable. As with BNC connectors, incorrect procedures or a wrong sized crimping tool can cause sloppy joints. This can lead to intermittent problems that are difficult to locate.

Again, a good test is to grab hold of the connector and to try and rip it off the cable with brute force. If the connector comes off, then it was not properly installed in the first place.

Dirty taps

The MAU transceiver is often installed on a thick coax by using a vampire tap, which necessitates pre-drilling into the cable in order to allow the center pin of the tap to contact the center conductor of the coax. The hole has to go through two layers of braided screen and two layers of foil. If the hole is not properly cleaned pieces of the foil and braid can remain and cause short circuits between the signal conductor and ground.

Open tap holes

When a transceiver is removed from a location on the cable, the abandoned hole should be sealed. If not, dirt or water could enter the hole and create problems in the long run.

Tight cable bends

The bend radius on a thick coax cable may not exceed 10 in. If it does, the insulation can deform to such an extent that reflections are created leading to CRC errors. Excessive cable bends can be detected with a TDR.

Excessive loop resistance

The resistance of a cable segment may not exceed 5 Ω. As in the case of thin coax, the easiest way to do this is to remove a terminator at one end and measure the loop resistance. It should be in a range of 50–55 Ω.

11b.4.4   UTP problems

The most commonly used tool for UTP troubleshooting is a cable meter or pair scanner. At the bottom end of the scale a cable tester can be an inexpensive tool, only able to check for the presence of wire on the appropriate pins of a RJ-45 connector. High-end cable testers can also test for noise on the cable, cable length, and crosstalk (such as near end signal crosstalk or NEXT) at various frequencies. It can check the cable against CAT5/5e specifications and can download cable test reports to a PC for subsequent evaluation.

The following is a description of some wiring practices that can lead to problems.

Incorrect wire type (solid/stranded)

Patch cords must be made with stranded wire. Solid wire will eventually suffer from metal fatigue and crack right at the RJ-45 connector, leading to permanent or intermittent open connection/s. Some RJ-45 plugs, designed for stranded wire, will actually cut through the solid conductor during installation, leading to an immediate open connection. This can lead to CRC errors resulting in slow network performance, or can even disable a workstation permanently. The length of the patchcords or flyleads on either end of the link may not exceed 5 m, and these cables must be made from stranded wire.

The permanently installed cable between hub and workstation, on the other hand, should not exceed 90 m and must be of the solid variety. Not only is stranded wire more expensive for this application, but the capacitance is higher, which may lead to a degradation of performance.

Incorrect wire system components

The performance of the wire link between a hub and a workstation is not only dependent on the grade of wire used, but also on the associated components such as patch panels, *surface mount units* (SMUs) and RJ-45 type connectors. A single substandard connector on a wire link is sufficient to degrade the performance of the entire link.

High quality fast and Gigabit Ethernet wiring systems use high-grade RJ-45 connectors that are visibly different from standard RJ-45 type connectors.

Incorrect cable type

Care must be taken to ensure that the existing UTP wiring is of the correct category for the type of Ethernet being used. For 10BASE-T, Cat3 UTP is sufficient, while fast Ethernet (100BASE-T) requires Cat5 and Gigabit Ethernet requires Cat5e or better. This applies to patch cords as well as the permanently installed ('infrastructure') wiring.

Most industrial Ethernet systems nowadays are 100BASE-X based and hence use Cat5 wiring. For such applications, it might be prudent to install screened Cat5 wiring (ScTP) for better noise immunity. ScTP is available with a common foil screen around the 4 pairs or with an individual foil screen around each pair.

A common mistake is to use telephone grade patch ('silver satin') cable for the connection between an RJ-45 wall socket (SMU) and the network interface card in a computer. Telephone patch cables use very thin wires that are untwisted, leading to high signal loss and large amounts of crosstalk. This will lead to signal errors causing retransmission of lost packets, which will eventually slow the network down.

Straight vs crossover cable

A 10BASE-T or 100BASE-TX patch cable consists of 4 wires (two pairs) with an RJ-45 connector at each end. The pins used for the TX and RX signals are typically 1, 2 and 3, 6. Although a typical patch cord has 8 wires (4 pairs), the 4 unused wires are nevertheless crimped into the connector for mechanical strength. In order to facilitate communication between computer and hub, the TX and RX ports on the hub are reversed, so that the TX on the computer and the RX on the hub are interconnected whilst the TX on the hub is connected to the RX on the hub. This requires a 'straight' interconnection cable with pin 1 wired to pin 1, pin 2 wired to pin 2, etc.

If the NICs on two computers are to be interconnected without the benefit of a hub, a normal straight cable cannot be used since it will connect TX to TX and RX to RX. For this purpose, a crossover cable has to be used, in the same way as a 'null' modem cable. Crossover cables are normally color coded (for example, green or black) in order to differentiate them from straight cables.

A crossover cable can create problems when it looks like a normal straight cable, an unsuspecting person may use it to connect a NIC to a hub or a wall outlet. A quick way to identify a crossover cable is to hold the two RJ-45 connectors side by side and observe the colors of the 8 wires in the cable through the clear plastic of the connector body. The sequence of the colors should be the same for both connectors.

Hydra cables

Some 10BASE-T hubs feature 50 pin connectors to conserve space on the hub. Alternatively, some building wire systems use 50 pin connectors on the wiring panels but the hub equipment has RJ-45 connectors. In both cases, hydra or octopus cable has to be used. This consists of a 50 pin connector connected to a length of 25 pair cable, which is then broken out as a set of 12 small cables, each with a RJ-45 connector. Depending on the vendor the 50 pin connector can be attached through locking clips, Velcro strips or screws. It does not always lock down properly, although at a glance it may seem so. This can cause a permanent or intermittent break of contact on some ports.

For 10BASE-T systems, near end crosstalk (NEXT), which occurs when a signal is coupled from a transmitting wire pair to a receiving wire pair close to the transmitter, (where the signal is strongest) causes most problems. On a single 4 pair cable, this is not a serious problem, as only two pairs are used but on the 25 pair cable, with many signals in close proximity, this can create problems. This can be very difficult to troubleshoot since it will require test equipment that can transmit on all pairs simultaneously.

Excessive untwists

On Cat5 cable, crosstalk is minimized by twisting each cable pair. However, in order to attach a connector at the end the cable has to be untwisted slightly. Great care has to be taken since excessive untwists (more than 1 cm) is enough to create excessive crosstalk, which can lead to signal errors. This problem can be detected with a high quality cable tester.

Stubs

A stub cable is an abandoned telephone cable leading from a punch-down block to some other point. This does not create a problem for telephone systems, but if the same Cat3 telephone cabling is used to support 10BASE-T, then the stub cables may cause signal reflections that result in bit errors. Again, a high quality cable tester only will be able to detect this problem.

Damaged RJ-45 connectors

On RJ-45 connectors without protective boots, the retaining clip can easily break off especially on cheaper connectors made of brittle plastic. The connector will still mate with the receptacle but will retract with the least amount of pull on the cable, thereby breaking contact. This problem can be checked by alternatively pushing and pulling on the connector and observing the LED on the hub, media coupler or NIC – wherever the suspect connector is inserted. Because of the mechanical deficiencies of 'standard' RJ-45 connectors they are not commonly used on Industrial Ethernet systems.

T4 on 2 pairs

100BASE-TX is a direct replacement for 10BASE-T in that it uses the same 2 wire pairs and the same pin allocations. The only prerequisite is that the wiring must be Cat5.

100BASE-T4, however, was developed for installations where all the wiring is Cat3, and cannot be replaced. It achieves its high speed over the inferior wire by using all 4 pairs instead of just 2. In the event of deploying 100BASE-T4 on a Cat3 wiring infrastructure, a cable tester has to be used to ensure that in fact, all 4 pairs are available for each link and have acceptable crosstalk.

100BASE-T4 required the development of a new physical layer technology, as opposed to 100BASE-TX/FX that used existing FDDI technology. It therefore only became commercially available a year after 100BASE-X, and never gained real market acceptance. As a result, very few users will actually be faced with this problem.

11b.4.5   Fiber-optic problems

Since fiber does not suffer from noise, interference and crosstalk problems there are basically only two issues to contend with namely attenuation and continuity.

The simplest way of checking a link is to plug each end of the cable into a fiber hub, NIC or fiber-optic transceiver. If the cable is OK, the LEDs at each end will light up. Another way of checking continuity is by using an inexpensive fiber-optic cable tester consisting of a light source and a light meter to test the segment.

More sophisticated tests can be done with an *optical time domain reflectometer* (OTDR). OTDRs can not only measure losses across a fiber link, but can also determine the nature and location of the losses. Unfortunately, they are very expensive but most professional cable installers will own one.

10BASE-FX and 100BASE-FX use LED transmitters that are not harmful to the eyes, but Gigabit Ethernet use laser devices that can damage the retina of the eye. It is therefore dangerous to try and stare into the fiber (all systems are infrared and therefore invisible anyway!).

Incorrect connector installation

Fiber-optic connectors can propagate light even if the two connector ends are not touching each other. Eventually, the gap between the fiber ends may be so far apart that the link stops working. It is therefore imperative to ensure that the connectors are properly latched.

Dirty cable ends

Because of the small fiber diameter (8–62 microns) and the low light intensity, a speck of dust or some finger oil deposited by touching the connector end is sufficient to affect communication. For this reason, dust caps must be left in place when the cable is not in use and a fiber-optic cleaning pad must be used to remove dirt and oils from the connector point before installation.

Component aging

The amount of power that a fiber-optic transmitter can radiate diminishes during the working life of the transmitter. This is taken into account during the design of the link but in the case of a marginal design, the link could start failing intermittently towards the end of the design life of the equipment. A fiber-optic power meter can be used to confirm the actual amount of loss across the link but an easy way to trouble shoot the link is to replace the transceivers at both ends of the link with new ones.

11b.4.6   AUI problems

Excessive cable length

The maximum length of the AUI cable is 50 m but this assumes that the cable is a proper IEEE 802.3 cable. Some installations use lightweight office grade cables that are limited to 12 m in length. If these cables are too long, the excessive attenuation can lead to intermittent problems.

DIX latches

The DIX version of the 15 pin D-connector uses a sliding latch. Unfortunately, not all vendors adhere to the IEEE 802 specifications and some use lightweight latch hardware which results in a connector that can very easily become unstuck. There are basically two solutions to the problem. The first solution is to use a lightweight (office grade) AUI cable, providing that distance is not a problem. This places less stress on the connector. The second solution is to use a special plastic retainer such as the 'ET Lock' made specifically for this purpose.

SQE test

The signal quality error (SQE) test signal is used on all AUI BASE-d equipment to test the collision circuitry. This method is only used on the old 15 pin AUI BASE-d external transceivers (MAUs) and sends a short signal burst (about 10 bit times in length) to the NIC just after each frame transmission. This tests both the collision detection circuitry and the signal paths. The SQE operation can be observed by means of an LED on the MAU.

The SQE signal is only sent from the transceiver to the NIC and not on to the network itself. It does not delay frame transmissions but occurs during the interframe gap and is not interpreted as a collision.

The SQE test signal must, however, be disabled if an external transceiver (MAU) is attached to a repeater hub. If this is not done the hub will detect the SQE signal as a collision and will issue a jam signal. As this happens after each packet, it can seriously delay transmissions over the network. The problem is that it is not possible to detect this with a protocol analyzer.

11b.4.7   NIC problems

Basic card diagnostics

The easiest way to check if a particular NIC is faulty is to replace it with another (working) NIC. Modern NICs for desktop PC's usually have auto-diagnostics included and these can be accessed, for example, from the device manager in Windows Some cards can even participate in a card-to-card diagnostic. Provided there are two identical cards, one can be set up as an initiator and one as a responder. Since the two cards will communicate at the data-link level, the packets exchanged will, to some extent, contribute to the network traffic but will not affect any other devices or protocols present on the network.

The drivers used for card auto-diagnostics will usually conflict with the NDIS and ODI drivers present on the host, and a message is usually generated, advising the user that the Windows drivers will be shut down, or that the user should re-boot in DOS.

With PCMCIA cards, there is an additional complication in that the card diagnostics will only run under DOS, but under DOS the IRQ (interrupt address) of the NIC typically defaults to 5, which happens to be the IRQ for the sound card! Therefore the diagnostics will usually pass every test, but fail on the IRQ test. This result can then be ignored safely if the card passes the other diagnostics. If the card works, it works!

Incorrect media selection

Some cards support more than one medium, for example, 10BASE-2/10BASE-5, or 10BASE-5/10BASE-T, or even all three. It may then happen that the card fails to operate since it fails to 'see' the attached medium.

It is imperative to know how the selection is done. Modern cards usually have an auto-detect function but this only takes place when the machine is booted up. It does NOT re-detect the medium if it is changed afterwards. If the connection to a machine is therefore changed from 10BASE-T to 10BASE-2, for example, the machine has to be re-booted.

Some older cards need to have the medium set via a setup program, whilst even older cards have DIP switches on which the medium has to be selected.

Wire hogging

Older interface cards find it difficult to maintain the minimum 9.6 μs *inter frame spacing* (IFS) and as a result of this, nodes tend to return to and compete for access to the bus in a random fashion. Modern interface cards are so fast that they can sustain the minimum 9.6 μs IFS rate. As a result of this, it becomes possible for a single card to gain repetitive sequential access to the bus in the face of slower competition and hence 'hogging' the bus.

With a protocol analyzer, this can be detected by displaying a chart of network utilization vs time and looking for broad spikes above 50%. The solution to this problem is to replace shared hubs with switched hubs and increase the bandwidth of the system by migrating from 10 to 100 Mbps, for example.

Jabbers

A jabber is a faulty NIC that transmits continuously. NICs have a built-in jabber control that is supposed to detect a situation whereby the card transmits frames longer than the allowed 1518 bytes, and shut the card down. However, if this does not happen, the defective card can bring the network down. This situation is indicated by a very high collision rate coupled with a very low or nonexistent data transfer rate. A protocol analyzer might not show any packets, since the jabbering card is not transmitting any sensible data. The easiest way to detect the offending card is by removing the cables from the NICs or the hub one by one until the problem disappears in which case the offending card has been located.

Faulty CSMA/CD mechanism

A card with a faulty CSMA/CD mechanism will create a large number of collisions since it transmits legitimate frames but does not wait for the bus to be quiet before transmitting. As in the previous case, the easiest way to detect this problem is to isolate the cards one by one until the culprit is detected.

Too many nodes

A problem with CSMA/CD networks is that the network efficiency decreases as the network traffic increases. Although Ethernet networks can theoretically utilize well over

90% of the available bandwidth, the access time of individual nodes increase dramatically as network loading increases. The problem is similar to that encountered on many urban roads during peak hours. During rush hours, the traffic approaches the design limit of the road. This does not mean that the road stops functioning. In fact, it carries a very large number of vehicles, but to get into the main traffic from a side road becomes problematic.

For office type applications, an average loading of around 30% is deemed acceptable while for industrial applications 3% is considered the maximum. Should the loading of the network be a problem, the network can be segmented using switches instead of shared hubs. In many applications, it will be found that the improvement created by changing from shared to switched hubs, is larger than the improvement to be gained by upgrading from 10 Mbps to fast Ethernet.

Improper packet distribution

Improper packet distribution takes place when one or more nodes dominate most of the bandwidth. This can be monitored by using a protocol analyzer and checking the source address of individual packets. Another way of easily checking this is by using the NDG software Web Boy facility and checking the contribution of the top 10 transmitters.

Nodes like this are typically performing tasks such as video-conferencing or database access, which require a large bandwidth. The solution to the problem is to give these nodes separate switch connections or to group them together on a faster 100BASE-T or 1000BASE-T segment.

Excessive broadcasting

A broadcast packet is intended to reach all the nodes in the network and is sent to a MAC address of ff-ff-ff-ff-ff-ff. Unlike routers, bridges and switches forward the broadcast packets throughout the network and therefore cannot contain the broadcast traffic. Too many simultaneous broadcast packets can degrade network performance.

In general, it is considered that if broadcast packets exceed 5% of the total traffic on the network, it would indicate a broadcast overload problem. Broadcasting is a particular problem with Netware servers and networks using NetBIOS/NetBEUI. Again, it is fairly easy to observe the amount of broadcast traffic using the WebBoy utility.

A broadcast overload problem can be addressed by adding routers, layer 3 switches or VLAN switches with broadcast filtering capabilities.

Bad packets

Bad packets can be caused by poor cabling infrastructure, defective NICs, external noise, or faulty devices such as hubs, devices or repeaters. The problem with bad packets is that they cannot be analyzed by software protocol analyzers.

Software protocol analyzers obtain packets that have already been successfully received by the NIC. That means they are one level removed from the actual medium on which the frames exist and hence cannot capture frames that are rejected by the NIC. The only solution to this problem is to use a software protocol analyzer that has a special custom NIC, capable of capturing information regarding packet deformities or by using a more expensive hardware protocol analyzer.

Faulty packets include:

Runts   Runt packets are shorter than the minimum 64 bytes and are typically created by a collision taking place during the slot time.

As a solution, try to determine whether the frames are collisions or under-runs. If they are collisions, the problem can be addressed by segmentation through bridges and switches. If the frames are genuine under-runs, the packet has to be traced back to the generating node that is obviously faulty.

CRC errors   CRC errors occur when the CRC check at the receiving end does not match the CRC check sum calculated by the transmitter.

As a solution, trace the frame back to the transmitting node. The problem is either caused by excessive noise induced into the wire, corrupting some of the bits in the frames, or by a faulty CRC generator in the transmitting node.

Late collisions   Late collisions are typically caused when the network diameter exceeds the maximum permissible size. This problem can be eliminated by ensuring that the collision domains are within specified values, that is, 2500 m for 10 Mbps Ethernet, 250 m for fast Ethernet and 200 m for Gigabit Ethernet.

Check the network diameter as outlined above by physical inspection or by using a TDR. If that is found to be a problem, segment the network by using bridges or switches.

Misaligned frames   Misaligned frames are frames that get out of sync by a bit or two, due to excessive delays somewhere along the path or frames that have several bits appended after the CRC check sum.

As a solution, try and trace the signal back to its source. The problem could have been introduced anywhere along the path.

Faulty auto-negotiation

Auto-negotiation is specified for

- 10BASE-T
- 100BASE-TX
- 100BASE-T2
- 100BASE-T4 and
- 1000BASE-T.

It allows two stations on a link segment (a segment with only two devices on it) e.g. an NIC in a computer and a port on a switching hub to negotiate a speed (10/100/1000 Mbps) and an operating mode (full-/half-duplex). If auto-negotiation is faulty or switched off on one device, the two devices might be set for different operating modes and as a result, they will not be able to communicate.

On the NIC side the solution might be to run the card diagnostics and to confirm that auto-negotiation is, in fact, enabled.

On the switch side, this depends on the diagnostics available for that particular switch. It might also be an idea to select another port, or to plug the cable into another switch.

10/100 Mbps mismatch

This issue is related to the previous one since auto-negotiation normally takes care of the speed issue.

Some system managers prefer to set the speeds on all NICs manually, for example, to 10 Mbps. If such an NIC is connected to a dual-speed switch port, the switch port will automatically sense the NIC speed and revert to 10 Mbps. If, however, the switch port is only capable of 100 Mbps, then the two devices will not be able to communicate.

This problem can only be resolved by knowing the speed(s) at which the devices are supposed to operate, and then by checking the settings via the setup software.

Full-/half-duplex mismatch

This problem is related to the previous two.

A 10BASE-T device can only operate in half-duplex (CSMA/CD) whilst a 100BASE-TX can operate in full-duplex OR half-duplex.

If, for example, a 100BASE-TX device is connected to a 10BASE-T hub, its auto-negotiation circuitry will detect the absence of a similar facility on the hub. It will therefore know, by default, that it is 'talking' to 10BASE-T and it will set its mode to half-duplex. If, however, the NIC has been set to operate in full-duplex only, communications will be impossible.

11b.4.8   Host-related problems

Incorrect host setup

Ethernet V2 (or IEEE 802.3 plus IEEE 802.2) only supplies the bottom layer of the DoD model. It is therefore able to convey data from one node to another by placing it in the data field of an Ethernet frame, but nothing more. The additional protocols to implement the protocol stack have to be installed above it, in order to make networked communications possible.

In industrial Ethernet networks this will typically be the TCP/IP suite, implementing the remaining layers of the ARPA model as follows.

The second layer of the DoD model (the Internet layer) is implemented with IP (as well as its associated protocols such as ARP and ICMP).

The next layer (the host-to-host layer) is implemented with TCP and UDP.

The upper layer (the application layer) is implemented with the various application layer protocols such as FTP, Telnet, etc. The host might also require a suitable application layer protocol to support its operating system in communicating with the operating system on other hosts, on Windows, that is NetBIOS by default.

As if this is not enough, each host needs a network 'client' in order to access resources on other hosts, and a network 'service' to allow other hosts to access its own resources in turn. The network client and network service on each host do not form part of the communications stack, but reside above it and communicate with each other across the stack.

Finally, the driver software for the specific NIC needs to be installed, in order to create a binding ('link') between the lower layer software (firmware) on the NIC and the next layer software (for example, IP) on the host. The presence of the bindings can be observed, for example, on a Windows 95/98 host by clicking 'settings' –> 'control panel' –> 'networks' –> 'configuration', then selecting the appropriate NIC and clicking 'Properties' –> 'Bindings'.

Without these, regardless of the Ethernet NIC installed, networking is not possible.

Failure to log in

When booting a PC, the Windows dialogue will prompt the user to log on to the server, or to log on to his/her own machine. Failure to log in will not prevent Windows from completing its boot-up sequence but the network card will not be enabled. This is clearly visible as the LEDs on the NIC and hub will not light up.

11b.4.9 Hub - related problems

Faulty individual port

A port on a hub may simply be 'dead'. Everybody else on the hub can 'see' each other, except the user on the suspect port. Closer inspection will show that the LED for that particular channel does not light up. The quickest way to verify this is to remove the UTP cable from the suspect hub port and plugging it into another port. If the LEDs light up on the alternative port, it means that the original port is not operational.

On managed hubs the configuration of the hub has to be checked by using the hub's management software to verify that the particular port has not in fact been disabled by the network supervisor.

Faulty hub

This will be indicated by the fact that none of the LEDs on the hub are illuminated and that none of the users on that particular hub are able to access the network. The easiest way to check this is by temporarily replacing the hub with a similar one and checking if the problem disappears.

Incorrect hub interconnection

If hubs are interconnected in a daisy-chain fashion by means of interconnecting ports with a UTP cable, care must be taken to ensure that either a crossover cable is used or that the crossover/uplink port on one hub ONLY is used. Failure to comply with this precaution will prevent the interconnected hubs from communicating with each other although it will not damage any electronics.

A symptom of this problem will be that all users on either side of the faulty link will be able to see each other but that nobody will be able to see anything across the faulty link. This problem can be rectified by ensuring that a proper crossover cable is being used or, if a straight cable is being used, that it is plugged into the crossover/uplink port on one hub only. On the other hub, it must be plugged into a normal port.

11b.5 Troubleshooting switched networks

Troubleshooting in a shared network is fairly easy since all packets are visible every where in the segment and as a result, the protocol analysis software can run on any host within that segment. In a switched network, the situation changes radically since each switch port effectively resides in its own segment and packets transferred through the switch are not seen by ports for which they are not intended.

In order to address the problem, many vendors have built traffic monitoring modules into their switches. These modules use either RMON or SNMP to build up statistics on each port and report switch statistics to switched management software.

Capturing the packets on a particular switched port is also a problem, since packets are not forwarded to all ports in a switch hence there is no place to plug in a LAN analyzer and view the packets.

One solution implemented by vendors is port aliasing, also known as port mirroring or port spanning. The aliasing has to be set up by the user and the switch copies the packets from the port under observation to a designated spare port. This allows the LAN user to plug in a LAN analyzer onto the spare port in order to observe the original port.

Another solution is to insert a shared hub in the segment under observation, that is, between the host and the switch port to which it was originally connected. The LAN analyzer can then be connected to the hub in order to observe the passing traffic.

11b.6   Troubleshooting fast Ethernet

The most diagnostic software is PC BASE-d and it uses a NIC with a promiscuous mode driver. This makes it easy to upgrade the system by simply adding a new NIC and driver. However, most PCs are not powerful enough to receive, store and analyze incoming data rates. It might therefore be necessary to rather consider the purchase of a dedicated hardware analyzer.

Most of the typical problems experienced with fast Ethernet, have already been discussed. These include a physical network diameter that is too large, the presence of Cat3 wiring in the system, trying to run 100BASE-T4 on 2 pairs, mismatched 10BASE-T/100BASE-TX ports, and noise.

11b.7   Troubleshooting Gigabit Ethernet

Although Gigabit Ethernet is very similar to its predecessors, the packets arrive so fast that they cannot be analyzed by normal means. A Gigabit Ethernet link is capable of transporting around 125 MB of data per second and few analyzers have the memory capability to handle this. Gigabit Ethernet analyzers such as those made by Hewlett Packard (LAN Internet Advisor), Network Associates (Gigabit Sniffer Pro) and WaveTek Wandel Goltemann (Domino Gigabit Analyzer) are highly specialized Gigabit Ethernet analyzers. They minimize storage requirements by filtering and analyzing capture packets in real time, looking for a problem. Unfortunately, they come with a rather high price tag.

12a

AS-interface (AS-i) overview

Objectives

When you have completed study of this chapter, you will be able to:

- Describe the main features of AS-i
- Fix problems with:
  - Cabling
  - Connections
  - Gateways to other standards.

12a.1 Introduction

The actuator sensor interface is an open system network developed by eleven manufacturers. These manufacturers created the AS-i association to develop the AS-i specifications. Some of the more widely known members of the association include Pepperl-Fuchs, Allen-Bradley, Banner Engineering, Datalogic Products, Siemens, Telemecanique, Turck, Omron, Eaton and Festo. The governing body is ATO, the AS-i Trade Organization. The number of ATO members currently exceeds fifty and continues to grow. The ATO also certifies products under development for the network that meet the AS-i specifications. This will assure compatibility between products from different vendors.

AS-i is a bit-oriented communication link designed to connect binary sensors and actuators. Most of these devices do not require multiple bytes to adequately convey the necessary information about the device status, so the AS-i communication interface is designed for bit-oriented messages in order to increase message efficiency for these types of devices.

The AS-i interface is just that, an interface for binary sensors and actuators, designed to interface binary sensors and actuators to microprocessor based controllers using bit length 'messages'. It was not developed to connect intelligent controllers together since this would be far beyond the limited capability of bit length message streams.

Modular components form the central design of AS-i. Connection to the network is made with unique connecting modules that require minimal, or in some cases no, tools and provide rapid, positive device attachment to the AS-i flat cable. Provision is made in the communications system to make 'live' connections, permitting the removal or addition of nodes with minimum network interruption.

Connection to higher level networks (e.g. Profibus) is made possible through plug-in PC and PLC cards or serial interface convertor modules.

The following sections examine these features of the AS-i network in more detail.

12a.2   Layer 1: the physical layer

AS-i uses a two-wire untwisted, unshielded cable that serves as both communication link and power supply for up to thirty-one slaves. A single master module controls communication over the AS-i network, which can be connected in various configurations such as bus, ring, or tree (see Figure 12a.1). The AS-i flat cable has a unique cross section that permits only properly polarized connections when making field connections to the modules. Alternatively, ordinary 2 wire cable (#16 AWG, 1.5 mm) can be used. A special shielded cable is also available for high noise environments.

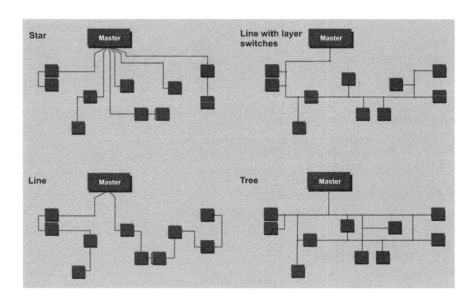

Figure 12a.1
Various AS-i configurations

Each slave is permitted to draw a maximum of 65 mA from the 30 V DC-power supply. If devices require more than this, separate supplies must be provided for each device. With a total of 31 slaves drawing 65 mA, a total limit of 2 A has been established to prevent excessive voltage drop over the 100 m permitted network length. A 16 AWG cable is specified to insure this condition. If this limitation on power drawn from the (yellow) signal cable is a problem, then a second (black) cable, identical in dimensions to the yellow cable, can be used in parallel for power distribution only.

The slave (or field) modules are available in four configurations:

- Input modules for 2-and 3-wire DC sensors or contact closure
- Output modules for actuators
- Input/output (I/O) modules for dual purpose applications
- Field connection modules for direct connection to AS-i compatible devices.
- 12-bit analog to digital converter.

The original AS-i specification (V2) allowed for 31 devices per segment of cable (see Figure 12a.2), with a total of 124 digital inputs and 124 digital outputs that is, a total of 248 I/O points. The latest specification, V2.1, allows for 62 devices, resulting in 248 inputs and 186 outputs, a total of 434 I/O points. With the latest specification, even 12-bit A to D converters can be read over 5 cycles.

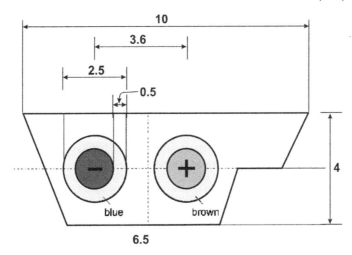

Figure 12a.2
Cross section of AS-i cable (mm)

A unique design allows the field modules to be connected directly into the bus while maintaining network integrity (see Figure 12a.3). The field module is composed of an upper and lower section, secured together once the cable is inserted. Specially designed contact points pierce the self-sealing cable providing bus access to the I/O points and/or continuation of the network. True to the modular design concept, two types of lower sections and three types of upper sections are available to permit 'mix-and-match' combinations to accommodate various connection schemes and device types. Plug connectors are utilized to interface the I/O devices to the slave (or with the correct choice of modular section screw terminals) and the entire module is sealed from the environment with special seals provided where the cable enters the module. The seals conveniently store away within the module when not in use.

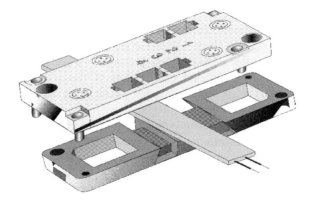

Figure 12a.3
Connection to the cable

The AS-i network is capable of a transfer rate of 167 kbps. Using an access procedure known as 'master–slave access with cyclic polling', the master continually polls all the slave devices during a given cycle to ensure rapid update times. For example, with 31 slaves and 124 I/O points connected, the AS-i network can ensure a 5 ms-cycle time, making the AS-i network one of the fastest available.

A modulation technique called 'alternating pulse modulation' provides this high transfer rate capability as well as high data integrity. This technique will be described in the following section.

12a.3   Layer 2: the data-link layer

The data-link layer of the AS-i network consists of a master call-up and slave response. The master call-up is exactly fourteen bits in length while the slave response is 7 bits. A pause between each transmission is used for synchronization. Refer Figure 12a.4, for example, call-up and response frames.

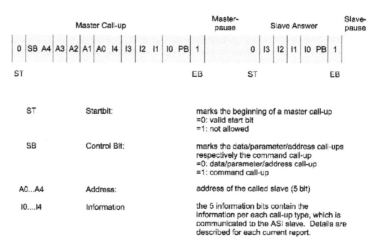

Figure 12a.4
Example call up and response frames

Various code combinations are possible in the information portion of the call-up frame and it is precisely these various code combinations that are used to read and write information to the slave devices. Examples of some of the master call-ups are listed in Figure 12a.5.   A detailed explanation of these call-ups is available from the ATO literature and is only included here to illustrate the basic means of information transfer on the AS-i network.

The modulation technique used by AS-i is known as 'Alternating Pulse Modulation' (APM). Since the information frame is of a limited size, providing conventional error checking was not possible and therefore the AS-i developers chose a different technique to ensure high level of data integrity.

Referring to the following figure, the coding of the information is similar to Manchester II coding but utilizing a 'sine-squared' waveform for each pulse (see Figure 12a.6). This waveform has several unique electrical properties, which reduce the bandwidth required of the transmission medium (permitting faster transfer rates) and reduce the end of line reflections common in networks using square wave pulse techniques. Also, notice that each bit has an associated pulse during the second half of the bit period. This property is utilized as a bit level of error checking by all AS-i devices. The similarity to Manchester II coding is no accident since this technique has been used for many years to pass synchronizing information to a receiver along with the actual data.

		5 Bit Address		5 Bit Information	

Data Call-Up	0	0	A4 A3 A2 A1 A0	0	D3 D2 D1 D0 PB	1
	ST SB			I4 I3 I2 I1 I0		EB

Parameter Call-Up	0	0	A4 A3 A2 A1 A0	1	P3 P2 P1 P0	1
	ST SB			I4 I3 I2 I1 I0		EB

Addressing Call-Up	0	0	0 0 0 0 0	A4 A3 A2 A1 A0 PB	1
	ST SB A4 A3 A2 A1 A0	I4 I3 I2 I1 I0		EB

Command Call-Up: Reset ASI Slave	0	1	A4 A3 A2 A1 A0	1	- 1 0 0 PB	1
	ST SB			I4 I3 I2 I1 I0		EB

Command Call-Up: Erase ASI Slave	0	1	A4 A3 A2 A1 A0	0	0 0 0 0 PB	1
	ST SB			I4 I3 I2 I1 I0		EB

Command Call-Up: Read I/O Configuration	0	1	A4 A3 A2 A1 A0	1	0 0 0 0 PB	1
	ST SB			I4 I3 I2 I1 I0		EB

Command Call-Up: Read \ID-Code	0	1	A4 A3 A2 A1 A0	1	0 0 0 1 PB	1
	ST SB			I4 I3 I2 I1 I0		EB

Command Call-Up: Read Status	0	1	A4 A3 A2 A1 A0	1	- 1 1 0 PB	1
	ST SB			I4 I3 I2 I1 I0		EB

Command Call-UP Read and Erase Status	0	1	A4 A3 A2 A1 A0	1	- 1 1 1 PB	1
	ST SB			I4 I3 I2 I1 I0		EB

Figure 12a.5
Some AS-i call-ups

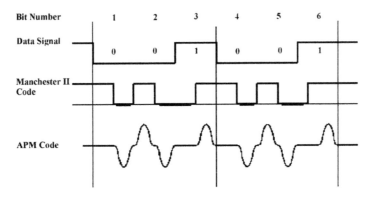

Figure 12a.6
Sine-squared wave form

In addition, AS-i developers also established a set of rules for the APM coded signal that is used to further enhance data integrity. For example, the start bit or first bit in the AS-i telegram must be a negative impulse and the stop bit a positive impulse. Two subsequent impulses must be of opposite polarity and the pause between two consecutive impulses should be 3 µs. Even parity and a prescribed frame length are also incorporated at the frame level. As a result the 'odd' looking waveform, in combination with the rules of the frame formatting, the set of APM coding rules and parity checking, work together to provide timing information and high-level data integrity for the AS-i network.

12a.4 Operating characteristics

AS-i node addresses are stored in nonvolatile memory and can be assigned either by the master or one of the addressing or service units. Should a node fail, AS-i has the ability to automatically reassign the replaced node's address and, in some cases, reprogram the node itself allowing rapid response and repair times.

Since AS-i was designed to be an interface between lower level devices, connection to higher-level systems enables the capability to transfer data and diagnostic information. Plug-in PC cards and PLC cards are currently available. The PLC cards allow direct connection with various Siemens PLCs. Serial communication converters are also available to enable AS-i connection to conventional RS-232, 422, and 485 communication links. Direct connection to a Profibus field network is also possible with the Profibus coupler, enabling several AS-i networks access to a high-level digital network.

Handheld and PC based configuration tools are available, which allow initial start-up programing and also serve as diagnostic tools after the network is commissioned. With these devices, on-line monitoring is possible to aid in determining the health of the network and locating possible error sources.

12b

AS-i troubleshooting

12b.1 Introduction

The AS-i system has been designed with a high degree of 'maintenance friendliness' in mind and has a high level of built-in auto-diagnosis. The system is continuously monitoring itself against faults such as:

- Operational slave errors (permanent or intermittent slave failure, faulty configuration data such as addresses, I/O configuration, and ID codes)
- Operational master errors (permanent or intermittent master failure, faulty configuration data such as addresses, I/O configuration, and ID codes)
- Operational cable errors (short circuits, cable breakage, corrupted telegrams due to electrical interference and voltage outside the permissible range)
- Maintenance-related slave errors (false addresses entered, false I/O configuration and false ID codes)
- Maintenance-related master errors (faulty projected data such as I/O configuration, ID codes, parameters, etc.)
- Maintenance - related cable errors (counter poling the AS-i cable).

The fault diagnosis is displayed by means of LEDs on the master.

Where possible, the system will protect itself. During a short-circuit, for example, the power supply to the slaves is interrupted, which causes all actuators to revert to a safe state. Another example is the jabber control on the AS-i chips, whereby a built-in fuse blows if too much current is drawn by a chip, disconnecting it from the bus.

The following tools can be used to assist in fault finding.

12b.2 Tools of the trade

12b.2.1 Addressing handheld

Before an AS-i system can operate, all the operating addresses must be assigned to the connected slaves, which store this on their internal nonvolatile memory (EEPROM). Although this can theoretically be done on-line, it requires that a master device with this addressing capability be available.

In the absence of such a master, a specialized battery powered addressing handheld (for example, one manufactured by Pepperl and Fuchs) can be used. The device is capable of reading the current slave address (from 0 to 31) as well as reprograming the slave to a new address entered via the keyboard.

The slaves are attached to the handheld device, one at a time, by means of a special short cable or plug directly into the handheld device. They are only powered via the device while the addressing operation takes place (about 1 s) with the result that several hundred slaves can be configured in this way before a battery change is necessary.

12b.2.2 Monitor

A monitor is essentially a protocol analyzer, which allows a user to capture and analyze the telegrams on the AS-i bus. A good monitor should have triggering and filtering capabilities, as well as the ability to store, retrieve and analyze captured data. Monitors are usually implemented as PC-based systems.

12b.2.3 Service device

An example of such a device is the SIE 93 handheld manufactured by Siemens. It can perform the following:

- Slave addressing, as described above
- Monitoring, that is, the capturing, analysis and display of telegrams
- Slave simulation, in which case it behaves like a supplementary slave, the user can select its operating address
- Master simulation, in which case the entire cycle of master requests can be issued to test the parameters, configuration and address of a specific slave device (one at a time).

12b.2.4 Service book

A 'service book' is a commissioning and servicing tool based on a notebook computer. It is capable of monitoring an operating network, recording telegrams, detecting errors, addressing slaves off-line, testing slaves off-line, maintaining a database of sensor/ actuator data and supplying help functions for user support.

Bus data for use by the software on the notepad is captured, preprocessed and forwarded to the laptop by a specialized network interface, a so-called 'hardware checker'. The hardware checker is based on an 80C535 single chip micro-controller and connects to the notepad via an RS-232 interface.

12b.2.5 Slave simulator

Slave simulators are PC-based systems used by software developers to evaluate the performance of a slave (under development) in a complete AS-i network. They can simulate the characteristics of up to 32 slaves concurrently and can introduce errors that would be difficult to set up in real situations.

13a

DeviceNet overview

Objectives

When you have completed study of this chapter you will be able to:

- List the main features of DeviceNet
- Identify and correct problems with:
  - Cable topology
  - Power and earthing
  - Signal voltage levels
  - Common mode voltages
  - Terminations
  - Cabling
  - Noise
  - Node communications problems.

13a.1   Introduction

DeviceNet, developed by Allen-Bradley, is a low-level device oriented network based on the controller area network (CAN) developed by Bosch (GmbH) for the automobile industry. It is designed to interconnect lower level devices (sensors and actuators) with higher level devices (controllers).

The variable, multi-byte format of the CAN message frame is well suited to this task as more information can be communicated per message than with bit-type systems. The Open DeviceNet Vendor Association, Inc. (ODVA) has been formed to issue DeviceNet specifications, ensure compliance with the specifications and offer technical assistance for manufacturers wishing to implement DeviceNet. The DeviceNet specification is an open specification and available through the ODVA.

DeviceNet can support up to 64 nodes, which can be removed individually under power and without severing the trunk line. A single, four-conductor cable (round or flat) provides both power and data communications. It supports a bus (trunk line drop line) topology, with branching allowed on the drops. Reverse wiring protection is built into all nodes, protecting them against damage in case of inadvertent wiring errors.

The data rates supported are 125, 250 and 500 kbaud, although a specific installation does not have to support all, as data rates can be traded for distance.

As DeviceNet was designed to interface lower level devices with higher level controllers, a unique adaptation of the basic CAN protocol was developed. This is similar to the familiar poll/response or master/slave technique but still utilizes the speed benefits of the original CAN.

Figure 13a.1 illustrates the positioning of DeviceNet and CANBUS within in the OSI model. Note that ControlNet and Ethernet/IP use the same application layer protocols. Because of this particular architecture, messages are routable between DeviceNet, ControlNet and Ethernet/IP systems.

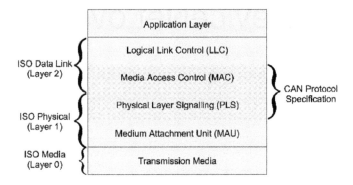

Figure 13a.1
DeviceNet vs the OSI model
[Note: Use Figure 19.11 from FE manual]

13a.2 Physical layer

13a.2.1 Topology

The DeviceNet media consists of a physical bus topology (Figure 13a.2). The bus or 'trunk' (white and blue wires) is the backbone of the network and must be terminated at either end by a 120 Ω 1/4 W resistor.

Drop lines of up to 6 m (20 ft) in length enable the connection of nodes (devices) to the main trunk line, but care has to be taken not to exceed the total drop line budget for a specific speed. Branching to multiple nodes is allowed only on drop lines.

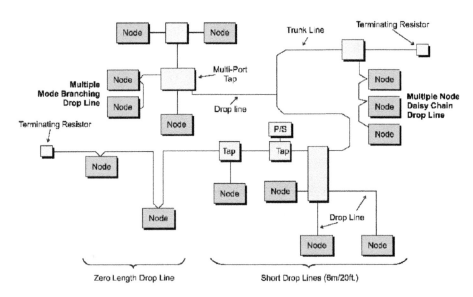

Figure 13a.2
DeviceNet topology

Three types of cable are available, all of which can be used as the trunk. They are thick, thin and flat wire.

13a.3   Connectors

DeviceNet has adopted a range of open and closed connectors that are considered suitable for connecting equipment onto the bus and drop lines. This range of recommended connectors is described in this section.

DeviceNet users can connect to the system using other proprietary connectors, the only restrictions placed on the user regarding the types of connectors used are as follows:

- All nodes (devices), whether using sealed or unsealed connections, supplying or consuming power, must have male connectors.
- Whatever connector is chosen, it must be possible for the related device to connect or disconnect from the DeviceNet bus without compromising the system's operation.
- Connectors must be upgraded to carry high levels (8 A or more at 24 V, or 200 VA) of current.
- A minimum of 5 isolated connector pins are required, with the possible requirement of a 6th, or metal body shield connection for safety ground use.

There are two basic styles of DeviceNet connectors that are used for bus and drop line connections in normal, harsh, and hazardous conditions. These are:

1. An open style connector (pluggable or hard-wired)
2. A closed style connector (mini or micro style).

13a.3.1   Pluggable (unsealed) connector

This is a 5 pin, unsealed open connector utilizing direct soldering, crimping, screw terminals, barrier strips or screw type terminations. This type of connector entails removing system power for connection (Figure 13a.3).

Important: DeviceNet requires that connectors on *devices* must have male contacts

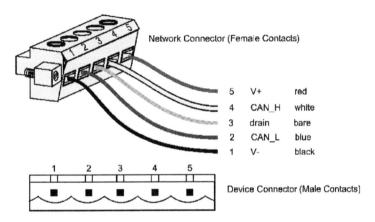

5	V+	red
4	CAN_H	white
3	drain	bare
2	CAN_L	blue
1	V-	black

Figure 13a.3
Unsealed screw connector

13a.3.2　Hard-wired (unsealed) connection

Loose wire connections can be used to make direct attachment to a node or a bus tap without the presence of a connector, although this is not a preferred method. It is only a viable option if the node can be removed from the trunk line without severing the trunk.

The ends of the cable are 'live' if the cable has been removed from the node in question and are still connected as part of the bus infrastructure. As such, care MUST be taken to insulate the exposed ends of the cable (Figure 13a.4).

Important: This hard-wired solution is an option, provided that the node can be removed from the network without severing the trunk.
Important: Wires should not be installed while the network is active. This will prevent problems such as shorting the network supply or disrupting communications

Figure 13a.4
Open wire connection

13a.3.3　Mini (sealed) connector

This 18 mm round connector is recommended for harsh environments (field connections). This connection must meet ANSI/B93.55M-1981. The female connector (attached to the bus cable) must have rotational locking. This connector requires a minimum voltage rating of 25 V, and for trunk use a current rating of 8 A is required. Additional options can include oil and water resistance (Figure 13a.5).

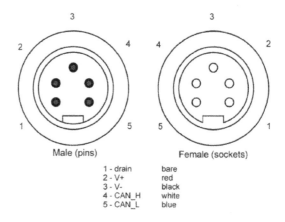

Male (pins)　　　　　　　　　Female (sockets)

1 - drain	bare
2 - V+	red
3 - V-	black
4 - CAN_H	white
5 - CAN_L	blue

Figure 13a.5
Sealed mini-type connector (face views)

13a.3.4　Micro (sealed) connector

This connector is effectively a 12 mm diameter miniature version of the mini style connector, except its suitability is for thin wire drop connections requiring reduction in both physical and current carrying capacity (Figure 13a.6).

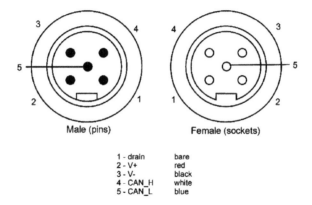

Figure 13a.6
Sealed micro-style connector (face views)

It has 5 pins, 4 in a circular periphery pattern and the fifth pin in the center. This connector should have a minimum voltage rating of 25 V, and for drop connections a current rating of 3 A is required. The male component must mate with Lumberg Style RST5-56/xm or equivalent, the female component part must also conform to Lumberg Style RST5-56/xm or equivalent. Additional options can include oil and water resistance.

13a.4   Cable budgets

DeviceNet's transmission media can be constructed of either DeviceNet thick, thin or flat cable or a combination thereof. Thick or flat cable is used for long distances and is stronger and more resilient than the thin cable, which is mainly used as a local drop line connecting nodes to the main trunk line.

The trunk line supports only tap or multiport taps that connect drop lines into the associated node. Branching structures are allowed only on drop lines and not on the main trunk line.

The following Figures 13a.7, 13a.8, 13a.9 show the distance vs length trade-off for the different types of cable.

DATA RATES	125 kbaud	250 kbaud	500 kbaud
Trunk distance	500 m (1640 ft)	250 m (630 ft)	100 m (328 ft)
Max. drop length	20 ft	20 ft	20 ft
Cumulative drop	512 ft	256 ft	128 ft
Number of nodes	64	64	64

Figure 13a.7
Constraints: thick wire

DATA RATES	125 kbaud	250 kbaud	500 kbaud
Trunk distance	100 m (326 ft)	100 m (326 ft)	100 m (328 ft)
Max. drop length	20 ft	20 ft	20 ft
Cumulative drop	512 ft	256 ft	128 ft
Number of nodes	64	64	64

Figure 13a.8
Constraints: thin wire

DATA RATES	125 kbaud	250 kbaud	500 kbaud
Trunk distance	420 m (1640 ft)	200 m (630 ft)	75 m (328 ft)
Max. drop length	20 ft	20 ft	20 ft
Cumulative drop	512 ft	256 ft	128 ft
Number of nodes	64	64	64

Figure 13a.9
Constraints: flat wire

13a.5   Device taps

13a.5.1   Sealed taps

Sealed taps are available in single port (T type) and multiport configurations. Regardless of whether the connectors are mini or micro style, DeviceNet requires that male connectors must have external threads while female connectors must have internal threads. In either case, the direction of rotation is optional (Figure 13a.10).

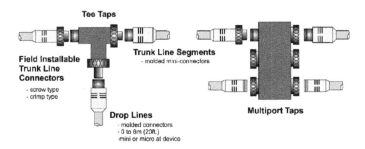

Figure 13a.10
Sealed taps

13a.5.2   IDC taps

Insulation displacement connectors (IDCs) are used for KwikLink flat cable (Figure 13a.11). They are modular, relatively inexpensive and compact. They are compatible with existing media and require little installation effort. The enclosure conforms to NEMA 6P and 13, and IP 67.

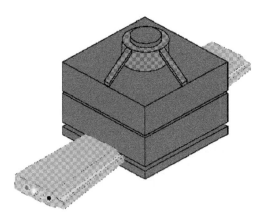

Figure 13a.11
Insulation displacement connector

13a.5.3   Open style taps

DeviceNet has three basic forms of open taps (Figure 13a.12). They are:

1. Zero length drop line, suitable for daisy-chain applications
2. Open tap, able to connect a 6 m (20 ft) drop line onto the trunk
3. An open style connector, supporting 'temporary' attachment of a node to a drop line.

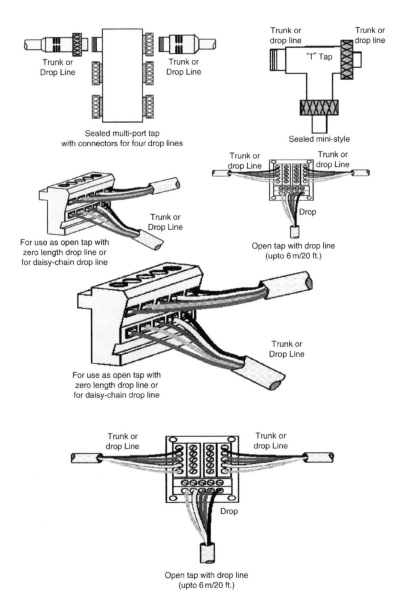

Figure 13a.12
Open and temporary DeviceNet taps

The temporary connector is suitable for connection both to and from the system when the system is powered. It is of similar construction to a standard telephone wall plug, being of molded construction and equipped with finger grips to assist removal, and is styled as a male pin-out. The side cheeks are polarized to prevent reversed insertion into the drop line open tap connector.

13a.5.4   Multi-port open taps

If a number of nodes or devices are located within a close proximity of each other, for example within a control cabinet or similar enclosure, an open tap can be used (Figure 13a.13).

Alternatively, devices can be wired into a DeviceBox multi-port tap. The drops from the individual devices are not attached to the box via sealed connectors but are fed in via cable grips and connected to a terminal strip.

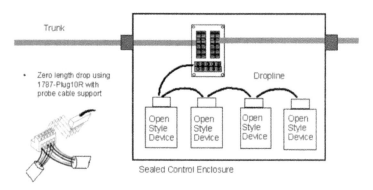

Figure 13a.13
Multi-port open taps

13a.5.5   Power taps

Power taps differ from device taps in that they have to perform four essential functions that are not specifically required by the device taps. These include:

- Two protection devices in the V+ supply
- Connection from the positive output of the supply to the V+ bus line via a Schottky diode
- Provision of a continuous connection for the signaling pair, drain and negative wires through the tap
- Provision of current limiting in both directions from the tap.

The following Figure 13a.14 illustrates the criteria listed above.

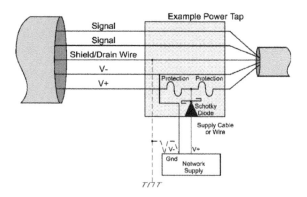

Figure 13a.14
Principle of a DeviceNet power tap

13a.6   Cable description

The 'original' (round) DeviceNet cable has two shielded twisted pairs. These are twisted on a common axis with a drain wire in the center, and are equipped with an overall braid.

13a.6.1   Thick cable

This cable is used as the trunk line when length is important (Figure 13a.15). Overall diameter is 0.480 in. (10.8 mm) and it comprises of:

- A signal pair, consisting of one twisted-pair (3 twists per foot) coded blue/white with a wire size of #18 (19×30 AWG) copper and individually tinned; the impedance is 120 Ω ±10% at 1 MHz, the capacitance between conductors is 12 pF /ft and the propagation delay is 1.36 nS/ft maximum.
- A power pair, consisting of one twisted-pair (3 twists per foot) coded black/red with a wire size of #15 (19×28 AWG) copper and individually tinned.

This is completed by separate aluminized Mylar shields around each pair and an overall foil/braided shield with an #18 (19×30 AWG) bare drain wire. The power pair has an 8 A power capacity and is PVC/nylon insulated. It is also flame resistant and UL oil resistant too.

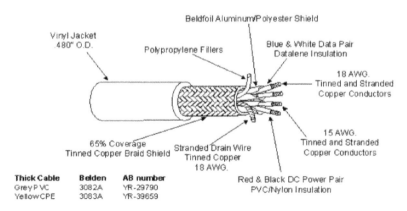

Figure 13a.15
DeviceNet thick cable

13a.6.2   Thin cable specification

This cable is used for both drop lines as well as short trunk lines. Its overall diameter is 0.27 in. (6.13 mm) and it comprises of:

- A signal pair, consisting of a twisted-pair (4.8 twists per foot) coded blue/white with a wire size of #24 (19×36 AWG) copper and individually tinned; the impedance is 120 Ω ±10% at 1 MHz, the capacitance between conductors is 12 pF/ft and the propagation delay is 1.36 nS/ft maximum.
- A power pair consisting of one twisted-pair (4.8 twists per foot) coded black/red with a wire size of #22 (19×34 AWG) copper and individually tinned.

This is completed by separate aluminized Mylar shields around each pair and an overall foil/braided shield with an #22 (19×34 AWG) bare drain wire. The power pair has a 3 A power capacity and is PVC insulated (Figure 13a.16).

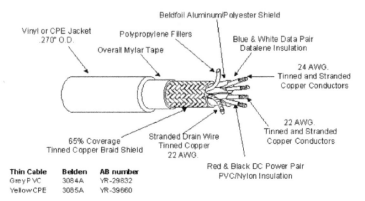

Figure 13a.16
DeviceNet thin cable

13a.6.3   Flat cable

DeviceNet flat cable is a highly flexible cable that works with existing devices (Figure 13a.17). It has the following specifications:

- 600 V 8 A rating
- A physical key
- Fitting into 1 in. (25 mm) conduit
- The jacket made of TPE/Santoprene.

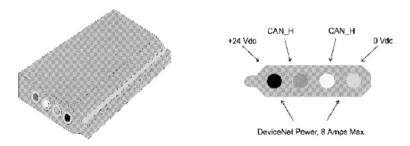

Figure 13a.17
DeviceNet flat cable

13a.7   Network power

13a.7.1   General approach

One or more 24 V power supplies can be used to power the devices on the DeviceNet network, provided that the 8 A current limit on thick/flat wire and the 3 A limit on thin wire is not exceeded. The power supplies used should be dedicated to the DeviceNet cable power ONLY!

Although, technically speaking, any suitable power supply can be used, supplies such as the Rockwell automation 1787-DNPS 5.25 A supply are certified specifically for DeviceNet.

The power calculations can be done by hand, but it is easier to use a design spreadsheet such as the Rockwell automation/Allen Bradley DeviceNet Power Supply Configuration toolkit running under Microsoft Excel.

The network can be constructed of both thick and thin cable as long as only one type of cable is used per section of network, comprising a section between power taps or between a power tap and the end of the network.

Using the steps illustrated below, a quick initial evaluation can be achieved as to the power requirements needed for a particular network.

Sum the total current requirements of all network devices, then evaluate the total permissible network length (be conservative here) using the following Table 13a.1.

Thick cable Network Current Distribution and Allowable Current Loading											
Network length in meters	0	25	50	100	150	200	250	300	350	400	450	500
Network length in feet	0	83.3	167	333	500	666	833	999	1166	1332	1499	1665
Maximum current in amperes	8	8	5.42	2.93	2.01	1.53	1.23	1.03	0.89	0.78	0.69	0.63

Thin Cable Network Current Distribution and Allowable Current Loading										
Network length in meters	0	10	20	30	40	50	60	70	80	90	100
Network length in feet	0	33	66	99	132	165	198	231	264	297	330
Maximum current in amperes	8	8	5.42	2.93	2.01	1.53	1.23	1.03	0.89	0.78	0.69

Table 13a.1
Thick and thin cable length and power capacity

Depending on the final power requirement cost and network complexity, either a single supply end or center connected can be used.

13a.7.2 Single supply – end connected

Total network length = 200 m (656 ft)
Total current = Sum of node 1, 2, 3, 4 and 5 currents = 0.65 A
Referring to Table 14.1 the current limit for 200 m = 1.53 A.

Configuration are correct as long as THICK cable is used (see Figure 13a.18).

13a.7.3 Single supply – center connected

Current in Section 1 = 1.05 A over a length of 90 m (300 ft)
Current in Section 2 = 1.88 A over a length of 120 m (400 ft)
Current limits for a distance of 90 m is 3.3 A and for 120 m is 2.63 A

Power for both sections is correct, and a 3 A (minimum) power supply is required (see Figure 13a.19).

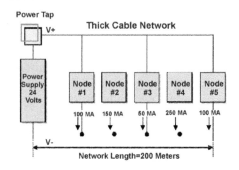

Figure 13a.18
Single supply – end connected

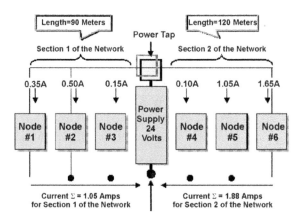

Figure 13a.19
Single supply – center connected

Tables 13a.2 and 13a.3 indicate parameters that control load limits and allowable tolerances as related to DeviceNet power.

System Power Load Limits	
Maximum voltage drop on both the –ve and +ve power lines	5.0 V on each line
Maximum thick cable trunk line current	8.0 A in any section
Maximum thin cable trunk line current	3.0 A in any section
Maximum drop line current	0.75 to 3.0 A
Voltage range at each node	11.0 to 25.0 V
Operating current on each product	Specified by the product manufacturer

Table 13a.2
System power load limits

Maximum Drop Line Currents	
Current limits are calculated by the following equations, where I = allowable drop line current and L = distance. In meters: $I = 4.57/L$ In feet $I = 15/L$	
Drop Length	**Maximum Allowable Current**
1.00	3.00
3.00	3.00
5.00	3.00
7.50	2.00
10.00	1.50
15.00	1.00
20.00	0.75

Table 13a.3
Maximum drop line currents

13a.7.4   Suggestions for avoiding errors and power supply options

The following steps can be used to minimize errors when configuring power on a network.

- Ensure the calculations made for current and distances are correct (be conservative)
- Conduct a network survey to verify correct voltages, remembering that a minimum of 11 V at a node is required and that a maximum voltage drop of 10 V across each node is allowed
- Allow for a good margin to have reserves of power to correct problems if needed
- If using multiple supplies, it is essential that they must all be turned on simultaneously to prevent both power supply and cable overloading
- Power supplies MUST be capable of supporting linear and switching regulators
- Supply MUST be isolated from both the AC supply and chassis.

13a.8   System grounding

Grounding of the system must be done at one point only, preferably as close to the physical center of the network as possible. This connection should be done at a power tap where a terminal exists for this purpose. A main ground connection should be made from this point to a good earth or building ground via a copper braid or at least a 8 AWG copper conductor not more than 3 m (10 ft) in length.

At this point of connection, the following conductors and circuits should be connected together in the form of a 'star' configuration.

- The drain wire of the main trunk cable
- The shield of the main trunk cable

- The negative power conductor
- The main ground connection as described above.

If the network is already connected to ground at some other point, do NOT connect the ground terminal of a power tap to a second ground connection. This can result in unwanted ground loop currents occurring in the system. It is essential that a single ground connection is established for the network bus and failure to ground the bus's –ve supply at ONE POINT will only result in a low signal to noise ratio appearing in the system.

Care must be exercised when connecting the drain/shield of the bus or drop line cable at nodes, which are already grounded. This can happen when the case or enclosure of the equipment, comprising the node, is connected to ground for electrical safety and/or a signaling connection to other self-powered equipment. In cases where this condition exists, the drain/shield should be connected to the node ground through a 0.01 µF/500 V capacitor wired in parallel with a 1 megohm 1/4 W resistor. If the node has no facility for grounding, the drain and shield must be left UNCONNECTED.

13a.9 Signaling

DeviceNet is a two wire differential network. Communication is achieved by switching the CAN_H wire (white) and the CAN_L wire (blue) relative to the V– wire (black). CAN_H swings between 2.5 V DC (recessive state) and 4.0 V DC (dominant state) while CAN_L swings between 2.5 V DC (recessive state) and 1.5 V DC (dominant state).

With no network master connected, the CAN_H and CAN_L lines should be in the recessive state and should read (with a voltmeter set to DC mode) between 2.5 and 3.0 V relative to V– at the point where the power supply is connected to the network. With a network master connected AND polling the network, the CAN_H to V– voltage will be around 3.2 V DC and the CAN_L to V– voltage will be around 2.4 V DC. This is because the signals are switching, which affects the DC value read by the meter.

The voltage values given here assume that no common mode voltages are present. Should they be present, voltages measured closer to the power supply will be higher than those measured furthest from the power supply. However, the differential voltages (CAN_H minus CAN_L) will not be affected.

DeviceNet uses a differential signaling system. A logical '1' is represented by CAN_H being Low (recessive) and CAN_L being High (recessive). Conversely, a logical '0' is represented by CAN_H being High (dominant) and CAN_L being Low (dominant). Figure 14.22 depicts this graphically.

The nodes are all attached to the bus in parallel, resulting in a wired–AND configuration. This means that as long as ANY one node imposes a Low signal (logical 0) on the bus, the resulting signal on the bus will also be low. Only when ALL nodes output a high signal (logical 1), the signal on the bus will also be high.

13a.10 Data-link layer

13a.10.1 Frame format

The format of a DeviceNet frame is shown in Figure 13a.20. Note that the data field is rather small (8 bytes) and that any messages larger than this need to be fragmented.

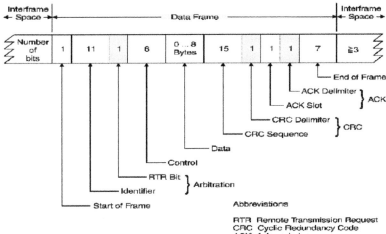

Figure 13a.20
DeviceNet frame

This frame will be placed on the bus as sequential 1s and 0s, by changing the levels of the CAN_H and CAN_L in a differential fashion.

In Figure 13a.21, A represents the CAN_H signal in its dominant (high) state (+3.5 to +4.0 V DC), C represents the CAN_L signal in its dominant (low) state (+1.5 to 2.5 V DC) and B represents both the CAN_H signal recessive (low) and the CAN_L signal recessive (high) states of +2.5 V–3.0 V DC.

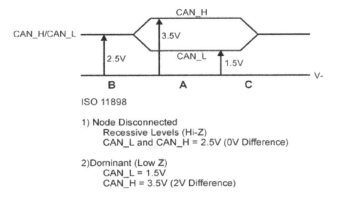

Figure 13a.21
DeviceNet transmission

13a.10.2 Medium access

The medium access control method is described as 'carrier sense multiple access with non-destructive bit-wise arbitration' (CSMA/NBA), where the arbitration takes place on a bit-by-bit basis on the first field in the frame (the 11 bit identifier field). If a node wishes to transmit, it has to defer to any existing transmission. Once that transmission has ended, the node wishing to transmit has to wait for 3 bit times before transmitting. This is called the interframe space.

Despite this precaution, it is possible for two nodes to start transmitting concurrently. In the following example (Figure 13a.22) nodes 1 and 2 start transmitting concurrently, with both nodes monitoring their own transmissions. All goes well for the first few bits since the bit sequences are the same. Then the situation arises where the bits are different. Since the '0' state is dominant, the output of node 2 overrides that of node 1. Node 1 loses the arbitration and stops transmitting. It does, however, still acknowledges the message by means of the ACK field in the frame.

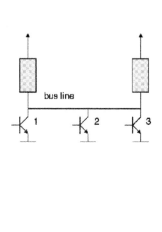 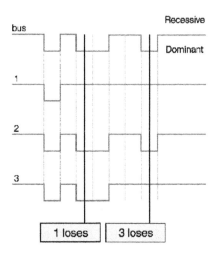

Figure 13a.22
DeviceNet arbitration

Because of this method of arbitration, the node with the lowest number (i.e. the most significant '0' s in its identifier field) will win the arbitration.

13a.10.3 Fragmentation

Any device that needs more than 8 bytes of data sent in any direction will cause fragmentation to occur. This happens since a frame can only contain 8 bytes of data. When fragmentation occurs, only 7 bytes of data can be sent at a time since the first byte is used to facilitate the reassembly of fragments. It is used as follows:

First byte	Significance
00	First fragment (number 0)
41–7F	Intermediate fragment (lower 6 bits of the byte is the fragment number)
80–FF	Last fragment (lower 6 bits of the byte is the fragment number)

Example:

Data packet	Description
00 12 34 56 78 90 12 34	First fragment, number 0
41 56 78 90 12 34 56 78	Intermediate fragment number 1
42 90 12 34 56 78 90 12	Intermediate fragment number 2
83 34 56	Last fragment number 3

13a.11 The application layer

The CAN specification does not dictate how information within the CAN message frame fields are to be interpreted – that was left up to the developers of the DeviceNet application software.

Through the use of special identifier codes (bit patterns) in the identifier field, master is differentiated from slave. Also, sections of this field tell the slaves how to respond to the master's message. For example, slaves can be requested to respond with information simultaneously in which case the CAN bus arbitration scheme assures the timeliest consecutive response from all slaves in decreasing order of priority. Or, slaves can be polled individually, all through the selection of different identifier field codes. This technique allows the system implementers more flexibility when establishing node priorities and device addresses.

The main protocol at the TCP application level (layers 5, 6 and 7 in the OSI model) is CIP the 'control and information protocol'. As shown in Figure 13a.1, CIP covers not only layers 5, 6 and 7 of the OSI model, but also the 'user layer' (layer 8), which includes the user device profiles. Apart from the common device profiles, CIP also includes the common object library, the common control services and the common routing services. The OSI model has no layer 8, but items such as device profiles do not fit within the conceptual structure of the OSI model hence vendors add a 'layer 8' above layer 7 for this purpose.

CIP gives generic DeviceNet an 'industrial functionality' and allows the control, collection and configuration of data. It also allows a producer-consumer model to run on CANBUS, or whatever technology being used at layers 1 and 2.

CIP provides the following common features for users of DeviceNet, ControlNet and Ethernet/IP:

- It provides the user with a standard set of messaging services for all three networks.
- It lets the user connect to any network and configure and collect data from any network.
- It saves time and effort during system configuration because no routing tables or added logic are necessary to move data between networks.
- It reduces the amount of training needed when moving personal between different networks by providing similar configuration tools and features.

13b

DeviceNet troubleshooting

13b.1 Introduction

Networks, in general, exhibit the following types of problems from time to time.

The first type of problem is of an electronic nature, where a specific node (e.g. a network interface card) malfunctions. This can be due to a component failure or to an incorrect configuration of the device.

The second type is related to the medium that interconnects the nodes. Here, the problems are more often of an electromechanical nature and include open and short circuits, electrical noise, signal distortion and attenuation. Open and short circuits in the signal path are caused by faulty connectors or cables. Electrical interference (noise) is caused by incorrect grounding, broken shields or external sources of electromagnetic or radio frequency interference. Signal distortion and attenuation can be caused by incorrect termination, failure to adhere to topology guidelines (e.g. drop cables too long), or faulty connectors.

Whereas these are general network-related problems, the following ones are very specific to DeviceNet:

- Missing terminators
- Excessive common mode voltage, caused by faulty connectors or excessive cable length
- Low power supply voltage caused by faulty connectors or excessive cable length
- Excessive signal propagation delays caused by excessive cable length.

These problems will be discussed in more detail.

13b.2 Tools of the trade

The following list is by no means complete, but is intended to give an overview of the types of tools available for commissioning and troubleshooting DeviceNet networks. Whereas some tools are sophisticated and expensive, many DeviceNet problems can be sorted out with common sense and a multimeter.

13b.2.1 Multimeter

A multimeter capable of measuring DC volts, resistance, and current is an indispensable troubleshooting tool. On the current scale, it should be capable of measuring several amperes.

13b.2.2   Oscilloscope

An inexpensive 20 MHz dual-trace oscilloscope comes in quite handy. It can be used for all the voltage tests as well as observing noise on the lines, but caution should be exercised when interpreting traces.

Firstly, signal lines must be observed in differential mode (with probes connected to CAN_H and CAN_L). If they are observed one at a time with reference to ground, they may seem unacceptable due to the common mode noise (which is not a problem since it is rejected by the differential mode receivers on the nodes).

13b.2.3   Handheld analyzers

Handheld DeviceNet analyzers such as the NetAlert NetMeter (Figure 13b.1) or DeviceNet Detective can be used for several purposes. Depending on the capabilities of the specific device, they can configure node addresses and baud rates, monitor power and signal levels, log errors and network events of periods ranging from few minutes to several days, indicate short circuits and poorly wired connections, and obtain configuration states as well as firmware versions and serial numbers from devices.

Figure 13b.1
NetAlert NetMeter

13b.2.4   Intelligent wiring components

Examples of these are the NetAlert traffic monitor and NetAlert power monitor. These are 'intelligent' tee-pieces that are wired into the system (Figure 13b.2). The first device monitors and displays network traffic by means of LEDs and gives a visual warning if traffic levels exceed 90%. The second device monitors voltages and visually indicates whether they are OK, too high, too low, or totally out of range.

The NetMeter can be attached to the above-mentioned tees for more detailed diagnostics.

Figure 13b.2
Power monitor tee

13b.2.5   Controller software

Many DeviceNet controllers have associated software, running under various operating systems such as Windows 2000 and NT4 that can display sophisticated views of the network for diagnostic purposes. The example given here is one of many generated by the ApplicomIO software (Figure 13b.3) and displays data obtained from a device, down to bit level (in hexadecimal).

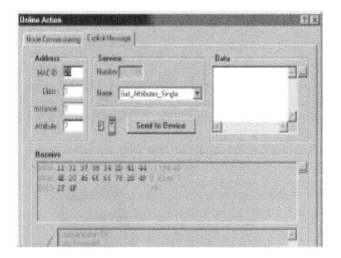

Figure 13b.3
ApplicomIO display

13b.2.6   CAN bus monitor

Since DeviceNet is based on the controller area network, CAN protocol analysis software can be used on DeviceNet networks to capture and analyze packets (frames). An example is Synergetic's CAN Explorer for Windows, running on a PC. The same vendor also supplies the ISA, PC/104, PCI and parallel port network interfaces for connecting the PC to the DeviceNet network.

A PC with this software can not only function as a protocol analyzer, but also as a data logger.

13b.3   Fault finding procedures

In general, the system should not be operating that is, there should be no communication on the bus, and all devices should be installed.

A low-tech approach to troubleshooting could involve disconnecting parts of the network, and observing the effect on the problem. This does, unfortunately, not work well for problems such as excessive common mode voltage and ground loops since disconnecting part of the network often solves the problem.

13b.3.1   Incorrect cable lengths

If the network exhibits problems during the commissioning phase or after modifications/additions have been made to the network, the cable lengths should be double-checked against the DeviceNet topology restrictions. The maximum cable lengths are as follows:

	125 kbaud	250 kbaud	50 kbaud
Thick trunk length	500 m	250 m	100 m
Thin trunk length	100 m	100 m	100 m
Single drop	6 m	6 m	6 m
Cumulative all drops	156 m	78 m	39 m

For simplicity, only the metric sizes are given here.

The following symptoms are indicative of a topology problem.

- If drop lines too long, that is, the total amount of drops exceeds the permitted length, variations on CAN signal amplitude will occur throughout the network.
- If a trunk line is too long it will cause 'transmission line' effects in which reflections in the network cause faulty reception of messages; this will result in CAN frame errors.

13b.3.2   Power and earthing problems

Shielding

Shielding is checked in the following way.

Connect a 16 A DC ammeter from DC common to shield at the end of the network furthest from the power supply. If the power supply is in the middle, then this test must be performed at both ends. In either case, there should be significant current flow. If practical, this test can also be performed at the end of each drop.

If there is no current flowing, then the shield is broken or the network is improperly grounded.

Grounding

In general, the following rules should be observed:

- Physically connect the DC power supply ground wire and the shield together to earth ground at the location of the power supply.
- In the case of multiple power supplies, connect this ground only at the power supply closest to the middle of the network.
- Ensure that all nodes on the network connect to the shield, the signal and power lines.

Note: CAN frame errors are a symptom of grounding problems. CAN error messages can be monitored with a handheld DeviceNet analyzer or CAN bus analyzer.

Break the shield at a few points in the network, and insert a DC ammeter in the shield.

If there is a current flow, then the shield is connected to DC common or ground in more than one place, and a ground loop exists.

Power

This can be measured with a voltmeter or handheld DeviceNet analyzer and is measured between V+ (red) and V− (black).

Measure the network voltage at various points across the network, especially at the ends and at each device. The measured voltage should ideally be 24 V, but no more than 25 V and not less than 11 V DC.

If devices draw a lot of current, then voltages on the bus can fluctuate hence bus voltages should be monitored over time.

If the voltages are not within specification, then:

- Check for faulty or loose connectors
- Check the power system design calculations by measuring the current flow in each section of cable.

On some DeviceNet analyzers, one can set a supply alarm voltage below which a warning should be generated. Plug the analyzer at locations far from the power supply and leave it running over time. If the network voltage falls below this level at any time, this low voltage event will be logged by the analyzer.

Note that 'thin' cable, which has a higher DC resistance, will have greater voltage drop across distance.

13b.3.3   Incorrect signal voltage levels

The following signal levels should be observed with a voltmeter, oscilloscope or DeviceNet analyzer. Readings that differ by more than 0.5 V with the following values are most likely indicative of a problem.

CAN_H can NEVER be lower than CAN_L and if this is observed, it means that the two wires have probably been transposed.

- If bus communications are OFF (idle) the following values can be observed with any measuring device

    - CAN_H (white) 2.5 V DC
    - CAN_L (blue) 2.5 V DC.

- If bus communications are ON, the following can be observed with a voltmeter:

    - CAN_H (white) 3.0 V DC
    - CAN_L (blue) 2.0 V DC.

Alternatively, the voltages can be observed with an oscilloscope or DeviceNet analyzer, in which case both minimum and maximum values can be observed.

These are:

- CAN_H (white) 2.5 V min., 4.0 V max.
- CAN_L (blue) 1.0 V min., 2.5 V max.

13b.3.4   Common mode voltage problems

This test assumes that the shield had already been checked for continuity and current flow and can be done with a voltmeter or an oscilloscope:

- Turn all network power supplies on
- Configure all nodes to draw the maximum amount of power from the network
- Turn on all outputs that draw current.

Now measure the DC voltage between V– and the shield. The difference should, technically speaking, be less than 4.65 V. For a reasonable safety margin, this value should be kept below 3 V.

These measurements should be taken at the two furthest ends (terminator position), at the DeviceNet master(s) and at each power supply. Should a problem be observed here, a solution could be to relocate the power supply to the middle of the network or to add additional power supplies.

In general, one can design a network using any number of power supplies, providing that:

- The voltage drop in the cable between a power supply and each station it supplies does not exceed 5 V DC.
- The current does not exceed the cable/connector ratings.
- The power supply common ground voltage level does not vary by more than 5 V between any two points in the network.

13b.3.5   Incorrect termination

These tests can be performed with a MultiMate. They must be done with all bus communications off (bus off) and the meter set to measure resistance.

Check the resistance from CAN_H to CAN_L at each device. If the values are larger than 60 Ω (120 Ω in parallel with 120 Ω) there could be a break in one of the signal wires or there could be a missing terminator or terminators somewhere. If, on the other hand, the measured values are less than 50 Ω, this could indicate a short between the network wires, (an) extra terminating resistor(s), one or more faulty transceivers or unpowered nodes.

13b.3.6   Noise

Noise can be observed with a loudspeaker or with an oscilloscope. However, more important than the noise itself, is the way in which the noise affects the actual transmissions taking place on the medium. The most common effect of EMI/RFI problems are CAN frame errors, which can be monitored with a CAN analyzer or DeviceNet analyzer.

The occurrence of frame errors must be related to specific nodes and to the occurrence of specific events, for example, a state change on a nearby variable frequency drive.

13b.3.7   Node communication problems

Node presence

One method to isolate defective nodes is to use the master configuration software or a DeviceNet analyzer to create a 'live list' to see which nodes are active on the network, and to compare this with the list of nodes that are supposed to be on the network.

Excessive traffic

The master configuration software or a DeviceNet analyzer can measure the percentage traffic on the network. A figure of 30–70% is normal and anything over 90% is excessive.

Loads over 90% indicate problems. High bus loads can indicate any of the following:

- Some nodes could be having difficulty making connections with other nodes and have to retransmit repeatedly to get messages through. Check termination, bus length, topology, physical connections and grounding.
- Defective nodes can 'chatter' and put garbage on the network.
- Nodes supplied with corrupt or noisy power may chatter.
- Change of state (COS) devices may be excessively busy with rapidly changing data and cause high percentage bus load.

- Large quantities of explicit messages (configuration and diagnostic data) being sent can cause high percentage bus load.
- Diagnostic instruments such as DeviceNet analyzers add traffic of their own; if this appears to be excessive, the settings on the device can be altered to reduce the additional traffic.

MACID/baud rate settings

A network status LED is built into many devices. This LED should always be flashing GREEN. A solid RED indicates a communication fault, possibly an incorrect baud rate or a duplicate station address (MACID).

Network configuration software can be used to perform a 'network who' to verify that all stations are connected and communicating correctly.

In the absence of indicator LEDs, a DeviceNet analyzer will only be able to indicate that one or more devices have wrong baud rates. The devices will have to be found by inspection, and the baud rate settings corrected. First disconnect the device with the wrong baud rate, correct the setting, and then reconnect the device.

In the absence of an indicator LED, there is no explicit way of checking duplicate MACIDs either. If two nodes have the same address, one will just passively remain off-line. One solution is to look for nodes that should appear in the live list, but do not.

14a

Profibus PA/DP/FMS overview

Objectives

When you have completed study of this chapter, you will be able to:

- List the main features of Profibus PA/DP/FMS
- Fix problems with:
  - Cabling
  - Fiber
  - Shielding
  - Grounding/earthing
  - Segmentation
  - Color coding
  - Addressing
  - Token bus operation
  - Unsolicited messages
  - Fine tuning of impedance terminations
  - Drop-line lengths
  - GSD files usage
  - Intrinsic safety concerns.

14a.1 Introduction

Profibus (PROcess FIeld BUS) is a widely accepted international networking standard, commonly found in process control and in large assembly and material handling machines. It supports single-cable wiring of multi-input sensor blocks, pneumatic valves, complex intelligent devices, smaller sub-networks (such as AS-i), and operator interfaces.

Profibus is nearly universal in Europe and also popular in North America, South America, and parts of Africa and Asia. It is an open, vendor-independent standard. It adheres to the OSI model and ensures that devices from a variety of different vendors can communicate together easily and effectively. It has been standardized under the German National standard as DIN 19 245 Parts 1 and 2 and, in addition, has also been ratified under the European national standard EN 50170 Volume 2.

The development of Profibus was initiated by the BMFT (German Federal Ministry of Research and Technology) in cooperation with several automation manufacturers in 1989. The bus interfacing hardware is implemented on ASIC (application specific integrated circuit) chips produced by multiple vendors, and is based on the RS-485 standard as well as the European EN50170 Electrical specification. The standard is supported by the Profibus Trade Organization, whose website can be found at *www.profibus.com*.

Profibus uses nine-pin D-type connectors (impedance terminated) or 12 mm quick-disconnect connectors. The number of nodes is limited to 127. The distance supported is up to 24 km (with repeaters and fiber-optic transmission), with speeds varying from 9600 bps to 12 Mbps. The message size can be up to 244 bytes of data per node per message (12 bytes of overhead for a maximum message length of 256 bytes), while the medium access control mechanisms are polling and token passing.

Profibus supports two main types of devices, namely, masters and slaves:

1. Master devices control the bus and when they have the right to access the bus, they may transfer messages without any remote request. These are referred to as active stations.
2. Slave devices are typically peripheral devices i.e. transmitters/sensors and actuators. They may only acknowledge received messages or, at the request of a master, transmit messages to that master. These are also referred to as passive stations.

There are several versions of the standard, namely, Profibus DP (master/slave), Profibus FMS (multi-master/peer-to-peer), and Profibus PA (intrinsically safe).

- Profibus DP (distributed peripheral) allows the use of multiple master devices, in which case each slave device is assigned to one master. This means that multiple masters can read inputs from the device but only one master can write outputs to that device. Profibus DP is designed for high-speed data transfer at the sensor/actuator level (as opposed to Profibus FMS which tends to focus on the higher automation levels) and is based around DIN 19 245 parts 1 and 2 since 1993. It is suitable as a replacement for the costly wiring of 24 V and 4–20 mA measurement signals. The data exchange for Profibus DP is generally cyclic in nature. The central controller, which acts as the master, reads the input data from the slave and sends the output data back to the slave. The bus cycle time is much shorter than the program cycle time of the controller (less than 10 ms).
- Profibus FMS (fieldbus message specification) is a peer-to-peer messaging format, which allows masters to communicate with one another. Just as in Profibus DP, up to 126 nodes are available and all can be masters if desired. FMS messages consume more overhead than DP messages.
- 'COMBI mode' is when FMS and DP are used simultaneously in the same network, and some devices (such as Synergetic's DP/FMS masters) support this. This is most commonly used in situations where a PLC is being used in conjunction with a PC, and the primary master communicates with the secondary master via FMS. DP messages are sent via the same network to I/O devices.
- The Profibus PA protocol is the same as the latest Profibus DP with V1 diagnostic extensions, except that voltage and current levels are reduced to meet the requirements of intrinsic safety (class I division II) for the process industry. Many DP/FMS master cards support Profibus PA, but barriers are required to convert between DP and PA. PA devices are normally powered by the network at intrinsically safe voltage and current levels, utilizing the transmission technique specified in IEC 61158-2 (which Foundation Fieldbus H1 uses as well).

14a.2 Profibus protocol stack

The architecture of the Profibus protocol stack is summarized in Figure 14a.1. Note the addition of an eighth layer, the so-called 'user' layer, on top of the seven-layer OSI model.

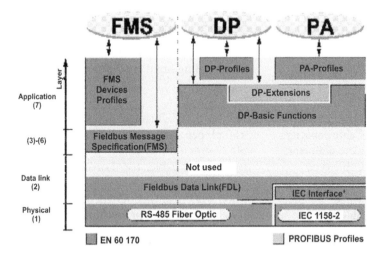

Figure 14a.1
Profibus protocol stack

All three Profibus variations namely FMS, DP, and PA use the same data-link layer protocol (layer 2). The DP and PA versions us the same physical layer (layer 1) implementation, namely RS-485, while PA uses a variation thereof (as per IEC 61158-2) in order to accommodate intrinsic safety requirements.

14a.2.1 Physical layer (layer 1)

The physical layer of the Profibus DP standard is based on RS-485 and has the following features:

- The network topology is a linear bus, terminated at both ends.
- Stubs are possible.
- The medium is a twisted-pair cable, with shielding conditionally omitted depending on the application. Type-A cable is preferred for transmission speeds greater than 500 kbaud. Type B should only be used for low baud rates and short distances. These are very specific cable types of which the details are given below.
- The data rate can vary between 9.6 kbps and 12 Mbps, depending on the cable length. The values are:

9.6 kbps	1200	m
19.2 kbps	1200	m
93.75 kbps	1200	m
187.5 kbps	600	m
500 kbps	200	m
1.5 Mbps	200	m
12 Mbps	100	m.

The specifications for the two types of cable are as follows:

Type A cable

Impedance:	135 up to 165 Ω (for frequency of 3–20 MHz)
Cable capacity:	<30 pF per meter
Core diameter:	>0.34 mm^2 (AWG 22)
Cable type:	twisted-pair cable. 1 × 2 or 2 × 2 or 1 × 4
Resistance:	<110 Ω per km
Signal attenuation:	max. 9 dB over total length of line section
Shielding:	Cu shielding braid or shielding braid and shielding foil

Type B cable

Impedance:	135 up to 165 Ω (for frequency >100 kHz)
Cable capacity:	<60 pF per meter
Core diameter:	>0.22 mm^2 (AWG 24)
Cable type:	twisted-pair cable. 1 × 2 or 2 × 2 or 1 × 4
Resistance:	<110 Ω per km
Signal attenuation:	Max. 9 dB over total length of line section
Shielding:	Cu shielding braid or shielding braid and shielding foil

For a more detailed discussion of RS-485, refer to the chapter on RS-485 installation and troubleshooting.

14a.2.2 Data-link layer (layer 2)

The second layer of the OSI model implements the functions of medium access control as well as that of the logical link control i.e. the transmission and reception of the actual frames. The latter includes the data integrity function i.e. the generation and checking of checksums.

The medium access control determines when a station may transmit on the bus and Profibus supports two mechanisms, namely, token passing and polling.

Token passing is used for communication between multiple masters on the bus. It involves the passing of software token between masters, in a sequence of ascending addresses. Thus, a logical ring is formed (despite the physical topology being a bus). The polling method (or master–slave method), on the other hand, is used by a master that currently has the token to communicate with its associated slave devices (passive stations).

Profibus can be set up either as a pure master–master system (token passing), or as a polling system (master–slave), or as a hybrid system using both techniques (Figure 14a.2).

The following is a more detailed description of the token-passing mechanism:

- The token is passed from master station to master station in ascending order.
- When a master station receives the token from a previous station, it may then transfer messages to slave devices as well as to other masters.
- If the token transmitter does not recognize any bus activity within the slot time, it repeats the token and waits for another slot time. It retires if it recognizes bus activity. If there is no bus activity, it will repeat the token frame for the last time. If there is still no activity, it will try to pass the token to the next but one master station. It continues repeating the procedure until it identifies a station that is alive.

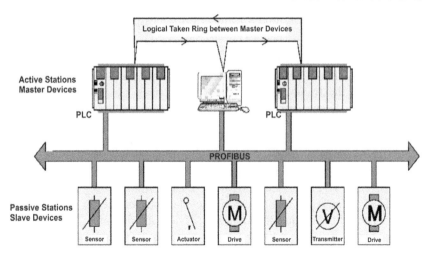

Figure 14a.2
Hybrid medium access control

- Each master station is responsible for the addition or removal of stations in the address range from its own station address to the next station. Whenever a station receives the token, it examines one address in the address range between itself and its current successor. It does this maintenance whenever its currently queued message cycles have been completed. Whenever a station replies saying that it is ready to enter the token ring it is then passed the token. The current token holder also updates its new successor.
- After a power up and after a master station has waited a predefined period, it claims the token if it does not see any bus activity. The master station with the lowest station address commences initialization. It transmits two token frames addressed to itself. This then informs the other master stations that it is now the only station on the logical token ring. It then transmits a 'request field data-link status' to each station in an increasing address order. The first master station that responds is then passed the token. The slave stations and 'master not ready' stations are recorded in an address list called the GAP list.
- When the token is lost, it is not necessary to re-initialize the system. The lowest address master station creates a new token after its token timer has timed out. It then proceeds with its own messages and then passes the token onto its successor.
- The real token rotation time is calculated by each master station on each cycle of the token. The system reaction time is the maximum time interval between two consecutive high-priority message cycles of a master station at maximum bus load. From this, a target token rotation time is defined. The real token rotation time must be less than the target token rotation time for low-priority messages to be sent out.
- There are two priorities that can be selected by the application layer, namely 'low' and 'high'. The high-priority messages are always dispatched first. Independent of the token rotation time, a master station can always transmit one high-priority message. The system's target token rotation time depends on the number of stations, the number of high-priority messages and the duration of each of these messages. Hence it is important only to set very important and critical messages to high-priority. The predefined target token rotation time should contain

sufficient time for low-priority message cycles with some safety margin built in for retries and loss of messages.

Basically the Profibus layer 2 operates in a connectionless fashion, i.e. it transmits frames without prior checking as to whether the intended recipient is able or willing to receive the frame. In most cases, the frames are 'unicast', i.e. they are intended for a specific device, but broadcast and multicast communication is also possible. Broadcast communication means that an active station sends an unconfirmed message to all other stations (masters and slaves). Multicast communication means that a device sends out an unconfirmed message to a group of stations (masters or slaves).

Layer 2 provides data transmission services to layer 7. These services are as defined in DIN 19241-2, IEC 955, ISO 8802-2 and ISO/IEC JTC 1/SC 6N 4960 (LLC Type 1 and LLC Type 3) and comprise three acyclic data services as well as one cyclic data service.

The following data transmission services are defined:

- Send-data-with-acknowledge (SDA) – acyclic.
- Send-data-with-no-acknowledge (SDN) – acyclic.
- Send-and-request-data-with-reply (SRD) – acyclic.
- Cyclic-send-and-request-data-with-reply (CSRD) – cyclic.

All layer 2 services are accessed by layer 7 in software through so-called service access points or SAPs. On both active and passive stations, multiple SAPs (service access points) are allowed simultaneously:

- 32 Stations are allowed without repeaters, but with repeaters this number may be increased to 127.
- The maximum bus length is 1200 m. This may be increased to 4800 m with repeaters.
- Transmission is half-duplex, using NRZ (non-return to zero) coding.
- The data rate can vary between 9.6 kbps and 12 Mbps, with values of 9.6, 19.2, 93.75, 187.5, 500, 1500 kbps, or 12 Mbps.
- The frame formats are according to IEC-870-5-1, and are constructed with a hamming distance of 4. This means that despite up to four consecutive faulty bits in a frame (and despite a correct checksum), a corrupted message will still be detected.
- There are two levels of message priority.

14a.2.3   Application layer

Layer 7 of the OSI model provides the application services to the user. These services make an efficient and open (as well as vendor independent) data transfer possible between the application programs and layer 2.

The Profibus application layer is specified in DIN 19 245 part 2 and consists of:

- The Fieldbus message specification (FMS)
- The lower layer interface (LLI)
- The Fieldbus management services layer 7 (FMA 7).

14a.2.4   Fieldbus message specification (FMS)

From the viewpoint of an application process (at layer 8), the communication system is a service provider offering communication services, known as the FMS services. These are basically classified as either confirmed or unconfirmed services (Figure 14a.3).

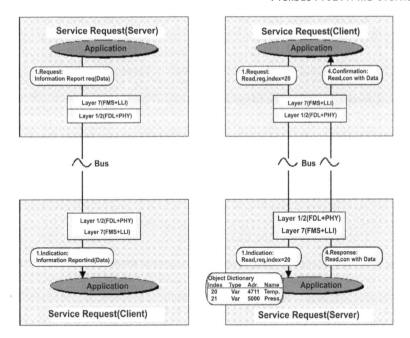

Figure 14a.3
Execution of confirmed and unconfirmed services

Confirmed services are only permitted on connection-oriented communication relationships while unconfirmed services may also be used on connectionless relationships. Unconfirmed services may be transferred with either a high or a low priority.

In the Profibus standard, the interaction between requester and responder, as implemented by the appropriate service, is described by a service primitive.

The Profibus FMS services can be divided into the following groups:

- Context management services allow establishment and release of logical connections, as well as the rejection of inadmissible services.
- Variable access services permit access (read and write) to simple variables, records, arrays, and variable lists.
- The domain management services enable the transmission (upload or download) of contiguous memory blocks. The application process splits the data into smaller segments (fragments) for transmission purposes.
- The program invocation services allow the control (start, stop, etc.) of program execution.
- The event management services are unconfirmed services, which make the transmission of alarm messages possible. They may be used with high or low priority, and messages may be transmitted on broadcast or multicast communication relationships.
- The VFD support messages permit device identification and status reports. These reports may be initiated at the discretion of individual devices, and transmitted on broadcast or multicast communication relationships.
- The (OD) management services permit object dictionaries to be read and written. Process objects must be listed as communication objects in an object dictionery OD. The application process on the device must make its objects visible and available before these can be addressed and processed by the communication services.

As can be seen, there are large amounts of Profibus FMS application services to satisfy the various requirements of field devices. Only a few of these (5, in fact) are mandatory for implementation in all Profibus devices. The selection of further services depends on the specific application and is specified in the so-called profiles.

14a.2.5   Lower layer interface (LLI)

Layer 7 needs a special adaptation to layer 2. This is implemented by the LLI in the Profibus protocol. The LLI conducts the data flow control and connection monitoring as well as the mapping of the FMS services onto layer 2, with due consideration of the various types of devices (master or slave).

Communications relationships between application processes with the specific purpose of transferring data must be defined before a data transfer is started. These definitions are listed in layer 7 in the communications relationship list (CRL).

The main tasks of the LLI are:

- Mapping of FMS services onto the data-link layer services
- Connection establishment and release
- Supervision of the connection
- Flow control.

The following types of communication relationships are supported by:

- Connectionless communication, which can be either
- Broadcast, or
- Multicast, and
- Connection-oriented communication, which can be either

    – Master/master (cyclic or acyclic), or
    – Master/slave – with or without slave initiative – (cyclic or acyclic).

Connection-oriented communication relationships represent a logical peer-to-peer connection between two application processes. Before any data can be sent over this connection, it has to be established with an initiate service, one of the context management services. This comprises the connection establishment phase. After successful establishment, the connection is protected against third party access and can then be used for data communication between the two parties involved. This comprises the data transfer phase. In this phase, both confirmed and unconfirmed services can be used. When the connection is no longer needed, it can be released with yet another context management service, the Abort service. This comprises the connection release phase (Figure 14a.4).

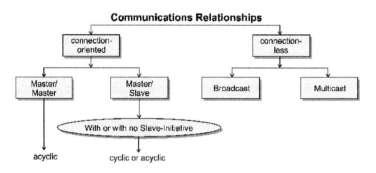

Figure 14a.4
Supported communication relationships

14a.2.6 Fieldbus management layer (FMA 7)

This describes object and management services. The objects are manipulated locally or remotely using management services. There are three groups here:

1. *Context management*: This provides a service for opening and closing a management connection.
2. *Configuration management*: This provides services for the identification of communication components of a station, for loading and reading the communi cation relationship list (CRL), and for accessing variables, counters, and the parameters of the lower layers.
3. *Fault management*: This provides services for recognizing and eliminating errors.

14a.3 The Profibus communication model

From a communication point of view, an application process includes all programs, resources, and tasks that are not assigned to one of the communication layers. The Profibus communication model permits the combination of distributed application processes into a common process, using communications relationships. This acts to unify distributed application processes to a common process. That part of an application process in a field device that is reachable for communication is called a virtual field device (VFD).

All objects of a real device that can be communicated with (such as variables, programs, data ranges) are called communication objects. The VFD contains the communication objects that may be manipulated by the services of the application layer via Profibus.

14a.4 Relationship between application process and communication

Between two application processes, one or more communication relationships may exist; each one having a unique communication end point as shown in Figure 14a.5:

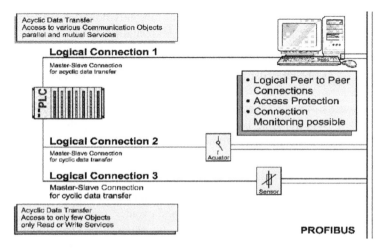

Figure 14a.5
Assignment of communication relationships to application process

Mapping of the functions of the VFD onto the real device is provided by the application layer interface. Figure 14a.6 shows the relationship between the real field device and the virtual field device.

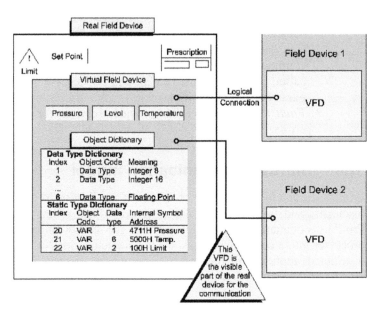

Figure 14a.6
Virtual field device (VFD) with object dictionary (OD)

In this example, only the variables pressure, fill level, and temperature may be read or written via two communication relationships.

14a.5   Communication objects

All communication objects of a Profibus station are entered into a local object dictionary. This object dictionary may be predefined at simple devices; however on more complex devices it is configured and locally or remotely downloaded into the device.

The object dictionary (OD) structure contains:

- A header, which contains information about the structure of the OD
- A static list of types, containing the list of the supported data types and data structures
- A static object dictionary, containing a list of static communication objects
- A dynamic list of variable lists, containing the actual list of the known variable lists, and a dynamic list of program invocations, which contains a list of the known programs.

Defined static communication objects include simple variable, array (a sequence of simple variables of the same type), record (a list of simple variables not necessarily of the same type), domain (a data range), and event.

Dynamic communication objects are entered into the dynamic part of the OD. They include program invocation and variable list (a sequence of simple variables, arrays, or records). These can be predefined at configuration time, dynamically defined, deleted, or changed with the application services in the operational phase.

Logical addressing is the preferred way of addressing of communication objects. They are normally accessed with a short address called an index (unsigned 16 bit). This makes for efficient messaging and keeps the protocol overhead down.

There are, however, two other optional addressing methods:

1. Addressing by name, where the symbolic name of the communication objects is transferred via the bus.
2. Physical addressing. Any physical memory location in the field device may be accessed with the services PhysRead and PhysWrite.

It is possible to implement password protection on certain objects and also to make them read-access only, for example.

14a.6 Performance

A short reaction time is one of the main advantages of Profibus DP. The figures are typical.

512 Inputs and outputs distributed over 32 stations can be accessed:

- In 6 ms at 1.5 Mbps and
- In 2 ms at 12 Mbps.

Figure 14a.7 gives a visual indication of Profibus performance.

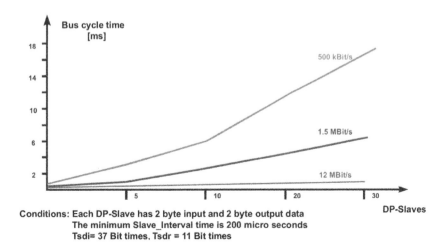

Conditions: Each DP-Slave has 2 byte input and 2 byte output data
The minimum Slave_Interval time is 200 micro seconds
Tsdi= 37 Bit times. Tsdr = 11 Bit times

Figure 14a.7
Bus cycle time of a Profibus DP mono-master system

The main service used to achieve these results is the send and receive data service of layer 2. This allows for the transmission of the input and output data in a single message cycle. Obviously, the other reason for increased performance is the higher transmission speed of 12 Mbps.

14a.7 System operation

14a.7.1 Configuration

The choice is up to user as to whether the system should be a mono-master or multi-master system. Up to 126 stations (masters or slaves) can be accommodated.

There are different device types:

- *DP-master class 1 (DPM1)*:   This is typically a PLC (programmable logical controller).
- *DP-master class 2 (DPM2)*:   These devices are used for programing, configuration or diagnostics.
- *DP-slave A*:   This is typically a sensor or actuator. The amount of I/O data is limited to 246 bytes.

The two configurations possible are shown in Figures 14a.8 and 14a.9.

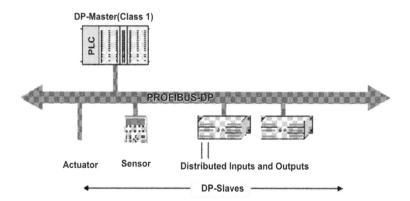

Figure 14a.8
Profibus DP mono-master system

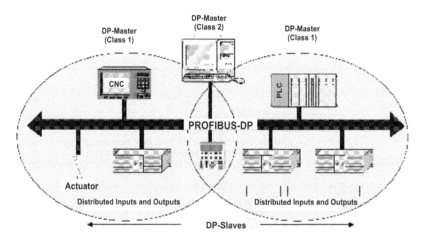

Figure 14a.9
Profibus DP multi-master system

The following states can occur with DPM1:

- *Stop*:   In this state, no data transfer occurs between the DPM1 and DP-slaves.
- *Clear*:   The DPM1 puts the outputs into a fail-safe mode and reads the input data from the DP-slaves.
- *Operate*:   The DPM1 is in the data transfer state with a cyclic message sequence where input data is read and output data is written down to the slave.

14a.7.2   Data transfer between DPM1 and the DP-slaves

During configuration of the system, the user defines the assignment of a DP slave to a DPM1 and which of the DP-slaves are included in the message cycle. In the so-called parameterization and configuration phases, each slave device compares its real configuration with that received from the DPM1. This configuration information has to be identical. This safeguards the user from any configuration faults. Once this has been successfully checked, the slave device will enter into the data transfer phase as indicated in Figure 14a.10.

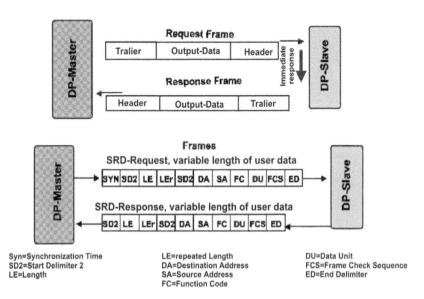

Figure 14a.10
User data exchange for Profibus DP

14a.7.3   Synchronization and freeze modes

In addition to the standard cyclic data transfer mechanisms automatically executed by the DPM1, it is possible to send control commands from a master to an individual or group of slaves.

If the 'sync' command is transmitted to the appropriate slaves, they enter this state and freeze the outputs. They then store the output data during the next cyclic data exchange. When they receive the next 'sync' command, the stored output data is issued to the field.

If a 'freeze' command is transmitted to the appropriate slaves, the inputs are frozen in the present state. The input data is only updated on receiving the next 'freeze' command.

14a.7.4   Safety and protection of stations

At the DPM1 station, the user data transfer to each slave is monitored with a watchdog timer. If this timer expires indicating that no successful transfer has taken place, the user is informed and the DPM1 leaves the OPERATE state and switches the outputs of all the assigned slave devices to the fail-safe state. The master changes to the CLEAR state. Note that the master ignores the timer if the automatic error reaction has been enabled (Auto_Clear = True).

At the slave devices, the watchdog timer is again used to monitor any failures of the master device or the bus. The slave switches its outputs autonomously to the fail-safe state if it detects a failure.

14a.7.5 Mixed operation of FMS and DP stations

Where lower reaction times are acceptable, it is possible to operate FMS and DP devices together on the same bus. It is also possible to use a composite device, which supports both FMS and DP protocols simultaneously. This can make sense if the configuration is done using FMS and the higher speed cyclic operations are done for user data transfer. The only difference between the FMS and DP protocols are of course the application layers (Figure 14a.11).

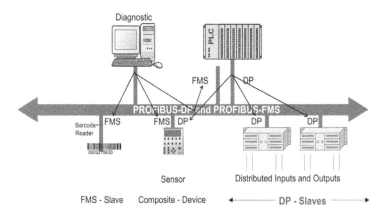

Figure 14a.11
Mixed operation of Profibus FMS and DP

14b

Profibus troubleshooting

14b.1 Introduction

Profibus DP and FMS use RS-485 at the physical layer (layer 1) and therefore all the RS-485 installation and troubleshooting guidelines apply. Refer to Chapter 14a. Profibus PA uses the same physical layers as the 61158-2 standard (which is the same as the Foundation Fieldbus H1 standard). This section will discuss some additional specialized tools.

14b.2 Troubleshooting tools

14b.2.1 Handheld testing device

These are similar to the ones available for DeviceNet, and can be used to check the copper infrastructure before connecting any devices to the cable. A typical example is the unit made by Synergetic.

They can indicate:

- A switch (i.e. reversal) of the A and B lines
- Wire breaks in the A and B lines as well as in the shield
- Short circuits between the A and B lines and the shield
- Incorrect or missing terminations.

The error is indicated via text shown in the display of the device.

These devices can also be used to check the RS-485 interfaces of Profibus devices, after they have been connected to the network. Typical functions include:

- Creating a list with the addresses of all stations connected to the bus (useful for identifying missing devices)
- Testing individual stations (e.g. identifying duplicate addresses)
- Measuring distance (checking whether the installed segment lengths comply with the Profibus requirements)
- Measuring reflections (e.g. locating an interruption of the bus line).

14b.2.2 D-type connectors with built-in terminators

For further location of cable break errors reported by a handheld tester, nine-pin D connectors with integrated terminations are very helpful. When the termination is switched to 'on' at the connector, the cable leading out of the connector is disconnected. This feature can be used to identify the location of the error, as follows.

If, for example, the handheld is connected at the beginning of the network and a wire break of the A line is reported, plug the D connector somewhere in the middle of the network and switch the termination to 'on'. If the problem is still reported by the tester, it means that the introduced termination is still not 'seen' by the tester and thus the cable break must be between the beginning of the network and the D connector.

14b.2.3   Configuration utilities

Each Profibus network must be configured and various products are commercially available to perform this task. Examples include the Profibus DP configuration tool by SST, the Allen Bradley plug & play software, and the Siemens COM package (Figure 14b.1). In many cases, the decision on the tool to be used for configuration is made automatically by choosing the controlling device for the bus. The choice of configuration tool should not be treated lightly because the easier the tool is to use, the less likely a configuration error will be made.

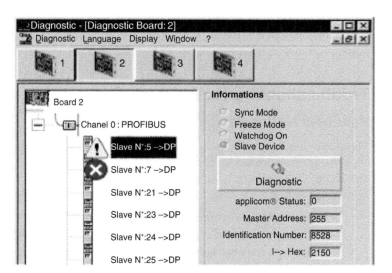

Figure 14b.1
Applicom configuration tool

With Profibus, all parameters of a device (including text to provide a good explanation of the parameters and of the possible choices, values and ranges) are specified in a so-called GSD file, which is the electronics data sheet of the device. Therefore the configuration software has all the information it needs to create a friendly user interface with no need for the interpretation of hexadecimal values.

14b.2.4   Built-in diagnostics

Several diagnostic functions were designed into Profibus. The standard defines different timers and counters used by the physical layer to maintain operation and monitor the quality of the network. One counter, for example, counts the number of invalid start delimiters received as an indication of installation problems or an interface not working properly. These timers and counters can be used by the Profibus device or by its configuration tool to identify a problem and to indicate it to the user.

For Profibus DP, a special diagnostic message is defined, which can be indicated by a Profibus DP slave or requested by a Profibus DP master. The first 6 bytes are implemented for all Profibus DP devices.

This information is used to indicate various problems to the user and could include:

- Configuration of the specific device incorrect
- Required features not supported on the device or
- Device does not answer.

The user normally gets access to all this information through the configuration tool. The user selects a device, the tool reads the diagnostic information from the device, and provides high-level text information.

During operation, a DP device automatically reports problems to the Profibus DP master. The master stores the diagnostic information and provides it to the user. This can, for example, be done by a PC-based system that utilizes diagnostic flow charts to evaluate the information and then make it available to the operator.

The definition of additional diagnostics enables each manufacturer to simplify matters for end-users. The additional information differentiates between a device-related, an identifier-related, and a channel-related part. The device-related part provides the opportunity to encode manufacturer-specific details. This can be used to report that the module place in slot #4 is not the same as the one configured. Module-related diagnostics provides an overview of the status of all modules; it identifies whether a module supports diagnostics or not. The channel-related part offers the possibility to report problems down to the bit level. This means a DP slave can indicate that channel #3 of the module in slot #5 has a short-circuit to ground.

With the additional diagnostics, a Profibus DP device can send very detailed error reports to the controlling device. As a result, the master device is able to provide details to the user such as 'ERROR oven control: lower temperature limit exceeded' or 'station address 23 (conveyor control): wire break at module 2, channel 5'. This feature provides not only the flexibility to report any kind of error at a device but also often how to correct it. Because the protocol for Profibus PA is identical to that for DP, the diagnostic mechanism is the same.

14b.2.5 Bus monitors

A bus monitor (protocol analyzer) is an additional tool for troubleshooting a Profibus network, enabling the user to perform packet content and timing verification. It is capable of monitoring and capturing all Profibus network activity (messages, ACKs, etc.) on the bus, and then saving the captured data to disk. Each captured message is time-stamped with sub-millisecond resolution. A monitor does not have a Profibus station address nor does it affect the speed or efficiency of the network.

A monitor provides a wide range of trigger and filter functions that allow capturing messages between two stations only or triggering on a special event like diagnostic requests. Such a tool can be used for the indication of problems with individual devices (e.g. wrong configuration) and also to visualize physical problems.

Bus monitors are typically PCs with a special Profibus interface card and the appropriate data capturing software. An example is the Profibus DP capturing utility by SST. Bus monitors are sophisticated tools and are recommending only for people with a reasonable knowledge of Profibus and its protocol.

14b.3　Tips

Profibus (especially DP) is straightforward from a user's point of view, as the messaging format is fairly simple.

However, the following notes will be helpful in identifying common problems:

- Profibus has a relatively high (12 Mbps) maximum data rate but it can also be operated at speeds as low as 9600 baud. If Profibus is to be used at high speeds, it might be necessary to use a scope or analyzer to check and fine-tune impedance terminations and drop-line lengths. Such problems are magnified at higher speeds. Users who initially intend to run their network at maximum speed often find that a lower speed setting performs just as well and is easier to get working.
- One of the most common problems encountered in configuring a Profibus network is selecting the wrong GSD (device description) file for a particular node. As GSD files reside in a separate disk and are not embedded in the product itself, files are sometimes paired with the wrong devices.
- When installing a new network, follow the Profibus installation guidelines:

  - Use connectors suitable for an industrial environment and according to the defined standard
  - Use only the specified (blue) cable
  - Make sure the cable has no wire break and none of the wires causes a short circuit condition
  - Do not crisscross the wires; always use the green wire for A and the red wire as B throughout the whole network
  - Make sure the segment length is according to the chosen transmission rate (use repeaters to extend the network)
  - Make sure the number of devices/RS-485 drivers per segment does not exceed 32 (use repeaters where necessary)
  - Check proper termination of all copper segments (an RS-485 segment must be terminated at both ends)
  - If so-called 'activated terminations' are used, they must be powered at all times
  - Avoid drop lines or make sure the overall length does not exceed the specified maximum. In case T-drops are needed, use repeaters or active bus terminals
  - In case the network connects buildings or runs in a hazardous environment, consider the use of fiber optics
  - Check whether the station addresses are set to the correct value
  - Check if the network configurations match the physical setup
  - For RS-485 implementations (Profibus FMS and Profibus DP), type A cable is preferred for transmission speeds greater than 500 kbaud; type B should only be used for low baud rates and short distances.

The specifications for the two types of cable are as follows:

Type A Cable		
Impedance:	135 up to 165 Ohm (for frequency of 3 to 20 MHz)
Cable Capacity:	<30 pF per Meter
Core Diameter:	>0.34 mm2 (AWG 22)
Cable Type:	twisted pair cable. 1 x2 or 2x2 or 1x4.
Resistance:	<110 Ohm per km
Signal Attenuation:	Max. 9dB over total length of line sectior
Shielding:	Cu shielding braid or shielding braid and shielding foil

Type B Cable		
Impedance:	135 up to 165 Ohm (for frequency > 100 kHz)
Cable Capacity:	<60 pF per Meter
Core Diameter:	>0.22 mm2 (AWG 24)
Cable Type:	twisted pair cable. 1 x2 or 2x2 or 1x4.
Resistance:	<110 Ohm per km
Signal Attenuation:	Max. 9dB over total length of line sectior
Shielding:	Cu shielding braid or shielding braid and shielding foil

- The connection between shield and protective ground is made via the metal cases and screw tops of the D-type connectors. Should this not be possible, then the connection should be made via pin 1 of the connectors. This is not an optimum solution and it is probably better to bare the cable shield at the appropriate point and to ground it with a cable, as short as possible, to the metallic structure of the cabinet.

15a

Foundation Fieldbus overview

Objectives

When you have completed study of this chapter, you will be able to:

- Describe how Foundation Fieldbus operates
- Remedy problems with:
    - Wiring
    - Earths/grounds
    - Shielding
    - Wiring polarity
    - Power
    - Terminations
    - Intrinsic safety
    - Voltage drop
    - Power conditioning
    - Surge protection
    - Configuration.

15a.1   Introduction to Foundation Fieldbus

Foundation Fieldbus (FF) takes full advantage of the emerging 'smart' field devices and modern digital communications technology allowing end-user benefits such as:

- Reduced wiring
- Communications of multiple process variables from a single instrument
- Advanced diagnostics
- Interoperability between devices of different manufacturers
- Enhanced field level control
- Reduced start-up time
- Simpler integration.

The concept behind Foundation Fieldbus is to preserve the desirable features of the present 4–20 mA standard (such as a standardized interface to the communications link, bus power derived from the link and intrinsic safety options) while taking advantage of the new digital technologies.

This will provide the features noted above because of:

- Reduced wiring due to the multi-drop capability
- Flexibility of supplier choices due to interoperability
- Reduced control room equipment due to distribution of control functions to the device level
- Increased data integrity and reliability due to the application of digital communications.

Foundation Fieldbus consists of four layers. Three of them correspond to OSI layers 1, 2, and 7. The fourth is the so-called 'user layer' that sits on top of layer 7 and is often said to represent OSI 'layer 8', although the OSI model does not include such a layer. The user layer provides a standardized interface between the application software and the actual field devices.

15a.2 The physical layer and wiring rules

The physical layer standard has been approved and is detailed in the IEC 61158-2 and the ISA standard S50.02-1992. It supports communication rates of 31.25 kbps and uses the Manchester Bi-phase L encoding scheme with four encoding states as shown in Figure 15a.1. Devices can be optionally powered from the bus under certain conditions. The 31.25 kbps (or H1, or low-speed bus) can support 2–32 devices that are not bus-powered, 2–12 devices that are bus-powered, or 2–6 devices that are bus-powered in an intrinsically safe area. Repeaters are allowed and will increase the length and number of devices that can be put on the bus. The H2 or high-speed bus options was not implemented as originally planned, but was superseded by the high-speed Ethernet (HSE) standard. This is discussed later in this section.

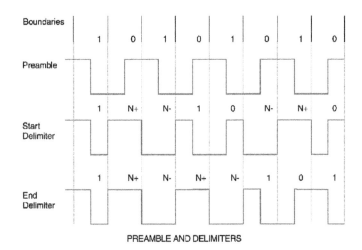

PREAMBLE AND DELIMITERS

Figure 15a.1
Use of N+ and N– encoding states

The low-speed (H1) bus is intended to utilize existing plant wiring and uses #22 AWG type-B wiring (shielded twisted pair) for segments up to 1200 m (3936 ft) and #18 AWG type-A wiring (shielded twisted pair) up to 1900 m (6232 ft). Two additional types of cabling are specified and are referred to as type C (multi-pair twisted without shield) and type D (multi-core, no shield).

Type C using #26 AWG cable is limited to 400 m (1312 ft) per segment and type D with #16 AWG is restricted to segments less than 200 m (660 ft).

- Type A: #18 AWG   1900 m (6232 ft)
- Type B: #22 AWG   1200 m (3936 ft)
- Type C: #26 AWG   400 m (1312 ft)
- Type D: #16 AWG multi-core   200 m (660 ft).

The Foundation Fieldbus wiring is floating/balanced and equipped with a termination resistor (RC combination) connected across each end of the transmission line (Figure 15a.2). Neither of the wires should ever be connected to ground. The terminator consists of a 100 Ω quarter Watt resistor and a capacitor sized to pass 31.25 kHz. As an option, one of the terminators can be center-tapped and grounded to prevent voltage buildup on the bus. Power supplies must be impedance matched. Off-the-shelf power supplies must be conditioned by fitting a series inductor. If a 'normal power supply' is placed across the line, it will load down the line due to its low impedance. This will cause the transmitters to stop transmitting.

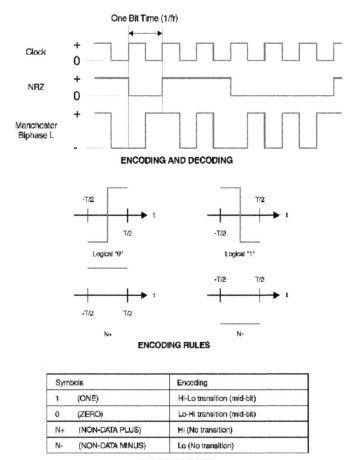

Symbols		Encoding
1	(ONE)	Hi-Lo transition (mid-bit)
0	(ZERO)	Lo-Hi transition (mid-bit)
N+	(NON-DATA PLUS)	Hi (No transition)
N-	(NON-DATA MINUS)	Lo (No transition)

ENCODING RULES

Figure 15a.2
Foundation Fieldbus physical layer

Fast response times for the bus were one of the FF goals. For example, at 31.25 kbps on the H1 bus, response times as low as 32 µs are possible. This will vary, based on the loading of the system, but will average between 32 µs and 2.2 ms with an average of approximately 1 ms.

Spurs can be connected to the 'home run'. The length of the spurs depends on the type of wire used and the number of spurs connected. The maximum length is the total length of the spurs and the home run.

The upper layers are defined by the Fieldbus Foundation as the 'communications stack' and the 'user layer' (Figure 15a.3). The following sections will explore these upper layers.

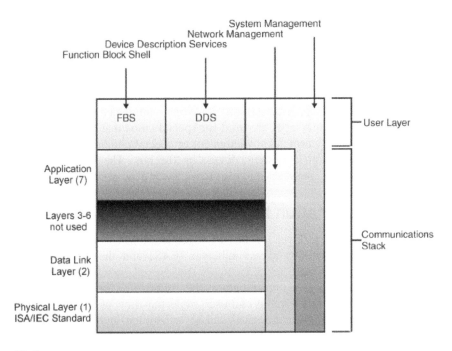

Figure 15a.3
The OSI model of the FF protocol stack

15a.3   The data-link layer

The communications stack, as defined by the FF, corresponds to OSI layers 2 and 7, the data-link and applications layers. The DLL (data-link layer) controls access to the bus through a centralized bus scheduler called the link active scheduler (LAS). The DLL packet format is shown in Figure 15a.4.

The LAS controls access to the bus by granting permission to each device according to predefined 'schedules'. No device may access the bus without LAS permission. There are two types of schedules implemented: cyclic (scheduled) and acyclic (unscheduled). It may seem odd that one could have an unscheduled 'schedule', but these terms actually refer to messages that have a periodic or non-periodic routine, or 'schedule'.

GENERAL PACKET LAYOUT

Preamble

Preamble	Start Delimiter	Overhead + User Data	Frame Check Sequence	End Delimiter
1 Octet	1 Octet	1 to 256 Octets	2 Octets	1 Octet

Figure 15a.4
Data-link layer packet format

The cyclic messages are used for information (process and control variables) that requires regular, periodic updating between devices on the bus. The technique used for information transfer on the bus is known as the publisher–subscriber method. Based on the user predefined (programed) schedule, the LAS grants permission for each device in turn access to the bus. Once the device receives permission to access the bus, it 'publishes' its available information. All other devices can then listen to the 'published' information and read it into memory (subscribe) if it requires it for its own use. Devices not requiring specific data simply ignore the 'published' information.

The acyclic messages are used for special cases that may not occur on a regular basis. These may be alarm acknowledgment or special commands such as retrieving diagnostic information from a specific device on the bus. The LAS detects time slots available between cyclic messages and uses these to send the acyclic messages.

15a.4   The application layer

The application layer in the FF specification is divided into two sub-layers: the Foundation Fieldbus access sublayer (FAS) and the Foundation Fieldbus messaging specification (FMS).

The capability to pre-program the 'schedule' in the LAS provides a powerful configuration tool for the end-user since the time of rotation between devices can be established and critical devices can be 'scheduled' more frequently to provide a form of prioritization of specific I/O points. This is the responsibility and capability of the FAS. Programing the schedule via the FAS allows the option of implementing (actually, simulating) various 'services' between the LAS and the devices on the bus.

Three such 'services' are readily apparent such as:

1. Client/server with a dedicated client (the LAS) and several servers (the bus devices)
2. Publisher/subscriber as described above
3. Event distribution with devices reporting only in response to a 'trigger' event, or by exception, or other predefined criteria.

These variations, of course, depend on the actual application and one scheme need not necessarily be 'right' for all applications, but the flexibility of the Foundation Fieldbus is easily understood from this example.

The second sub-layer, the Foundation FMS, contains an 'object dictionary' that is a type of database that allows access to Foundation Fieldbus data by tag name or an index number. The object dictionary contains complete listings of all data types, data type descriptions, and communication objects used by the application. The services allow the object dictionary (application database) to be accessed and manipulated.

Information can be read from or written to the object dictionary allowing manipulation of the application and the services provided.

15a.5 The user layer

The Fieldbus Foundation specifies an eighth layer called the user layer that resides 'above' the application layer of the OSI model; this layer is usually referred to as layer 8. In the Foundation Fieldbus, this layer is responsible for three main tasks viz. network management, system management, and function block/device description services. Figure 15a.5 illustrates how all the layer's information packets are passed to the physical layer.

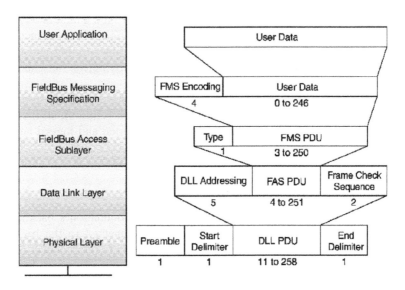

MESSAGE ENCODING/DECODING EXAMPLE

Figure 15a.5
The passage of information packets to the physical layer

The network management service provides access to the other layers for performance monitoring and managing communications between the layers and between remote objects (objects on the bus). The system management takes care of device address assignment, application clock synchronization, and function block scheduling. This is essentially the time coordination between devices and the software, and ensures correct time stamping of events throughout the bus.

Function blocks and device description services provide pre-programed 'blocks', which can be used by the end-user to eliminate redundant and time-consuming configuration. The block concept allows selection of generic functions, algorithms, and even generic devices from a library of objects during system configuration and programing. This process can dramatically reduce configuration time since large 'blocks' are already configured and simply need to be selected. The goal is to provide an open system that supports interoperability and a device description language (DDL), which will enable multiple vendors and devices to be described as 'blocks' or 'symbols'. The user would select generic devices then refine this selection by selecting a DDL object to specify a specific vendor's product. Entering a control loop 'block' with the appropriate parameters would nearly complete the initial configuration for the loop. Advanced control functions and mathematics 'blocks' are also available for more advanced control applications.

15a.6   Error detection and diagnostics

FF has been developed as a purely digital communications bus for the process industry and incorporates error detection and diagnostic information. It uses multiple vendors' components and has extensive diagnostics across the stack from the physical link up through the network and system management layers by design.

The signaling method used by the physical layer timing and synchronization is monitored constantly as part of the communications. Repeated messages and the reason for the repetition can be logged and displayed for interpretation.

In the upper layer, network, and system management is an integral feature of the diagnostic routines. This allows the system manager to analyze the network 'on-line' and maintain traffic loading information. As devices are added and removed, optimization of the LAS routine allows communications optimization dynamically without requiring a complete network shutdown. This ensures optimal timing and device reporting, giving more time to higher-priority devices and removing, or minimizing, redundant, or low-priority messaging.

With the device description (DD) library for each device stored in the host controller (a requirement for true interoperability between vendors), all the diagnostic capability of each vendors' products can be accurately reported and logged and/or alarmed to provide continuous monitoring of each device.

15a.7   High-speed Ethernet (HSE)

High-speed Ethernet (HSE) is the Fieldbus Foundation's backbone network running at 100 Mbits/second. HSE field devices are connected to the backbone via HSE-linking devices. A HSE-linking device is a device used to interconnect H1 Fieldbus segments to HSE to create a larger network. A HSE switch is an Ethernet device used to interconnect multiple HSE devices such as HSE-linking devices and HSE field devices to form an even larger HSE network. HSE hosts are used to configure and monitor the linking devices and H1 devices. Each H1 segment has its own LAS located in a linking device. This feature enables the H1 segments to continue operating even if the hosts are disconnected from the HSE backbone. Multiple H1 (31.25 kbps) Fieldbus segments can be connected to the HSE backbone via linking devices (Figure 15a.6).

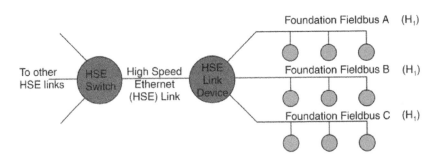

Figure 15a.6
High-speed Ethernet and Foundation Fieldbus

15a.8   Good wiring and installation practice

15a.8.1   Termination preparation

If care is taken in the preparation of the wiring, there will be fewer problems later and minimal maintenance required.

A few points to be noted here are:

- Strip 50 mm of the cable sheathing from the cable and remove the cable foil.
- Strip 6 mm of the insulation from the ends. Watch out to avoid wire nicking or cutting off strands of wire. Use a decent cable-stripping tool.
- Crimp a ferrule on the wire ends and on the end of the shield wire. Crimp ferrules are preferable as they provide a gas-tight connection between the wire and the ferrule that is corrosion resistant. It is the same metal as the terminal in the wiring block.
- An alternative strategy is to twist the wires together and to tin them with solder. Wires can be put directly into the wire terminal but make sure all strands are in and they are not touching each other. Make sure that the strands are not stretched to breaking point.
- Do not attach shield wires together in a field junction box. This can be the cause of ground loops.
- Do not ground the shield in more than one place (inadvertently).
- Use good wire strippers to avoid damaging the wire.

15a.8.2   Installation of the complete system

Other system components can be installed soon after the cable is installed. This includes the terminators, power supply, power conditioners, spurs and in some cases, the intrinsic safety barriers. Some devices already have terminator built-in. In that case, be careful that you are not doubling up with terminators.

Check whether the grounding is correct. There should only be one point for the shield ground point. Once these checks have been performed, switch on the power supply and check the wiring system.

The Fieldbus tester (or an alternative simpler device) can be used to indicate:

- Polarities are correct
- Power-carrying capability of the wire system is ok
- The attenuation and distortion parameters are within specification.

A few additional wiring tips and suggestions with reference to the diagram in Figure 15a.7.

- It is not possible to run two homerun cables in parallel for redundancy under the H1 standard. H1 Fieldbus is a balanced transmission line that must be terminated at each end. In some cases, it is a good idea to run a parallel cable for future use. In case of physical damage, you need to disconnect the damaged cable and put in the undamaged one. Ensure that, if this is the philosophy, you do not route both cables in the same cable tray.
- Do not ground the shield of the cable at each Fieldbus device. The shield of the cable at the transmitter (for example) should be trimmed and covered with insulating tape or heat-shrinkable tubing. The only 'ground' that occurs on the segment is usually at the control room Fieldbus power conditioner.

FIELDBUS SEGMENT

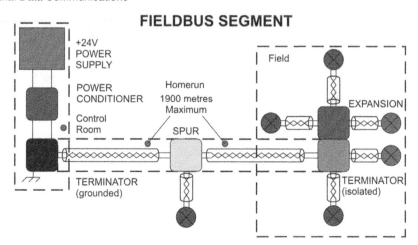

Figure 15a.7
Overall diagram of Fieldbus wiring configuration (courtesy Relcom Inc.)

- Note that the ground that is connected to the isolated terminator at the far end of the segment does not connect the shields of the Fieldbus. It only allows for a high-frequency path for AC currents.
- There has been no provision made for lightning strikes. However, you should specify a terminator that has some type of spark gap arrestor, which will clamp the shields to about 75 V in such a high-voltage surge.
- A quick way to check that the grounding is correct before powering up is, doing a resistance measurement from the ground bolt on the power conditioner to the earth ground connection point. This measurement should be of the order of megohms. You can then connect the earth-protective ground to the power conditioner bolt. Once this has been done, measure the resistance from the cable shields on the isolated terminator at the far end of the segment to a nearby earth ground point. A very low value of resistance should be seen.
- A standard power supply cannot be used to power a Fieldbus segment. A standard power supply absorbs most of the Fieldbus signals due its low internal impedance. It is possible for a standard power supply to provide power to a Fieldbus power conditioning device as long as it has sufficient current is a floating power supply and has very low ripple and noise.
- Use wiring blocks that hold the wiring securely and will not vibrate loose.

Regular testing of an operational Fieldbus network

A Fieldbus tester can be used to get a view on the operation of the network. It is generally connected as follows:

- Red terminal to the (+) wire
- Black terminal to the (–) wire
- Green terminal to the shield.

When the network is operating, the tester will build up a record of operational devices and then builds up a record of their signal characteristics. During later routine network maintenance, the results will be compared. If there is deterioration, this will be indicated, and could be wiring problems, additional noise, or a device, whose transmitter is starting to fail.

15b

Foundation Fieldbus troubleshooting

15b.1 Introduction

Estimates are that 70% of network downtime is caused by physical problems. Foundation Fieldbus is more complicated to troubleshoot most networks because it can, and often does, use the communication bus to power devices. The troubleshooter needs to know not only whether the communication is working but also whether there is enough power for the devices. Figure 15b.1 is a diagram of a typical system. Notice that the power supply on the left is supplying power to the devices in the system.

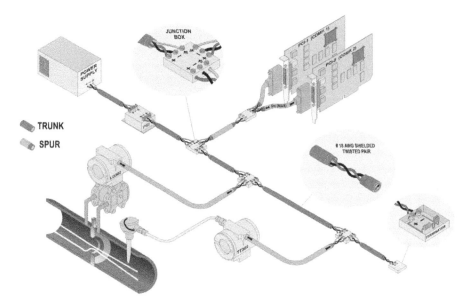

Figure 15b.1
A typical Foundation Fieldbus system

When troubleshooting a Foundation Fieldbus system, it is necessary to first determine whether the problem is a power problem or a communications problem. In new systems, it may be found that the problem is both. In working systems it is usually one or the other.

15b.2   Power problems

Power problems in a FF system can be divided into two types. One where the system is new and never worked and the other where the system has been up and running for a while. When new devices are added to an existing system and the communications immediately fails, it is easy to realize that the new device had something to do with the problem. If the system has never worked, then the problem could be anywhere and could be caused by multiple devices. The problem could also be with the design itself.

The following need to be known when troubleshooting the power system of a FF system.

- What is the layout of the system? Does each device have at least 9 V DC?
- What is the supply current?
- What is the supply voltage?
- What is the current draw of each device?
- What is the resistance of each cable leg?

The easiest way of determining a power problem is to do the following (Figure 15b.2):

- Check each device to see if the power light is on
- Measure the voltage at each device
- Check the connections for opens, corrosion or loose connections
- Measure the current draw of each device to see if it conforms to the manufacturer's specifications.

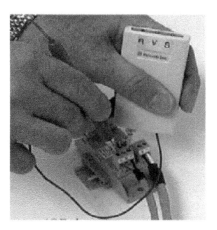

Figure 15b.2
Testing the system (courtesy Relcom Inc.)

Notice that the home run in Figure 15b.3 connects the control room equipment with the devices via common terminal blocks (chickenfoot or crowsfoot). The signal cable also provides the power to the devices. There is a terminator at each end of the cable. Power supplies require power conditioners.

Power example
Here is an example of the power requirements for a system:

- The power supply output is 20 V
- The two wires are 1 km long with 22 Ω per wire (44 Ω total)

FIELDBUS SEGMENT

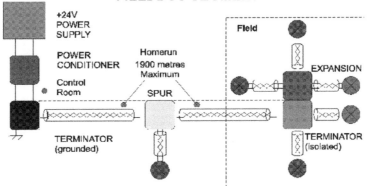

Figure 15b.3
Layout of a system

- Each device draws 20 mA
- Minimum voltage at each device 9 V $(20 - 9 = 11$ V$)$
- 11 V/44 Ω = 250 mA.

Therefore

- 250 mA/20 mA = 12 devices on the system.

15b.3   Communication problems

Once the power is ruled out as a problem, it can be assumed that the communication system is at fault (Figures 15b.4 and 15b.5). Initially, it is important to check the following items:

- Are the wires connected correctly?
- Is the shield continuous throughout the system?
- Is the shield grounded at only one place?

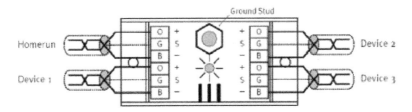

Figure 15b.4
Schematic of a terminal block (courtesy Relcom Inc.)

Once these basics are verified, the next step is to check to make sure that the cables are not too long. To measure the losses through the cable, a FF transmitter device is placed at one end and a receiver test device at the other. The maximum loss is usually around −14 dB. The typical characteristics of a twisted-pair cable is:

- Impedance: 100 Ω
- Wire size: 18 GA (0.8 mm²)

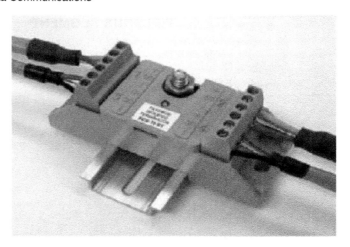

Figure 15b.5
Terminal block (courtesy Relcom Inc.)

- Shield: 90% coverage
- Capacitive unbalance: 2 nF/km
- Attenuation: 3 dB/km.

Using an ungrounded oscilloscope, it is possible to look at the signal. A good transmitter signal might look like Figure 15b.6.

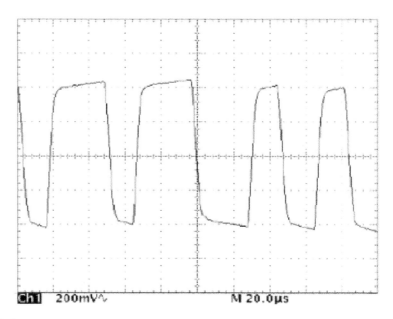

Figure 15b.6
A good transmitted signal (courtesy Relcom Inc.)

When it is received it might look like Figure 15b.7.

Notice that the waveform is a bit distorted and lower in amplitude but still good. Figure 15b.8 is what the whole packet might look like.

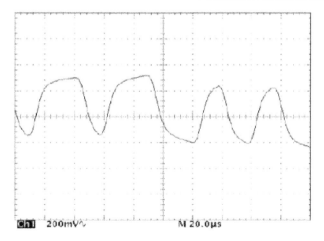

Figure 15b.7
Received FF signal (courtesy Relcom Inc.)

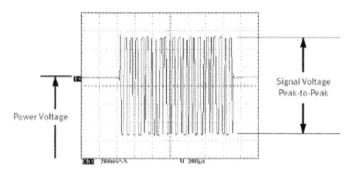

Figure 15b.8
Bipolar FF signal (courtesy Relcom Inc.)

15b.4   Foundation Fieldbus test equipment

There are a few manufacturers that have brought out test equipment specifically designed for testing FF systems. Some of the test equipment can be used while the system is working and others are used when the system is offline.

Some of the things the test equipment can check for are:

- DC voltage levels
- Link active scheduler probe node frame voltage
- Number of devices on the network
- If devices have been added or removed
- The lowest voltage level transmitted by a device
- Noise level between frames
- Device response noise level.

One of the best troubleshooting tools are the LEDs provided on the devices. These LEDs show many different conditions of the system. If the troubleshooter becomes familiar with them, then LEDs can often indicate what is wrong with the system.

16a

Modbus Plus protocol overview

Objectives

When you have completed study of this chapter, you will be able to:

- Describe the main features of Modbus Plus
- Fix problems with:

    - Cabling
    - Grounding/earthing
    - Shielding
    - Terminations.

16a.1 General overview

Besides the standard Modbus protocol, there exist two other Modbus protocol structures:

- Modbus Plus
- Modbus II.

The more popular one is the Modbus Plus. It is not an open standard as the classical Modbus has become. Modbus II is not used much due to additional cabling requirements and other difficulties.

The Modbus Plus protocol was developed to overcome the 'single master' limitation of the Modbus protocol. As described earlier, in order to share information across various Modbus networks, a designer would have had to employ a complex hierarchical network structure in order to achieve system-wide networking.

Modbus Plus is a local area network system for industrial control applications. Networked devices can exchange messages for the control and monitoring of processes at remote locations in the industrial plant. The Modbus Plus network was one of the first token-passing protocol networks that pioneered the development of other more advanced deterministic protocols of today.

Each device on a network segment must be assigned a unique network address within the range 1 through 64 inclusive. Multiple network segments may be bridged together to form large systems. Messages are passed from one device to another by the appropriate use of a route within the message. The route will include the network address of the target device, and any inter-network addresses required. The route field of a message may be up to five layers deep, is terminated with the value 00, and all unused drops are also set to 00 (Figure 16a.1).

Master Output Path	Router Counter	Transaction Sequence No.	Routing Path	Modbus Frame (without CRC / /LRC)
1 Byte	1 Byte	1 Byte	5 Bytes	Variable

Destination Address	Source Address	MAC Function	Byte Count	LLC Field (including Modbus Command)
1 Byte	1 Byte	1 Byte	2 Bytes	Variable

Preamble	Opening Flag	Broadcast Address	MAC / LLC Data	Error Check Field	Closing Flag
1 Byte	1 Byte	1 Byte	Variable	2 Bytes	1 Byte

Figure 16a.1
Format of Modbus Plus message frame

Each network supports up to 64 addressable node devices. Up to 32 nodes can connect directly to the network cable over a length of 1500 ft (450 m). Repeaters can extend the cable distance to its maximum of 6000 ft (1800 m) and the node count to its maximum of 64 (Figure 16a.2). Fiber-optic repeaters are available for longer distances.

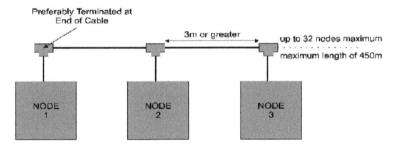

Figure 16a.2
Typical Modbus Plus network with termination

Multiple networks can be inter-networked through bridge plus devices. Messages originating on one network are routed through one or more bridges to a destination on another network. Bridges do not permit deterministic timing of I/O processes. In networks requiring deterministic I/O timing, messages remain on that network only, and do not pass through bridges (Figure 16a.3).

Network nodes are identified by addresses assigned by the user. Each node's address is independent of its physical site location. Addresses are within the range of 1–64 decimal and do not have to be sequential. Duplicate addresses are not allowed.

Network nodes function as peer members of a logical ring, gaining access to the network upon receipt of a token frame. The token is a grouping of bits that is passed in a rotating address sequence from one node to another. Each network maintains its own token rotation sequence independent of the other networks. Where bridges join multiple networks, the token is not passed through the bridge device.

While holding the token, a node initiates message transactions with other nodes. Each message contains routing fields that define its source and destination, including its routing path through bridges to a node on a remote network.

SETUP OF BRIDGES

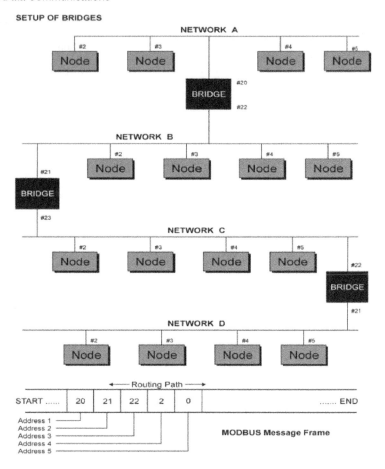

Figure 16a.3
Modbus Plus network with bridges

When passing the token, a node can write into a global database that is broadcast to all nodes on the network. Global data is transmitted as a field within the token frame. Other nodes monitor the token pass and can extract the global data if they have been programed to do so. Use of the global database allows rapid updating of alarms, setpoints, and other data. Each network maintains its own global database, as the token is not passed through a bridge to another network.

The network bus consists of twisted-pair shielded cable that is run in a direct path between successive nodes. The two data lines in the cable are not sensitive to polarity; however a standard wiring convention is followed in this guide to facilitate maintenance.

On dual-cable networks (Figure 16a.4), the cables are known as cable A and cable B. Each cable can be up to 1500 ft (450 m) long, measured between the two extreme end devices on a cable section. The difference in length between cables A and B must not exceed 500 ft (150 m), measured between any pair of nodes on the cable section.

The token passing sequence is determined by the node addresses. Token rotation begins at the network's lowest number active node, proceeding consecutively through each higher number node, until the highest number active node receives the token. That node then passes the token to the lowest one to begin a new rotation.

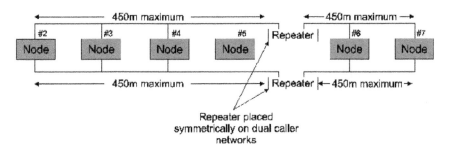

Figure 16a.4
Typical Modbus Plus network with dual cabling

If a node leaves the network, a new token-passing sequence will be established to bypass it, typically within 100 ms. If a new node joins, it will be included in the address sequence, typically within 5 s (worst case time is 15 s). The process of deleting and adding nodes is transparent to the user application.

Where multiple networks are inter-connected with bridges, tokens are not passed through a bridge device from one network to another. Each network performs its token passing process independently of the other networks.

While a node holds the token, it sends its application messages if it has any to transmit. The other nodes monitor the network for incoming messages. When a node receives a message, it sends an immediate acknowledgment to the originating node. If the message is a request for data, the receiving node will begin assembling the requested data into a reply message.

When the message is ready, it will be transmitted to the requestor when the node receives a subsequent token granting it access to transmit. After a node sends all of its messages, it passes the token on to the next node. Protocols for token passing and messaging are transparent to the user application.

16b

Modbus Plus troubleshooting

16b.1   Common problems and faults

The Modbus Plus network is a 3-wire (one pair and a shield) twisted-pair cable with the nodes connected in a daisy-chained configuration. There is no polarity requirement at the node's transceiver, so the data cable pair may be connected either way at a node. A 220 Ω terminator is required at each end of the network cable. There are limits upon the maximum number of nodes per segment, the number of repeaters, and the lengths of cable segments on the Modbus Plus network. For more information, refer to the Modicon Modbus Plus network planning and installation guide (GM-MBPL-001).

The most common hardware-related problems have already been discussed in the previous section. Please refer to the hardware-related troubleshooting list for the Modbus protocol. You should configure the node address of the Modbus Plus port on the nodes before connecting them to the network. This should avoid possible duplicate address problems with other units on the network.

Most problem issues arise from the use of invalid slave addresses, illegal slave memory addressing, illegal data formats and even perhaps use of unrecognized function codes. Other issues are related to the actual configuration of the communication hardware itself, for example, the SA85 Modbus Plus network interface card that is used to provide an IBM compatible personal computer access to the Modbus Plus network.

The following are typical error messages reported by a controller:

- Remote PC not listening for call
- Slave xx reported an illegal data address
- Slave xx reported an illegal data value
- Slave xx reported an illegal function
- Card SA85: 0 not found.

Often, problems could be easily be identified by referring to the user manual, and looking up the meanings of the various status indicators provided on the front panel of the Modbus Plus device. For example, there is usually a Modbus Active LED provided on the node.

Table 16b.1 is an example of such a Modbus Plus network status indicator for a specific device.

16b.1.1   Modbus active LED

The Modbus active LED on the node flashes repetitive patterns to display node status. Table 16b.1 lists typical Modbus active LED blinking patterns and their description.

Blinking Patterns	Description
Flash every 160 ms normal operation	This node is successfully receiving and passing the token. All nodes should blink at this rate under when working properly
Flash every 1 s	This node is in the MONITOR_OFFLINE state. It must remain in this state for 5 s and is not allowed to transmit messages onto the network. While in this state, the node is listening to all other nodes and building a table of the known nodes
Two flashes, off 2 s	This node is in the MAC_IDLE state. It is hearing other nodes get the token but it is never receiving the token itself. This node may have a bad transmitter
Three flashes, off 1.7 s	This node is not hearing any other nodes and it is periodically claiming the token and finds no other nodes to pass it to. This node may be the only active node on the network or it may have a bad receiver
Four flashes, off 1.4 s	This node has heard a duplicate address packet. There is another node on the network with the same address as this node. This node is now in the DUPLICATE_OFFLINE state where it will passively monitor the link until it does not hear the duplicate node for 5 s

Table 16b.1
Typical list of Modbus active LED blinking patterns

16b.2   Description of tools used

Apart from the standard set of tools that have been listed in the previous section while discussing Modbus protocols to troubleshoot hardware-related problems, there are only the manufacturer-supplied application packages that report any software errors that occur in the Modbus Plus communication networks.

Section 16b.3 discusses the cause of some of the most common Modicon Modbus and Modbus Plus error messages that you may encounter when attempting to establish communications with one of the various off-the-shelf Modbus Plus-based applications packages such as the Wonderware® Modicon Modbus or Modicon Modbus Plus I/O server (*Source*: http://www.wonderware.com).

16b.3   Detailed troubleshooting

16b.3.1   Remote PC not listening for call

This error means that the Modbus or Modbus Plus I/O server is unable to 'see' a slave device. That is, it is unable to get to the specified node(s), which has been defined in the topic slave path. Either the slave path does not have the correct path defined or one or more of the node addresses in the slave path do not match the addresses of the PLCs.

If you are unable to establish communications through more than one Modbus Bridge Plus (BP), then start with the first bridge plus listed in the slave path and access a slave device on that Modbus Plus network. For example, if your slave path is defined as '24.32.16.10' and you are getting the 'Remote PC not listening for call' error, then begin by establishing communications to a node through BP 24.

If you are addressing a slave device with an address of 25 on the first network, then set the Slave Path to '24.25.0.0'. Then, establish communications to node 25 on the first network (i.e. advise a point on node 25 and verify that the data is being retrieved). If you are successful, then move onto the next BP and communicate to a node within that network. Then, modify the slave path to '24.32.x.0' where x represents the address of a node within the next network. Repeat this step until the target PLC is reached.

By following this technique, it will help you to verify two things:

1. The correct node addresses are being used.
2. The slave path is defined correctly.

16b.3.2   Slave xx reported an illegal data address

This error message means that a tagname's DDE item name has the correct format and was accepted by the Modbus or Modbus Plus I/O Server, but the PLC (slave device) rejected the DDE item name because the register has not been defined. 'xx' refers to the node address of the slave device. That is, the referenced address, or DDE item name, was not a defined address for the slave device.

For example, say we had the following configuration:

- The I/O table for a Modbus 984 PLC is defined up to register 45999
- A DDE topic in the I/O Server is defined with a slave type of '584/984'
- A DDE tagname is defined with an item of 49999.

Since register 49999 is not defined in the I/O table when the I/O server attempts to advise this register, the error 'slave xx reported an illegal data address' is logged in the Wonderware Logger (WWLogger).

To resolve this error, verify the DDE items to be advised, fall within the range of the defined I/O table for the PLC.

Note that this error does not mean the same thing as getting an 'Advised Failed' error. The 'slave xx reported an illegal data address' error means that the DDE item of a tagname is not addressing a register defined in the PLC's I/O map.

16b.3.3   Slave xx reported an illegal data value

(The xx refers to the node address of the slave device.) This error message means the data which is being read from or written to a register in the slave device does not match the expected data type for that register ('xx' refers to the node address of the slave). That is, the data is not the same data type that the Modbus or Modbus Plus I/O server expects for that register.

For example, if a I/O server topic is defined with a slave type of '584/984' and the I/O server tries to write to Coil 9999, but the data from the tagname is something other than a discrete data type, then the error 'slave xx reported an illegal data value' occurs. This error could also occur if the slave type selected is not correct for the type of PLC that is being advised. For example, if you try to write data to a Modbus 984 PLC but the slave type selected was '484', then this error will occur.

16b.3.4 Slave xx reported an illegal function

This error message occurs when the slave device cannot perform a particular Modbus function that was issued by the master node because either the slave device does not understand the function or it is unable to execute the function. The computers that have either the Modbus or Modbus Plus I/O server installed are considered to be a 'master' node. 'xx' refers to the node address of the slave device.

When receiving this type of error, verify that the slave device support the Modbus function that it is being requested to execute. You can verify the Modbus function code that the I/O server issued and the response that was received from the slave device by enabling the I/O server's 'show send' and 'show receive' menu options.

To enable the 'show send' and 'show receive' menu options, follow these steps:

- Edit the Win.ini file in the C:\Windows\System directory and depending on the server you are using, i.e., the Modbus or Modbus Plus I/O server, locate either [Modbus] or [MBPLUS] file section. Look for a 'DebugMenu = x' entry in the file section. If it exists, modify the entry as follows:

  DebugMenu = 1

- If it does not exist, add this entry to the end of the file section.
- Restart the Modbus or Modbus Plus I/O server and click the window's control menu box. You should now see the 'show send' and 'show receive' menu options. Single click each option and the option 'all topics' (or a list of the current active topics defined in the I/O server) will display to the right of the 'show send' or 'show receive' menu option. Enable either 'all topics' or one or more of the topics for which the problem is occurring.
- Initiate communications to the slave device again.
- With the 'show send' and 'show receive' menu options enabled, the I/O server will log all Modbus protocol messages in WWLogger when it attempts to communicate 's' to the slave device, such as the following send request examples (those issued by the I/O server to the slave device):

  ```
  S:  :0301005601683D\r\n
  S:  :0101001101E20A\r\n
  ```

The Modbus and Modbus Plus I/O servers use the standard Modbus protocol and here are the function codes that the I/O server will issue (Table 16b.2) (which are tied to the protocol messages):

For information on how to correctly read the Modbus send requests in WWLogger and decipher the Modbus function code that is listed as part of the message, see the document titled 'Interpreting the Modbus Protocol' which is part of the Wonderware Knowledge Base.

Or, you may go to the Modicon Website at http://www.modicon.com/.

Note: The 'show send' and 'show receive' menu options will generate frequent writes to WWLogger, and therefore both should be enabled during troubleshooting only. If 'show send' and 'show receive' are left activated during the normal operation of the I/O server, then the performance of your computer will slow considerably.

Control Code	Function Code
Read coil	01
Read contact	02
Read holding register	03
Read input register	04
Force coil	05
Load register	06
Force multiple coils	15
Load multiple registers	16
Read general reference	20
Write general reference	21

Table 16b.2
Function codes issued by Modbus Plus I/O server

16b.3.5   Card SA85:0 not found, bad NCB_LANA_NUM – device not found

This error message means that the Modbus SA85 adapter card is not being acknowledged by the Modbus Plus I/O server. This error may result when the SA85 adapter card does not initialize during the startup of the computer. If this card does not initialize properly, then the I/O server will not be able to communicate with any slave device on the Modbus Plus network.

To resolve this error, if you are running Windows, Windows for Workgroups or Windows 95, then make sure the following device statement is in the config.sys file which is located in the root (C:\) directory:

Device = MBPHOST.SYS /mXXXX /nY /r2 /sZZ

Where XXXX represents the 'memory window' setting that is set with the switches on the SA85 adapter card, Y represents the number of the adapter card that is installed (examples: n0, n1), and ZZ is the hexadecimal address of the software interrupt that is to be used by the device driver. Note the spaces between the parameters in the device statement. Once this SA85 device statement is defined correctly, the SA85 adapter card should initialize properly. (See tech note number 5, solving Modbus Plus channel allocation errors for specific instructions on how to define this device statement.)

Note that release 5.2a and later of the Modbus Plus I/O server will automatically add this device statement to the config.sys file (earlier releases of the I/O server require that you enter the device statement in the config.sys file, as well as edit the Modicon.ini file). If you are running release 5.2a or later, then make sure that the Mbphost.sys file is located in the root directory.

Note: Wonderware technical support suggests that you install version 3.4 or later of the Mbphost.sys file instead of the SA85.sys file in the root directory. To obtain the latest Mbphost.sys file, contact your Group Schneider/Modicon representative or go to the Modicon website.

Verify that the Mbphost.sys file is being loaded to the SA85 Adapter card during startup of the computer by manually stepping through the startup procedure of the operating system. For Windows and Windows for Workgroups, you do this by pressing the <F8> key when the operating system proceeds from its self-diagnostic test to the execution of the config.sys file. For Windows 95, you do this by pressing the <F8> key at the beginning of startup and select 'step by step confirmation' from the Windows 95 startup menu screen. This will allow you to step through the execution of each line of the config.sys and autoexec.bat files. (For Windows NT 3.51 and 4.0, see the section 'Troubleshooting the SA85 adapter card under Windows NT' below.)

After you enter the manual step through execution mode, look for information that is displayed after the 'Device=' statement in which the Mbphost.sys file is executed. It should indicate that the SA85 device driver was loaded correctly, as shown in this example:

```
SA85 Device Driver Version 3.4
<<PG-MBPL-500>>
Copyright (c) 1989-1994 Modicon In. All Rights Reserved.
set for polled mode, SW int:0x5D Memory at 0xD000. LAN
adapter #0
node address = 31
This example shows that the SA85 adapter card is:
Set for polled mode (which is required for the SA85 Adapter
card);
Using interrupt 5D;
Using memory location D000;
```

Set to address 31 on the Modbus Plus network. (Note that for both 'c' and 'd', the memory and node address numbers must always match the dip switch settings on the SA85 adapter card.)

Following the procedure in this section, you will be able to help determine why the SA85 adapter card did not initialize properly, and thus, you will be able to resolve the error 'Card SA85:0 not found, bad NCB_LANA_NUM – device not found'.

16b.3.6   Troubleshooting the SA85 adapter card under Windows NT

Troubleshooting the cause of the error 'Card SA85:0 not found, bad NCB_LANA_NUM – device not found' under Windows NT 3.5 or 4.0 is performed differently than under Windows or WFW.

Note: When installing or troubleshooting any communication problems with the Modbus or Modbus Plus I/O server under Windows NT 3.5 or 4.0, make sure that you log on as 'administrator' to ensure that all files are copied and updated as necessary.

During the installation of the Modbus Plus I/O server, updates are added to the Windows NT registry. If you are not logged on as 'administrator', then the registry will not be updated, and thus, the I/O server will not work properly. The I/O server under Windows NT does not rely on the config.sys file during startup of the computer. Instead, during the installation of the I/O server, the file Mbplus.sys is installed into the \%SystemRoot%\System32\Drivers directory. Then, once you configure the I/O server's adapter card settings and reboot the computer, the parameters for the Mbplus.sys file are automatically defined and the registry will be updated.

Start up the Windows NT Event Viewer that is located under the Administrative Tools program group. Verify that Windows NT acknowledged the SA85 Adapter card with no errors. (That is, there are not 'STOP' errors for 'MBPLUS'.)

Further verify that Windows NT acknowledged the SA85 Adapter card by double clicking the Devices program group from the Control Panel window. Then, scroll down the Device list and locate the 'MBPLUS' device. Verify that the status of the device is listed as 'Started' and the startup is defined as 'Automatic'. If these statuses are not listed and the Modbus Plus I/O server attempts to communicate with a slave device, then the error 'Card SA85:0 not found, bad NCB_LANA_NUM – device not found' will result.

Data Highway Plus/DH485 overview

Objectives

When you have completed study of this chapter, you will be able to:

- Describe the main features of data highway plus
- Fix problems with:
  - Cabling
  - Grounding/earthing
  - Shielding
  - Terminations
  - Token passing timing.

17a.1 Allen Bradley Data Highway (Plus) protocol

17a.1.1 Overview of Allen Bradley protocol

There are three main protocol standards used in Allen Bradley data communications:

The Data Highway protocol

This is a *local area network* (LAN) that allows peer-to-peer communications up to 64 nodes. It uses a half-duplex (polled) protocol and rotation of link mastership. It operates at 57.6 kbaud.

The Data Highway Plus protocol

This is similar to the data highway network although designed for fewer PCs and operates at a data rate of 57.6 kbaud. This has peer-to-peer communications with a token passing scheme to rotate link mastership among the nodes connected to that link.

Note that both protocol standards implement peer-to-peer communications through a modified token passing system called the floating master. This is a fairly efficient mechanism as each node has an opportunity to become a master at which time it can immediately transmit without checking with each mode for the requisite permission to commence transmission.

The Allen Bradley Data Highway Plus uses the three layers of the OSI layer model:

- Hardware (a physical layer)
- Data-link layer protocol
- Application layer.

DH-485

This is used by the SLC range of Allen Bradley controllers and is based on RS-485.

17a.1.2 Physical layer (hardware layer)

This is based on twin axial cable with three conductors essentially in line with the RS-485 specifications. The troubleshooting and specifications for RS-485 are covered in an earlier chapter.

17a.1.3 Full-duplex data-link layer

Note that the asynchronous link can use either a full-duplex (unpolled) protocol or a master slave communication through a half-duplex (unpolled) protocol. Although both types of protocols are available the tendency today is to use the full-duplex protocol as this explains the high performance nature of the link. Hence this protocol will be examined in more detail in the following sections.

Full-duplex protocol is character orientated. It uses the ASCII control characters listed in the following table, extended to eight bits by adding a zero for bit number seven (i.e. the eighth bit).

The following ASCII characters are used (Table 17a.1):

Abbreviation	Hex Value
STX	02
ETX	03
ENQ	05
ACK	06
DLE	10
NAK	11

Table 17a.1
ASCII control characters

Full-duplex protocol combines these characters into control and data symbols. Table 17a.2 lists the symbols used for full-duplex implementation.

Symbol	Type	Description
DLE STX	Control symbol	Sender symbol that indicates the start of a message
DLE ETX BCC/CRC	Control symbol	Sender signal that terminates a message
DLE ACK	Control symbol	Responses symbol which signals that a message has been successfully received
DLE NAK	Control symbol	Response symbol which signals that a message was not received successfully

Symbol	Type	Description
DLE ENQ	Control symbol	Sender symbol that requests retransmission of a response symbol from the receiver
APP DATA	Data symbol	Single character data values between 00-OF and 11-FF includes data from the application layer including user programs and common application routines
DLE DLE	Data symbol	Symbol that represents the data value 10 Hex

Table 17a.2
Symbols used for full-duplex mode

Format of a message

Note that response symbols transmitted within a message packet are referred to as embedded responses (Figure 17a.1).

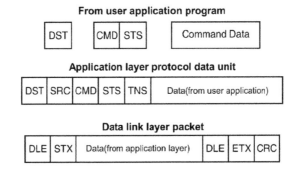

Figure 17a.1
Protocol structure

The CRC-16 calculations is done using the value of the application layer data bytes and the ETX byte. The CRC-16 results consists of two bytes.

Note that to transmit the data value of 10H, the sequence of data symbols DLE must be used. Only one of these DLE bytes and no embedded responses are included in the CRC value.

Message limitations

- Minimum size of a valid message is six bytes.
- Duplicate message detection algorithm – receiver compares the second, third, fifth and sixth bytes of a message with the same bytes in the previous message.

P = Recovery procedure
T = Ready to transmit next message
* = Default values.

Depending on the highway traffic and saturation level, there may be a wait for a reply from the remote node before transmitting the next message (Figure 17a.2).

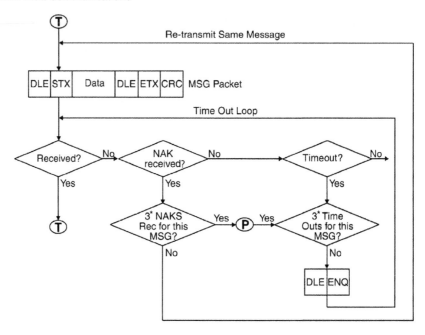

Figure 17a.2
Software logic for transmitter

Software logic for receivers

The following figures (Figures 17.3, 17.4 and 17.5) show typical events that occur in the communications process. 'xxxx' indicates information transmitted while 'x??x' indicates that errors have occurred during transmission.

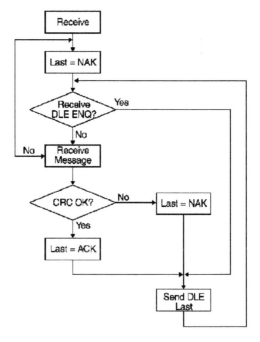

Figure 17a.3
Software logic for receivers

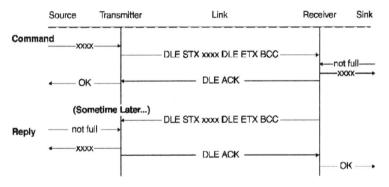

Figure 17a.4
Normal message transfer

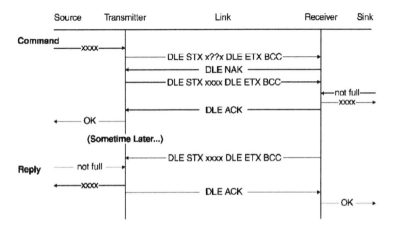

Figure 17a.5
Message transfer with NAK

There are two types of application programs:

1. Command initiators
2. Command executors.

Command initiators specify which command function to execute at a particular remote node. The command executor must also issue a reply message for each command it receives. If the executor cannot execute a command, it must send the appropriate error code. The reply message may contain an error. The command initiator must check for this condition and depending on the type of error, retransmit the message or notify the user.

If the command executor reply is lost due to noise, the command initiator should maintain a timer for each outstanding command message. If the timer expires, the command initiator should take appropriate action (notify the user or retransmit to executor).

If the application layer software cannot deliver a command message, it should generate a reply message with the appropriate error code and send the reply to the initiator. If it cannot deliver a reply message, the application layer should destroy the reply without notification to the command executor (Figure 17a.6).

Note that not all command messages have FNC, ADR, SIZE or DATA bytes. Not all reply messages have DATA or ETX STS bytes.

Command

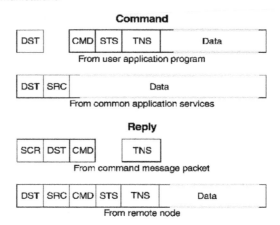

Figure 17a.6
Application program

Explanation of bytes

- *DST*:   Destination byte. This contains the ultimate destination of the node
- *SRC*:   Source node of the message
- *CMD*:   Command byte
- *FNC*:   Function byte.

These together define the activity to be performed by the command message at the destination node. Note that bit five of the command byte shall always be zero (normal priority).

STS and ETX SYS – status and extended status bytes

In command messages, the STS byte is set to zero. In reply messages, the STS byte may contain a status code. If the four high bits of the STS byte are ones, there is extended status information in an ETX STS byte.

TNS – transaction bytes (two bytes)

The application level software must assign a unique 16-bit transaction number (generated via a counter). When the command initiator receives reply to one of its command messages, it can use the TNS value to associate the reply message with its corresponding command.

Whenever the command executor receives a command from another node, it should copy the TNS field of the command message into the same field of the corresponding reply message.

ADDR

Address field contains the address of a memory location in the command executor where the command is to begin executing. The ADDR field specifies a byte address (not a word address as in PLC programing).

Size

The size byte specifies the number of data bytes to be transferred by a message.

Data

The data field contains binary data from the application programs.

PLC-5 command set message packet fields

- *Packet offset*: This field contains the offset between the DATA field of the current message packet and the DATA field of the first packet in the transmission.
- *Total trans*: This field contains the total number of PLC-5 data elements transferred in all message packets initiated by a command.

Basic command set

The asynchronous link message packet formats to be used are delivered below (see Figure 17a.7).

In the lists below, privileged commands are initiated by computer and executed by PLCs. A PLC or a computer initiates non-privileged commands. The CMD values listed are for non-priority command message packets.

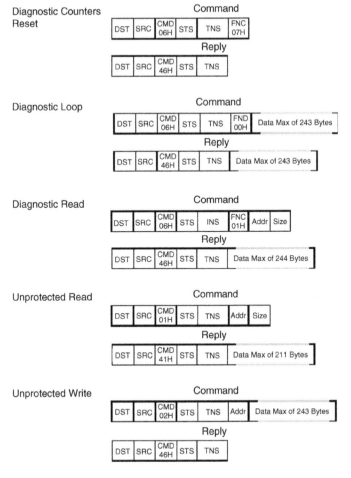

Figure 17a.7
Basic command set for PLC-5

Synchronous link status code (STS, ETX STS)

The TS bytes provide information about the execution or failure of the corresponding command that was transmitted from the computer. If the reply returns a code of 00, the command was executed at the remote node.

All other codes are divided into two types:

1. *Local error*: Local node is unable to transmit a message to the remote node.
2. *Remote error*: Remote node is unable to execute the command.

Local STS error code

Code	Description
00	Success – no error
01	Destination node out of buffer space
02	Remote node does not ACK command message
03	Duplicate token holder detected
04	Local port is disconnected

Remote STS error codes

Code	Description
00	Success – no errors
10	Illegal command or format
20	Host has a problem and will not communicate
30	Remote node is missing, disconnected
40	Host could not complete function due to hardware fault
50	Addressing problem or memory protect rungs
60	Function disallowed due to command protection selection
70	Processor is in program mode
80	Compatibility mode file is missing or communication zone problem
A0	Not used
B0	Remote node problems due to download
F0	Error in the ETX STS byte
C0 to E0	Not used

There is only an ETX STS byte if the STS code is F0. If the command code is 00–08, there is not an ETX STS byte. Commands used in this implementation are in this range; hence the ETX STS byte is not being used.

Diagnostic counter for each module

Diagnostic counters are bytes of information stored in RAM in each data highway and data highway plus module. When using the 'diagnostic read' command, a dummy value should be used for the address. The reply contains the entire counter block.

17b

Data Highway Plus/DH485 troubleshooting

17b.1 Introduction

This section is broken down into the following sections:

- Data Highway Plus wiring troubleshooting
- Data Highway Plus network diagnostics.

Note that the rules for troubleshooting the physical side of these two cables are very similar to that of RS-485. In fact, DH485 physical layer is identical to RS-485 whilst data highway plus uses a transformer-isolated version.

The difficult part in diagnosing problems with the data highway plus is in the operation of the protocol.

17b.2 Data Highway Plus wiring troubleshooting

One should inspect the cable closely for wiring problems if the operation of the network appears intermittent. Typical problems that should be examined are:

- Damage to the cable
- No termination resistance (or removed) at the end of the line
- Screen removed or damaged.

A few suggestions to look for on the wiring are described below.

17b.2.1 Wiring recommendations

- Ensure that twin axial cable has been used for trunklines and drop lines (Belden 9463 or equivalent)
- Connect ground wire from station connector to the earth ground
- Route cables away from sources of electrical interference.

17b.2.2 Station connector wiring

- Connect trunklines to the upper side of the station connector
- Connect drop lines and earth to the lower connections.

17b.2.3   Cable preparation

- Cut the drop line to required length
- Remove 1 in. of insulation, foil, braid, and filler cord
- Strip about one-eighth of an inch of insulation off each of the insulated wires
- Insert the cable through hood of D-shell connector
- Fit about half an inch of heatshrink tubing over each of the conductors.

17b.2.4   Solder wires to connector

Solder as following:

- Blue wire to Pin 6
- Drain wire to Pin 7
- Clear wire to Pin 8
- Slide heatshrink over soldered connections and shrink with a heat gun
- Assemble the 15-pin connector to the D-shell hood.

Prepare other end of the drop line cable

- Remove about 3 in. of insulation, foil, braid, and filler
- Free drain wire, clear and blue insulated wires
- Strip about 1/4 in. of insulation off each conductor.

17b.2.5   Trunk line preparation

Remove cover and terminal block from enclosure and mount enclosure where you want to add the drop line. Cut trunk line cable. Feed incoming and outgoing cables through the respective cable clamps at the top of the enclosure.

Wiring enclosure

- Twist the wires of the same color together from each trunk line cable
- Secure the wires under their respective screw clamp terminals.

Note: It is easier to do this with the terminal block out of the enclosure.

Terminating stations

- Install a 150 Ω resistor at the first and last station connectors on the trunkline
- Use a 1 in. length of heatshrink to protect resistor and connect between terminals 1 and 3.

17b.3   Data Highway Plus network diagnostics

There are literally hundreds of possible errors, but there are a few important ones worth highlighting in this section.

Many of them are the result of excessive noise on the network and can be corrected by examining the actual wiring and removing the source of noise, if possible. If not (for example, due to the data highway running parallel to a power cable in a cable tray), consideration will have to be given to the use of fiber cabling as a replacement for the copper-based cable.

A few errors (which are identified in the diagnostics registers on the interface module) worth mentioning are:

- *ACK Time out*: This indicates where a sender has been transmitting packets and has not received any acknowledgment responses. This is often due to long cable or the presence of reflections and low-level noise.
- *Contention*: This occurs on noisy or overlength cables. A similar remedy to the one above.
- *False poll*: This indicates the number of times this station has tried to relinquish bus mastership, and the station that was expected to take over didn't do so. This is often the case on a noisy highway.
- *Transmitted messages and received messages*: While these are not errors, they are worth examining (and recording) to see the level of activity (number of packets sent and received) against the level of errors.
- *Data pin allocation*: Not all data highway plus equipment use the same pin configuration on the 15-pin connector! With certain types of Allen Bradley PLCs the allocation of pins 6 and 8 are transposed.

18a

HART overview

Objectives

When you have completed study of this chapter, you will be able to:

- Describe the fundamental operation of HART
- Fix problems with:

    - Cabling
    - Configuration.

18a.1 Introduction to HART and smart instrumentation

Smart (or intelligent) instrumentation protocols are designed for applications where actual data is collected from instruments, sensors, and actuators by digital communication techniques. These components are linked directly to programmable logic controllers (PLCs) and computers.

The HART (highway addressable remote transducer) protocol is a typical smart instrumentation fieldbus that can operate in a hybrid 4–20 mA digital fashion.

HART is, by no means, the only protocol in this sphere. There are hundreds of smart implementations produced by various manufacturers – for example, Honeywell – that compete with HART. This chapter deals specifically with HART.

At a basic level, most smart instruments provide core functions such as:

- Control of range/zero/span adjustments
- Diagnostics to verify functionality
- Memory to store configuration and status information (such as tag numbers, etc.).

Accessing these functions allows major gains in the speed and efficiency of the installation and maintenance process. For example, the time consuming 4–20 mA loop check phase can be achieved in minutes, and the device can be readied for use in the process by zeroing and adjustment for any other controllable aspects such as the damping value.

18a.2 HART protocol

This protocol was originally developed by Rosemount and is regarded as an open standard, available to all manufacturers. Its main advantage is that it enables an instrumentation engineer to keep the existing 4–20 mA instrumentation cabling and to use, simultaneously, the same wires to carry digital information superimposed on the analog signal. This enables most companies to capitalize on their existing investment in 4–20 mA instrumentation cabling and associated systems and to add further capability of HART without incurring major costs.

HART is a hybrid analog and digital protocol, as opposed to most fieldbus systems, which are purely digital.

The HART protocol uses the frequency shift keying (FSK) technique based on the Bell 202 communications standard. Two individual frequencies of 1200 and 2200 Hz, representing digits 1 and 0 respectively, are used (Figure 18a.1). The average value of the sine wave (at the 1200 and 2200 Hz frequencies), which is superimposed on the 4–20 mA signal, is zero. Hence, the 4–20 mA analog information is not affected.

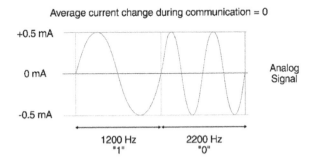

Figure 18a.1
Frequency allocation of HART protocol

The HART protocol can be used in three ways:

1. In conjunction with the 4–20 mA current signal in point-to-point mode
2. In conjunction with other field devices in multi-drop mode
3. In point-to-point mode with only one field device broadcasting in burst mode.

Traditional point-to-point loops use zero for the smart device polling address. Setting the smart device polling address to a number greater than zero creates a multi-drop loop. The smart device then sets its analog output to a constant 4 mA and communicates only digitally.

The HART protocol has two formats for digital transmission of data:

- Poll/response mode
- Burst (or broadcast) mode.

In the poll/response mode the master polls each of the smart devices on the highway and requests the relevant information. In burst mode the field device continuously transmits process data without the need for the host to send request messages. Although this mode is fairly fast (up to 3.7 times/s), it cannot be used in multi-drop networks.

The protocol is implemented with the OSI model using layers 1, 2, and 7. The actual implementation is covered in this chapter.

18a.3 Physical layer

The physical layer of the HART protocol is based on two methods of communication.

- Analog 4–20 mA
- Digital frequency shift keying (FSK).

The basic communication of the HART protocol is the 4–20 mA current system. This analog system is used by the sensor to transmit an analog value to the HART PLC or HART card in a PC (Figure 18a.2). In a 4–20 mA system, the sensor outputs a current value somewhere between 4 and 20 mA that represents the analog value of the sensor. For example, a water tank that is half full – say 3400 kL – would put out 12 mA. The receiver would interpret this 12 mA as 3400 kL. This communication is always point-to-point, i.e. from one device to another. It is not possible to do multi-drop communication using this method alone. If two or more devices put some current on the line at the same time, the resulting current value would not be valid for either device.

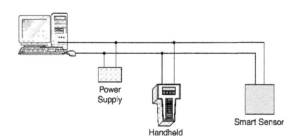

Figure 18a.2
HART point-to-point communications

18a.3.1   Digital multi-drop communications

For multi-drop communications, the HART protocol uses a digital/analog modulation technique known as frequency shift keying (FSK). This technique is based on the Bell 202 communication standard (Figure 18a.3). Data transfer rate is 1200 baud with a digital '0' frequency (2200 Hz) and a digital '1' frequency (1200 Hz). Category 5 shielded, twisted-pair wire is recommended by most manufacturers. Devices can be powered by the bus or individually. If the bus powers the devices, only 15 devices can be connected. As the average DC current of an ac frequency is zero, it is possible to place a 1200 or 2200 Hz tone on top of a 4–20 mA signal. The HART protocol does this to allow simultaneous communications on a multi-drop system.

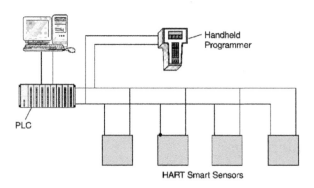

Figure 18a.3
HART multi-point communications

18a.3.2   The HART handheld communicator

The HART system includes a handheld control device (Figure 18a.4). This device can be a second master on the system. It is used to read, write, range, and calibrate devices on the bus. It can be taken into the field and used for temporary communications. The battery-operated handheld has a display and key input for specific commands.

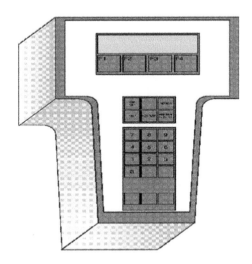

Figure 18a.4
HART handheld controller

The HART field controller in Figure 18a.5 is wired in series with the field device (valve positioner or other actuator). In some cases, a bypass capacitor may be required across the terminals of the valve positioner to keep the positioner's series impedance below the 100 Ω level required by HART specifications. Communications with the field controller requires the communicating device (handheld terminal or PC) to be connected across a loop impedance of at least 230 Ω. Communications is not possible across the terminals of the valve positioner because of its low impedance (100 Ω). Instead, the communicating device must be connected across the transmitter or the current sense resistor.

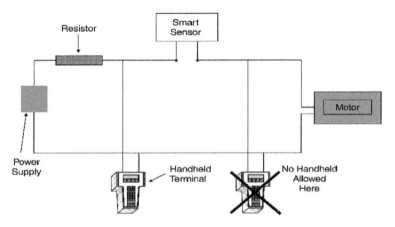

Figure 18a.5
HART handheld connection method

	Layer	Description	HART™
7	Application	Serves up formatted data	Hart Commands
6	Presentation	Translates Data	
5	Session	Controls Dialogue	
4	Transport	Ensures Message Integrity	
3	Network	Routes Information	
2	Data Link	Detects Errors	Protocol Rules
1	Physical	Connects Device	Bell 202

Figure 18a.6
HART protocol implementation of OSI layer model

18a.4 Data-link layer

The data-link frame format is shown in Figure 18a.7.

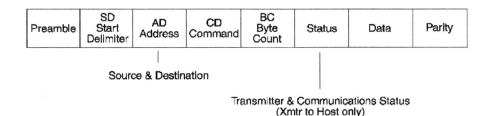

Figure 18a.7
HART data-link frame format

Two-dimensional error checking, including vertical and longitudinal parity checks, is implemented in each frame. Each character or frame of information has the following parameters:

- 1 start bit
- 8 data bits
- 1 odd parity bit
- 1 stop bit.

18a.5 Application layer

The application layer allows the host device to obtain and interpret field device data (Figure 18a.8). There are three classes of commands:

1. Universal commands
2. Common practice commands
3. Device-specific commands.

Examples of these commands are listed below.

18a.5.1 Universal commands

- Read manufacturer and device type
- Read primary variable (PV) and units
- Read current output and percent of range

- Read up to four predefined dynamic variables
- Read or write 8-character tag, 16-character descriptor, date
- Read or write 32-character message
- Read device range, units and damping time constant
- Read or write final assembly number
- Write polling address.

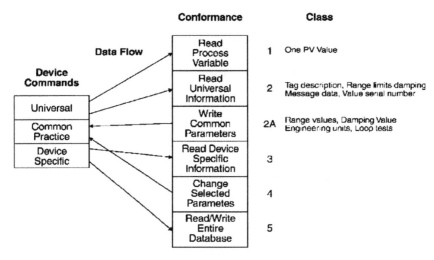

Figure 18a.8
HART application layer implementation

18a.5.2 Common practice commands

- Read selection of up to four dynamic variables
- Write damping time constant
- Write device range
- Calibrate (set zero, set span)
- Set fixed output current
- Perform self-test
- Perform master reset
- Trim PV zero
- Write PV units
- Trim DAC zero and gain
- Write transfer function (square root/linear)
- Write sensor serial number
- Read or write dynamic variable assignments.

18a.5.3 Instrument specific commands

- Read or write low flow cut-off value
- Start, stop or clear totalizer
- Read or write density calibration factor
- Choose PV (mass flow or density)
- Read or write materials or construction information
- Trim sensor calibration.

18a.5.4   Summary of HART benefits

- Simultaneous analog and digital communications
- Allows other analog devices on the highway
- Allows multiple masters to control same smart instrument
- Multiple smart devices on the same highway
- Long distance communications over telephone lines
- Two alternative transmission modes
- Flexible messaging structure for new features
- Up to 256 process variables in any smart field device.

18a.5.5   Hardware recommendations

Minimum cable size: 24 AWG, (0.51 mm diameter)
Cable type: Single-pair shielded or multiple-pair with overall shield.

18b

HART troubleshooting

18b.1 Troubleshooting HART systems

Beside the actual instruments that require calibration, the only major problem that can occur with HART is the cable length calculation.

The HART protocol is designed to work over existing analog signal cables but the reliable length of cable depends on:

- Loop load resistance
- Cable resistance
- Cable capacitance
- Number and capacitance of field devices
- Resistance and position of other devices in the loop.

The main reason for this is that network must pass the HART signal frequencies (1200 and 2200 Hz) without excessive loss or distortion. A software package such as H-Sim can be used to calculate whether you are operating with the correct signal level. In addition, you should ensure that you have the correct bandwidth of at least 2500 Hz. You can do this by ensuring that the product of the cable resistance and capacitance is less than 65 µs.

19

Wireless technologies

19.1 Satellite systems

Satellite systems are a form of microwave radio transmission whereby the transmitter sends the signal up to the satellite, where it is amplified and then transmitted back to the earth on another frequency. This provides a point-to-multi-point transmission system where each terminal accesses its signal out of the common beam. The satellite is located in a *geostationary earth orbit* (GEO) at some 36 000 km above the earth's equator where it appears to be stationary relative to an observer on the earth. This is illustrated in Figure 19.1. This means that the satellite antenna at all of the terminals can have fixed alignment. In this chapter, the principles of satellite operation and methods of access will be introduced and the design of *very small aperture satellite* (VSAT) systems will be discussed.

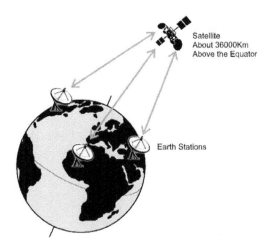

Figure 19.1
Geostationary earth orbit satellite communication

19.1.1 Satellite-operating principles

Satellite electronics

The satellite comprises a number of transponders that receive the signal from the earth, amplify it, convert it to a lower frequency and then amplify the signal for retransmission back to earth. A block diagram showing these components is given in Figure 19.2.

The *low noise amplifier* (LNA) is one of the most critical components in the satellite link since it is required to extract very low signals and the same time provide very large gain, up to 50 dB. The *high power amplifier* (HPA) in the satellite transponder may produce 10–50 W depending on the configuration. This power is limited by international agreement, to prevent interference with terrestrial microwave systems and such systems are said to be 'down-link limited'. By comparison, the equivalent HPA at the earth station may be running at power levels between 100 and 600 W.

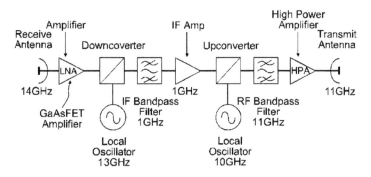

Figure 19.2
Block diagram of satellite transponder

Satellite frequency bands

The main frequency bands used for commercial satellite communication are listed in Table 19.1. It will be noted that the up-link frequencies, which are used from the earth to the satellite, are higher than the corresponding down-link frequencies. The reason for this is that the higher frequencies have a greater path loss and therefore require greater transmitter power. This is easily provided by the mains-powered earth stations, whereas the satellite transmitters are reliant on limited battery and solar energy resources; so use the lower frequencies.

Frequency Band Usage		Uplink Frequency (GHz)	Downlink Frequency (GHz)
L	Mobile	1.550–1.600	1.500–1.550
S	Military/Government	5.925–6.055	2.535–2.655
C	Commercial	5.2625–26.0265	3.2600–4.800
X	Military/Government	26.900–8.400	26.250–26.2650
Ku	Commercial	12.265–18.10	10.260–13.25
Ka	Military/Government	226.00–31.00	18.30–22.2

Table 19.1
Satellite frequency bands

The reasons for using particular frequency bands are as follows:

- *C band*: This is the most popular because it is least affected of all the bands by man-made and natural noise. Because it is shared with terrestrial services, satellite transmit power is limited to reduce interference.
- *Ku band*: As the C band is crowded, the Ku band is becoming more popular. It is affected by rain attenuation and high natural noise levels. Greater data rates are possible with higher frequencies.

- *L band*: This is used for mobile low capacity terminals. It is affected by man-made noise. Less pointing accuracy and lower power is required.
- *S, X and Ka bands*: These are restricted to military, government, and experimental users.

VSAT antenna diameter

The diameter of the antenna used at the earth station limits the amount of bandwidth that a station is able to access. VSAT systems use antennae ranging from 5 to 11 m in diameter at the hub and at the remote terminal antenna diameter ranges from 0.5 m (1.6 ft) to 2.5 m (8 ft). The outbound traffic from the hub may reach 2 Mbps, while the inbound traffic is typically 9600 bps.

Satellite access techniques

Satellite systems can be accessed in either the frequency domain (FDMA) or the time domain (TDMA). This access can also be assigned permanently (i.e. dedicated) for heavy traffic routes or dynamically as in demand-assigned multiple access (DAMA) systems. In DAMA systems the master station assigns traffic circuits to an earth station on demand. When the call terminates, the DAMA circuit is returned to the pool for re-assignment to other users.

Frequency division multiple access (FDMA)

In FDMA systems, each transponder – which typically has 36 MHz bandwidth – assigned divided into various frequency segments. Each earth station is assigned one or more frequency segments. For example, 14 earth stations could access one 36 MHz transponder with each having 24 analog voice channels. These allocations can be on a *single channel per carrier* (SCPC) basis whereby an individual user can transmit and receive on particular pre-allocated channels from his remote terminal. This is normally the simplest method of providing access to large numbers of small users.

The advantages in using FDMA are that no network timing is required and that the channel assignment is simple. The disadvantages are that up-link power levels need to be closely coordinated for efficient use of transmitter RF output power and inter-modulation becomes a problem as the number of separate RF carriers increases.

Time division multiple access (TDMA)

TDMA is used with digital transmission and is shared by the satellite transponder on a time basis. Individual time slots are assigned to the earth stations in sequence and each station has full and exclusive access to the whole of the transponder bandwidth during its assigned time slot. During its access period, the earth station transmits a burst of digital information. All stations on the network need precise time synchronization. This is done using a synchronization burst at the start of each frame. A typical INTELSAT TDMA system has a frame period of 2650 µs.

The advantages of TDMA are that only one earth station is providing input to the satellite at any one instant, so inter-modulation does not occur, the system allows greater flexibility with the different user's EIRP and data rates, and is able to cope quickly with the dynamically changing traffic patterns. The disadvantages of TDMA are that very accurate timing is required for all stations on the network, there is some loss of throughput due to the frame overhead, and large buffer storage is needed to cope with long frame lengths.

19.1.2   Satellite system design concepts

Receiving system figure of merit (*G/T*)

The receiving system figure of merit (*G/T*) describes the capability of a satellite or earth station to receive a signal. This is defined as follows:

$$G/T = G - 10 \log T$$

Where:
G/T is the figure of merit measured in dB per degree Kelvin (dB/K)
G is the net antenna gain up to the reference plane, which is normally the input to the LNA, in dB
T is the effective noise temperature of the receiving system in degrees Kelvin.

Net antenna gain

The net antenna gain is the gross gain of the antenna less the losses of all of the components making up the down-link receive chain, namely the radome loss, feed loss, directional coupler loss, wave guide loss, the band pass filter loss, and transition losses. These components are illustrated in Figure 19.3.

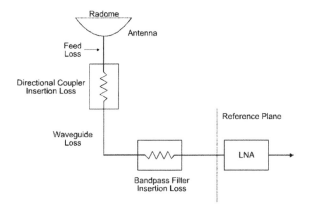

Figure 19.3
Components in receiver down-link chain

System noise temperature

The system noise temperature in degrees Kelvin is given by the following formula:

$$T_{sys} = T_{sys} + T_{feed} + T_{recv}$$

Where:
T_{sys} is the sky noise
T_{feed} is the thermal noise generated by the receive chain components
T_{recv} is the thermal noise generated by the LNA.

Sky noise

Sky noise varies in proportion to frequency and inversely in proportion to the elevation angle. Some representative values of sky noise are given in Table 19.2. Earth stations generally have minimum elevation angles at which they will work satisfactorily. Below the minimum angles the radio beam is subject to much greater atmospheric refraction and there is greater noise pickup from terrestrial sources and the sky noise increases dramatically. The minimum elevation angles are 5° at 4 GHz and 10° at 12 GHz.

Frequency (GHz)	Elevation Angle (°)	Sky Noise (K)
4.0	5	28
4.0	10	16
26.5	5	33
26.5	10	18
11.26	10	23
11.26	15	18
20.0	10	118
20.0	15	100
20.0	20	80

Table 19.2
Some sky noise figures

Noise figure

The *noise figure* (NF) in dB is the thermal noise generated by the losses of all devices inserted in the receive chain and it can be related to the noise temperature by the following formula:

$$NF = 10 \log \left(1 + \frac{T_e}{290}\right)$$

Where T_e is the effective noise temperature measured in degrees Kelvin (K).

19.1.3   Satellite down-link design procedure

To design the satellite down-link a similar process is followed to the design of microwave radio links as discussed in Section 19.3.

The objective is to calculate the carrier-to-noise ratio (C/N_0) using the following methodology:

- The effective power produced by the satellite or earth station is calculated (EIRP).
- The free space loss along the radio path is calculated (L_{FS}).
- An allowance is made for the other losses along the radio path (L_{other}).
- The figure of merit for the receiver system is calculated (G/T).
- Boltzmann's constant (k) = − 228.6 dBW/Hz is subtracted.
- The algebraic sum of all the above gains and losses can be calculated as follows:

$$C/N_0 = \text{EIRP} - L_{FS} - L_{other} + G/T - k \, \text{dB}$$

A *fade margin* of 4 dB is added to compensate for propagation anomalies and to allow for aging in the components.

The other losses in the radio path can include:

- *Polarization loss (0.5 dB)* at both the earth station and the satellite (0.5 dB each). This is to compensate for any antenna misalignment.

- *Off-contour loss* to compensate for variation in received signal strength at the terminal location. This information is obtained from the satellite service provider in the form of an antenna footprint, which shows the down-link-received signal strength (EIRP) for the specific spot or zone beam from the satellite. An example is shown for the Aussat 160E satellite in Figure 19.4.
- *Gaseous absorption loss* is caused by atmospheric absorption and increases with frequency, is inversely proportional to the elevation angle, and the elevation of the earth station. At higher altitudes the air is less dense and therefore the path loss is reduced. The elevation angle is compensated for by allowing 0.5 dB for 4 GHz systems at less than eight degrees elevation and 1.0 dB for 20.25 GHz systems at less than 10°elevation.
- *Rainfall attenuation* is significant for systems operating above 10 GHz. The amount of excess attenuation is dependent on the rainfall intensity and the frequency.

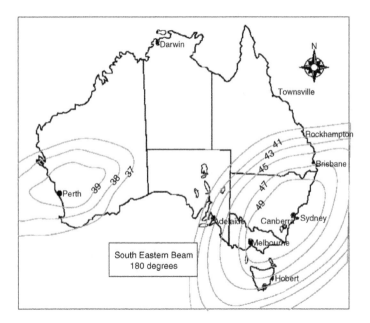

Figure 19.4
Example of satellite down-link footprint

19.1.4   Applications of satellite systems

Satellite systems have a number of advantages plus a few disadvantages. The advantages of satellite include:

- Systems only require a transmitting and a receiving site, and the distance between them on the earth is irrelevant.
- Systems can be installed in very remote locations where the provision of other services such as fiber-optic cables is impractical or prohibitively expensive.
- Systems can be installed on mobile equipment.
- System security involves only the protection of the transmitting and receiving sites, without the need to protect cable along the total path length.
- System installation can be much quicker with only the two terminals to install.

- VSAT systems are often installed to bypass the PSTN to create private data networks, ensuring data security. They are also used for telemetry links in isolated rural areas. An example of a VSAT network topology is shown in Figure 19.5.

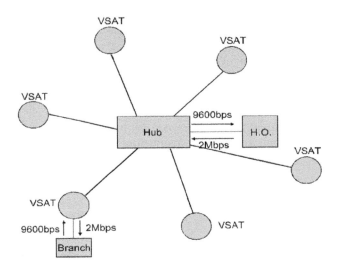

Figure 19.5
Typical VSAT network configuration

The disadvantages of using satellite systems are as follows:

- Satellite systems have limited bandwidth, thereby restricting the achievable data rates.
- The radio path is very long, and receive power is very low making systems susceptible to interference.
- The length of the radio path, some 36 000 km each way, causes a propagation delay of about 256 ms in one direction (512 ms return).
- Only limited radio frequencies are available in certain areas.
- GEO satellite orbital positions are limited and radio frequency interference is possible if an earth station antenna is incorrectly aligned or has too wide a beam width.

19.2   Wireless LANs (WLANs)

19.2.1   Topologies

A WLAN can be configured in three possible ways namely in star topology, peer-to-peer topology or hierarchical topology. Each topology has its own advantages and the choice of topology depends on the user's needs.

Star topology

In a star topology, the communication takes place over two separate channels. The node at the centre of the star is known as the central hub, while the surrounding nodes are known as network nodes. The communication from the central hub to the network nodes takes place on one channel while the other channel is used for communication in the opposite direction.

It is important to note that star topology has only one hop between the network node and the central hub. This characteristic provides the star topology with predictability and extra reliability. However, if that connection is weak, then there are no alternatives. One of the biggest advantages that a star topology WLAN offers is the use of central control functions at the hub. These functions include channel estimations, routing, and resource allocation.

Such centralized topology results in an efficient and reliable network service to the client devices. Hence, most commercial wireless networks, for instance commercial cellular and paging systems, prefer a star WLAN topology.

A hub-based LAN is said to operate in *infrastructure* mode.

Peer-to-peer topology

This topology interconnects a set of nodes, embedded with wireless adapters. The nodes self-configure to form an integrated network utilizing distributed control. This is known as *ad hoc* mode.

The connection between any two nodes in the network consists of one or more peer-to-peer communication links. Peer-to-peer topology can use multiple hops for the end-to-end connection, which results in the advantage of extending the network range. However, if one of the hops fails the entire end-to-end connection is lost. This disadvantage is compensated for by the possibility of each node having multiple paths to other nodes.

Peer-to-peer networks also do not require any existing infrastructure for establishing the network. These are also easily configurable. These features have made peer-to-peer networks ideal for military applications.

Hierarchical topology

As the name suggests, a hierarchical topology is ideal for networks that span a range of coverage regions. These regions are related to each other in the form of a hierarchy, for instance, town, city, state, and so forth.

Since the coverage regions define a natural hierarchy of the overall network, hierarchical network architecture along with protocols, routing, and identifying locations are more suited to this type of system.

19.2.2   WLAN components

The following components are necessary to set up a WLAN.

Wireless NIC

Wireless network interface cards interface the computer to the wireless network by modulating the data signal with the spreading sequence and implementing a carrier sense multiple access protocol (Figure 19.6). If a machine on the network wishes to transmit data onto network, the NIC listens for other transmissions. If it does not sense any transmission, the card will transmit its data in a frame. Other stations, listening to the incoming data, capture the frame and check the address of the intended recipient. The station whose address matches the frame address accepts the data frame, while the others discard it.

Wireless NICs plug into the ISA bus of a desktop PC or into the PCMCIA slot of a portable computer. Most wireless NICs have a built-in antenna, while some have provision for an external antenna as well.

Figure 19.6
Wireless NIC

Examples of commercial WLAN NICs include RangeLAN (Proxim Inc.) and WaveLAN (Lucent Technologies).

Wireless network bridges (access points)

Network bridges play a vital role in any kind of network. They interconnect multiple LANs at the MAC (medium access control) layer, the layer responsible for providing access functions. Bridges interface multiple wireless and wired LANs, provided they are identical at layer 2 of the OSI model. Another important function that a bridge provides is packet filtering based on the MAC address. This function allows organizations to create network segments in an enterprise network.

Assume that there are two network segments, A and B, both part of the enterprise network. If workstation A1 in segment A wishes to send the data to workstation A2 in the same segment A, then the bridge will not allow the packet (frame) to propagate to other segments of the network or to the backbone of the enterprise network. On the other hand, if A1 wishes to send data to workstation B1 in segment B2, the packet will be allowed to pass through the bridge. This process is called segmentation. It makes the better use of network bandwidth and increases overall performance.

Examples of commercial wireless bridges are RangeLAN Access Point (Proxim Inc.) and WavePOINT (Lucent Technologies).

There are several parameters that need to be set up on an access point. On most new models this can be done remotely via a browser.

Types of bridges

Based on the distances between the segments of an enterprise network that a bridge can cover, it can be classified as local bridges or remote bridges. Local bridges connect segments located at close proximities. For instance, two rooms in an office on a single floor can be connected using a local bridge. Remote bridges, on the other hand, are installed in pairs. They connect segments located a large distance apart, beyond the LAN's capability. For instance, two separate buildings can be connected using remote bridges.

19.2.3   Cell coverage

In a wireless network, the two basic components are wireless network interface cards and bridges (access points). These components can be used to create either a single cell or multiple cell WLAN networks.

Single cell WLAN

This configuration is ideal for small regions such as single floor factories. Under ideal conditions a single cell can cover up to 30 000 sq.m.

One of the characteristics of a single cell WLAN is the possible elimination of access points (Figure 19.7). In the absence of access points, the NICs on the wireless devices (PCs, laptops, etc.) can establish peer-to-peer connections with the other wireless devices in the same cell coverage area. This, however, requires that there should not be to too many nodes. It also eliminates some of the convenient functionalities of an AP, such as dynamic host configuration (DHCP). Wireless NICs have to be specifically configured to operate in *ad hoc* mode.

Figure 19.7
Access point

Multiple cell WLAN

If an organization requires its wireless device users to operate at greater distances, beyond the scope of a single cell coverage area, a multiple cell scenario using wireless local bridges can serve the purpose.

In a multiple cell configuration, a set of access points along with a wired network backbone creates multiple cells, overlapping with each other. It results in increasing the coverage of the wireless network to the desired extent. This configuration allows users, belonging to different cells, communicate with each other. All the users have also the privilege to access the common wired network resources. Multiple cell coverage is ideal for multi-floor buildings, college campuses, and so forth.

In the multiple cell scenario, a portable device with a wireless LAN adapter can also roam within the cells while maintaining a live connection to the corporate Intranet.

In the case of multiple cells, care must be taken not to operate adjacent access points at the same frequency (channel). The channel selection has to be done on the access point itself. Care must also be taken to eliminate interference where there are access points on different floors as sufficient frequency diversity in a horizontal plane does not preclude access points vertically separated (on different floors) from interfering with each other.

Roaming

Similar to the cellular networks, the concept of 'roaming' is applicable to WLANs. To make this a reality, most commercial wireless network APs support a roaming protocol that works in the MAC layer. The handoff process of a WLAN is similar to the handoff process in cellular networks. There is also a roaming version of IP for use on WLANs. If, on a fixed network, a workstation moves beyond a router on to a new network, its NetID has to change. On a mobile station this is not practical, as a user may not even know that he/she is on a different network. IP roaming enables the packet to be forwarded to the host's current location.

19.2.4 Devices

There are many types of wireless devices that can operate in a WLAN environment. At present, new WLAN-compatible devices are being rolled out everyday.

Some of the characteristics of WLAN devices include portability, a small screen size limited storage capacities, and multimedia support. Some of the well-known devices that satisfy these criteria include handheld (PDAs), laptops, tablet PCs (by Microsoft), notebook PCs, and cell phones.

The area of WLAN devices is considered to have immense potential. In future, mobile device manufactures are planning to develop their own range of WLAN devices.

19.2.5 Accessories

Antennas

These devices control the signal channels to ensure a clear, interference-free transmission of all types of data including audio, video, and digital images. Most NICs have built-in antennas giving a range of up to 100 m without amplification. Some have a socket for an external antenna. These are available from various vendors and include Yagi antennas, parabolic grids, and parabolic dishes. A properly designed parabolic antenna can improve the range to about 8–10 km without amplification.

Power

WLAN access points need external power to operate. To obviate the need for separate electrical wiring to power access points, the concept of PoE (power over Ethernet) has been developed. This delivers power to the AP via the unused pairs of the Cat5 cabling.

19.2.6 IEEE 802.11 specifications

In 1996 the IEEE finalized the initial standard for wireless LANs, IEEE 802.11. This standard specified a 2.4 GHz operating frequency with data rates of 1 and 2 Mbps. Users had the option of using either *frequency hopping spread spectrum* (FHSS) or *direct sequence spread spectrum* (DSSS).

Since the ratification of the initial 802.11 standard, the IEEE 802.11 working group (WG) has made several revisions through various task groups. Task groups are designated through a suffix after the 802.11, for example 802.11b designates task group B.

Here follows a brief summary of the various IEEE 802.11 standards.

IEEE 802.11a

IEEE 802.11a is a physical layer standard that specifies operating in the 5 GHz UNII band using *orthogonal frequency division multiplexing* (OFDM). It supports data rates ranging from 6 to 54 Mbps. It offers much less potential for radio frequency interference than other PHYs (e.g. 802.11b and 802.11g) that utilize 2.4 GHz frequencies.

IEEE 802.11b

IEEE 802.11b uses *direct sequence spread spectrum* (DSSS) in the 2.4 GHz band. It includes 5.5 and 11 Mbps data rates in addition to the 1 and 2 Mbps data rates of the initial standard. To provide the higher data rates, 802.11b uses CCK (complementary code keying), a modulation technique that makes efficient use of the radio spectrum.

IEEE 802.11b is the basis for Wi-Fi certification from the Wireless Ethernet Compatibility Alliance (WECA).

IEEE 802.11c

IEEE 802.11c provides required information to ensure proper bridge operations. Product developers utilize this standard when developing access points.

IEEE 802.11d

IEEE 802.11d deals with global harmonization in terms of 802.11. In order to support a widespread adoption of 802.11, the 802.11d task group has an ongoing charter to define PHY requirements that satisfy regulatory within countries other than the US, Europe, and Japan, which already had the necessary regulations in place at the beginning. This is especially important for operation in the 5 GHz bands because the use of these frequencies differ widely from one country to another. This standard mostly applies to companies developing 802.11 products.

IEEE 802.11e

This standard deals with MAC enhancements for quality of service (QoS). This is required for optimum transmission of voice and video, which is achieved by mechanisms to prioritize traffic within 802.11. The 802.11e task group refined the 802.11 medium access layer to improve QoS for better support of audio and video such as MPEG-2 applications. Because 802.11e falls within the MAC Layer, it is common to all 802.11 PHYs and backward compatible with existing 802.11 wireless LANs.

IEEE 802.11f

This is the inter-access point protocol. The original 802.11 standard did not specify the communications between access points in order to support users roaming from one access point to another. The problem, however, was that access points from different vendors did not always interoperate when supporting roaming. IEEE 802.11f specifies an inter-access point protocol that provides the necessary information to support roaming.

19.2.7 WLANs (wireless local area networks) vs WPANs (wireless personal area networks)

IEEE 802.11 is an example of a WLAN. However, Bluetooth (IEEE 802.15), a WPAN, is gaining popularity as well. The key differences between a WLAN (IEEE 802.11) and a WPAN (IEEE 802.15) are listed here. Bluetooth is essentially a replacement for infrared technology and will be used to link computers, peripherals, and handheld devices in an office environment.

WLAN	WPAN
Environment	
It is appropriate for applications that require MAC provisions (ability to support large numbers of nodes involved in concurrent communication, mechanism to avoid interference) and high range (10–100+ meter) necessary to support LAN applications	WPANs are appropriate for applications which are limited to the WPAN range (0–10 m), do not require the complexity of a LAN-style MAC scheme, and are extremely sensitive to power consumption and per-unit cost

WLANs support segments at least 100 m in length. The specifications for WPANs focus on short-distance wireless networks with a range of 0–10 m.

Medium Access Control Mechanism (MAC)	
IEEE 802.11 calls for a carrier sense multiple access with collision avoidance (CSMA/CA) MAC scheme	The Task Group 1 (TG1 – Bluetooth) specification calls for a time division multiple access (TDMA) scheme. This mechanism provides no 'listen before transmission' type of interference avoidance as in CSMA/CA
Cost Factor	
No specific cost constraints for 802.11	Cost factors are critically important in the WPAN arena; for example, the unit cost to manufacturers for TG1 (Bluetooth) devices is targeted in the $10 (or under) range in volume
Power Consumption	
No specific power consumption constraints for 802.11	802.15 standards are intended to address power consumption issues critical to this class of small portable/mobile device

19.3 Radio and wireless communications

19.3.1 Introduction

A significant number of industrial protocols are transferred using radio telemetry systems. Radio is often chosen in preference to using landlines for a number of reasons:

- Costs of cable can far exceed that of radio telemetry systems
- Radio systems can be installed faster than landline systems
- Radio equipment is very portable and can be easily moved
- Radio can be used to transmit the data in any format required by the user
- Reasonably high data rates can be achieved compared to some landline applications
- Radio can be used as a back-up for landlines.

This chapter briefly examines some of the issues that have to be considered if the industrial protocols are used over a radio link. It is broken down into:

- Components of a radio link
- Radio spectrum and frequency allocation
- Summary of radio characteristics for VHF/UHF radio telemetry systems
- Radio modems
- How to prevent inter-modulation problems
- Implementing a radio link
- Miscellaneous considerations.

19.3.2 Components of a radio link

A radio link consists of the following components:

- Antennas
- Transmitters
- Receivers
- Antenna support structures
- Cabling
- Interface equipment.

Figure 19.8 illustrates how these elements are connected together to form a complete radio link.

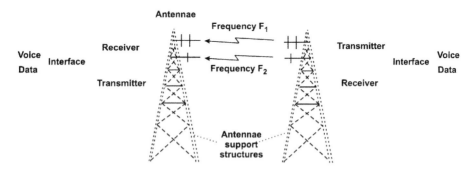

Figure 19.8
Basic elements of a radio link

Antenna

This is the device used to radiate or detect the electromagnetic waves. There are many different designs of antennas available. Each one radiates the signal (electromagnetic waves) in a different manner. The type of antenna used depends on the application and on the area of coverage required.

Transmitter

This is the device that converts the voice or data signal into a modified (modulated) higher frequency signal. Then it feeds the signal to the antenna where it is radiated into the free space as an electromagnetic wave at radio frequencies.

Receiver

This is the device that converts the radio frequency signals (fed to it from the antenna detecting the electromagnetic waves from free space) back into voice or data signals.

Antenna support structure

An antenna support structure is used to mount antennas, in order to provide a height advantage, which generally provides increased transmission distance and coverage. It may vary in construction from a 3 m wooden pole to 1000 m steel structure.

A structure that has guy wires for support is generally referred to as a mast. A structure that is free standing is generally referred to as a tower (Figure 19.9).

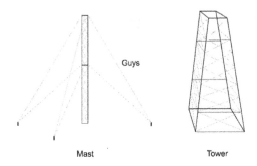

Figure 19.9
Mast and tower

Cabling

There are three main types of cabling used in connecting radio systems:

1. Coaxial cable for all radio frequency connections
2. Twisted-pair cables for voice, data and supervisory connections
3. Power cables.

Interface equipment

This allows connection of voice and data into the transmitters and receivers from external sources. It also controls the flow of information, timing of operation on the system, and control and monitoring of the transmitter and receiver.

19.3.3 The radio spectrum and frequency allocation

There are very strict regulations that govern the use of various parts of the radio frequency spectrum. Specific sections of the radio frequency spectrum have been allocated for public use. All frequencies are allocated to users by a government regulatory body. Table 19.3 illustrates the typical sections of the radio spectrum allocated for public use around the world. Each section is referred to as a band.

Certain sections of these bands will have been allocated specifically for telemetry systems.

Ultra High Frequency (UHF)	Mid band UHF	960 MHz 800 MHz
	Low band UHF	520 MHz 335 MHz
Very High Frequency (VHF)	High band VHF	225 MHz 101 MHz
	Mid band VHF	100 MHz 60 MHz
	Low band VHF	59 MHz 31 MHz
High Frequency (HF)		30 MHz 2 MHz

Table 19.3
The radio spectrum for public use

In some countries, a deregulated telecommunications environment has allowed sections of the spectrum to be sold off to large private organizations to be managed, and then sold to smaller individual users.

Application must be made to the government body, or independent groups that hold larger chunks of the spectrum for on selling, to obtain a frequency, and no transmission is allowed on any frequency unless a license is obtained.

19.3.4 Summary of radio characteristics of VHF/UHF

Tables 19.4 and 19.5 summarize the information discussed in this section.

19.3.5 Radio modems

Radio modems are suitable for replacing wire lines to remote sites or as a back-up to wire or fiber-optic circuits, and are designed to ensure that computers and PLCs, for example, can communicate transparently over a radio link without any specific modifications required.

Modern radio modems operate in the 400–900 MHz band. Propagation in this band requires a free line of sight between transmitting and receiving antennae for reliable communications. Radio modems can be operated in a network, but require a network management software system (protocols) to manage network access and error detection. Often, a master station with hot change-over, communicates with multiple radio field stations. The protocol for these applications can use a simple poll/response technique (Figure 19.10).

	Low Band VHF	**Mid Band VHF**	**High Band VHF**
Propagation mode	Mostly LOS some surface wave	LOS Minimal surface wave	LOS
Data rates	600 baud	1200 baud	2400 baud
Diffraction properties	Excellent	Very good	Good
Natural noise environment	High	Medium	Low
Affected by man-made noise	Severe	Bad	Some
Penetration of solids	Excellent	Very good	Good
Fading by ducting	Long term	Medium term	Short term
Absorption by wet vegetation	Negligible	Low	Some
Equipment availability	Minimal	Reasonable	Excellent
Relative equipment cost	High	Medium	Low
Uses	– In forested areas – Mostly mobile – Very hilly	– Very hilly and Forested areas – Mostly mobile – Over water	– Long distance/LOS/hilly areas – LOS links – Mobile – Borefields – Over water

Table 19.4
VHF radio characteristics

	UHF 1	**UHF 2**
Propagation mode	LOS	LOS
Data rates	4800 baud (9600?)	9600 baud (19.2 K?)
Diffraction properties	Some	Minimal
Natural noise environment	Low	Negligible
Affected by man made noise	Low	Very low
Penetration of solids	Low	Negligible
Reflection and absorption by solids	Good (enhanced multi-pathing)	Excellent (excellent multi-pathing)
Absorption by wet vegetation	High	Very high
Interference by ducting	Some	Some
Equipment availability	Excellent	Reasonable
Relative equipment costs	Low	Medium
Uses	– Telemetry – Mobile	– Telemetry – Mobile – Links

Table 19.5
UHF radio characteristics

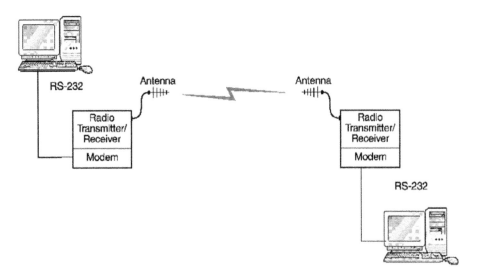

Figure 19.10
Radio modem configuration

The more sophisticated peer-to-peer network communications applications require a protocol based on carrier sensing multiple access with collision detection (CSMA/CD) or carrier sensing multiple access with collision avoidance (CSMA/CA). A variation on the standard approach is to use one of the radio modems as a network watchdog to periodically poll all the radio modems on the network and to check their integrity. The radio modem can also be used as a relay station to communicate with other systems that are out of the range of the master station.

The interface to the radio modem is typically RS-232 but RS-422, RS-485, and fiber-optics are also options. Typical speeds of operation are up to 9600 bps. A buffer is required in the modem and is typically a minimum of 32 kB. Hardware and software flow control techniques are normally provided in the radio modem firmware, ensuring that there is no loss of data between the radio modem and the connecting terminal.

Typical modulation techniques are two level direct FM (1200–4800 bps) to three level direct FM (9600 bps). A typical schematic of a radio modem is given in Figure 19.11.

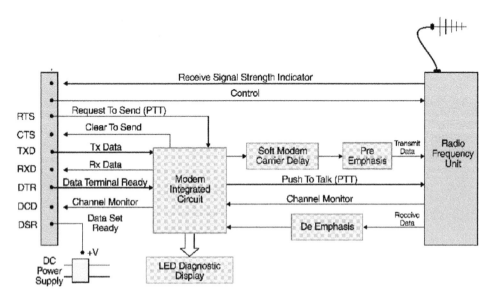

Figure 19.11
Block diagram of a radio modem

The following terms are used in relation to radio modems:

PTT	Push to talk signal
RSSI	Receive signal strength indicator – indicates the received signal strength with a proportionally varying DC voltage
Noise squelch	Attempts to minimize the reception of any noise signal at the discriminator output
RSSI squelch	Opens the receive audio path when the signal strength of the RF carrier is of a sufficiently high level
Channel monitor	Indicates if the squelch is open
Soft carrier delay	Allows the RF transmission to be extended slightly after the actual end of the data message which avoids the end of transmission bursts that occur when the carrier stops and the squelch almost simultaneously disconnects the studio path
RTS, CTS, DCD, DCD, Clock, TxD, RxD	All relate to RS-232.

The radio modem has a basic timing system for communications between a terminal and the radio modem, indicated in Figure 19.12.

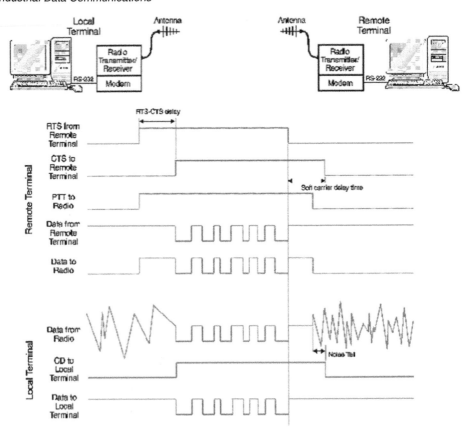

Figure 19.12
Radio modem timing diagram

Data transmission begins with the RTS line becoming active at the remote terminal side. The radio modem then raises the CTS line to indicate that transmission can proceed. At the end of the transmission, the PTT is kept active to ensure that the receiving side detects the remaining useful data before the RF carrier is removed.

Modes of radio modems

Radio modems can be used either in point-to-point mode or in point-to-multi-point mode.

A point-to-point system can operate in continuous RF mode, which has a minimal turn on delay in transmission of data, and non-continuous mode where there is a considerable energy saving. The RTS to CTS delay for continuous and switched carriers is of the order of 10 and 20 ms respectively.

A point-to-multi-point system generally operates with only the master and one radio modem at a time.

In a multi-point system when the data link includes a repeater, data regeneration must be performed to eliminate signal distortion and jitter. Regeneration is not necessary for voice systems where some error is tolerable.

Regeneration is performed by passing the radio signal through the modem, which converts the RF analog signal back to a digital signal and then applies this output binary data stream to the other transmitting modem, which repeats the RF analog signal to the next location (Figure 19.13).

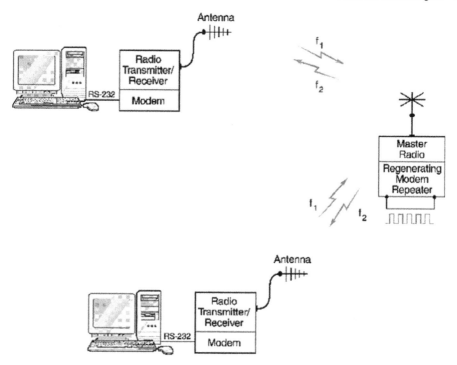

Figure 19.13
Regeneration of a signal with a radio modem

Features of a radio modem

Typical features that have to be configured in the radio modem are:

Transmit/receive radio channel frequency

In a point-to-point configuration running in a dual frequency/split channel assignment, two radios will operate on opposing channel sets.

Host data rate and format

Data rate/character size/parity type and number of stop bits for RS-232 communications.

Radio channel data rate

Data rate across the radio channel defined by the radio and bandwidth capabilities. Note that these specifications are generally set at the time of manufacture.

Minimum radio frequency signal level

Should not be set too low on the receiver otherwise noise data will also be read.

Supervisory data channel rate

Used for flow control and therefore should not be set too low otherwise the buffer on the receiver will overflow. Typically one flow control bit to 32 bits of serial data is the standard.

Transmitter key up delay

The time for the transmitter to energize and stabilize before useful data is sent over the radio link. Transmitter key up delay should be kept as low as possible to minimize overheads.

Spread spectrum radio modems

Several countries around the world have allocated a section of bandwidth for use with spread spectrum radio modems. In Australia and America, this is in the 900 MHz area.

In brief, a very wide band channel is allocated to the modem, for example, approximately 3.6 MHz wide. The transmitter uses a pseudo random code to place individual bits, or groups of bits, broadly across the bandwidth and the receiver uses the same random code to receive them. Because they are random, a number of transceivers can operate on the same channel and a collision of bits will be received as noise by a receiver in close proximity.

The advantage of 'spread spectrum' radio modems is very high data security and data speeds of up to 19.2 kbps. The disadvantage is the very inefficient use of the radio spectrum.

19.3.6   Inter-modulation and how to prevent it

Introduction

Besides noise and interference that emanates from man-made sources (cars, electrical motors, switches, rectifiers, etc.), there are three other main causes of RF interference. These are produced from other radio equipment. The first and the most obvious source, is another radio user operating close by on the same frequency as the system suffering from interference. Unfortunately, besides using special coding techniques to minimize the problem there is little that can be done, short of complaining to the regulatory government body that issues licenses, or finding out who it is and asking them to stop transmissions.

The second source of interference comes from noisy transmitters that emit spurious frequencies outside their allocated bandwidth. These spurious emissions will tend to fall on other users' channel bandwidths and cause interference problems. Aging transmitters and those that are not well maintained are normally the culprits.

The third source of interference is known as inter-modulation. This is normally the most common source of interference and generally the most difficult to locate and the most costly to eliminate. The following section will examine this phenomenon in more detail.

Inter-modulation

Inter-modulation occurs where two or more frequencies interact in a non-linear device such as a transmitter, receiver or their environs, or on a rusty bolted joint acting as an RF diode to produce one or more additional frequencies that can potentially cause interference to other users. When two electromagnetic waves meet and inter-modulate in a non-linear device, they produce a minimum of two new frequencies – one being the sum of the frequencies and the other being the difference of the frequencies.

A nearby receiver may be on or close to one of the inter-modulation frequency products, receive it as noise and interference and then could retransmit it as further noise and interference. For example, if two frequencies 'a' and 'b' interact, then they will produce two new frequencies 'c' and 'd' where $a + b = c$ and $a - b = d$. c and d are referred to as inter-modulation products.

Of course c and d will be of significantly less magnitude than a and b and their exact magnitude depends on the magnitude of a and b, at the point a and b meet, and on the efficiency of the non-linear device at which the inter-modulation takes place.

Fortunately, this problem is only significant when the two transmitters for a and b are within close proximity. However, consideration should be given to inter-modulation products produced at a distant location as these have been known to cause noticeable background noise. If there are more than two frequencies at one location then the number of inter-modulation products possibly increases dramatically.

For example, if there are transmitters on frequencies a, b, and c at one location then the inter-modulation products become:

$$a+b=f_1$$
$$a+b=f_2$$
$$b+c=f_3$$
$$b-c=f_4$$
$$a+c=f_5$$
$$a-c=f_6$$
$$a+b-c=f_{26}$$
$$a+b-c=f_8$$
$$a-b+c=f_9$$
$$a-b-c=f_{10}$$

This illustrates that the number of potential inter-modulation products becomes prodigious as the number of frequencies increases. Unfortunately, the scenario gets worse. Each frequency from a transmitter will produce a significant harmonic at twice, three times, four times, etc., its carrier frequency (this is particularly true with FM systems). Each sequential harmonic will be of a lesser magnitude than the previous one.

Therefore if the transmitter is operating on frequency a, then harmonics will be produced at $2a$, $3a$, $4a$, etc. The $2a$ and $3a$ harmonics can be quite large. These harmonics are produced because of resonant properties of antennas, cables, buildings, and tuned circuits in the receivers and transmitters themselves and also due to the harmonic side bands produced in FM.

Taking these harmonics into account, inter-modulation products such as $(2a - b)$ and $(3b - 2c)$ are examples of what can be produced. (i) is referred to as a third order product and (ii) as a fifth order product. This refers to the total of multiples of each frequency.

These inter-modulation products can cause severe interference in radio systems that are located at the same site. Taking these into account, there are numerous permutations of a small number of base frequencies that may cause inter-modulation interference.

Generally, inter-modulation products greater than fifth orders are too small to be of consequence and generally, radio systems are engineered only to take into account possible inter-modulation distortion up to and including fifth order products. At sites where there are many sensitive receivers on different channels in one building, then calculations to seventh order may be carried out.

Software has been provided with this book for calculations of inter-modulation products, from any number of transmitters at a site.

For transmitters that are 1 km or more apart, the inter-modulation products are generally so small that it would not be a problem. The exception may be for first or second order products.

If a system is experiencing, unexplainable interference problems, a check should be made for distant inter-modulation products.

Another source of harmonics sometimes comes from old buildings or masts where rusty bolts or nails act as RF diodes (nonlinear devices) to produce inter-modulation products. These are then detected by nearby receivers and may be retransmitted as noise and interference.

A number of devices have been developed to assist in preventing the formation of inter-modulation products and to prevent these products, spurious transmissions and harmonics from causing interference to nearby receivers or transmitters. All these devices are connected between the transmitter and the antenna. The following sections provide details on these devices and how they are used to eliminate interference problems.

19.3.7   Implementing a radio link

There is an important methodology that must be followed when designing and implementing a radio link if it is to work satisfactorily. It is relatively straightforward and will provide successful radio communications if followed closely.

Software has been provided with this manual that carries out the necessary calculations. Reference should be made to the book when using the software. In general, the software will follow a procedure as is described in this section.

The design methodology in a sequential order is as follows:

- Carry out a radio path profile
- Calculate RF losses for the radio path
- Calculate effects of transmitter power
- Decide on required fade margin
- Choose cable and antenna
- Purchase equipment
- Install equipment.

Path profile

The first requirement in establishing a successful radio link is to draw up a radio path profile. This is basically a cross-sectional drawing of the earth for the radio propagation path showing all terrain variations, obstructions, terrain type (water, land, trees, buildings, etc.) and the masts on which the antenna are mounted. For distances less than a kilometer or two, profiles are not normally required, as the RTU can quite often be clearly seen from the master site (but all other calculations and choices described in the design methodology must be carried out). The Figure 19.14 illustrates a typical path profile.

The first step in this process is to obtain a contour map of the location. These survey maps are readily available from government departments that oversee land administration and private companies that carry out surveys and publish their material, for most areas of developed countries and many areas in developing countries. It is recommended that the map have a minimum of 20 m contour lines, with 2 m, 5 m, or 10 m being preferred.

Locate the RTU and master site locations on the map and draw a ruled line between the two locations with a pencil. Then assuming that the master site is at distance 0 km, follow the line along noting the kilometer marks and where a contour line occurs and at that point, also note the contour height.

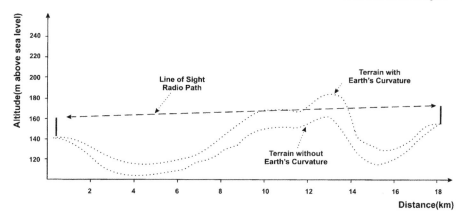

Figure 19.14
Typical path profile

The surface of the earth is of course not flat but curved. Therefore, to plot the points you obtained from the map directly would not be a true indication of the path. The formula below provides a height correction factor that can be applied to each point obtained from the map to mark a true earth profile plot.

$$h = \frac{(d_1 \times d_2)}{12.265K}$$

Where:

    H = height correction factor that is added to the contour height (in m)
    d_1 = the distance from a contour point to one end of the path (in km)
    d_2 = the distance from the same contour point to the other end of the path (in kilometers)
    K = the equivalent earth radius factor.

The equivalent earth radius factor K is required to account for the fact that the radio wave is bent towards the earth because of atmospheric refraction. The amount of bending varies with changing atmospheric conditions and therefore the value of K varies to account for this.

For the purposes of radio below 1 GHz it is sufficient to assume that for greater than 90% of the time K will be equal to 4/3. To allow for periods where a changing K will increase signal attenuation, a good fade margin should be allowed for.

The K factor allows the radio path to always be drawn in a straight line and adjusts the earth's contour height to account for the bending radio wave. Once the height has been calculated and added to the contour height, the path profile can be plotted.

From the plot it can now be seen if there are any direct obstructions in the path. As a general rule, the path should have good clearance over all obstructions. There is an area around the radio path that appears as a cone that should be kept as clearance for the radio path. This is referred to as the 'Fresnel zone'.

Fresnel zone clearance (Figure 19.15) is of more relevance to microwave path prediction than to radio path prediction. The formula for the Fresnel zone clearance required is:

$$F = 0.55 \left[\frac{(d_1 \times d_2)}{(G \times D)} \right]^{1/2}$$

Where:

F = Fresnel zone clearance in meters (i.e. radius of cone)
d_1 = distance from contour point to one end of path (in km)
d_2 = distance from contour point to other end of path (in km)
D = total length of path (in km)
G = frequency in MHz.

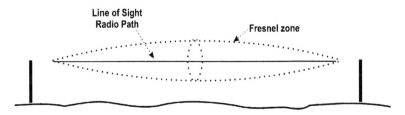

Figure 19.15
Fresnel zone clearance

If from the plot it appears that the radio path is going dangerously close to an obstruction, then it is worth doing a Fresnel zone calculation to check for sufficient clearance. Normally, the mast heights are chosen to provide a clearance of 0.6 times the Fresnel zone radius. This figure of 0.6 is chosen because it firstly gives sufficient radio path clearance and secondly assists in preventing cancellation from reflections. At less than 0.6F, attenuation of the line of sight signal occurs. At 0.6F, there is no attenuation of the line of sight signal and therefore there is no gain achieved by the extra cost of providing higher masts.

Another important point to consider is that frequencies below 1 GHz have good diffraction properties. The lower the frequency the more diffraction that occurs. Therefore, for very long paths it is possible to operate the link with a certain amount of obstruction. It is important to calculate the amount of attenuation introduced by the diffraction and determine the affect it has on the availability (i.e. fade margin) of the radio link. The mathematics for doing this calculation is relatively complex and has been included in the software provided.

As an example, Figure 19.14 shows a hill obstructing the radio path. Therefore a calculation needs to be carried out to determine the attenuation due to diffraction at this hill. This would then be added to the total path loss to determine if the link will still operate satisfactorily.

One further point of note is that this discussion and the formulas and software provided are for fixed radio links only. Mobile (moving RTU) radio uses a completely different set of criteria and formula. The greater majority of telemetry links are fixed and analysis of mobile radio is not provided here.

RF path loss calculations

The next step is to calculate the total attenuation of RF signal from the transmitter antenna to the receiver antenna.

This includes:

- Free space attenuation
- Diffraction losses
- Rain attenuation
- Reflection losses.

Free space attenuation and diffraction losses are calculated using the industry standard formulas. Rain attenuation is negligible at frequencies below 1 GHz.

Reflection losses are difficult to determine. Firstly, the strength of the reflected signal depends on the surface it is reflected off (for example, water, rock, sand). Secondly, the reflected signal may arrive in phase, out of phase or at a phase angle in between. So reflected waves can be anything from totally catastrophic to enhancing the signal. Good engineering practice should always assume the worst case, which would be catastrophic failure. Therefore, when designing a link, a check is made for reflections and if they exist, measures should be taken to remove the problem (Figures 19.16 and 19.17).

This can be done by moving antennas or masts to different locations and heights or by placing a barrier in the path of the reflection to absorb it. For example, place the antenna behind a hill, house, billboard, etc.

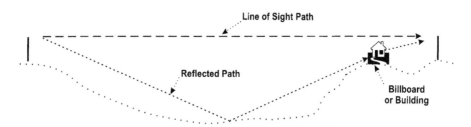

Figure 19.16
Removing potential reflections

With reference to Figure 19.10, the total loss would be calculated as follows:

(a) Free space loss $= 32.5 + 20 \log_{10} F + 20 \log_{10} D$
$= 32.5 + 53.1 + 24.6$
$= 110.2$ dB
(b) Diffraction loss $= 23$ dB
(c) Total loss $= (a) + (b)$
$= 133.2$ dB

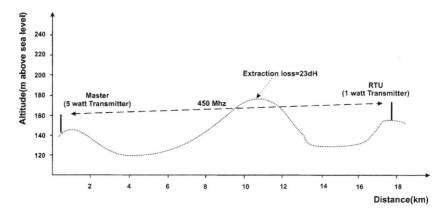

Figure 19.17
Example link

Transmitter power/receiver sensitivity

The next step is to determine the gain provided by the transmitters. If in a link configuration one transmitter operates with less power than the other, the direction with the least power transmitter should be considered. Therefore, as the ACA regulation requires that RTUs be allowed to transmit a maximum of 1 W into the antenna, while master stations can transmit 5 W into the antenna (sometimes higher), the path direction from the RTU to the master should be considered.

The transmit power should be converted to a dBm figure. For an RTU this would be as follows:

$$\text{Power} = 10 \log [1/10^{-3}] \text{ dBm}$$
$$= 10 \log [103] \text{ dBm}$$
$$= 30 \text{ dBm}$$

The next step is to determine the minimum RF level at the receiver input that will open the front end of the receiver (i.e. turn it on). This is referred to as the 'receiver threshold sensitivity level' or sometimes as the 'squelch level'. This figure can be obtained from the manufacturer's specification sheets.

For a radio operating at 450 MHz, this would be approximately –123 dBm. At this level, the signal is only just above noise level and is not very intelligible. Therefore, as a general rule, a figure slightly better than this is used as a receiver sensitivity level. A *de facto* standard is used where the RF signal is at its lowest but still intelligible. This level is referred to as the 12 dB SINAD level.

Again, this figure is obtained from manufacturer's data sheets. For a typical 450 MHz radio, this level is approximately –1126 dBm.

Using these figures, a simple calculation can be performed to determine the links performance for the example link in Figure 19.10.

Tx Pwr	= Transmit power at RTU
	= +30 dBm
Loss	= RF Path attenuation
	= 133.2 dB
Rx Sen	= Receiver sensitivity for 12 dB SINAD
	= −1126 dB
Tx Pwr − Loss	= Available power at receiver
	= +30 − 133.2 = −103.2 dBm

Since the receiver can accept an RF signal down to –1126 dBm, then the RF signal will be accepted by the receiver. In this case, we have 13.8 dBm of spare RF power.

Signal to noise ratio and SINAD

The most common measure of the effect of noise on the performance of a radio system is signal to noise ratio (SNR). This is a measure of the signal power level compared to the noise power level at a chosen point in a circuit. In reality, it is the signal plus noise compared to noise.

$$\therefore \text{ SNR} = \frac{P_{\text{signal}} + P_{\text{noise}}}{P_{\text{noise}}}$$

SNR is often expressed in dBs. Therefore:

$$\text{SNR} = 10 \log_{10}\left(\frac{P_{\text{signal}} + P_{\text{noise}}}{P_{\text{noise}}}\right)$$

The real importance of this measurement is at the radio receiver. As the receive signal at the antenna increases, the noise level at the audio output of the receiver effectively decreases. Therefore, a measure of SNR at the receiver audio output for measured low level of RF input to the receiver front end is a good measure of the performance of a receiver.

The highest level of noise at the audio output will be when the RF input signal is at its lowest level. That is when the RF input signal just opens the receiver. At this point, the SNR will be between 3 and 6 dB.

A measurement has been developed as a *de facto* standard that measures the receiver input signal level for an SNR of 12 dB at the audio output. It is often referred to as the 12 dB SINAD level (signal to noise and distortion). The measurement is made with a device called SINAD meter.

The SINAD measurement is carried out by feeding the input of the receiver with a RF signal that is modulated by a 1 kHz input audio signal. The 1 kHz signal will produce harmonics and unwanted distortion in the audio output. A SINAD meter is placed at the receiver audio output. The SINAD meter measures the power level of the 1 kHz plus the noise and distortion. It then filters the 1 kHz signal and measures the broadband level of noise power without the 1 kHz signal. It then divides the two measurements and provides a reading of SNR in dBs. The level at the receiver RF input is slowly increased until the SNR at the audio output is 12 dB. The RF input level is then noted and this is referred to as the 12 dB SINAD level. Some manufacturers refer to it as *sensitivity at 12 dB SINAD* or sometimes just as *sensitivity*. The latter can be very deceptive and care must be taken. The equipment configuration for measurement of SINAD is shown in Figure 19.18.

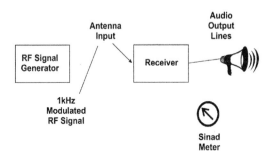

Figure 19.18
Measuring SINAD

Some typical 12 dB SINAD sensitivity figures for modern radios in the VHF and UHF bands are 0.25 to 0.35 μV. The receiver opening sensitivity is normally 0.18 to 0.2 μV (i.e. the squelch level).

Another measurement also used to determine receiver performance is the '20 dB quieting' measurement. This is not used as often as the 12 dB SINAD method.

Here, the receiver squelch is set so that it is just open. A level meter is connected to the speaker and the noise level measured. The audio volume control is set for a convenient level (0 dBm). A signal generator is then connected to the receiver input and an unmodulated RF signal is fed into the receiver and increased slowly until the noise level at the audio output has dropped by 20 dB.

The disadvantage of this method is that it only measures the ability of the receiver to receive an unmodulated RF carrier signal. Poor design, component aging or improper alignment can provide a circuit response that admits the carrier signal perfectly but provides poor quality reception of modulated signals.

Fade margin

Radio is statistical by nature and it is therefore impossible to predict with 100% accuracy as to how it is going to perform. For example, due to degrading effects of reflections, multi-pathing, ducting, and RF interference, a link may lose or gain signal by up to 15 dB over short of long periods. It is because of this unpredictability, it is important to have a safety margin to allow for intermittent link degradation. This safety margin (or spare RF power) is generally referred to as the fade margin.

It should be the intention to design most links to have a fade margin of approximately 30 dB. This means that if there was a 30 dB drop in RF signal level then the RF signal at the receiver input would drop below the 12 dB SINAD sensitivity. Therefore, in the example in the previous section there is insufficient fade margin. This is overcome by using high gain antennas. For example, if we use a 13 dB gain Yagi at the RTU and a 6 dB gain omni-directional antenna at the master site, we add an extra 19 dB gain to our signal. Therefore, the total fade margin in our example would become:

$$13.8 + 19 = 32.8 \text{ dB}$$

Finally, we must consider other losses introduced by cables, connectors, multi-couplers, etc. In this example, if we have 20 m of 3 dB/100 m loss cable at each end, total connector losses of 0.5 dB at each end and a multi-coupler loss of 3 dB at the master site then:

Extra losses:

Cables: 2 (0.2 × 3 dB)	= 1.2 dB
Connectors: 2 × 0.5 dB	= 1 dB
Multi-coupler	= 3 dB
Total extra losses	= 3 + 1 + 1.2
	= 5.2 dB

Therefore the fade margin for the link is:

$$32.8 - 5.2 = 226.6 \text{ dB}$$

Summary of calculations

The following equation is a summary of the requirements for calculation of fade margin: Fade margin = − (free space attenuation) − (diffraction losses) + (transmitter power) + (receiver sensitivity) + (antenna gain at master site) + (antenna gain at RTU) − (cable and connector loss at master) − (cable and connector loss at RTU) − (multi-coupler filter or duplexer loss) + (receiver pre-amplifier gain).

Miscellaneous considerations

When implementing a radio link, there are other important considerations. The following is a list of some of the main considerations:

- It is important to obtain specification sheets from radio supplier before purchasing any equipment and ensuring that all parameters meet your requirements.

- The audio frequency output and input for a radio is normally a balanced 600 Ω connection. Depending on the equipment provided, it will accept levels of between −30 dBm and +15 dB and will output levels from −15 to +15 dBm. These are normally adjustable internally.
- Most radios operate at +12 V DC (or 13.2 V DC if it is floated across a battery). Depending on the RF output power level the current consumption may vary from 1 A for 1 W output to 10 A for 50 W output. This should be taken into consideration when sizing power supplies and batteries.
- The size and weight of the radio equipment should be noted so that correct mechanical mounting and rack space can be provided. Multi-couplers and duplexers can be very large and may need to be mounted on walls outside the radio equipment racks or in separate racks. In order to minimize inter-modulation, multi-couplers and filters should be as close as possible to the transmitter and receiver.
- It is beneficial to obtain *mean time between failure* (MTBF) figures from manufacturers because if the radio is to be placed in a remote location that is difficult to regularly access, it is vital that the radio is reliable.
- If the telemetry communication protocol requires the radio to be switched on and off at regular intervals, it is best to avoid having relays in the inline RF circuit. Discrete transistor RF switching is preferred.

20

System design methodology

20.1 Introduction

Ideally, the project should be implemented with a systems engineering approach as described in Chapter 1. This involves drawing up a functional specification first, followed by the validation of any techniques or technologies of which perfect operation is not a foregone conclusion. After this come the detailed design, procurement, installation/integration, commissioning/testing, and long-term maintenance.

With that in mind, the functional requirements have to be established up front. It involves specifying environmental requirements as well as the inputs, outputs, and transfer functions of all systems and sub-systems to be procured. If any systems or subsystems (for example, data acquisition units) have to be built from scratch for some or other reason, then the EC and ST structures (in other words, how the system is put together and how it operates) will also be designed.

Often more than one solution satisfies the functional requirements. If this is the case, and the cost of the system is substantial, there may be a requirement that an economic analysis be done as well. For each system, all expenditures (capital expenditures as well as operating costs) will be estimated and then referred to the present time by means of a process called discounting. This will be done at an interest rate called the 'cost of capital' or the 'hurdle rate'. The final decision is made, for example, on the internal rate of return (IRR) or the net present value (NPV). Unfortunately, these techniques are totally beyond the scope of this book.

As part of the specification process, the following will need to be formalized.

20.1.1 Environment

Before embarking on a design of the system itself, the environment in which it will operate has to be specified, as this imposes very specific constraints on the system design.

The environment involves everything surrounding, affecting, or supporting the system and its sub-systems, but does not include the system itself. For the purpose of this discussion we will view the system as all communicating devices as well as the interconnecting medium.

The following questions need to be asked. The points listed here are not in any specific order:

- What is the range of temperatures to be experienced by individual components? Whereas a network device (e.g. Ethernet switch) in an enclosure within a control room may be kept more or less permanently at 25 °C, for example, the same device mounted outside in the open (with maybe some form of covering to keep out rain) may experience from −10 °C in winter to +50 °C in summer.

- What is the maximum level of humidity/water to be experienced? Some equipment for use on oilrigs may need to be immersable, for example, whilst components mounted outside in a partially open enclosure with a roof will need to be able to withstand occasional raindrops being blown in from the side. This applies to devices as well as cable assemblies and connectors.
- Is the environment very dusty? In the vicinity of mines, especially open (surface) mines, the dust levels in an unfiltered environment can be immense.
- How corrosive is the atmosphere? In marine environments, the salt in the air can create large-scale corrosion. Wiring suitable for use in a building will not last long on a ship.
- Is there a possibility of people, equipment or other objects (e.g. stones) impacting on the equipment or its enclosure and thereby damaging it?

In the presence of dust, moisture, and impact as described above, the appropriate IP ratings for individual components have to be determined:

- What power infrastructure is available, if any? Is there alternating current (AC)? If so, is it 110 V or 220 V? Is there direct current (DC)? If so, is it 12 V or 24 V? Is there a proper earth ground available? Is there a proper protective (chassis) ground available? How 'clean' is the latter? Is there any need for or provision of redundant supplies? Are there differences in the earth potentials?
- Are cables running outside, e.g. between two buildings? If so, are they exposed to water in some or other form? Are they exposed to UV radiation (sunlight)? Are they running in a protected channel or do they need to be armored?
- What is the possibility of a nearby lightning strike?
- Are there any existing ('legacy') systems to be considered?
- Are there any corporate directives/policies in terms of preferred vendors and/or technologies?
- Is there a risk of explosion caused by electrical sparks? This could be the case where flammable vapors or a high concentration of airborne combustible dust (e.g. sawdust) is present. In this case the data communications electronics will have to be intrinsically safe, i.e. the energy in the signals will have to be limited to such an extent that sparks cannot be created if a physical connection is made or broken.
- Are there any cost/budgetary constraints?
- What level of vendor support is available locally?
- Is there an existing maintenance infrastructure, and if so, which technologies are supported?

Once these facts have been established, we can turn our attention to the functional requirements of the actual data communications systems.

20.2 Point-to-point links

20.2.1 Functional requirements

If there is any point-to-point (or point-to-multipoint) communications required, the following needs to be ascertained:

- Is it purely point-to-point communication between two nodes, a multi-drop (bus) configuration with only one transmitter but several receivers, or a multidrop configuration with several transmitters and receivers?

- Is the communication simplex, half-duplex or full-duplex?
- What distance needs to be covered? Is it a few meters? A few hundred meters? A few kilometers?
- If the communicating devices are a few kilometers apart are the two sites within line-of-sight? What is the terrain like in terms of the path profile? Is there any existing communications infrastructure?
- If line-of-sight operation is not possible, are both stations within the footprint of a specific satellite?
- Are they far apart but can, for some reason, not be be serviced by satellite?
- What transmission rate is required (bits per second)?
- What data rate (on average) is expected?
- Are remote stations stationary or mobile?

Once these facts are known, the options could be as follows.

20.2.2   RS-232

If the two communicating devices are close together (say, in the same building), there is very little electrical interference (noise) present and there is a good grounding system with both end systems at the same reference potential, RS-232 is an option.

Refer to the chapter on RS-232 for permissible distances. The distance has to be reduced as the bit (baud) rate goes up, and at 110 baud, a distance of 850 m is possible but at 115 kbaud, this distance is reduced to 20 m. Charts, similar to the one for RS-485 shown further on, are available for RS-232 on different types of wire.

Since RS-232 uses separate lines for TX and RX, full-duplex is possible in theory as long as the upper layer protocols can support it. Keep in mind that RS-232 only implements layer 1 (the physical layer) of the OSI model.

20.2.3   RS-422/485

If the two end stations are up to 1200 m (4000 ft) apart and/or there is a fair amount of noise present, RS-422 or 485 may be a solution. However, at 1200 m a data rate of no more than 90 kbps may be possible. The data rate decreases at a straight line on a log/lin scale until at 10 Mbps a distance of no more than 15 m may be possible.

Refer to Figure 20.1, which shows the data-signaling rate vs cable length for 24 AWG twisted-pair wire with a shunt capacitance of 16 pF/ft and terminated in 100 Ω. This curve is based on signal quality requirements of a signal rise and fall time equal to or less than one-half unit interval at the applicable bit rate, and a maximum voltage loss between driver and load of 6 dB. Simple charts like this enable users to select the proper cable without a technical understanding of the cable parameters. The charts for RS-422 and RS-485 are identical.

The losses in a transmission line are a combination of AC losses (skin effect) in the conductor, DC losses in the conductor, leakage, and AC losses in the dielectric. In high-quality cable, the losses in the conductor and the losses in the dielectric are more or less the same. Figure 20.2 shows the difference in losses (in terms of attenuation vs frequency) between different types of cable. Polyethylene cables offer much lower attenuation than PVC cables.

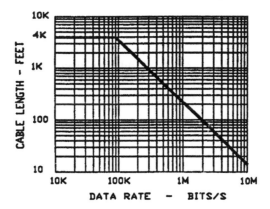

Figure 20.1
Data-signaling rate vs cable length

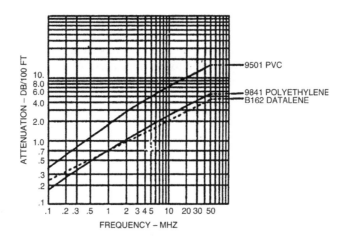

Figure 20.2
Attenuation vs frequency for various cable types

Another approach to choosing the cable is the so-called 'E-GRADE' program, established by Anixter Bros. Inc., a worldwide distributor of wiring products. Under this system, there are four categories viz.:

- E-GRADE 1: Limited distance
- E-GRADE 2: Standard distance
- E-GRADE 3: Extended distance
- E-GRADE 4: Maximum distance.

For reliable operation, it is imperative that surge suppressors be installed on both sides. However, the capacitance of the suppression devices may adversely affect the maximum bit rate of the link. If this becomes a problem, fiber might be the only way out.

If the earth potentials between the two end sites are significantly different, it might also be necessary to revert to fiber.

An RS-422 system only supports simplex operation. RS-485 with one pair of wires only supports half-duplex, while RS-485 with two pairs of wire supports full-duplex. However, as in the case of RS-232, this depends on the capabilities of the upper layer communication protocols since RS-422 and 485 only implement layer 1 of the OSI model.

20.2.4 Fiber

If the earth potentials of the two end stations are significantly different, or there is a severe noise problem, or the cable runs outside and there is a high incidence of lightning strikes, then it will be necessary to revert to fiber.

The cheapest fiber solution is to use two low-cost (1 mm) plastic fibers with an RS-232 to fiber converter at each end as a replacement for the copper link. Power stealing converters (drawing power from the control lines on the RS-232 connector) will be the cheapest option but will limit the distance to around 10 m. Using external power supplies for the converters will increase this distance to around 40 m.

A slightly more expensive solution will be to use multimode fiber (e.g. 50/120/900) with appropriate interfaces. This will operate typically up to 1.8–2 km.

If larger distances are required, single-mode fiber will be necessary and, depending on the driver and the wavelength used, segments of up to 100 km can be implemented. Ultimately, distance is not a limitation as repeaters can be used to link segments; the only problem is to supply power to the repeaters. At present the high-speed Internet links between the East Coast of the USA and South Africa, for example, are undersea fiber-optic links.

A single fiber can only support simplex operation as the fiber plus is transmitter and receiver only allows light to travel in one direction. For full- or half-duplex operation, two fibers are necessary.

20.2.5 Other solutions

Here is a brief summary of alternative methods used to transfer data from one location to another. The cost and reliability will differ from method to method.

- *Cable modems*: Cable modems can create a permanent connection between two devices (DTEs) across a twisted-pair cable (landline). The cable can be privately owned and installed between two locations, or it can be leased from a telephone utility. The hosts (DTEs) communicate with the modems (DCEs) via RS-232, whilst the two modems use a different protocol, such as the point-to-point protocol (PPP) between themselves.
- *Wireless modems*: Wireless modems are suitable for replacing wireless lines to remote sites or as a back-up to wire or fiber-optic circuits. They are designed to ensure that computers and PLCs, for example, can communicate transparently over a radio link without any specific modifications required. The interface to the radio is typically RS-232, but RS-22 or 485 are also options. Typical speeds of operation are 9600 bps. A buffer is built into the modem and is typically 32 kB in size. Typical modulation techniques are two level FM (1200 to 4800 bps) to three level FM (9600 bps).
- *IEEE 802.11 wireless LAN with suitable long-range antennas*: With suitable antennas (40–50 cm parabolic dish) a remote station can communicate with an IEEE 802.11 wireless hub over a range of several kilometers without the need for power amplification. The data rate depends on the version (802.11, 802.1b

or 802.11a) and the quality of the signal, but 1–10 Mbps over distances up to 8 km is attainable.

- *VSAT (very small aperture terminals)*: This technology is a solution where remote stations have to link up to a base station in a remote area where the distances are large (beyond line of sight) and there is no established infrastructure. A typical example would be data acquisition systems used by geologists in the oilfields in the north of Canada.

The following methods use third-party links supplied by telecommunications utilities. They are not truly 'industrial' links, but could nevertheless be used to link industrial sites at the enterprise level.

- Cellular data systems such as CDPD (cellular digital packet data) and GPRS (general packet radio service).
- Other public transport network (WAN) technologies such as T1, E1, Switched 56, ISDN-BRI (integrated services data network-basic rate interface), ISDN-PRI (ISDN primary rate interface), Frame Relay, B-ISDN (broadband ISDN), X.25, ATM (synchronous transfer mode), and SDH/SONET (synchronous digital hierarchy/synchronous optical network). The costs of the various technologies vary, commensurate with the data rate.
- The Internet as the 'cloud'. In this case it would be advisable to use an industrial Internet service provider (iISP) instead of a commercial ISP, as well as proper authentication and encryption schemes. The creation of a virtual private network (VPN) might be advisable for security reasons, as all communication through the Internet will take place in logical 'tunnels', which make it impossible to intercept the data.

20.3   Networked systems

Networked systems in a plant can be placed conceptually in one of the three levels. These areas are not rigorously defined, so it is possible for two vendors to place heir products at slightly different positions in this hierarchy.

The lowest (bottom layer) is often referred to as the device layer. Systems at this level are deployed on the plant floor and link sensors and actuators, both digital and analog, with controllers. Required response times could be fast, and often a high degree of deterministic behavior is required. Data packets (frames) are generally small, and often bit-oriented. Typical systems at this level include DeviceNet, Foundation Fieldbus H1, Profibus DP/PA, HART, and AS-i. This layer is not necessarily implemented by one large system, but can consist of several smaller systems, linked with bridges, routers, or gateways. For example, smaller AS-i automation islands can be connected via gateways to a larger Profibus DP network. Systems at this level could be involved in PID control.

The middle layer is referred to as the control layer, and this layer typically interconnects PLCs, SCADA systems, and HMIs. Typical systems at this level are ControlNet, Ethernet/IP, Foundation Fieldbus HSE, ProfiNet, Modbus Plus, and Data Highway Plus. Systems at this level are involved in supervisory control, and there is less emphasis on deterministic behavior. Response times can be slower, and data packets (frames) are generally larger, and byte-oriented.

The upper layer is referred to as the enterprise or information layer. Typical networks at this level include Ethernet and Token ring, connecting various computer systems (mainframes, etc.). Systems interconnected include financial systems, MRP systems, and various other database-type applications. There is no need for deterministic behavior and messages could be large.

Ideal solutions would offer the following:

- The use of common protocols across all three layers, for example, TCP/IP
- The same network standard (e.g. Ethernet) across all three layers, or at least the upper two. This simplifies maintenance, and facilitates the use of off-the-shelf network components (e.g. routers and switches).

Keeping the above model in mind, the following questions need to be asked:

- At what level is the system being designed (device, operator, or enterprise)?
- *Inputs*: What types, e.g. digital input, analog input? How many? How distributed across the plant?
- *Outputs*: What types, e.g. analog output, digital output (relay contact or open collector transistor, etc.)? How many? How dispersed across the plant?
- Functionality required:

    - Real-time control (PID)? If so, how many loops?
    - Logging?
    - SCADA functions?
    - What degree of determinism is required?
    - What degree of redundancy is required and if any where? Redundant links? Redundant network devices? Redundant controllers?
    - Is it a real-time application? If so, what constitutes 'real time'? On the steering system of an oil tanker, a 30 s response time is real time. On a computer numerically controlled milling machine, a 5 ms response time might be 'real time'.
    - Is power via the bus a requirement? If so, to what degree? Is it only for networking devices or also for field devices?
    - Are built-in OPC servers a requirement? If so, which ones? DA, DX, etc.? OPC DX allows controllers from multiple vendors to be configured via a standard web interface.

Once these requirements have been finalized, it is time to look at the various options.

20.3.1   Device level

Ethernet has truly come of age and is often used at the device level in applications as demanding as marine applications (for example, controlling the position of the floats of the barge used to raise the submarine Kursk), on ships and on avionics systems for fighter aircraft. Applications like this tend to use deterministic Ethernet with dual redundant switched fiber rings. Ethernet interfaces are available right down to sensor level. Limited device power is available with PoE (Power over Ethernet).

However, Ethernet is not a cure-all. It cannot supply large amounts of current via the bus (due to the small wire gage) and it implements only the bottom two layers of the OSI model. Agreed, TCP/IP runs well over Ethernet, but still only accounts for layers 3 and 4. There is no agreed upper layer control protocol in layers 5–7, and no 'user' layer above it so there are no functional building blocks for process control applications. Ethernet frames have a large overhead, but the high speeds (typically 100 Mbps for industrial applications) compensate for that.

For smaller applications with primarily digital inputs, a very strong need for determinism and a fast cycle rate, AS-i could be an option. Note that there are a somewhat limited number of inputs, and the maximum diameter of the network is relatively small; so that in many applications it has to be bridged into another network, e.g. Profibus to make data accessible throughout the plant.

For applications with intrinsic safety requirements, the choices are narrowed down to systems with IEC 61158-2 capability. This includes Foundation Fieldbus H1 and Profibus PA. Note that Profibus PA encompasses only the physical and data-link layers, it still needs Profibus PA or FMS for its 'intelligence'.

For applications requiring power on the bus, DeviceNet or Foundation Fieldbus could be options, with DeviceNet allowing up to 8 A of current and FF up to 2.5 A. However, DeviceNet supports up to 500 kbps while FF only allows 31.25 kbps due to its intrinsic safety design.

The degree of determinism required is a contentious issue, more so because many people do not really understand the issues and are confused by proponents of the various technologies as well as misleading advertising. Deterministic does not mean fast! The degree of determinism is an indicator of the predictability of the access time of a given device to the bus, not the actual waiting time before it gains access. For example, on a token passing network with several hundred nodes the access time could be guaranteed to be a maximum of 200 ms. Whereas the operation could be labeled as deterministic, it is by no means fast. On the other hand, on an IEEE 802.1p/Q Ethernet VLAN switch, a specific node could always gain immediate access by virtue of the fact that it has the highest priority, yet many people do not regard Ethernet as being deterministic!

Full-duplex operation (i.e. simultaneous reading from and writing to a device) may also be an issue for some high-speed applications. Ethernet (100 Mbps and up) is the ONLY base band network technology capable of this since it uses a hub topology with separate transmit and receive paths. Virtually all device level networks use a bus topology, which makes full-duplex impossible.

20.3.2　Control level

Systems at this level include Modbus Plus, Data Highway Plus, ControlNet, Profibus FMS, etc. Ethernet features strongly here, though not on its own but rather as the OSI layers 1 and 2 of other control networks. For example, Rockwell automation has brought out its Ethernet/IP (Ethernet/Industrial Protocol), which is essentially an Ethernet version of DeviceNet. The Profibus organization brought out ProfiNet, which is essentially Profibus FMS running on Ethernet (although its functionality goes way beyond that of profibus). In similar fashion, the Fieldbus Foundation brought out Foundation Fieldbus HSE, which is essentially Foundation Fieldbus on Ethernet. An added feature of these Ethernet-based systems are that they support TCP/IP. This makes it possible to access devices freely across the network, and even from outside the network, provided that the required access devices and security measures are in place. In addition, the products mentioned here will also support OPC DX, which means that all controllers on the network, regardless of vendor, can be configured in exactly the same way via a common browser interface. In the final analysis, it only makes sense to complement the device layer systems with control layer systems from the same vendor where possible. In this way we will have DeviceNet supplemented with Ethernet/IP, Profibus with ProfiNet, and FF H1 with FF HSA.

Whatever the case, it is important to be able to source an off-the-shelf device (gateway) to connect the device level network with the control level network.

All the new products support TCP/IP. TCP/IP not only supports OPC, but also HTTP so web servers can be embedded in devices such as PLCs. In addition, *de facto* protocols like Modbus (Modbus over TCP/IP) can be supported.

Enterprise network

Typical technologies employed at the upper (enterprise) layer include Token Ring and Ethernet, although for new applications Ethernet would be the preferred choice, for several reasons:

- It is by far the fastest LAN technology available today.
- If Ethernet is used at the control level, interconnection between the middle and upper layers can be established through standard off-the-shelf switches and routers.
- The protocol suite used here would also be TCP. Note that the network at this level is a generic 'IT'-type installation and that none of the industrial prerequisites apply.

Detailed planning

Once a decision has been made on the product to be used, extreme care has to be taken with the design.

Detailed planning and installation manuals are available for the various systems. For example, Allen Bradley publishes an 80-page guide on DeviceNet installation planning. The wiring types, maximum wire lengths and connector types are no cause for concern as they are strictly defined by the standards.

Installation, commissioning, troubleshooting

21.1 Introduction

The following section offers some guidelines for getting a system to work. It does assume that the troubleshooter has the appropriate tools for the job and a thorough understanding of the technology involved. Troubleshooting, for example, a TCP/IP-based system requires the use of a suitable protocol analyzer as well as a thorough understanding of the interrelationships of the various protocols (e.g. IP, ICMP, ARP) and the composition of the various headers.

21.2 Methodology

21.2.1 Old vs new systems

The approach to troubleshooting will vary slightly depending on whether it is a new system being commissioned or an old system being troubleshooted. In a new system the wiring has to be checked to confirm that it has been installed according to specifications. However, in an operational system it can be assumed that the wiring has been installed correctly and that any wiring problems could be attributed to a damaged cable.

21.2.2 Systems approach

A good idea is to use a systems approach when commissioning a plant or trying to find a fault. View a system in terms of its environment, divide the overall system into subsystems, and then view the subsystems in terms in inputs, outputs, and transfer functions.

When troubleshooting, check that the following environmental factors do not create problems:

- Water/humidity
- Electrical noise
- Dirt/dust
- Vibration
- Temperature
- Power (no power, under voltage, over voltage, power fluctuations, voltage transients).

Then view the system as a collection of subsystems interconnected with the appropriate media. If individual subsystems are operating correctly and the media has been properly installed, the subsystems should be able to communicate with each other.

21.2.3   OSI model

Follow the sequence of the OSI layers when troubleshooting instead of approaching the problem in a haphazard fashion. If two systems cannot communicate with each other at the application (client/server) level, start by checking the medium ('layer 0'). If the medium is in order, proceed by checking the physical layer (layer 1) in the case of RS-232/485 or the network interfaces (layers 1 and 2) in the case of networks such as Ethernet. If it function correctly, the problem could be protocol-related. Proceed by checking out the protocol layers in ascending numerical order, in other words, first confirm that the routing (layer 3) is operational – if it is present. If there is no problem at this level, proceed to check the transport layer protocols (layer 4), etc. If all protocol layers seem to be functioning correctly, the problem must be at the application level. (*Note*: not to be confused with the seventh layer of the OSI model!)

It should be obvious that the higher one ventures into the OSI layer, the more complex the problem and the more difficult the search for it becomes. It is therefore imperative to start at the bottom. It is estimated that 60–70% of problems can be traced to the medium and layer 1.

Miscellaneous

Here are some additional tips:

- Remove all non-critical devices from the system under test.
- Use onboard diagnostics wherever they are available.
- Be systematic.
- Good documentation, especially wiring diagrams, is critical.
- Baseline statistics, i.e. system measurements such as traffic density (bytes per second) under normal operating conditions are helpful. In the case of a suspected problem, the current measurements can be compared against the baseline measurements and that can point towards the problem.

21.3   Common problems

21.3.1   Media problems

These problems have been dealt with in detail in other chapters, but a summary at this point in time is in order. The following problems may be encountered:

- Damaged or broken cables
- Connector-related problems
- Excessive attenuation
- Insufficient bandwidth
- Reflections/ringing.

Problems related to attenuation, bandwidth, and reflections can usually be eliminated altogether by choosing the correct type of cable and installing it as per the suppliers' guidelines using appropriate tools. When using an external installer, it is wise to insist on a certificate of approval from the cable manufacturer. This may not be obtainable in all cases but it is normally done with Cat5 cabling for network installations.

Most problems at this level can be detected with a multi-meter and/or a handheld cable tester. Persistent reflection-related problems might require the use of an oscilloscope or time domain reflectometer.

Network interface problems

Problems at this level can be categorized as follows:

- *Total failure (layer 1)*:   This is very rare but it can happen when a network interface simply stops working due to an electronic fault. More often, however, this damage is caused by a high voltage transient, for example, due to lightning finding their way into the circuitry. Any cabling prone to high voltage transients should be fitted with transient protection devices to protect the circuitry.
- *Incorrect set-up*:   In this case, the circuitry does not work but it is fully operational. It simply has not been set up properly. This is a very common problem with 10/100 Ethernet cards that have not been set up correctly or where the auto negotiation process has failed.
- *Traffic-related problems (layer 2)*:   If too many devices try to access the medium or the aggregate traffic levels become too high, problems may occur (e.g. packets dropped or too many collisions). Nothing in the system has failed but the situation has arisen due to an oversight on the part of the system designer. This can only be observed with the help of a protocol analyzer and similar tools.

Protocol problems

These are software problems related to layers 3–7 of the OSI model as well as 'layer 8' as defined by various vendors. Problems at this level require a thorough understanding of the protocols used and require the use of a protocol analyzer.

Index

Printed and bound by CPI Group (UK) Ltd, Croydon, CR0 4YY

03/10/2024

01040338-0014